VIRGIN MOTHER GODDESSES OF ANTIQUITY

Also by Marguerite Rigoglioso

The Cult of Divine Birth in Ancient Greece (Palgrave Macmillan 2009)

VIRGIN MOTHER GODDESSES OF ANTIQUITY

Marguerite Rigoglioso

VIRGIN MOTHER GODDESSES OF ANTIQUITY
Copyright © Marguerite Rigoglioso, 2010.

First published in hardcover in 2010 by PALGRAVE MACMILLAN® in the
United States—a division of St. Martin's Press LLC, 175 Fifth Avenue,
New York, NY 10010.

Where this book is distributed in the UK, Europe and the rest of the world,
this is by Palgrave Macmillan, a division of Macmillan Publishers Limited,
registered in England, company number 785998, of Houndmills,
Basingstoke, Hampshire RG21 6XS.

Palgrave Macmillan is the global academic imprint of the above companies
and has companies and representatives throughout the world.

Palgrave® and Macmillan® are registered trademarks in the United States,
the United Kingdom, Europe and other countries.

ISBN: 978–1–137–29342–8

The Library of Congress has cataloged the hardcover edition as follows:

Rigoglioso, Marguerite.
    Virgin mother goddesses of antiquity / Marguerite Rigoglioso.
      p. cm.
    Includes bibliographical references and index.
    ISBN 978–0–230–61886–2
      1. Mother goddesses. I. Title.

BL325.M6R54 2010
202'.1140938—dc22   2010013321

A catalogue record of the book is available from the British Library.

Design by Newgen Imaging Systems (P) Ltd., Chennai, India.

First PALGRAVE MACMILLAN paperback edition: December 2012

10 9 8 7 6 5 4 3 2 1

To my grandmother Elena
my mother Marie
and my aunt Elizabeth,
with admiration and thanks.

CONTENTS

ACKNOWLEDGMENTS

I would like to thank many people for their support in association with this book: my dissertation committee members, who read several of these chapters as part of my doctoral dissertation at the California Institute of Integral Studies (CIIS)—Associate Professor Jorge Ferrer (chair), Professor Lucia Chiavola Birnbaum, and Marvin Meyer, Griset Professor of Bible and Christian Studies at Chapman University; CIIS Professor Charlene Spretnak, for getting us started on the topic of the lost history of goddesses of the ancient Mediterranean world and for her invaluable mentorship; Angeleen Campra, for her chapter on the Gnostic Sophia, included in this volume; Gregory Shaw, for unflagging encouragement, insights, and scholarly references; Burke Gerstenschlager and Samantha Hasey at Palgrave Macmillan, for their professional editorial support and guidance; Rohini Krishnan at Newgen Imaging Systems for typesetting assistance; Suzanne Sherman Aboulfadl for her indexing skills; librarians Adolfo (AJ) Real, Jr., Kenneth Fish, and Shaun Barger (Dominican University of California), for their patient assistance with my interlibrary loan requests; Irene Young and Laurelin Remington-Wolf, for their beautiful cover image; and Robert Owings, for invaluable insights and support over many years.

NOTE ABOUT CITATION STYLE

For this book, *The Chicago Manual of Style's* author-date system of documentation has been used so that the reader may discern the sources being referenced without having to flip constantly to the endnotes. This should be particularly helpful for classical citations. Where citations contain more than two authors or are otherwise visually cumbersome, however, they have been placed in the notes section.

Since I frequently reference my first book, *The Cult of Divine Birth in Ancient Greece,* I abbreviate that volume as *CDB* throughout the text for the sake of convenience.

INTRODUCTION

The goddesses have stories to tell. One such story—far too long ignored—is that, in their original, unadulterated form, they were parthenogenetic. The word *parthenogenesis* comes from the Greek *parthenos,* "virgin," more or less, and *gignesthai,* "to be born." It means, essentially, to be born of a virgin—that is, without the participation of a male. For a goddess to be "parthenogenetic" thus means that she stands as a primordial creatrix who requires no male partner to produce the cosmos, earth, life, matter, and even other gods out of her own essence. Plentiful evidence shows that in their earliest cults, before they were subsumed under patriarchal pantheons as the wives, sisters, and daughters of male gods, various female deities of the ancient Mediterranean world were indeed considered self-generating, virgin creatrixes. This is the first book to explore that evidence comprehensively.

Understanding goddesses of Graeco-Roman antiquity in this way allows us to resolve the seemingly confounding paradox, noted by various observers,[1] of the simultaneous virginity and generativity attributed to certain deities in their earliest mythological and cultic material. How can a "virgin" create life? How can a creatrix be "virgin"? The information presented throughout this volume suggests that, rather than being contradictory, these two co-existent aspects form a complex of "virgin motherhood" in which goddesses procreated despite being consortless. It allows us to see the "virginity" of various goddesses as representing not sterility, but inviolable and sovereign creative power. In revealing some of our oldest divinities in the West to be Virgin Mothers, this book offers a fresh angle on the original nature and agency of these deities, thereby complementing and, in a sense, completing earlier feminist analyses of such goddesses.[2]

Virgin Mother Goddesses of Antiquity also provides evidence to support progressive feminist theories that early ancient Mediterranean cults were based in a matriarchal ethos. Moreover, by exposing a little-explored theological development—the appropriation of parthenogenetic power on the part of the divine Masculine in religious stories—the book offers new insights about the ferocity of the gender wars that took place under the cultural transition to patriarchy. It explores the ramifications of such theological appropriation for the priestesshoods dedicated to Virgin Mother goddesses, as well as for women and culture more broadly.

The Larger Purpose of This Book

Why is it important to argue that goddesses originally did not need male consorts? Is it to invalidate the Masculine principle? Denigrate male gods? Insult human men by making them feel unneeded and unwanted in the cosmic scheme?

The answer to all three questions is a firm "no."

First, we must remember that, for those of us who have grown up under patriarchal monotheisms, the tables have long been reversed—some would argue for millennia. We have been raised under the strange specter of *male* creator gods who, we are told, produced the universe spontaneously. I say "strange," because even some of the ancient myths hint that, like human males, Masculine deities in fact lacked the proper apparatus for creation. Although divine, they still had to locate a "womb" for the gestation of their issue. For the Egyptian gods Atum and Re, for example, it was their mouths, into which they ejaculated semen to create the cosmos. For Zeus, it was first his belly, into which he swallowed the pregnant Metis, and then his cranium, from which he "birthed" Athena. Then, we have the case of the famous male god who simply "created" the heavens and the earth, as though by means of a giant erector set.

In short, we have been programmed with stories of male parthenogenesis that defy or contradict the very processes of birth that are woven into the fabric of the universe as we understand it on an essential level. The resulting cognitive dissonance has, I would argue, created a gross confusion within our psyches. Deep down, we sense that something is wrong from the start. From there, the stories of the father gods proceed with strains of aggression and violence particularly directed toward the Feminine. As numerous scholars, from Jane Ellen Harrison to Mary Daly to Carol Christ to many others, have argued, this has led to an unhappy state of affairs for humanity.

So why is it important to show that the goddess doesn't—or didn't—need a man? As a male-honoring woman, I continue to ponder this question. What I have arrived at is this: It is necessary for us to turn the conceptual tables back to the idea of a virgin female creator deity, even if only for a moment, because in the process we may spark something evolutionary. By acknowledging the autonomous capacity of the Feminine, which the ancient stories indicate was primarily benevolent, not violent, we restore and honor a critical piece of our psychology and our world that has gone missing. A point made by three contemporary Greek writers, Neoklis Georgopoulos, George Vagenakis, and Apostolos Pierris (2003) is particularly apt here. In discussing the notion of duality in the female-centered universe depicted in the myth of Demeter and Persephone, they note, "One pole in the pair of opposites enjoys a certain priority, in that it better expresses the original unity." That is, in origin stories in which the goddess is a Virgin Mother, the "whole" is understood to be "Feminine," even though the Masculine is included *as an equal part*. Or, as the contemporary Hindu mystic Ammachi says, "Is God a Man or a Woman? The answer to the question is *Neither—God is That*. But if you must give God a gender, God is more female than male, for *he* is contained in *She*" (in Canan 2004, 169).

Georgopoulos et al. echo that in a cosmos in which god is a Virgin Mother, "malehood emerges from the womb of Ur-femininity"—that is, from original, primordial femininity. It is important to note that in this condition the Masculine is not annihilated, but rather understood to be contained *within* the Feminine and to function as a cosmic emanation of it (as, in fact, biological reality reminds us each time a boy is born). Allowing ourselves to embrace the concept of a universe in which the Feminine, rather than the Masculine, is seen to "better express the original unity" may help us to right our relationships with one another and inspire us to adopt new models of relating that establish harmony and respect among the genders and between humans, Mother Earth, and all her creatures. Stimulating such thinking is my ultimate aim in restoring awareness about the original parthenogenetic nature of goddesses of Western antiquity.

Outline of This Book

I begin the study with the oldest divine entities described in Hesiodic and Orphic theogony—Chaos, Nyx/Night, and Ge/Gaia (Earth)—highlighting details of their autogenetic (self-creating) and parthenogenetic (self-generating) activities. I discern in their stories an older subtext in which such goddesses held positions of primacy in cult, which I argue corresponded with an earlier period of matriarchal social structure. I move to Athena, the goddess who most famously held the epithet *Parthenos*, "Virgin." I offer a pioneering examination of her relationship to the Greek Metis and the Egyptian Neith to show that Athena was originally not the sterile, father-serving deity of classical Greece, but rather a parthenogenetic creatrix in her own right. My extended analysis of the mythology associated with Athena's "mother" Metis highlights material generally ignored or glossed over in the scholarly literature, particularly details suggestive of Metis's own parthenogenetic powers, as well as of her masculinization as the god Phanes in Orphic theology. My analysis of Neith's autogenetic/parthenogenetic nature similarly serves as one of the more comprehensive portraits of this Libyo-Egyptian goddess to date. In short, it reveals the tremendous original power and cultic importance of this goddess and exposes the arrogation of her self-generative capacities to the male sphere in Egyptian theogony, and the corresponding shift from matriarchy to patriarchy during the pharaonic era.

By detailing Athena's identification with Neith, I not only restore the lost "motherhood" of this Greek goddess in her earliest phase, but also provide the most detailed argument to date attesting to her African origins, a topic that has been sidestepped by all but a few scholars. This work includes laying out important evidence attesting to the possible historicity of the female warrior Amazons who venerated Neith/Athena in North Africa. In my treatment of Athena's "Grecization," I further expose the transition from matriarchy to patriarchy in Greece, which most likely occurred during the Mycenean period, as the independent goddess was made the "daughter" of the new universal creator god, the male Zeus.

I then analyze a second Greek goddess who possessed the title *Parthenos*: Artemis. I explore her mythology to argue that she, like Athena, originally was considered a parthenogenetic creator deity. In doing so, I resolve the seeming paradox of Artemis's dual role as a goddess who rejected heterosexual eroticism yet protected women's birthing process. I also examine her connections with Athena/Neith, looking at her relationship as the goddess of the Thermadon Amazons and their links, in turn, with the Libyan Amazons. I introduce here consideration of the possible emergence of the West Asian/Thermadon Amazons from the North African/Libyan Amazons, thereby opening the door to future study about possible links between the cults of Artemis and Athena.

I next turn to the third Greek goddess known as *Parthenos*, Hera, and probe her myths to provide evidence that, before she was made the wife of Zeus in Olympian mythology, she was considered a virgin creatrix, as well. These include stories of her parthenogenetic birthing of Ares, Hephaestus, and Typhon, and legends associating her with the apples of the Hesperides, which, I argue, were symbols of virgin birth. My analysis allows for a unique interpretation of the famous myth of the "Judgment of Paris" as representing a theological moment in which the goddess Hera "lost" her parthenogenetic power as the sought-after "apple" migrated to the realm of Aphrodite, where it became forever fixed as a symbol of heterosexual eroticism. Further, I offer an original argument that the accounts of several of Heracles' famous twelve labors, which involved what I propose were symbols with parthenogenetic associations (such as the hydra, lion, stag, and woman's *zônê*, or "belt"), represented a male theological attack on human female parthenogenetic ability. I also show that they quite possibly referred to an aggression against what I argue was an entire priesshood dedicated to divine birth, a topic upon which I have elaborated in my first book, *The Cult of Divine Birth in Ancient Greece* (Palgrave Macmillan 2009).

Having explored the three goddesses known as *Parthenoi*, I consider two other Greek goddesses with parthenogenetic stories: Demeter, the goddess of the grain, and Persephone, her daughter and Queen of the Underworld. I provide evidence that their myth encodes a story of female self-replication. I further posit that this element served as the great "mystery" associated with the two goddesses' oldest cult, one that found expression in the rituals dedicated to them, among them the Thesmophoria and the Eleusinian Mysteries. By applying various aspects of the theory that a cult of divine birth existed in ancient Greece, I am able to offer the most coherent reconstruction of these rites to date, one that explicates their purpose, meaning, and function in startling new ways.

I elucidate, in particular, that the Thesmophoria was originally a celebration of the parthenongenetic capacity of not only the two goddesses, but also their virgin priestesses. I argue that Persephone's rape served as the cosmic paradigm for the interruption of women's mysteries in this regard and corresponded with the transfer of divine birth practices in service of producing holy males, literally considered to be the sons of gods, who ushered in the patriarchal era. I detail evidence that the installation of this new phenomenon was the *raison d'etre* for the Eleusinian Mysteries but show how the rite nevertheless retained its roots in female-centered reality. By carefully sifting through mythological motifs and the testimony of ancient writers, I present the case that both male and female initiates of the Mysteries had to undergo an altered-state descent into the underworld that involved their experiencing the rape of Persephone through the ritual use of an artificial phallus. The experience, I show, forced initiates to confront the violence of the Masculine and resolve the "inner" gender war through a journey into paradox and, ultimately, wholeness.

The book concludes with a chapter by Angeleen Campra on the goddess Sophia as portrayed in Gnostic texts. Exploring the Valentinian creation story, the *Thunder, Perfect Mind*, and *On the Origin of the World*, Campra offers a feminist critique of the Gnostic framing of various parthenogenetic motifs in Sophia's mythologem, including the goddess's spontaneous generation of the demiurge Ialdabaoth. She argues that the rendering of such female generativity as "transgressive" and the transfer-ring of "legitimate" parthenogenetic capacity to the male creator god sig-naled a final theological moment in the demotion of the Virgin Mother as primal creatrix in the West.

Readers familiar with my first book, *The Cult of Divine Birth in Ancient Greece,* will recognize some overlap between it and the present volume. In that book, I also discuss the parthenogenetic nature of Athena/Neith, Artemis, and Hera. However, the explorations in the present study are far more comprehensive. Moreover, the new material on Demeter, Persephone, and Sophia, goddesses who were given only a passing men-tion in the earlier work, fleshes out this book and makes a unique contri-bution to the literature on goddesses of antiquity.

Who's Missing?

This book might have included chapters on the great mother goddess Cybele, worshipped in ancient Anatolia and West Asia, as well as Anat/Anath, popular in West Asia from Ugaritic times into the Roman era, but space would not permit it. It might also have discussed the beau-tiful Aphrodite, who, despite her late and circumscribed role as a god-dess of sexuality, has roots as a Great Mother and even a virgin (see Harrison [1903] 1957, 307–14; Baring and Cashford 1991, 349–64). I do not include her here because the focus in this volume is on goddesses whose virginity and/or miraculous birth aspect was seen as *primary* to their identity in the ancient Mediterranean world *and* who were con-nected with priestesshoods that, as I argue in *The Cult of Divine Birth in Ancient Greece*, attempted virgin birth. I have left Hestia, an avowed vir-gin in the Greek pantheon, for consideration in a forthcoming volume, *Miraculous Birth across the Ancient Mediterranean World*, where I will discuss her Roman manifestation as Vesta, the hearth goddess associated with the Vestal Virgins. In that book, I will also discuss Isis, another goddess with a divine birth story, as well as the most famous Virgin Mother of all, Mary.

Critical Concepts from *The Cult of Divine Birth in Ancient Greece*

Given that in this book I frequently refer to my previous volume, *The Cult of Divine Birth in Ancient Greece* (hereafter, *CDB*), it is important to review the main thesis of that study, as well as a few relevant concepts. Readers who do not subscribe to the theories I put forth in *CDB* will still find the present book useful as a text that illuminates our understanding

of various ancient goddesses. Familiarity with some of those earlier theoretical points, however, will afford a fuller appreciation of the nuances
of the current work.

In *CDB*, I make the case that certain specialized priestesshoods in
ancient Greece attempted to conceive children in various non-ordinary
ways as an elevated form of spiritual practice. I show that the intended
purpose of this practice was to give birth to a hero or heroine, gifted spiritual leader, or purported supernatural being—an individual who, it was
believed, could not enter the human stream through "normal" sexual
channels. This miraculously born individual was considered a special soul
capable of benefiting humanity significantly in some way or of heralding
or reinforcing particular value systems (sometimes highly spiritual, often
patriarchal) for the human race.

I argue that attempting to produce offspring through various asexual
and/or magical methods was thought to be a specialized sacerdotal activity for women and that those who believed that the phenomenon was real
considered it the most advanced form of magico-spiritual achievement
possible. Its intended purpose was to transport the human race to a new
level of functioning and awareness through the influence of the incarnated individual. I also provide plentiful evidence that the purported
birth of a specially conceived child was thought to result in the apotheosis, or literal divinization, of the priestess herself, and led to her corresponding veneration. I show that, similarly, the child of this conception
was considered to be of a divine nature and likewise became the focus
of worship.

A key piece of my argument is my contention that the cult of divine
birth proceeded in stages as matriarchal social conditions gave way to
patriarchy. In *CDB*, I present the case that in the earliest practice of the
cult, under matriarchy, priestesses were focused on achieving parthenogenetic conception of female-only offspring—what I call "pure parthenogenesis." What is important to the present book is the concept that
*these holy women attempted to mimic the parthenogenetic ability of goddesses they
served.* Thus, the idea of the Virgin Mother goddess goes hand in hand
with that of the virgin birth priestess: the woman was the human representation of the Great Mother, who could conceive without the inter-
action of the male. I posit that this priestesshood initially focused on
producing *female* avatars—that is, manifestations of the goddess on earth
in human form. In a later stage, perhaps as male gods started to come to
ascendancy, it began to produce male holy children as well. I return to
this idea again and again throughout the book.

Another critical piece of the book is the argument that, as the parthenogenetic power of the goddesses was usurped or interrupted by forced

or coerced intercourse on the part of the male gods on the cosmic level, so the parthenogenetic power of the virgin priestesses was appropriated by male priesthoods and channeled into a different type of miraculous birth activity. This new activity involved the priestesses engaging in sexual relations with male gods in a trance state for the purpose of conceiving the gods' progeny on the planet. Put another way, the "stealing" and denigrating of goddesses' parthenogenetic capacity corresponded with the seizing of the divine birth priestesshoods by male religious authorities, who pressured priestesses into attempting to give birth miraculously to male heroes as a means of fueling the patriarchal enterprise. I call this stage of the practice divine birth through *hieros gamos*, or "sacred union"—that union taking place between the human priestess and what was believed to be a disincarnate male entity. As mentioned briefly previously, in this present book I assert that Persephone's rape by Zeus symbolized the transition of these priestesshoods from pure parthenogenesis to what I term divine birth through *hieros gamos* with male gods. The last stage of the taxonomy proposed in *CDB* is what I call *hieros gamos* by surrogate. This involved priestesses engaging in sexual unions with gods through the medium of human males, who served as receptacles for the spirits of particular deities during trance rituals. It is through this type of practice that ancient Egypt, for example, claimed to generate its pharaohs.

A critical point I make in *CDB* is that several terms used to describe girls and women in ancient Greek myths, legends, and historical texts originally were titles denoting "virgin priestess of divine birth." One was *parthenos,* which later came to refer a girl, particularly an adolescent, who had not had sexual relations or was unmarried. (To avoid any ambiguity, I use "holy *parthenos*" to make it clear that I am referring to a priestess of virgin birth.) Another was *nymph,* which was the name for particular class of female deity usually associated with nature. Yet another was *heroine,* often used to describe a major figure or ancestress in Greek legend. I show how all of the difficulties and contradictions in the current definitions of such terms are resolved if we understand them to have been titles in the cult of divine birth. I refer to these terms liberally throughout this book and argue, in my discussion of Persephone in chapter 5, that another such title should be added to the list: *kore.*

The methodological approaches I use in *CDB* are also worth noting, as they are relevant to my analysis in this book, as well. I first and foremost analyze ancient materials from a feminist hermeneutical perspective. I critically read primary and secondary texts to discover where women and the Feminine have being ignored, misrepresented, diminished, or distorted so as to reconstruct meanings about female agency that are hidden in such writings. In doing so, I attempt to draw a more accurate portrait of ancient goddesses and the priestesses who served them.

Moreover, I frequently explore literary artifacts through a neo-euhemeristic lens. That is, I look to mythology and legends as sources of important clues about historical events and ancient cultural and cultic practices. The term *neo-euhemerism* derives from the name of the fourth–century-B.C.E. writer Euhemerus, who concluded that gods were merely ancestors who had been divinized because they brought some great benefaction to humanity. I do not go so far as to reduce deities completely to human status, but rather posit that myths of gods "walking the earth" reflect beliefs that these beings could have (sometimes successive) human incarnations—namely, by being birthed through the bodies of specialized priestesses of virgin birth, as mentioned earlier. Indeed, the ancient Greeks themselves wrote of there being "several versions" of various divinities who entered the terrestrial plane, such as Dionysus, whom I discuss in more detail in this regard in chapter 5. Seen in this light, stories of immortals' "interactions" with human beings in some cases may be read as accounts of the actions of the supposed avatars of such deities on earth. In other cases, they may be read as accounts of the actions of specific priests or priestesses, who, as I argue in *CDB*, were at times understood to assume the identity of the deities themselves. In general, I take myths seriously as a repository for relics or traces of genuine historical events and cultic practices.[3]

The Meanings of Matriarchy

Critics of the theory that a matriarchal phase of human history preceded patriarchy will no doubt deride the fact that I am even considering such a concept as basis for this book. Haven't we thoroughly trounced the notion and shown it to be archaeologically and anthropologically untenable or unprovable, after all? Haven't we shown, in fact, that matriarchies never existed?[4]

I would argue, no.

Continued research on human societies, past and present, in the burgeoning field of matriarchal studies clearly indicates that the idea of ancient matriarchy should hardly be dismissed. Three master volumes by Göttner-Abendroth (1995, 1999, 2001) and an anthology entitled *Societies of Peace* (Goettner-Abendroth 2009) featuring contributions by numerous scholars, including some who were raised in contemporary matriarchal cultures, provide plentiful evidence that matriarchies have long persisted—and that they have deep roots in prehistory. Such study has also been cultivated through two world congresses on matriarchal studies, in 2003 in Luxembourg and 2005 in Austin, Texas, as well as related conferences on the gift economy and motherhood studies.[5]

An important part of the work of matriarchal studies has involved defining *matriarchy* appropriately, for misunderstandings about this term have continued to provoke acrimony in academic circles. The problem stems in part from the popular notion that a matriarchy is the flipside of a patriarchal dictatorship, the simple reverse of a male-oriented "power-over" culture in which women now dominate and abuse men. However, extensive historical and anthropological studies by Göttner-Abendroth (1987, 1995, 1999, 2000, 2001) and others[6] have revealed that this has never been the case. The very persistence of the notion that matriarchy is simply the mirror reverse of patriarchy, has, in part, led to its obfuscation. According to Göttner-Abendroth (2001), classical matriarchy is a sophisticated system possessing specific traits at four levels: the economic, social, political, and cultural. It is worth detailing them briefly here, given the importance of the concept of matriarchy to the present volume.

At the economic level, a matriarchy is characterized by reciprocity. Women have the power of distribution of goods, and inheritance is passed down through the mother's line. Yet the society is egalitarian and includes mechanisms for distributing wealth to prevent goods from being accumulated by special individuals or groups. At the social level, a matriarchy is matrilocal; people live in large clans, and kinship is acknowledged exclusively in the female line.

At the political level, decision making in a matriarchy is communal, consensual, and characterized by leadership that is shared in complementary fashion between the genders. Decisions begin in the clan house and are carried to the village level by delegates, either the oldest women of the clan or the brothers and sons they have chosen as representatives. At the cultural level, a matriarchy is characterized by religious traditions in which divinity is seen as imminent in the earth, nature, and the cosmos, and there is no separation between sacred and secular. Everyday tasks take on ritual meaning, the cycles of the seasons and other astronomical events are celebrated, and frequently the universe is conceived as a female, divine Mother.

In essence, a classical matriarchy is an egalitarian society in which the female principle is considered foundational and central. Thus, Peggy Reeves Sanday (1998, para. 2) has proposed the term *matriarchy* itself be redefined as "mother origin," since it derives from the Greek *mêtêr* (mother) and *archê*, which can mean "beginning," "origin," or "first principle."

There is every reason to use this broader, more expansive understanding of "matriarchal" when referring to the matrifocal, matrilineal social system that seems to have characterized the earliest substratum of Greek culture, according to prominent scholars of ancient Greek religion such as Jane Ellen Harrison, Karl Kerenyi, and Lewis Farnell. These classicists assert that this older system was indeed matriarchal. Before the Greeks as we know them existed, a series of invaders from the east and northeast successively overran the Greek peninsula throughout the second-millennium B.C.E.[7] Such invasions culminated with the Indo-European Dorians, who entered Greece about 1100 B.C.E. and brought what became the language of Greece. They also brought a patriarchal social structure and religion. As Harrison ([1903] 1957, 261) notes, "In historical days in Greece, descent was for the most part traced through the father.... [P]rimitive goddesses reflect another condition of things, a relationship traced through the mother, the state of society known by the awkward term matriarchal."

The idea that Greek mythology preserves hints of the older matriarchal substratum in which a Great Goddess was the primary deity prior to the installation of the Olympian pantheon, as codified by Hesiod and Homer, forms the basis of much twentieth century scholarly interpretation, and is the thread I pursue in this book. Guthrie (1967, 52–53), for example, writes, "the contrast between [the earlier] Aegean and [the later] Homeric cults was, generally speaking, a contrast between a religion of the soil, a worship of the fertility of the earth [Ge/Gaia] not unmixed with magical practices to secure its continuance, and a religion of the sky, whose chief god [Zeus] was the sender of thunder and lightning upon those who displeased him."

Gimbutas (1982, 1989, 1991, 1999) has provided archaeological evidence to support the theory that an earlier civilization that was not only based on a Great Goddess, but also held women in high positions of cultural leadership in tandem with men, predated that of patriarchal civilization in Old Europe and surrounding regions.[8] She dates the beginnings of the transition between the late fifth and early fourth millennia B.C.E. Following Gimbutas (1989, xx–xvi), I assume that, as Guthrie, Harrison, and others posited, patriarchal peoples invaded the Greek peninsula from the east or northeast throughout the second millennium B.C.E. to create the beginnings of Greek civilization. I further assume that these peoples encountered pre-existing hybrid societies in which matriarchal traits were still prominent. The second-millennium invasions would have intensified the patriarchal nature of such societies and systematically erased the vestiges of matriarchy.

As I show time and again in this book, as well as in *CDB*, there is plentiful evidence in the ancient legendary and historical texts to support the idea that matriarchy was forcibly dismantled in ancient Greece and beyond.

I will mention here just one major indicator that Greece emerged out of an earlier matriarchal culture: the motif of "resistance to marriage" that persisted in ancient Greek wedding rites into the Hellenistic period. Details along these lines include the custom of women trying to "rescue" the bride and being "roared at" by the doorkeeper of the house (Pollux *Onomasticon* 3.42), the burning of the axle of the wagon that carried the newly married woman to her house in Boeotia, and wedding songs expressing her resistance to marriage and her reluctance to lose her virginity or leave her mother (Catullus 62.21–22, 24, 39–48, 59; see Foley 1994, 81n8). These elements, I posit, express symbolic resistance to forced patrilocality, which would have reversed the condition under matriarchy of women staying on their own homestead. Such resistance was also encoded, I propose, in the shared common features of marriages and funerals, such as garlands, ritual ablutions, the cutting of hair, songs, a feast, and the emphasis on passage from the house (of the bride or deceased) to a particular destination (the bride's new house or the deceased's grave) (Foley 1994, 81n8). Equating marriage with death represents what I suggest was an embedded grieving over the massive cultural shift that had taken place to reduce women's autonomy. Preserved in the mock dramatizations of old customs, such resistance and grief motifs served as a vague memory of an earlier, more female-empowered way of life.

The Primordial Parthenogenetic Goddess

Key to the present study are the plentiful signs in the archaeological, historical, and literary record that, concomitant with Greek social matriarchy, female deities enjoyed a far greater prominence and stature in pre-Greek culture than they did in Olympian religion. Again, what becomes apparent, as I explicate in the chapters that follow, is that nearly all such pre-Greek goddesses were understood to be both generative mothers and virgins simultaneously.

These goddesses were no doubt in the lineage of female creatrix deities who originated in the Paleolithic period of Old Europe, where the concept of a parthenogenetic goddess appears to be encoded in the archaeological record. As Gimbutas (1989, xix) writes, "Symbols and images cluster around the parthenogenetic (self-generating) Goddess and her basic functions as Giver of Life, Wielder of Death, and, not less importantly, as Regeneratrix, and around the Earth Mother, the Fertility Goddess young and old, rising and dying with plant life." Following Gimbutas's work, Reis (1991, 34–53) also discerns the conjunction of vulva and phallus appearing on some ancient figures as indicative of the European Paleolithic goddesses's perceived parthenogenetic nature.

A handful of authors have already discerned the parthenogenetic power of ancient Mediterranean goddesses, but their treatment is sporadic and fleeting. Davis (1971, 33) may have been the first to characterize Greek goddesses as originally parthenogenetic in her passing mention that the Greek goddesses Metis and Gaia represented the original creative principle, which generated the world without a male partner. Spretnak (1978, 20) also briefly notes that pre-patriarchal Mediterranean goddesses were always understood to reproduce parthenogenetically. Looking to religious systems farther east, Ruether (1992, 18) gives a nod to the idea that the Babylonian creation story recounting the battle between the mother goddess Tiamat and the patriarchal hero Marduk depicts a "matriarchal" world in which "the earliest model of generation is parthenogenetic gestation." A comprehensive analysis of the virgin motherhood of female deities is long overdue, however, and this volume is a beginning step in that direction.[9]

The conclusion that all of the goddesses discussed in this volume were originally Virgin Mothers leads us to the natural question: Were all goddesses originally one, as Gerhard (in Harrison [1903] 1957, 266n1), in pondering the Greek pantheon, posited more than a century and a half ago? A consideration of this possibility, although interesting, is beyond the scope of this book. I am content to present evidence for the parthenogenetic nature of multiple goddesses without trying to tether them in any kind of monotheistic sense. What I feel is more useful, and perhaps more reflective of regional variances in ancient times, is simply to show that each one was considered a universal creatrix in her own right before she was assigned a more circumscribed role under the patriarchal schema. Although one could argue that assigning a personified aspect to the great forces of life and nature is a modern, Western distortion that misconstrues how European ancestors conceived of the cosmos, I follow Harrison ([1903] 1957), who asserts that the earliest Greeks conceived of the generative forces as a "Great Mother of the dead as well as the living" (266), that each area had its own localized version of this Great Mother, and that from this great constellation the familiar goddesses of the Greek pantheon emerged (257–321). The European archaeological record, with its abundance of images of the sacred female in human and animal form (see, e.g., Gimbutas 1989), indeed suggests that the great cosmic forces were personified going back deep into Paleolithic times.[10]

With these theoretical and philosophical underpinnings established, let us proceed to the analysis of some of our ancient divine Virgin Mothers in the West.

CHAPTER 1

IN THE BEGINNING: CHAOS, NYX, AND GE/GAIA

In discussing the earliest divinities named in the Greek pantheon, most literature glosses over the fact that three of the most primordial—Chaos, Nyx, and Ge/Gaia—were parthenogenetic. The lack of commentary on the tremendous female power embedded in some of our oldest religious stories has rendered virgin motherhood essentially invisible from the start. In this chapter, I attend to the details of these stories and analyze their theological significance from a feminist perspective.

I show that Chaos, the deity representing the first state of the universe, parthenogenetically produced Erebus and Nyx. Nyx/Night similarly bore a number of offspring without male assistance, including the nymphs known as the Hesperides, and also, possibly, in an earlier iteration of Orphic theogony, the god Phanes. I provide textual evidence that Ge/Gaia was, like Chaos, considered to be an *autogenetic* (self-generated) being who bore offspring independently, including the Ourean mountains and their nymphs, and the Pontus sea. She is also credited in various traditions with having parthenogenetically produced all life on earth, including human beings. Moving to Orphic myth, I posit that Phanes' identification as "male," despite his bisexual nature, as well as his being assigned creator god status, may mark a theological moment in which parthenogenetic power was no longer considered the exclusive province of the female deity.

Chaos

I begin with Chaos, the first divine entity described in Hesiod's *Theogony* (116–20). Chaos was one of four divinities who were spontaneously generated without source or cause, the others being Ge/Gaia,[1] Tartarus, and Eros. Thus these four divinities were first and foremost *autogenetic* beings—that is, they were self-generated, having been created out of themselves/the void/nothingness/the All.[2] Chaos, whose name literally means "Opening" or "Gap," was the void, the abyss, the infinite space and darkness, unformed matter. Caldwell (in Hesiod 1987, 35) notes that the etymology of the verb to which Chaos's name is related, *chaskô* ("open, yawn, gape"), "may suggest a womb [that] opens to bring forth life." I would therefore argue that despite the fact that in Greek *chaos* is a Masculine noun, in the divine entity of Chaos, the first state of the universe, we have an intimation of a specifically female goddess of the void. Chaos as "cosmic womb" continued to reproduce parthenogenetically, bearing the male Erebus (Darkness) and his sister, Nyx (Black Night). In the Hesiodic account, these children were fatherless; it was not until Nyx joined in love with Erebus that divine "sexual" reproduction began.

Nyx/Night

In Orphic theogony,[3] Nyx/Night was the mother of Ge/Gaia and Uranus, that is, of Earth and Heaven (frag. 109 in Guthrie [1952] 1993, 138). Although scholars have generally interpreted the Orphic fragments to indicate that Nyx/Night conceived her children through sexual union with the god Phanes (e.g., Guthrie, 80; Cook 1914–40, 2.2: 1020), in fact such fragments do not specify this. The primary fragment in question (frag. 109 in Guthrie, 80) merely reads, "She in her turn bore Gaia and broad Ouranos [Uranus]," leaving the door open, in my view, to the possibility that she was understood to have done so parthenogenetically. In Hesiodic theogony, Nyx/Night unequivocally possessed parthenogenetic powers. She produced a great number of children parthenogenetically, despite the fact that her first progeny, Aether (Brightness) and Hemera (Day), were born of her sexual union with Erebus (Darkness) (Hesiod *Theogony* 211–32). Nyx/Night's parthenogenetically conceived children were personifications related to death, sleep, and other abstract qualities and conditions: Moros (Doom), Ker (Destiny), Thanatos (Death), Hypnos (Sleep), Oneiroi (Dreams), Momos (Blame), Oizys (Pain), Hesperides (Daughters of the Night), Moirai (Fates), Keres (Death Spirits), Nemesis (Retribution), Apate (Deceit), Philotes (Love), Geras (Old Age), and Eris (Discord). The Hesperides, the "nymphs" who guarded the tree of golden apples that Ge/Gaia gave to the goddess Hera, become important in relation to the discussion about Hera's own parthenogenetic nature in chapter 4.

In the Orphic theogony, it is clear that Nyx/Night initially held sway over all the gods (frag. 111 in Guthrie [1952] 1993, 138). She reared

Cronus, or Time (frag. 129 in Guthrie, 139), who, with Rhea/Demeter, subsequently became the father of Zeus (frags. 144, 145 in Guthrie, 139). In a cosmogony attributed to Epimenides of the seventh century B.C.E., it was Nyx/Night who produced the "wind-born" World Egg (Guthrie, 92–93). The fact that "wind-born" eggs were thought to be produced without male fertilization[4] suggests that Nyx/Night was understood to have produced the World Egg parthenogenetically. Aristophanes (*Birds* 693ff.) presents a fragment of a presumably Orphic theogony that it was this egg from which Eros, creator of gods and men, was born (see Guthrie, 92–93). As Guthrie (95–96, 102–4) notes, the "Eros" of this fragment may be identified with the Orphic god Phanes (whose name means "Light"). Guthrie thus posits the existence of an older, pre-classical version of the Orphic theogony in which Nyx/Night was the progenitor of this principal Orphic deity. This contrasts with another, presumably later, Orphic fragment (frag. 98 in Guthrie, 138) that may imply that she was his daughter.[5]

The extant Orphic fragments present a number of threads indicative of this earlier theogony. Fragment 86 (in Guthrie, 138), for example, states that when Phanes first emerged "none saw [him]... unless it were holy Night alone." Nyx/Night would of necessity have preceded Phanes in order to be able to "see" the new god. Nyx/Night's older, first-place status in the Orphic theogony is also indicated in the later-born god Zeus's referring to her reverently as "Mother, highest of the gods" and "immortal" (frag. 164 in Guthrie, 139). Even Homer (*Iliad* 14.259) presents Nyx/Night as a formidable power who was superior to the gods. Moreover, that Nyx/Night (darkness) would precede Phanes (light) in the procession of cosmological developments corresponds with the order of events in other neighboring cosmogonies (see, e.g., Genesis 1:1–5).

I would further argue that one of Phanes's epithets, *Protogonos* (Guthrie, 96), or "First Born," indicates that (1) he was understood to have been *born*, as opposed to autogenetically brought into existence (again, implying the pre-existence of Nyx/Night as birth mother), and (2) he was the *first* such being born. Phanes was famously pictured as a hermaphroditic entity, uniting in himself the characteristics of both sexes (frag. 81 in Guthrie, 137).[6] As such, he represented the first division into male and female. Hence Phanes's other epithet "Eros," the force of erotic attraction and love, perhaps demonstrates that Phanes represented a transition from parthenogenetic creation to sexual procreation in the order of the universe. Another important aspect of Phanes is that, although he was bisexual, he specifically took on a "male" identity. This stands in contrast to his probable mother Nyx/Night, who, although she was parthenogenetic, retained "female" status. I submit that Phanes's characterization as "male" and his being assigned power as the primary creator being were part of a theological transition marking the arrogation of parthenogenetic capacity to the realm of the Masculine. I return to this point in chapter 2, when I discuss the Orphic myth of Zeus's "swallowing or absorption" of Phanes as symbolic of a further trend in this regard.

Ge/Gaia

As we have seen, in Hesiodic theogony, Ge/Gaia, or the Earth Goddess, was also an autogenetically produced entity. According to this same tradition (*Theogony* 126–32), she had parthenogenetic capacity, as well, having borne starry Uranus, the god of the heavens, without a partner. She produced three other sets of progeny in similar fashion: (1) Ourea, or the mountains; (2) the accompanying nymphs of the mountains; and (3) the barren sea Pontus. It is not until after this point that Ge/Gaia began engaging in sexual union, mating with her son Uranus to bear the Titans, the Cyclopes, and the three hundred-handed sons (133–53).

Ge/Gaia's Titan children included the males Oceanus, Coeus, Creius, Hyperion, Iapetos, and Cronus, and the females Theia, Rhea, Themis, Mnemosyne, Phoebe, and Tethys (133–37). The Titans subsequently united in pairs sexually to create the first generation of Olympian gods, among whom Zeus came to be the chief deity. Ge/Gaia, however, fomented the rebellion of the Titans against Uranus, who despised their children. The son Cronus thus subsequently castrated Uranus. From the drops of Uranus's blood that fell to earth, Ge/Gaia also spontaneously produced the Erinyes, the giants, and the nymphs called the Meliai (185–87).

Hesiod (*Works and Days* 563) calls Ge/Gaia "mother of all." Not only was she credited with creating a number of the above-mentioned primordial beings parthenogenetically, but she was also understood to have created all life on earth in the same manner. Aeschylus calls her (*Libation Bearers* 127) "Earth, the mother of all things, and foster-nurse, and womb."[7] Cicero comments, "All things fall back into the earth and also arise from the earth" (*De Natura Deorum* 2.26, 1933, trans. Rackham).

Plutarch (*Table-Talk* 2.3.3/637B) notes the ancient Greek belief that the earth parthenogenetically produced creatures such as mice, snakes, frogs, cicadas, and locusts. Herodotus (1.78) reports a related belief that the snake was similarly born of Earth. Centuries later, Artemidorus (*Oneirocritica* 2.13) likewise asserts, "the serpent itself is a child of the earth and spends most of its time on the ground" (Artemidorus 1975, 97, trans. White). Pliny (*Natural History* 8.84) also remarks, "small serpents at Tiryns...are said to be sprung from the earth." Ge/Gaia is said to have spontaneously brought forth a great scorpion to kill Orion when the hunter went on a rampage to slay every beast on the planet (Pseudo-Eratosthenes *Constellations* 32; Ovid *Fasti* 5.540–44). Ovid (*Metamorphoses* 1.438–40) writes that, after the time of the legendary flood, Ge/Gaia parthenogenetically produced Python, the great serpent who guarded the Oracle at Delphi, and about whose own relationship to parthenogenesis, particularly in connection with the oracular priestesses at that site, I speak of at more length in *CDB* (Rigoglioso 2009, 188–89).

Besides being endowed with the capacity to produce animals and plants spontaneously from her own being, Ge/Gaia was also credited in some traditions with having created humans themselves parthenogenetically. A lyrical fragment attributed to Pindar and thought to come from the *Hymn to Zeus Ammon* states that in the beginning men sprang from Mother Earth (Cook 1914–40, 1:366–67). Archelaus of Athens supposedly believed that the first men appeared from the earth, were nurtured on the primordial ooze, and only later came to reproduce. Empedocles says that "shoots of miserable men and women" were born "from the earth, having a portion of both water and heat," and Democritus held that the first men were created of water and mud (Hesiod 1987, 61, trans. Caldwell). The concept is echoed by Plato (*Symposium* 191b), who relates a belief that humans used to spawn from the earth in the manner of crickets. He also reports (190b) a presumably ancient legend that the earth originally gave birth to women, in particular. Writing later, Plutarch (*Table-Talk* 2.3.3/637B) similarly speaks of a story that earth spawned the first humans as fully formed, grown, and self-sufficient creatures who thenceforth reproduced sexually.[8]

The poet Asius (in Pausanias 8.1.4) specifically mentions that "black earth" brought forth "divine Pelasgus" as the first mortal. The Arcadians likewise believed that Pelasgus was born of the earth itself (Plutarch *Roman Questions* 92/286A).

Legends recount that when the Greek "Noah," Deucalion, landed his ark on Mt. Parnassus, he and his wife Pyrrha consulted the (Delphic) oracle there on how to repopulate the earth. The goddess Themis, Ge/Gaia's daughter, cryptically instructed them to throw over their shoulders "the bones of their mother." Realizing that stones were the "bones of the earth mother," they followed the instructions, and new men and women sprang up from those bones (Apollodorus 1.7.2; Ovid *Metamorphoses* 1.368–410). Ge/Gaia's parthenogenetic capacity is also implied in the story of Erichthonius, who was "produced from the earth" when Hephaestus's semen fell there as a result of his unsuccessful attempted rape of Athena (Scholiast on *Iliad* 2.547; Euripides *Ion* 20, 266; Apollodorus 3.14.6; Pausanias 1.2.6).

In light of the argument that certain Greek priestesses produced off-spring parthenogenetically, Plato's comment (*Menexenus* 238a) about the relationship between the reproductive capacities of Ge/Gaia and women is perhaps significant. He states, "the woman in her conception and generation is but the imitation of the earth, and not the earth of the woman" (1892, 2:521, trans. Jowett). This not only demonstrates the primacy granted by the Greeks to Ge/Gaia as the template for all motherhood but may also point to an occult belief that women, too, had the capacity to reproduce as earth did—that is, parthenogenetically—a possibility I explore in depth in *CDB*. That Plato may have intended this is not such a far-fetched idea when one considers that the philosopher himself was legendarily thought to have been parthenogenetically conceived (see Rigoglioso 2007, 510–18).

It should also be noted that Ge/Gaia's generativity was attributed in some traditions to her *hieros gamos* union with Uranus. The classical expression of this belief is a fragment of Aeschylus's play *The Daughters of Danaus*, which formed part of a trilogy of which only the first play, *The Suppliants*, remains intact. In the fragment of this mostly lost work, the goddess Aphrodite declares,

> The pure Sky longs passionately to pierce the Earth, and passion seizes the Earth to win her marriage. Rain falling from the bridegroom sky makes pregnant the Earth. Then brings she forth for mortals pasture of flocks and corn, Demeter's gift, and the fruitfulness of trees is brought to completion by the dew of their marriage. Of these things am I part-cause. (in Guthrie 1967, 54)

A formula expressing this belief is preserved by the Neoplatonist Proclus (*On Plato's Timaeus* 5.293), who remarks that Orpheus speaks of the Earth as the first bride, and her union with the Sky as the first marriage. He further states that at the Eleusinian rites the Athenians "looked up to the sky and shouted *hye!* ('Rain!'), then down to the earth and shouted *kye!* ('Conceive!')," as I discuss further in chapter 5. The addition of Uranus to Gaia's story may have been a theological manipulation, however. As Guthrie (1967, 59) notes,

> For a settled agricultural people particularly, it is the earth on which they live, and from which they draw the means of living—it is she whom they primarily love and worship, just as it is she to whom they must devote their labor and their attention if they are to enjoy the fruits of her fertility. The male consort plays a minor part.... Whatever the reason, a characteristic of Mediterranean religion was the supremacy of the female principle in nature, the earth-mother. The reason may...lie in a state of society when

in human relationships too the mother occupied the chief place....Male
spirits of fertility existed, but they were subordinate figures, satellites of
the mother and no more.

Indeed, as I argue throughout this book, there is evidence that for early
Greek or pre-Greek society, in particular, the male consort in fact played
no part at all in goddess cosmogony. Moreover, the larger Aeschylus
drama cycle in which Aphrodite's message appears, mentioned earlier, concerns the story of the legendary Danaids, the fifty daughters of
Danaus of Egypt who refused to sacrifice their virginity in a forced marriage arrangement, and who killed their suitors on their so-called wedding night. The Danaids were descendants of Io, who I argue in *CDB*
(Rigoglioso 2009, 130–33) was a historical priestess of Hera conscripted
into sexual union with Zeus. According to my argument, this indicates
that she was a parthenogenetic priestess. The Danaids were also descendants of a second legendary figure with a parthenogenetic story, Danaë,
who was also impregnated by Zeus against her will, and who subsequently bore the Greek hero Perseus (Homer *Iliad* 14.319–20). This suggests that Danaë, too, was a priestess of divine birth. The "fifty daughters"
of Danaus were priestesses of Athena/Neith, Demeter, and Persephone,
as well, who I argue throughout this work were Virgin Mother goddesses.[9] I return to this argument in chapter 5. Here, I will but briefly suggest that, as devout virgin priestesses of these parthenogenetic goddesses,
and as descendants of parthenogenetic priestesses, the Danaids themselves
may well have been priestesses of divine birth. The story of their forced
marriage may therefore represent the disempowerment of their virgin
birth priestesshood. Thus, Aphrodite's statement at the dramatic conclusion of their story—that Ge/Gaia's fecundity only comes about *through
mating with Uranus*—may represent a corresponding patriarchal theological attempt to demote the original parthenogenetic nature of the Earth
Goddess herself.

CHAPTER 2

ATHENA/NEITH/METIS: PRIMORDIAL CREATRIX OF SELF-REPLICATION

In the Greek tradition, Athena was the goddess who most famously held the epithet *Parthenos*, Virgin. In this chapter, I explore her relationship to the Greek Metis and the Egyptian Neith to show that this title was a holdover of Athena's original status as a parthenogenetic creatrix. Demonstrating the connections between the goddesses Metis, Athena, and Neith, I argue that that all three were virgin mothers who, in their earliest mythological strata, may have been equated or esoterically considered overlays or octaves of one another.

In this chapter, I show that clues from both the Orphic and Hesiodic theogonies point to Metis's tremendous antiquity and her autogenetic/parthenogenetic status. These clues include her depiction as the creatrix who held the "seed" of—and preceded—the Orphic god Phanes, her identification with Phanes as hermaphroditic creator, the presence of her name in a Hesiodic catalogue of holy virgins who had the task of birthing and rearing the children of gods on earth, and a textual hint that her conception of Athena may have occurred independently of Zeus.

I also show that Neith was unequivocally portrayed as an autogenetic/parthenogenetic creatrix in the inscriptions of the middle and later periods in Egypt, a depiction that may have characterized the goddess in her earliest cult, as well. She specifically was both creator and "virgin," a being whose *peplos*, or dress, no one had lifted. As one of the oldest deities of Egypt, who most likely was worshipped throughout ancient Libya, she thus represents one of the earliest appearances of the archetype of the Virgin Mother goddess in the ancient Mediterranean world. Symbols and attributes related to her, including the weaving function, the bee, the vulture, and the beetle, all had either direct or indirect parthenogenetic meanings. Her symbols of the bow and arrow, and her veneration by the warrior-maiden Auses, may also indicate that she was specifically the goddess of what I argue were the historical Amazon women of Libya.

I present evidence that Athena was widely considered in antiquity to be the same goddess as the Egyptian Neith and that many aspects of her iconography, mythology, and cult indicate that she was not just the "Greek equivalent" of a foreign deity, but that she *was* Neith, transplanted to Greece from Egypt. Her birthplace was considered to be the legendary Lake Tritonis in North Africa, and it was there that she was said to have killed her comrade Pallas. The act resembles the combat ritual that the historical Ausean maidens of Libya enacted to determine who among them were "true" *parthenoi*, a detail that may subtly indicate that the Auseans once attempted the practice of divine birth. Like Neith, Athena was a "virgin," warrior goddess, and patroness of weaving, whose virginal *peplos* was a main feature of her cult at Athens. Like her "mother" Metis, she was considered a goddess of wisdom. The numerous correspondences among these parthenogenetic goddesses, combined with the motif of Metis's "motherhood" of Athena, may suggest that all *three* goddesses were one and that the "birth" of Athena represented a moment of pure parthenogenetic self-generation on the part of this being. Whether or not the argument can be pushed this far, it seems likely that, based on Athena's correspondences with Neith, the Greek warrior goddess also must have been venerated as a Virgin Mother in her most ancient aspect.

Finally, I point to clues in the myths associated with both Metis and Neith indicating that at some point both goddesses were ontologically demoted from their position as parthenogenetic creatrixes and placed in subordinate, wifely positions to male gods: Metis to Zeus and Neith to Re. Although they remained "mother" goddesses (of Phanes and Re, respectively), their parthenogenetic authority was usurped by the male gods Phanes, Zeus, and Re, among others, who came to assume self-generative powers. Similarly, Athena was cast as a "daughter" of Zeus and a protectress of the patriarchal Greek *polis* itself. These cosmic changeovers may have corresponded with a transition from a dedication to the practice of pure parthenogenesis to that of divine birth through *hieros gamos* on the part of priesthoods associated with Neith in Egypt and Neith/Athena in Greece. I now flesh out the details of these arguments.

Metis

In Orphic theogony, Metis, whose name means "wisdom" or "counsel," was identified with the god Phanes (Guthrie [1952] 1993, 97). Yet the extant Orphic fragments indicate that she also preceded him and overlapped with Nyx/Night as the being who was considered to have conceived and given birth to him. Specifically, Metis is called "An awful *daimon*...bearing the honored seed of the gods, whom the blessed on tall Olympus were wont to call Phanes, the Firstborn" (frag. 85, in Guthrie, 136). Elsewhere in the Orphic theogony (e.g., frags. 70–75, in Guthrie), it is implied that Phanes was born of the World Egg. Thus, if Metis bore Phanes, and Phanes was born of the World Egg, Metis must have produced this egg. As I suggested in chapter 1, in the oldest stratum of Orphic theogony Nyx/Night probably created this egg. This overlapping therefore points to a probable ancient identification between Metis and Nyx/Night. Certainly fragment 85, mentioned previously, at least implies that, with or without an egg, Metis conceived Phanes parthenogenetically. Her role in doing so would have rendered her a creatrix in her own right.

In the Hesiodic account (*Theogony* 337–58), Metis was an Oceanid, a child of the Titans Tethys and Oceanos, and thus a granddaughter of Ge/Gaia. Significantly, Hesiod (346–48) calls the first forty-one of the female offspring of Tethys and Oceanos, of which Metis was one, "a holy race of *Kourai* who on earth raise youths to manhood, with Lord Apollo and the Rivers" (Hesiod 1987, 48, trans. Caldwell). This charge was given to them by Zeus. What Hesiod implies here is that these holy *Kourai*—that is, "maidens" or, more to the point, "virgins"—either took earthly form or had human counterparts; in either case, the task of the holy daughters was to rear boys. I suggest their charges were not just *any* boys, but the progeny of male deities, among them Zeus and Apollo. I also suggest that the *Kourai* were tasked not only with raising these boys, but also with mating with the gods to bring such boys onto the earth plane to begin with. Indeed, an examination of the names of these *Kourai* reveals that quite a number of them are identical with those of female figures who, as I show in *CDB*, were depicted in myth as holy *parthenoi* or priestesses of parthenogenetic goddesses. Among them are Admete, a priestess of Hera (Rigoglioso 2009, 119–21); Kallirhoe, whose name was interchangeable with that of Io, another priestess of Hera, who bore Epaphus through union with Zeus (130–33); Dione, the primary female deity at Dodona, where I argue a parthenogenetic priesshood was located (139–69), and Europa, who, also by Zeus, bore both the namesake of Dodona, Dodon, and other important male heroes (145–46). Thus, I propose that Hesiod's lines here are the oldest extant reference to virgin motherhood and the divine birth priesthood. Although he describes this phenomenon in androcentric terms—as being at the bidding of male gods and, presumably, involving *hieros gamos* unions—we can read with a hermeneutics of suspicion that this may be a patriarchal gloss over what was originally conceived as a pure parthenogenetic function by goddesses and

their earthly priestesses. I would also argue that Hesiod's use of the term
Kourai (sing. *Kourê*) establishes it as one of the special titles for "virgin
mothers"—be they deities or the human women who attempted to imitate their miraculous mode of reproduction. This becomes significant
in chapter 5, where I discuss Persephone, who most famously bore the
Ko(u)rê title to the point where it was used interchangeably as her name.
By including Metis among the *Kourai*, the ancient mythographer, I contend, affirms the goddess's parthenogenetic nature.

Significantly, Hesiod (*Theogony* 886) also names Metis as the mother of
Athena, whom the Greeks widely acknowledged to be identical with the
North African/Egyptian goddess Neith. This is attested by Herodotus
(2.62), Plato (*Timaeus* 21e), Plutarch (*On Isis and Osiris* 9/354C), Diodorus
Siculus (5.58), and Pausanias (2.36.8, 9.12.2). According to Origen (*Contra
Celsum* 5.29), the Egyptians themselves believed that the goddess whom
the Greeks knew as Athena and perceived to "possess" Attica was also the
same goddess who had "obtained" Saïs, her most holy city in Egypt. On
Mt. Potinus in Argolis, Athena was known as Athena Saïtis (Pausanias
2.36.8), probably in recognition of her North African origins. What is
particularly interesting to the argument of this book is that Neith was a
parthenogenetic goddess par excellence: As the deity of the first essence,
she was autogenetic. This state of affairs suggests that, as Athena/Neith's
"mother," Metis herself may in some earlier substratum of myth have
been recognized as an autogene who gave birth to herself.

Neith

It is important in discussing Neith as autogene, or self-created Virgin
Mother, and her relationship to Metis and Athena first to establish her
preeminence in the Egyptian pantheon. Neith, also sometimes transliterated as *Nit* or *Net* (Budge [1904] 1969, 1:30), was one of the oldest of all
Egyptian deities and one of the most important divinities during the early
historic period. There is strong evidence that her worship was widespread
even in predynastic times (Budge 1:450; Hollis 1994–95, 46). She is first
documented iconographically in the last phase of the predynastic period
(c. fourth millennium B.C.E.), where her emblem of crossed bows appears
on some decorated pottery (Petrie 1901, pl. 20 no. 11; B. Adams 1988, 51).
Near the beginning of the First Dynasty (c. 2920–2770 B.C.E.), Aha, the
first historical king of Egypt, dedicated a temple to her at Saïs (Emery
1961, 51).

That Neith was worshipped in the earliest dynastic period and enjoyed
a dominant role at the Egyptian royal court is evident from the fact that
nearly forty percent of early dynastic personal names incorporate her

name, particularly those of four royal women of the First Dynasty—two of them clearly queens and related to the last predynastic and first three dynastic kings (Hollis 1994–95, 46).[1] Among them is Nit-hotep, the probable wife of King Aha (Budge [1904] 1969, 1:453). On an ivory tablet found among the burial goods of Aha, in Upper (southern) Egypt, the earliest portrayal of what is thought to be a sacred shrine associated with Neith's cult is depicted (Spencer 1993, fig.; Hollis, 48). Thus, it is clear that the religion associated with Neith must have been of considerable antiquity even in the First Dynasty.

A text from the Ramesside period of the New Kingdom (1304–1075 B.C.E.) affirms that Neith was held to be the "great, divine mother" of primeval times who wisely adjudicated the dispute between Horus and Seth for divine kingship (Lichtheim 1973–80, 2:215). Neith's cult is first documented at Abydos and flourished particularly in the northern town of Saïs[2] on the western delta, where King Aha built a temple to her. However, that the ivory drawing from his burial was found in the south and that pottery depicting her symbols was much more widely dispersed indicate her cult could not originally have been so limited (Lesko 1999, 47). In dynastic times, she was the most important goddess, and possibly the most important divinity in general, of the northern kingdom (47). Her cult reached its height during the Old Kingdom at Saïs (c. 2525–2134 B.C.E.), and remained important, though to a lesser extent, in the Middle and New Kingdom. It regained political and religious prominence during the Twenty-Sixth Dynasty (c. 672–525 B.C.E.) at Saïs and in Esna in Upper Egypt (Griffis-Greenberg 1999, para. 5).

Kees (1961, 28) notes that during the Old Kingdom the Egyptians characterized this goddess as "Neith from Libya, as if she were the chieftaness of this neighboring people with whom the inhabitants of the Nile valley were at all times at war." Herodotus and other Greek writers saw her as originating in Libya as well (Sayed 1982, 192–93). Two symbols associated with her suggest that her worship indeed may have originated in prehistoric times in ancient "Libya," the Greek term for all of North Africa to the west and southwest of Egypt. The first is the image of crossed arrows, sometimes laid over a shield-like sign. Budge ([1904] 1969, 1:31) believes that this image, the dynastic sign of Neith, is the equivalent of a similar sign found in the predynastic period, thus stressing its great antiquity. In her anthropomorphic form, Neith frequently holds in her hand a bow and two arrows, and in later times she was called Mistress of the Bow and Ruler of the Arrows (Lesko 1999, 46). Egyptologists agree (e.g., Budge 1:451; Hollis 1994–95, 47), that such symbolism indicates that Neith was originally a goddess of either war or the hunt, although there is little mythological reference supporting this concept.

Images of the hunt and warfare waged with bow and arrow indeed proliferate in the prehistoric rock art of the expanse of ancient Libya, indicating that these symbols in Egypt were likely a holdover from the Libyan worship of this goddess (see Lhote 1959, e.g., figs. 12, 31, 42, 44, and Lajoux 1963, 98, 158, 160–69). One Egyptian text speaks of Neith as having set her arrow to her bow and of her enemies falling daily under her arrows (Budge [1904] 1969, 1:462). In her funerary mode, Neith is depicted as shooting arrows at evil spirits that might attack the deceased (Sayed 1982, 81–85). At her temple in the later period at Esna, four arrows were shot toward the cardinal points to indicate that her power was universal and that her—and Egypt's—enemies could expect to be annihilated (Bleeker 1975, 136–37). The German philologist Kurt Sethe has posited (1906, 145) that Neith's original name may have been something close to NTR, namely Nr.t, meaning "the terrifying one," with i sometimes being a modification of the letter r, resulting in Nit. Writing in the fifth century B.C.E., Herodotus (4.180) confirms that Neith was worshipped by the "Libyan" Ause tribe of his day and that her veneration involved a combat ritual among the tribe's maidens, a topic to which I return later in the chapter. That Herodotus situates the Auses in what has been identified as contemporary Tunisia indicates that, at least in the Classical Greek period, worship of Neith extended far west of Egypt.

A second symbol associated with Neith, the cow, further suggests that her worship likely originated in prehistoric Libya. In Egypt, Neith appears in one depiction as a cow with eighteen stars on one side and a collar around her neck (Budge [1904] 1969, 1:451). She is similarly depicted as a great bovine goddess in Coffin Text spell 15, in Herodotus's (2.133) description of her festival at Saïs, and on the wall of the temple to the god Khnum at Esna (Lesko 1999, 55, 60). Rock art throughout the northern part of the African continent dating as far back as 6000 B.C.E. widely depicts sacred bovines and female figures wearing horns, which may represent early forms of Neith and later goddesses with whom she was identified, such as Hathor and Isis.[3]

Beginning in the Third and Fourth Dynasties, Neith came to be regarded as a form of Hathor,[4] but, as Budge ([1904] 1969, 1:451) notes, "at an earlier period she was certainly a personification of a form of the great, inert, primeval watery mass." Indeed, he writes (459), "the Egyptians regarded Net[/Neith] as the 'Being' *par excellence*, i.e., the Being who was eternal and infinite, and was the creative and ruling power of heaven, earth, and the underworld, and of every creature and thing in them." He speculates (283) that as "Net," her name may even be related in meaning to "Nut," the primordial Egyptian goddess of the "watery mass of the sky." In the Pyramid Texts and in a creation text inscribed on a temple at Esna, she was closely identified with the waters of chaos, or Great Flood (*Mehet-Weret*). In this context, she was characterized as a cow who rose from the primeval waters (Lesko 1999, 62). Again, the text from the Ramesside period, mentioned earlier, calls her "the eldest, the Mother of the gods, who shone on the first face," implying that she was considered the original, primordial deity who predated all others (57). Elsewhere, she is described as "the great goddess, the mother of all the gods," and as "Rat [the female sun], the lady of heaven, the mistress of all the gods, who came into being in the beginning" (Budge 1:457–58).[5] Griffis-Greenberg (1999, para. 7) interprets Egyptian myths to indicate that male gods to whom primacy of position in creation was ascribed, such as Atum and Ptah, acted *after* emerging from the void, whereas Neith was a "representation of the first conscious Act of Creation from the Void, who [took] the inert potential . . . and [caused] creation to begin." She thus identifies Neith as Egypt's "deity of the First Principle," the highest and unmoved mover.

Neith as an Autogenetic Deity

As a divinity of the First Principle, Neith was an autogenetic goddess who, in the ultimate mystery, created herself out of her own being. Budge notes ([1904] 1969, 1:458) that an inscription on a statue of Utchat-Heru, a high priest of Neith, relates that she "was the first to give birth to anything, and that she had done so when nothing else had been born, and that she had never herself been born." We see her autogenetic aspect echoed in both Egyptian and Greek texts. Plutarch (*On Isis and Osiris* 9) refers to an inscription on her statue in Saïs,[6] where, as Herodotus (2.59–62) writes, a great and mystical annual festival was held to honor her: "I am everything that has been, and that is, and that shall be, and no one has ever lifted my garment (*peplos*)." The existence of this inscription is confirmed by Proclus (*On Timaeus* 1.30): "[T]he Egyptians relate, that in the adytum of the Goddess there was this inscription, *I am the things that are, that will be, and that have been. No one has ever laid open the garment by which I am concealed. The fruit which I brought forth was the sun*" (Proclus 1820, 1:82, trans. Taylor). The inscription may be a development of a play on her name, *Net*, and the Egyptian *ent* or *entet*, that is, a person or thing that is, that exists, or that has being (Budge [1904] 1969, 1:459). As such, it linguistically would connect her very name with Being and with self-becoming—that is, autogenesis. Plutarch further remarks on the autogenetic nature of Neith later in his treatise *On Isis and Osiris* (62), where he notes that the Egyptians often referred to Isis (that is, Neith) by the name Athena, which signifies "I have come from myself" (*élthon 'ap' 'emautês*).

That in the above-noted Saïtic inscription Neith's "garment" remained perpetually "unlifted" is also a sexual reference (Plutarch 1970, 284–85, ed. Griffiths), as the Greek word used is *peplos*, a robe typically worn by women. The inscription therefore communicates that Neith never engaged in any kind of sexual union; that is, she was eternally a virgin.[7] Yet, as the primordial Being, she was also generative. Thus, in Neith we have one of the earliest appearances of the archetype of the Virgin Mother, the Holy *Parthenos*, in her original, unadulterated form.

The Saïtic inscription has echoes in an Egyptian prayer, whose ideas Budge believes date possibly back to the early dynastic period (c. 2920 B.C.E.), in which the goddess Neith/Net is addressed as follows:

> Hail, great mother, thy birth hath not been uncovered!
> Hail, great goddess, within the underworld which is doubly hidden,
>   thou unknown one!
> Hail thou great divine one, whose garment hath not been unloosed!
> O unloose thy garment.
> Hail, Hapt [hidden one], to whom I am not given entrance, come,
>   receive the soul of Osiris [i.e., the deceased person], protect it within
>   thy two hands. (Budge [1904] 1969, 1:459–61)

In this petition, we have an even more direct reference to the mysterious nature of Neith's (autogenetic) birth, her virginity, and her power over not only the realms of life, but also the realms of death. Here, she is depicted as receiving the deceased back to her deepest "uncovered" aspect, the part of her that must be "unloosed" for the task—in short, her cosmic womb. This prayer likely relates to one of Neith's other early titles, *Apt-uat*, "Opener of the Ways." The text of Unas indicates that she was believed to perform important ceremonies of a magical character in connection with the dead (Budge [1904] 1969, 1:454). As mentioned previously, in her funerary mode Neith is depicted as shooting arrows at evil spirits that might attack the deceased (Sayed 1982, 81–85). Thus, she was also a queen of the Underworld, a guide and protector for the soul in its cosmic and otherworldly journeys. I suggest that her warrior attributes, more broadly, also represent her "death-and-destroyer" aspect, which, paradoxically, simultaneously stands for peace. In containing the forces of destruction and terror within herself, she serves as a touchstone for human consciousness to honor the fierce energies so as not to be subsumed by them. Thus, in Neith we have both the generative and loving autogene and the terrifying yet protective death goddess—the embodiment of opposites, duality, and paradox. This renders Neith a deity of totality, much like the Hindu Kali.

According to Budge ([1904] 1969, 1:451), Net/Neith's name may have derived from the root of the Egyptian *netet*, "to knit, to weave." Thus, a mysterious ovoid or square symbol sometimes depicted above her head in iconography is thought by some to represent a weaving shuttle. Whether or not such an interpretation is correct, Neith was indeed thought to have invented weaving (Sayed 1982, 1:17–18). She was regarded as the divine patron of weavers; the weaving of the meters of cloth needed to wrap mummies came under her protection. An Eighteenth-Dynasty tomb text mentions such linen wrappings as having been produced by the weavers of Neith (Lesko 1999, 56), which also suggests that there may have been a special section of the priesthood devoted to this activity. The Neoplatonist Porphyry (*On the Cave of the Nymphs* 14) notes that in the esoteric Pythagorean tradition, weaving was understood to symbolize the process of incarnation of the soul. Given what I have shown was Neith's preeminence as an autogenetic/parthenogenetic goddess, I suggest that the "weaving" aspect associated with her—a symbol of manifestation and "becoming"—was by definition a parthenogenetic reference. This will become particularly important when I discuss Athena later in this chapter, Hera in chapter 4, and Persephone in chapter 5, all of whom are connected to weaving either in their mythology or cult, thereby underscoring their parthenogenetic nature.

Another parthenogenetic symbol associated with Neith was the bee. I discuss more fully the parthenogenetic aspects of the bee in *CDB* in association with the Pythia, or oracular priestess of Delphi, one of whose titles was *Melissa*, or "Bee" (Rigoglioso 2009, 192–202). Here, I simply note that bees were associated with parthenogenesis because they were believed to be born spontaneously from the carcasses of bulls (see, e.g., Plutarch *Cleomenes* 39; Pliny *Natural History* 11.23; Aelian *On Animals* 2.57). Neith's temple at Saïs was sometimes known as the House of the Bee (Lesko 1999, 48).

The earliest symbol associated with Neith, the image of two click beetles head to head, also may well have had parthenogenetic meaning. Click beetles, which belong to the Elateridae family, were most likely seen by the Egyptians as parthenogenetic because their young appear to emerge in full adult form "spontaneously" from the earth (in fact, they arise from eggs laid there by the female) (Hollis 1994–95, 49). This motif in later times may have been abstracted into Neith's oblong "figure-eight" shield, which sometimes appeared overlaid by her crossed arrows (Lesko 1999, 46; Hollis 1994–95, 48–49; Sayed 1982, 23–24).

Budge ([1904] 1969, 1: 458) suggests that Neith's titles honoring her as the original primordial deity, and her epithet as the "One,"[8] prove that "at a certain period of her history she was to goddesses what Re was to gods." I argue that her documented antiquity, combined with her depictions as the "oldest" of the gods, suggest that she predated Re (later Amun-Re) altogether as supreme being. In fact, she is frequently depicted as having given birth to Re, which, by logic, demonstrates her precedence.[9] Although Re as sun god came to be described as Neith's husband, who "makes fertile with his seed," the fact that Neith was not consistently identified with a consort indicates that such an arrangement had little mythological weight and was likely made by political or regional associations only (Griffis-Greenberg 1999, n13). Whereas evidence for the cult of Neith dates back to the First Dynasty and possibly earlier, Re and his associated priesthood did not come to ascension until the Second, Third, and Fourth Dynasties (Hollis 1994–95, 49). Again, this activity postdates Neith's presence in Egyptian religion, underscoring her probable status as a much older deity.

I submit that the rise in the supremacy of Re marked for the Egyptians the arrogation of female parthenogenetic capacity to the male. For, in his form as Khepera, Re was granted autogenetic and parthenogenetic powers and was said to have made all of creation, including the divinities, by masturbating and ejaculating semen into his mouth (Budge [1904] 1969, 1:308–11).[10] In iconography, Re/Khepera is frequently depicted with a head in the form of a beetle of the *Scarabaeus sacer* species, that is, a scarab or dung beetle. Several ancient writers of the late Greek and Roman periods echo an Egyptian belief in their (erroneous) observation that all beetles were male, and that they were, like the sun god Re, parthenogenetic.[11] This belief arose from the observation that scarab beetles lay a vast number of eggs (incorrectly assumed by the ancients to be sperm deposits [e.g., Aelian *On Animals* 10.15]) in a mass of dung, which they roll into a ball and push into a hole they have dug; there, the larvae are hatched by the heat of the sun. This rendered scarab beetles, in the eyes of the Egyptians, "sun born"—that is, parthenogenetically born of Re and in the manner of his own self-creation (Budge [1904] 1969, 1:356). The beetles in their larval form also represented to the Egyptians the germ of the living soul, which existed in the dead body of the human and burst into a new life in the other world. Thus, Re/Khepera symbolized the resurrection of the body, and this idea was at the root of the Egyptian custom of wearing figures of the beetle and placing them in the tombs and on the bodies of the dead (Budge [1904] 1969, 1:357).

Hollis (1994–95, 49) observes that the ascension of Re, the scarab beetle, and Hathor occurred during the Third and Fourth Dynasties just as Neith seems to have been declining in importance, and she questions whether the simultaneous occurrence of these trends was more than coincidental. I assert that the ascension of Re as beetle indeed marked the assumption by the male god of Neith's autogenetic/parthenogenetic status, as well as the demoting of the goddess from exclusively creatrix to "wife" and "daughter." We see this demotion, for example, in a Fourth-Dynasty sarcophagus: Apa-Ankh addresses Neith together with Anunu and Nesert, two very ancient goddesses, declaring that Neith came forth from Re and that the god came forth from her (Budge [1904] 1969, 1:454). Hathor absorbed these attributes as mother, wife, and daughter of the god and came to serve as the primary female deity involved in queens' *hieros gamos* rituals with gods (see Rigoglioso 2007, 70–71, 75).

Another development in later times was the conception of Neith as bisexual, rather than strictly female. According to Horapollo (*Hieroglyphics* 1.12), the Egyptians continued to include the beetle in the hieroglyph of Neith's name (whom, significantly, he refers to as *Athena*)—in the later era as a scarab beetle. The scarab was said to symbolize Neith's "male" element, and, thus, was always paired with a vulture that symbolized her "female" element. As I have discussed at length elsewhere (Rigoglioso 2007, 76–78), the vulture was a symbol of parthenogenesis. In contrast to scarab beetles, which were believed to be exclusively male, all vultures were considered to be female and to impregnate themselves by flying against the south wind or opening their beaks to the east wind (Aelian *On Animals* 2.46; Horapollo *Hieroglyphics* 1.11). Thus, Neith was represented as a parthenogenetic deity, but now in bisexual form. At Esna, Neith was depicted as "two thirds masculine" and "one-third feminine," and as both "Father of the father and Mother of the mothers" (Lesko 1999, 61). I argue, however, that such bisexual imagery reflects an androcentrically influenced view of her originally female totality. Certainly, the idea of her being "two-thirds" masculine—that is, claimed more for the male side than the female side—should be a clue to probable theological tampering with her story. As Lesko (62) observes, "It is difficult to accept this goddess as androgynous when again and again the text refers to her as 'the cow goddess' and she is called Mother."[12]

A point that should not be overlooked is that this change in Neith's ontological status from "mother" to "wife" under patriarchy may have had profound implications in the cultic realm. In moving from self-generator to "partner" of the god, capable of reproducing through "sexual" engagement with him only, Neith (later Hathor) was made to produce "reincarnated" epiphanies of the god himself. We see this esoteric arrangement reflected in the well-documented Egyptian schema of the priestess/queen mother who was thought to copulate with the god (as her husband, the present pharaoh) in order to give birth to the god (as her son, the new pharaoh; again, see Rigoglioso 2007, 70–94). Perhaps the theological transition of the goddess from pure parthenogenetic creatrix to *hieros gamos* partner paved the way for the use of women's bodies as receptacles for what was believed to be divine (male) seed.[13] As I argue in chapter 5, this cosmic trajectory is similarly embedded in Persephone's story as the *Kourê* whose own parthenogenetic plans were interrupted by rape.

Identification of Metis and Neith

I now return to Metis to argue that she was likely a Greek conception of Neith.[14] According to Hesiod (*Theogony* 887), Metis "knew more than all the gods or mortals." Thus she was a source of supreme wisdom. In Apollodorus (1.2.1), we hear that Zeus enlisted her to serve as a counselor in his power play against his father, Cronus. Cronus had swallowed all of his children to escape a prophecy that one would be greater than he, but Rhea had kept Zeus from this fate by hiding him in a cave after giving birth to him (Hesiod, *Theogony* 477–91). Zeus consulted with Metis on the situation of his siblings, and she gave Cronus a drug by which he was forced to vomit all of the children he had swallowed (Apollodorus 1.2.1). Zeus is depicted as subsequently taking Metis as the first of his six "wives" and engaging in sexual intercourse with her (Hesiod *Theogony* 886). In Hesiod's rendition (*Theogony* 890–900), Ge and Uranus then told Zeus of a prophecy that Metis would eventually give birth to a son who would supersede Zeus as king over gods and mortals. They advised him to put Metis inside his belly so that no other god should ever be given kingly position.

From these fragments, it is clear that Metis was an older and more powerful divinity than Zeus: She both was born before him and possessed wisdom he did not have. As Kerenyi (1978, 11–12) argues, she also represented the matriarchal order. This is hinted at, he says, by the fact that it was *her* descendant, in particular, who posed a threat to the ascendancy of Zeus, indicating that the privilege of mother right was in operation. That Metis was associated with the origination of a lineage can be further seen in an Attic tale describing a royal line known as the *Metionidai*, and a corresponding ancestral progenitor, *Metion*. Kerenyi contends these names derive from *Metis*. Moreover, Apollodorus (1.3.6) says it was Metis herself, not Ge and Uranus, who delivered to Zeus the prophecy of the "feared son," which corresponds more accurately with her authority as the wisest of the deities.[15] Such a pronouncement on her part also hints at a power struggle between her and Zeus.[16]

Apollodorus goes on to report that Metis's union with Zeus resulted in her becoming pregnant with Athena but notes that she turned herself into many forms to try to avoid the encounter. Her reluctance is arguably understandable in light of her likely desire to keep her matriarchal autonomy. A second Hesiodic narrative about Metis and Zeus, contained in a fragment preserved by Chrysippus (908),[17] may contain a vague hint that Metis was parthenogenetic: in this version Metis is portrayed as conceiving Athena *after* she is fully inside of Zeus's belly. The lines read as follows:

[Zeus]...had lain in love with...Metis, whom he deceived, for all she was so resourceful, for he snatched her up in his hands and put her inside his belly for fear that she might bring forth a thunderbolt stronger than his own; therefore the son of Cronus, who dwells on high, seated in the bright air, swallowed her down of a sudden, but she *then* conceived Pallas Athene...(italics mine)

That Zeus's swallowing of Metis—and Metis's conception of Athena—occur here at an indeterminate time after his intercourse with her opens the door to the possibility that the conception was understood to be unrelated to the sex act. I submit that this is but a shard of a reference to Metis's own parthenogenetic capacity,[18] a characteristic that is given fuller expression in the Orphic story, as I discussed earlier, and on which I elaborate in what follows. Given that in the biological condition of mother-daughter parthenogenesis, the daughter created is symbolically seen as a genetic "double" of the mother, we could read Metis's becoming pregnant with Athena as equivalent to her becoming "pregnant with herself." Because, as I established earlier in this chapter, Athena was widely identified by the Greeks with the North African Neith, what emerges from this analysis is the syllogism Metis = Athena; Athena = Neith; therefore, Metis = Neith.

Whether the identification among these three female beings can indeed be pushed this far or not, what is fruitful for the argument of this book is simply the evidence indicating that Metis was parthenogenetic in her own right. The hint of Metis being a virgin mother both in the Chrysippus fragment referenced previously and in her identification as one of the holy *Kourai* (which I have proposed were parthenogenetic female beings) allows one to conclude that the Hesiodic Metis and the Orphic Metis were, in their earliest conceptions, one and the same—for the latter, too, was depicted as autogenetic/parthenogenetic. As mentioned earlier, in the extant Orphic fragments, Metis is said to have given birth to Phanes by virtue of her own possession of the "seed of the gods." The implication is that no one put that seed within her but, rather, that she already contained it within herself—i.e., that she possessed the capacity to give birth out of herself spontaneously. That Metis in this story is depicted as an autogene, a self-generated being, is underscored by the fact that Phanes was understood to be "identical" with her, that is, a parthe-nogenetic "double." Indeed, one of Phanes's very names in Orphic theogony was *Metis*. The identification of these two figures is also expressed in Orphic fragments that simultaneously call Phanes both "Metis, the first father," and "Metis, first mother" (Guthrie [1952] 1993, 97). Guthrie (98) notes a passage of John Malalas (*Chronicle* 4.9, 1986, trans. Jeffreys et al.), an Antiochene historian of the sixth century C.E., further equating Phanes with Metis:

> and the name of the Light [i.e., the god Phanes]...Orpheus, having heard it by his gift of prophecy, declared [this god] to be Metis, Phanes, Erikepaios; which being interpreted in the common tongue is Counsel, Light, Lifegiver.

Thus, Metis = Phanes, just as Metis = Athena. In both Orphic and Hesiodic renderings, she is the autogene who reproduced herself.

As indicated earlier, however, in the Orphic tradition there was a twist. As the offspring of Metis, Phanes was no longer considered a female "double." Rather, he was rendered as explicitly bisexual. Yet, importantly, he was predominantly identified as male. This points to a cosmic transfer of female parthenogenetic capacity to the male element, for generative power was subsequently ascribed to Phanes-as-male/hermaphrodite. Later, Zeus appropriated parthenogenetic power by "swallowing" Metis in the Hesiodic version (*Theogony* 886–90) and Phanes in the Orphic version (frag. 167 in Guthrie [1952] 1993, 140). Such a motif once again affirms that Phanes was considered identical with Metis. In Hesiod, Zeus's acquiring of the parthenogenetic capacity of the female is expressed in the story of his "giving birth" to Athena from his head as a result of the presence of the pregnant Metis in his belly. That this was indeed perceived as a parthenogenetic episode is affirmed by the goddess Hera, who vociferously denounces it as a grave transgression of female power (*Hymn to Apollo* 311–24). I return in chapter 4 to Hera's response to this transgression by producing parthenogenetic offspring of her own.

The Greek Athena's Roots in North Africa

The story of Athena's birth from Zeus's head appears in Hesiod (*Theogony* 924). There, we learn that Zeus was relieved of his progeny by having his head split open by an axe. Pindar (*Olympian Ode* 7.35) assigns the role of axe wielder to Hephaestus and depicts Athena as springing forth with a mighty war shout. Other traditions add that the goddess emerged from Zeus's head in full armor.[19]

Several accounts of the story (e.g., Apollodorus 1.3.6) indicate that Athena's birth took place at the river Triton, which confirms her origins in North Africa. Apollonius Rhodius (*Argonautica* 4.1310) reports unambiguously that the pre-Hellenic peoples in Greece, the Pelasgians, believed that Athena was born beside Lake Tritonis/River Triton in ancient Libya.[20] Writing about the geography of his day, Herodotus (4.175–80) confirms the existence of a large river called "Triton," which flowed into "the great lake of Tritonis" in North Africa far west of Egypt. Apollonius Rhodius (4.1307) further records a legend that Athena was found and nurtured at the river Triton by three nymphs dressed in goat skins, an outfit that Herodotus (4.188) affirms was the typical garment worn by Libyan women. Herodotus (4.180) notes a specifically Libyan tradition that Athena/Neith was the daughter of Poseidon and Lake Tritonis itself. Apollonius Rhodius (4.1493) also speaks of a "Tritonian nymph" who gave birth to Nasamon, the eponym of the Nasamonians of North Africa. A connection is thus implied between this "Tritonian nymph" and the "nymphs" who helped rear Athena. As I argue more fully in *CDB* (Rigoglioso 2009, 88–92), the epithet "nymph" was often a marker for a parthenogenetic priestess. Thus, I contend that these myth fragments regarding the birth and homeland of Athena point to the existence of a parthenogenetic priesthood associated with Athena/Neith at Lake Tritonis (see Rigoglioso 55–59).

We see the first signs of support for this idea in a detail in Apollodorus (3.12.3): The Pelasgians maintained that, while engaged in combat as a girl, Athena killed her playmate, Pallas, the "daughter" of the river god Triton. As a "daughter" of a river, Pallas herself would have had "nymph" status, given that, as Larson (2001 *passim*) demonstrates, legendary daughters of waterways were always nymphs. Thus, we are at once alerted to the possibility that Pallas was a parthenogenetic priestess. Apollodorus goes on to report that the Pelasgians contended that Zeus intervened to prevent Pallas from striking Athena, thereby causing Athena to mortally wound her comrade.[21] As a token of her grief, Athena placed Pallas's name before her own, becoming Pallas Athena, and carved from a tree trunk a statue of Pallas known as the Palladium, which in Greek legend was venerated as an image of the goddess herself.

The African provenance for the birth of Athena supports her identification with the Libyo-Egyptian Neith, as well as the subsequent implication that she was brought to Greece by Egyptian or Libyan colonizers. Athena's probable African origins are further underscored by the fact that the first coins to show her head portrayed her as resembling a black African woman (Bernal 1987–2006, 3:548). Another tradition held by the Libyan Ause tribe of the fifth century B.C.E. further points in this direction. As just mentioned, according to Herodotus (4.180), the ancient Libyans—and the Ause tribe in particular—believed that Athena/Neith was the daughter of Poseidon and Lake Tritonis but that, because of a quarrel with Poseidon, she turned her loyalties to Zeus, who made her his own daughter. A possibly older genealogy for Athena in North Africa, however, is related by Diodorus Siculus (3.70.2–3). The historian confirms the tradition that Athena was born beside the river Triton but relates an ancient belief that she was "born of the earth," Ge/Gaia herself. Not only does this mythologem stress Athena's affiliation with Africa, it also connects her, once again, with a pure daughter-bearing partheno-genetic story. As one of the only explicitly acknowledged parthenoge-netic beings in the Greek tradition, Ge/Gaia could be seen as a proxy for Metis/Neith in this tradition.

Another mythological detail supports the argument for Metis's identi-fication with Neith, as well. According, again, to the fragment preserved by Chrysippus (908), Metis fashioned Athena's armor while both were in the belly of Zeus. In this detail, Metis herself is shown to possess the warrior attributes of the African Neith.

The Relationship of Neith/Metis/Athena to the Libyan Amazons

I will diverge here briefly from the focus thus far on the parthenoge-netic nature of Neith, Metis, and Athena to establish their connection to early matriarchy in North Africa and, by extension, the Greek regions to which they migrated. I contend that exploring the interplay between their mythology and the early cultural complexes in which they played a key role illuminates our understanding of each and allows us to appreciate more fully the importance of the concept of virgin motherhood in both.

The mythologem of Metis's making armor for Athena hints at a rit-ual of passing the mantle of warriorhood and the accoutrements of war-fare that may have been part of Libyan matriarchal culture. The story of Athena battling her friend Pallas in Libya indeed suggests a tradition of armed female combat in North Africa. According to the Suda (s.v. *Pallas*), the very name *Pallas* comes from *pallein*, "to brandish," as in a spear. Kerenyi (1978, 26) further claims, "It was once the name for robust maidens and implied the meaning of the masculine word *pallas* . . . 'robust young man.'" Thus, the name Pallas itself connoted a robust, masculine fighting woman: in short, an Amazon.

This is highly significant to my argument, for a tradition of women warriors in prehistoric North Africa is affirmed archeologically in the ancient rock art of the Tassili mountains, located in contemporary

Algeria. One scene depicted at Sefar, dating approximately 3550 to 2500 B.C.E., is clearly one of pitched battle in which female combatants with small breasts attack with bows and arrows opponents of ambiguous gender (Lajoux 1963, 164–68). This image supports the claims of Diodorus Siculus (3.52–55) that historical warrior women known as the Amazons dwelt in the region of Lake Tritonis and had an important influence on North African geopolitics many generations before the Trojan War (i.e., before 1275 B.C.E.).[22] Female warriorhood is furthermore documented ethnographically by Herodotus (4.180). Writing in the fifth century B.C.E., the historian reports that Libyan girls of the Ause tribe, who lived on the shores of Lake Tritonis near the Triton River, engaged in armed ritual combat. He specifically relates,

> They hold an annual festival in honor of Athena [Neith], at which the girls divide themselves into two groups and fight each other with stones and sticks; they say this rite had come down to them from time immemorial, and by its performance they pay honor to their native deity [Neith]— which is the same as our Greek Athena. If any girl, during the course of the battle, is fatally injured and dies, they say it is a proof that she is no maiden [*pseudoparthenos*]. Before setting them to fight, they pick out the best looking girl and dress her up publicly in a full suit of Greek armor and a Corinthian helmet;[23] then they put her in a chariot and drive her round the lake.

Herodotus then describes the nature of Auscan social structure:

> The women of the tribe are common property; there are no married couples living together, and intercourse is casual—like that of animals. When a child is fully grown, the men hold a meeting, and it is considered to belong to the one it most closely resembles. (Herodotus 1972, 331, trans. Sélincourt)

If we penetrate through the androcentric and derogatory tone in this passage (e.g., portraying women as "common property" presumably *of men*, and likening members' sexual habits to that of animals), it becomes apparent that what Herodotus is describing is a classical matriarchal society in which childrearing was communal, monogamous marriage was not practiced, lineage was reckoned through the mother's line, and paternity was of little consequence.[24] The Auses also retained memory of a tradition of female warriorhood, as suggested by the maiden ritual being fought *to the death* and the custom of parading a maiden around the lake in full combat gear. The fact that they held that the tradition was a survival "from time immemorial" further supports the idea of a probable deep history of female military tradition in their culture and in the larger North African region. I am suggesting, in short, that the Auses were a remnant of the Amazon tribes of North Africa about which Diodorus wrote and that were depicted in the rock art. I also suggest that their maidenly combat ritual echoes the myth of Athena slaying her friend Pallas in Libya. That the Auses carried out their old ritual specifically in honor of Neith, and that Athena and Pallas were associated with the rite, suggests that Neith/Athena was most likely the primary deity of the Libyan Amazons more broadly, dating from the remotest of times. I propose that it is this connection with female Amazons, in particular, that the symbols of the crossed arrows and the bow and arrows in Neith's early iconography reference. In short, I am suggesting that, originally, Neith was no generic "warrior goddess," but rather the goddess of the Libyan Amazons, specifically.

Bates (1970, 104) posits that the armed maiden who mounted the chariot in fact "represented" the goddess Neith/Athena herself. I agree, and I suggest that the criteria for her selection probably had to do with more than beauty. I posit, in fact, that the young woman may have been a victorious combatant from the previous year who had been selected for the position of high virgin priestess for a special reason. The clue to that— and its full meaning—may be found in the detail that the maidens who died in combat were considered *pseudoparthenoi*, false virgins. I propose that for the Auses, the opposite of a *pseudoparthenos*, that is, an *authentic parthenos* (maiden, virgin), was not considered simply a girl who had not engaged in sexual intercourse. From Herodotus's description of the Auses as a people among whom sex was casual and unfettered, it is clear that this tribe was not interested in virginity in a moralistic sense as a measure of a girl's purity and "value" in the brokering of marriage. Indeed, in this tribe there was no marriage, certainly not in the monogamous sense that the Greeks had in mind. This was clearly a people for whom sex was a natural act that had few taboos attached to it.

I propose, instead, that the Ause ritual originally may have served as a means of divining which maidens among them were fit to become priestesses of parthenogenetic conception in the manner of their parthenogenetic goddess, Neith/Athena. Not having engaged in sexual intercourse may have been one physical criterion for the priestesshood, but there was undoubtedly much more required on the spiritual level. I submit that those who perished in the combat were considered "false virgins" in that they were assumed to be the ones the goddess herself had determined were unfit for the role of holy *parthenos*, as I define in *CDB* (Rigoglioso 2009, 39–43), a priestess of divine birth.[25] Thus, I suggest that the ritual originally served as a divinatory "test" to determine which girls had the proper constitution to participate in the greatest mystery practice of their religion.

Such "tests of virginity" are documented elsewhere in Greek writings. Aelian (*On Animals* 11.16), for example, describes a tradition carried out at Hera's cult site of Rome in which the virginity of priestesses dedicated to the goddess was verified only if snakes accepted the young women's food offerings. As I argue in *CDB* (Rigoglioso 2009, 127–38), it is likely that Hera's cult at some phase included a parthenogenetic priestesshood. Thus, I posit that this snake ritual, like the Ause mock battle, was the vestige of a divinatory practice originally designed to determine which young women were either (1) suited to be holy *parthenoi* in the first place, or (2) dutifully maintaining their virginity for such a purpose. By the late Roman period, however, as Aelian reports it, the practice had devolved into a punitive one that emphasized the women's "purity" in a moralistic sense.

I propose that, in the earliest phase of Ausean culture, the *parthenos* who was crowned with the helmet of Neith/Athena before the battle may have been considered a particularly worthy priestess. Perhaps this was by virtue of the courage and physical prowess she had displayed in the combat ritual the year before. Perhaps, too, at some remote period, she was a *parthenos* who was believed to have conceived in miraculous fashion. Whether the Auses were attempting parthenogenesis in Herodotus's day (fifth century B.C.E.) remains an open question. I suspect it is more likely that by that late period the rite had become merely a symbolic one that preserved the memory of an original cultic practice.

That parthenogenesis may have been the actual or symbolic focus of the ritual is further suggested by a detail related some four centuries after Herodotus by the Roman geographer Pomponius Mela (1.35). The annual festival, he writes, was celebrated on Neith/Athena's birthday. As we will recall, the earliest substratum of Neith's story related that the goddess gave birth to herself out of herself—that is, autogenetically. Although, according to Herodotus, the Auses believed Neith/Athena to have been the child of Poseidon and the river Triton, I submit that the motif of celebrating the day of Neith's "birth" was a remnant of an archaic memory of the goddess's autogenetic origins.

If it is true that the Ause ritual centered around the selection of maidens for the parthenogenetic priesthood associated with Neith/Athena, the fact that combat was an integral part of the rite may signal that parthenogenetic birth was originally practiced by the earlier Libyan Amazons, as well. Furthermore, given that the primary familial relationship in a cultural condition of Amazony, the one imbued with the greatest importance and sacrality, was the mother-daughter bond,[26] it may be that the cult of the earlier Amazons was dedicated to pure daughter-bearing parthenogenesis, in particular. I suggest it may even be the case that the "quarrel" the Auseans reported between Athena and Poseidon reflected the imposition of the Poseidon cult into the culture. Given that, in the Greek tradition, Poseidon fathered numerous children by way of mortal women, it may be that the advent of the Poseidon cult in the region involved what I have argued was a transition from pure parthenogenesis to *hieros gamos* parthenogenesis and a corresponding power struggle between the clergy involved.

Support for this idea may be found in the work of Eva Meyerowitz, who, through extensive field work in the mid-twentieth century, identified what she believed was a survival of ancient "Libyan" religion in the beliefs and practices of the Akan peoples of contemporary Ghana. According to Meyerowitz,[27] the oldest substratum of Akan religion and culture, which probably reflects early Libyan customs most closely, indeed resembles in some senses the parthenogenetic Amazony that I posit here. During the earliest phase of their religion, the Akan worshipped a goddess, Nyame or Atoapoma, who, Meyerowitz observes, was nearly identical with the early Neith. She was an exclusively female, self-creating Mother Goddess of the moon believed to have brought forth the universe through parthenogenesis. She was venerated as the ruler of the Sky, the Earth, and the Underworld. Known as the "Ever-Ready Shooter," she gave life to humans and all living things on earth by shooting into their inert bodies particles of her *kra*, or "vitalizing moon fire." She also took them back to herself after death.

Women could become "possessed" by the *kra*, or animating life-force, of Nyame and, thereby, give birth to a "daughter" of the goddess, a being thought to subsequently incarnate in an animal (or insect) or representative totem, which would be venerated. The mediating divinity might show itself to the people in its animal shape (as an antelope, falcon, or the like) in times of danger to lead them to water, show them food, help them escape an enemy, and so forth. By giving birth to this goddess/animal being, the woman herself was rendered "divine," and was honored as a ruler of a clan. Although Meyerowitz does not report a claim that such a woman was believed to give birth to a *human* child parthenogenetically, the mechanism of this "spirit birth" in all other ways resembles what I posit in *CDB* took place in Greek cult: the woman entered into a trance state (see Rigoglioso 2009, 16–18) and was visited and "entered" by the moon. We similarly see the motif of impregnation by the moon in the ancient accounts of the conception of the Egyptian divine bull Apis and the story of Io's parthenogenetic impregnation with Epaphus (132–33). The divinization of the woman also supports my argument in *CDB* that women who were believed to have achieved miraculous birth were thought to ascend to goddesshood.

The Libyo-Akan female ruler could unite her clan with others to form a state, thereby becoming a queen mother. In order to be considered fit to rule, she was required to sacrifice her own child, preferably a daughter at the age of puberty; the sacrificial victim had to die willingly in order for the desired blessings to be achieved. In this motif we see echoes of the Ause combat ritual, which could also be read as a form of ritual sacrifice of the virgin.

The Libyo-Akan queen mother governed her state assisted by a council of head women from other clans and sub-clans. Although all adults in a village could join the council meetings, decisions rested with the women elders, and the queen mother's word was final. The queen mother was also the supreme war leader before the time when kingship was introduced, and maintained that role during later, more androcentric periods if the king died and no successor had been appointed. She accompanied her warriors into battle, a tradition that continued until 1900, when Yaa Asantewa became the last queen mother to lead an army in the Asante's war against the British (Clarke 1988, 133).

The Libyo-Akan queen mother was also a high priestess. She served as an intermediary both to the supreme goddess and the deceased ancestors, offering rituals and prayers to secure the well-being of her people. She was a rainmaker, as well, propitiating the goddess with offerings. In this, her role calls to mind that of the Danaids, priestesses from ancient North Africa who brought to Argos rainmaking and the Thesmophoria dedicated to Demeter and Persephone, which I discuss in chapter 5. The Libyo-Akan queen mother intervened ritually in the case of fire and epidemics and conducted girls' menarche rites. She passed her position down through her female line.

Meyerowitz hypothesizes a progression from matriarchy to a more patriarchal social structure over time, possibly due to the Akan uniting with other peoples who worshipped a father god. The queen mother moved from giving birth to what were believed to be exclusively female deities to producing bisexual ones; correspondingly, a father god came to share rule with the Mother Goddess. It is at this period and not before, Meyerowitz posits, that the sacred marriage to celebrate the union of the god with the goddess was instituted. This involved a ritual sexual rite between the queen mother (or her younger proxy) and a lover. As time went on, kingship also was introduced, with the king personifying the god. With the expansion of the city-state, the king was no longer regarded as the male aspect of the Mother Goddess moon, but rather an incarnation of the sun (akin to Re). Men now also claimed equality with women as givers of life. Although the king and queen mother continued to coexist as leaders, the king established his supremacy. Patrilocal marriage was also instituted. These developments correspond with the trajectory that I posit independently in *CDB*, of the divine birth cult's transition under patriarchy from attempts at pure parthenogenesis to conception rituals involving human male actors ritually invoking male gods.

Meyerowitz's work suggests the existence of a widespread matriarchy in North Africa in antiquity, in which women served as political leaders, warriors, priestesses, and purported birthers of supernatural beings, all in the service of their autogenetic goddess of the bow and arrow.[28] Her account corresponds with the profile of the ancient Auses in relationship to Neith/Athena that I have discerned from mythology and historical text. It illuminates what the relationship that between the Virgin Mother goddess and her holiest priestesses may have looked like.

The Grecization of Neith/Athena and Her Cult

The numerous correspondences between Neith and Athena support the argument that the cult of the former was transported from North Africa to Greece. Athena's springing from Zeus's head "fully grown," for example, echoes the idea of the click beetle that originally belonged to Neith emerging fully grown from the earth. Her association with the lake/river Triton, highlighted in two of her epithets, *Tritogeneia* (born of Triton) (Homer *Iliad* 4.515, *Odyssey* 3.378; Hesiod *Theogony* 895) and *Tritonis* (Apollonius Rhodius 1.109) recalls Neith's aspect as the goddess of the watery chaos. The various associations of Athena with the owl connected her with the realm of the dead, which, as we have seen, was Neith's domain, as well.[29] The symbol of the owl may also be parallel with that of Neith's vulture icon (Bernal 1987–2006, 3:578).

Athena was also, like Neith, widely acknowledged to be a virgin.[30] Various other elements associated with her suggest that she retained hints of autogeneity, as well. We recall Plutarch's (*On Isis and Osiris* 62/376A) claim that the name Athena signified "I have come from myself" (*êlthon 'ap' 'emautês*), an unequivocal autogenetic reference. The Orphic *Hymn to Pallas* (Athena) begins by addressing Athena as *monogenês*, which is generally translated as "only-begotten," but which can also mean "only born sole offspring," "unique in kind," and "singly born" (Long 1992, 49). In short, it connotes a self-born, self-created being, which corresponds perfectly with Athena's identification with the autogenetic Neith.[31] Athena also wore the lizard or crocodile on her breast in certain gems. This is likely a vestige of her association with Neith, whose mythology, mentioned earlier, included a story that she gave birth to the crocodile god Sobek. What is particularly interesting here is that the lizard was believed to conceive by the ear and bring forth its young from the mouth (King

1887, 107). Thus, Athena's wearing of the lizard/crocodile would connect her with both Neith and parthenogenesis.

Athena also retained Neith's function as goddess of weaving (e.g., Hesiod *Works and Days* 63–64; Aelian *On Animals* 6.57), which, as I posited earlier, was symbolic of parthenogenetic creation. Athena's role as virgin patron of weaving was acknowledged during her most important festival at Athens, the Panathenaia, which was held in the summer and celebrated as the new year. As part of this event, four women were elected from those of noble birth to weave the goddess's woolen *peplos*, or ceremonial robe, and present it to her statue at the Acropolis at the culminating moment of the grand procession (Suda, s.v., *arrephorein*; *peplos*). The *peplos* motif calls vividly to mind the inscription to Neith mentioned earlier, "no one has ever lifted my *peplos*," a direct reference to Neith's parthenogenetic nature.[32]

Cecrops, the legendary first king of Attica, is said to have introduced the cult of Athena in Athens, probably from Egypt. Diodorus Siculus (1:28.4–5) affirms that the Athenians believed they themselves were "colonists from Saïs in Egypt," Neith's primary cult center, and that Cecrops was Egyptian. The twelfth century Byzantine scholar Tzetzes quotes Charax of Pergamon, a priest and historian of the earlier centuries of the common era, as echoing the claim that Cecrops colonized Athens from Saïs (in Bernal 1987–2006, 3:566). Thus, there is much direct evidence to suggest that Cecrops brought the worship of Neith with him from Africa to Greece, where she took on the name *Athena*. Bernal (571) plausibly dates Athens's first foundation to the first half of the nineteenth century B.C.E.

Cecrops's establishment of the cult of Athena at Athens is further indicated in legends relating that he was the first to erect a statue to Athena (Eusebius *Preparation for the Gospel* 10.9.22), that he was "called upon" by Athena to witness her planting the olive tree there, and that his testimony persuaded the Olympian gods to grant the goddess supremacy in Attica over Poseidon (Apollodorus 3.14.1). According to Varro (in St. Augustine *City of God* 18.9), Cecrops is said to have called the citizens together to cast their vote in favor of one deity or another. As women of that period participated in civic affairs (in contrast to later Greek women, who were barred from such participation), they all voted for Athena. By virtue of their outnumbering the men by one person, they won the vote for the goddess. Shortly after this victory, Athena laid down the large "rock" on which the Acropolis was to be built in the city that was to bear her name, Athens (Callimachus *Hecale* frag. 260.18–29, trans. Trypanis]).

I suggest, then, that Cecrops's "establishment" of the Athena cult reflects the period in which the Neith cult of Africa was made part of the "official" state religion on Greek soil. Yet I also agree with Cook (1914–40, 3.1: 189–226), who believes that Athena was a pre-Greek divinity of the Athenian Acropolis and that she was an antecedent to Zeus. Thus, I suggest that what the legend of Cecrops depicts is the moment in which Athena was theologically "demoted." Cecrops was also credited as the first to apply the name *Zeus* to the masculine god (Eusebius *Preparation for the Gospel* 10.9) and the first to give him the epithet *Hypatos*, "Highest," indicating that under his rule Zeus was established as supreme deity (Kerenyi 1978, 19). As we have seen from the Greek myths about Athena, the once powerful creator goddess of Africa was made to come into a subordinate relation with this god. Perhaps the corresponding Ausean legend reported by Herodotus, that Athena broke with Poseidon and was made Zeus's "daughter" reflected a political bargain whereby the Athena cult was able to reign with supremacy over the Poseidon cult in Attica on the condition that it remained secondary to that of the religion of the "father," Zeus.

On the cosmic level, the drama was played out in the mythologem of Zeus's "swallowing" Metis-Athena/Metis-Phanes, thereby acquiring the generative powers of the universe, in addition to his kingship. This masculine appropriation of parthenogenetic capacity[33] is most clearly expressed in Orphic fragment 167 (in Guthrie [1952] 1993, 140), where Zeus's incorporation of Phanes is described as follows:

> Thus then engulfing the might of Erikepaios [Phanes], the Firstborn, [Zeus] held the body of all things in the hollow of his own belly; and he mingled with his own limbs the power and strength of the god. Therefore together with him all things in Zeus were created anew, the shining height of the broad *Aither* and the sky, the seat of the unharvested sea and the noble earth, great Ocean and the lowest depths beneath the earth, and rivers and boundless sea and all else, all immortal and blessed gods and goddesses, all that was then in being and all that was to come to pass, all was there, and mingled like streams in the belly of Zeus.

Zeus's parthenogenetic capacity is expressed here in the idea that all of existence was "created anew" in the moment of his ingesting of the older god. Fragment 168 (in Guthrie, 140) underscores this concept:

> Zeus became first, Zeus of the bright lightning last. Zeus is head, Zeus middle, and from Zeus all things have their being. Zeus became male, Zeus was an immortal maiden. Zeus is foundation of earth and starry heaven. Zeus is king and Zeus himself first father of all....and Metis the primeval father, and all-delightful Eros. All these things are united in the vast body of Zeus.[34]

Here again, by incorporating Phanes into himself, Zeus also incorporated Metis, the *original*, primeval mother (now called a "father"). Thus,
we see a male being having acquired the power of the female creatrix.
This is underscored in the very language used here, which echoes the
aretology attributed to the autogenetic/parthenogenetic Neith at Saïs: "I
am everything that has been, and that is, and that shall be, and no one has
ever lifted my garment (*peplos*)."

Zeus's usurping of female parthenogenetic power is also illustrated
elsewhere in the myth of Dionysus's birth. The mortal Semele was
impregnated with Dionysus by Zeus and died of fright when the god
appeared to her in his full splendor. Zeus subsequently took the fetus and
incubated it in his "thigh"—no doubt a euphemism for his penis—until
it was ready to be born (Apollodorus 3.4.2–3). As Zeitlin (1984, 189n21)
notes, the struggle of the male to control or usurp female reproductive
power could already be seen in the two divine generations prior to Zeus.
In Hesiod's *Theogony* (155–200), Zeus's grandfather Uranus, she writes,
"begrudges female productivity by refusing to allow his children to be
born, and, more importantly, he creates [Aphrodite] alone from the blood
and semen of his severed genitals." Zeus's father, Cronos, subsequently
swallowed his own children "in imitation of pregnancy," but was forced
to disgorge them (*Theogony* 453–500). In this light, it is thus particularly
significant that Zeus conscripted Metis, whom, as I have argued, was
parthenogenetic herself, into determining how to make Cronos expel
his progeny. He no doubt shrewdly discerned that part of her "wisdom"
would have been the knowledge of how to induce "labor"!

It is interesting to note that in Orphic fragment 168, mentioned above,
the gender opposite to Zeus (as "male") is rendered not as what one
would expect, that is, simply "female," but rather something much more
specific: the "immortal maiden." The actual transliteration is *Zeus ambro-
tos epleto numphe*, "Zeus was an immortal *nymph*." Thus, what has been
rendered as "maiden" by some translators is, in the original, literally,
"nymph." Expressed here is the idea that the female equivalent of the
male creator god, the gender counterpart who was on par with him, was
the *nymph/parthenos/kourê*. As I show in *CDB*, in cultic terms all three
words originally referred to the "holy virgin," the human priestess of
divine birth with whom gods were believed to unite sexually to produce
their children on earth (see, e.g., Rigoglioso 2009, 39–43; 88–106). Thus,
Zeus-as-male is being paired here with nymph/maiden as his opposite
sexual pole—and the one with whom he will copulate. I propose that
what we see here is the laying of the groundwork for what turns out
to be not a consensual union with, but rather the rape of, the *parthenos/
kourê/korê/nymph* on the cosmic realm. As I discuss in chapter 5, in the

Orphic story Zeus raped the *kourê* par excellence—Persephone—to bring forth his "double," the god Dionysus. As I also argue in that chapter, this travesty was the cosmic paradigm that translated on the earth plane as the usurping of the human divine birth priestesshoods. Through sexual unions with gods that were akin to rapes, the priestesses were conscripted into conceiving the sons of the male deities—their "doubles" who would serve as heroes and kings on earth.

In the Hesiodic myth (*Theogony* 900), Zeus put Metis away inside his own belly "so that this goddess might advise him on good and evil" (Hesiod 1987, 76, trans. Caldwell). Here we have the appropriation not only of female parthenogenetic capacity, but also of wisdom, personified by Metis. Despite interpretations of the word *mêtis* as nothing more than "cunning intelligence" (see, e.g., Detienne and Vernant 1978, 11, 21, 27, 107–9, etc.), I argue that the ideas that Metis was capable of advising Zeus on matters of "good and evil" (*agathon te kakon te*) and that she "knew more than all the gods or mortals" (Hesiod *Theogony* 887) indicate that her type of wisdom was much more than "cunning." Rather, these descriptions suggest that Metis's wisdom was all-powerful, mystical insight, or *gnosis*. This position is strengthened by the fact that Athena subsequently became the goddess not of "cunning," but of "wisdom" in its fuller sense. Such wisdom also included prophetic ability, as seen in the ancient belief that Athena introduced both prophecy and medicine to Greece (Plato *Timaeus* 24c).

Thus, with Zeus's swallowing of Metis, we have the entrapment of women's wisdom within the patriarchal entity, leading to the perpetual siphoning off of female energy by the male.[35] This, then, was the "most high" Zeus who was established in Attica during the reign of Cecrops, a god who had subsumed the wisdom and parthenogenetic capacity of the matriarchy in order to fuel the patriarchal enterprise.

That the Athenians attempted to fully cast Metis/Athena/Neith in her role as the pale shadow of Zeus—and, simultaneously, the female as the shadow of the male—can be seen on the temple to her they named the *Parthenon*, "Precinct of the Virgin." Located on the sacred site of the Acropolis at Athens, the fifth century B.C.E. edifice depicted on its pediment the "parthenogenetic" story of Athena's birth from Zeus's head (Pausanias 1.24.5). The pedestal of Athena's ivory statue, housed within, showed the misogynistic Hesiodic account of the birth of Pandora, whom the poet identified as the "first woman" to be born when men supposedly roamed the planet in female-less paradise (Hesiod *Theogony* 570–615, *Works and Days* 70–105).[36] On the shield of Athena's statue was a scene from the Athenians' legendary war to vanquish the Amazons (Pausanias 1.17.2), an image also depicted on the *metopes* of the building (Brouscaris

1978, 62–63). This last completes the picture of the disempowerment of the parthenogenetic matriarchy.[37]

Thus, the Parthenon, a victory monument celebrating the Greek defeat of the Persians and Athenian military dominance,[38] was simultaneously a monument to the patriarchal fantasy of male parthenogenesis and the male creation of women. This doctrinal program completely reversed the biological reality of the male's emergence (i.e., physical birth) from the female.[39] The ivory statue of Athena was known as *Athena Parthenos*, "Athena the Virgin" (Pausanias 5.11.10), here representing a virgin who was no longer generative and autogenetic, like the Libyan Neith, but masculinized and sterile. In his play *Eumenides* (658–66), Aeschylus even goes so far as to use the example of Athena's birth from Zeus's head to support the following statements: "The mother of what is called her child is not its parent, but only the nurse of the newly implanted germ.... [F]atherhood there may be when motherhood there is none" (Aeschylus 1926, 2:335, trans. Smyth). Callimachus (*Hymn 3, Bath of Pallas* 134) similarly depicts her as a goddess whom "no mother bore." Later in *Eumenides* (736–38), Aeschylus even has Athena utter a complete disavowal of her connection with women altogether: "For mother I have none that gave me birth, and in all things, save wedlock, I am for the male with all my soul, and am entirely on the father's side" (Aeschylus 1926, 2:344–45, trans. Smyth). The conscious recognition of Athena's older identity as generative mother persisted in only one small location of Greece: Elis. According to Pausanias (5.3.2), there the women founded a temple of Athena, surnamed *Mother*, to whom they prayed to conceive at their first unions with their husbands so that they would quickly repopulate a land that had lost many of its men in war.

In Greek religion, Athena thus operated as an exteriorized male projection of the female wisdom being Metis. Athena's creative energies were now harnessed in service to the Athenian state. She absorbed all of the warrior attributes of the Libyo-Egyptian Neith. In addition to being depicted as born in armor and uttering a mighty war cry, as mentioned earlier, she is described in various writings as cultivating and excelling in the arts of war; loving the war cry, the din of horses, and the sack of cities; and protecting those who went to war.[40] However, unlike Neith, who may well originally have been invoked to protect the matriarchate, Athena was appropriated to advance patriarchy, and the Greek patriarchy, in particular. She is depicted as coming to the assistance of many a violent Greek hero who was instrumental in advancing Greek political hegemony and the Zeus cult, including Achilles, Odysseus, Jason, and Bellerophon, as well as Perseus and Heracles (Blundell 1995, 27). She was recorded by many ancient writers as having "supported" the Greeks in their war against Troy (see, e.g., Theoi Project 2000–2007, specifically "Athena Myths 2" and "Athena Myths 3"). So potent was she considered to be in her warrior aspect that legends recount that Troy could not be sacked as long as the statue known as the Palladium, the likeness of Pallas with lance poised in one hand and distaff and spindle in the other, which Athena herself was said to have created, remained in Troy's possession.[41] The Orphic tradition pointedly says Athena was "made the dread accomplisher of the will of [Zeus]" (frag. 177 in Guthrie [1952] 1993, 140). The goddess joined Zeus in his victorious battles against the gods of the older generation to which Metis belonged, which, again, may have represented a pre-patriarchal order. Athena served the god as a shrewd warrior and tactician, helping to vanquish beings who tried to re-establish pre-Zeusian rule: the Titans (Hyginus *Fabulae* 150), the Giants (Apollodorus 1.6.2, 2.7.1; Pausanias 8.47.1), and Typhon, the winged and snake-like parthenogenetic son of either Ge/Gaia or Hera (Antonius Liberalis *Metamorphoses* 28; Valerius Flaccus *Argonautica* 4.236–38). In short, the Athena of classical Greece, whose story still dominates our understanding of her today, was an appropriated, diminished, and distorted version of the generative Virgin Mother she once was.

CHAPTER 3

ARTEMIS: VIRGIN MOTHER OF THE WILD, PATRON OF AMAZONS

Artemis was another Greek goddess who possessed the title *Parthenos*. In this chapter, I explore her mythology to argue that she, like Athena, was originally considered a Virgin Mother. I also consider her connections with Athena/Neith and, continuing the argument of the historicity of the Amazons who venerated these deities, offer a unique analysis of the possible relationship of the Thermadon Amazons of West Asia and the Libyan Amazons of North Africa.

In brief, Artemis was variously imaged as the twin sister of Apollo, the goddess of the Arcadian "nymphs," the fierce patroness of Tauris and Brauron, and the nurturing nature goddess of Ephesus. Underneath such imagery, one may discern a much older, pre-Hellenic goddess who was a parthenogenetic creatrix. The argument that in her earliest manifestation Artemis was understood to be a self-generative goddess is supported by the fact that in her most primitive aspect she was considered simultaneously a Mistress of the Wild Animals, a goddess of fertility and nature, and a *Parthenos* (Virgin). She also demanded women's chasteness, yet protected those who gave birth. These seeming paradoxes are resolved if one understands her to be a Virgin Mother who produced life from within herself without a male consort. As in the case of Athena and Metis, Artemis also had a mother, Leto, whose attributes suggest that she, too, was in a parthenogenetic relationship with her daughter.

In this chapter, I show that Artemis's many similarities with the autogenetic Neith/Athena further supports the position that she was originally considered parthenogenetic and lends credence to the idea that she may even have had roots in North Africa. Iconographically, both goddesses shared the symbols of the bow and arrow and the bee, for example. Like Neith, Artemis was depicted in many instances as a warrior goddess and patron of the Amazons. I argue that the Thermadon Amazons who venerated Artemis may, in fact, have been descendants of the Libyan Amazons reported to have colonized much of the West Asian region, where the Thermadon Amazons were later believed to have dwelt. Evidence pointing in this direction includes the presence of the city name *Myrina* in ancient Anatolia, which I suggest may have referenced the Libyan queen Myrina as an ancient ancestress. That both Libyan and Thermadon Amazons may have shared a common cultural heritage again points to the possibility that the two virgin mother goddesses whom they venerated may have had common roots in Africa.

Artemis as Creatrix

As she was known in Greece, Artemis seems to have had four distinct and overlapping identities, which may reflect how she was seen and adopted during different time periods and in various regions. In one of her aspects, she was the twin sister of Apollo and daughter of the Leto (e.g., *Hymns to Artemis* 9.2 and 27.3). In a second, she was the goddess of the nymphs of Arcadia, the mountainous, forested center of the Peloponnesus. In a third form, she was centered in Tauris and Bauronia, where at one time human sacrifices may have been offered to her.[1] In her fourth aspect, she was the Asiatic fructifying and all-nourishing nature goddess of Ephesus in Anatolia.

Classics scholars generally agree that the goddess Artemis originated in the pre-Greek era.[2] Her name does not appear to be Greek, and, according to Guthrie (1967, 99), in her early form she was "one of the greatest, if not the greatest, of the deities worshipped by the inhabitants of pre-Hellenic Greece, of Western Asia Minor, and of Minoan Crete." He thus contends (101) that the patriarchal northern invaders who established what was ancient Greece found this goddess already in place when they came to occupy these regions, and incorporated her into what became the Olympian pantheon. Artemis's identification with the Phrygian Cybele, who yoked lions to her chariot,[3] and the Cappadocian Ma, has prompted suggestions of her possible Asiatic origin; she also may have derived from the Minoan Mistress of the Animals or from an Arcadian cult (Guthrie 1967, 99, 106). On Crete, she was identified with the mother goddesses Britomartis, Dictynna, and Eileithyia.[4]

Artemis's probable pre-Greek aspect as goddess of nature may be reflected in her Homeric title *Potnia Theron*, Mistress of the Wild Animals (Homer *Iliad* 21.470). In Greek mythology, her realms were always the mountains, where she was said to have dwelt (Callimachus *Hymn 3 to Artemis* 19–20). Numerous animals were sacred to her or depicted by her side in text and iconography, including deer, leopards, lions, bears, fish, buzzards, and snakes.[5] Pausanias (8.22.4–8) further relates that in Stymphalus in Arcadia, where a great festival was held to Artemis, her sanctuary contained carvings of the Stymphalian birds. These were the deadly creatures that Heracles slew as one of his twelve labors, which were considered sacred to her. Behind the temple stood marble statues of maidens with the legs of birds, underscoring her ornithological associations. Such imagery suggests a connection between Artemis and what appears to have been a Bird Goddess of the Neolithic period in Old Europe, confirming Artemis's great antiquity (Gimbutas 1999, 155–57).

In Ephesus, where a monumental temple famous throughout the ancient world stood in her honor, Artemis's statue reflected her attributes as a goddess of animals, fertility, and nurture. Numerous large protrusions suggestive of breasts emanated from her chest, and a variety of animals and insects were depicted in relief covering her entire body and crown (see, e.g., Baring and Cashford 1991, 329). Such imagery leads Farnell ([1896–1909] 1977, 2:455–56) to conclude that Artemis was in the earliest Greek religion an earth goddess, associated chiefly with wildlife, growth of the field, and human birth. At Ephesus, she was worshipped in this "old way" right through classical times (Guthrie 1967, 103).

Given, as I argue in chapter 1, that the other primal Greek goddess who was similarly characterized, Ge/Gaia, was the parthenogenetic creatrix of all of nature's animal manifestations, I propose that in her original form, Artemis, too, was a parthenogenetic goddess. Indeed, I find various efforts on the part of scholars to connect Artemis with a "consort" unconvincing (see, e.g., Harrison [1912] 1963, 502; Guthrie 1967, 103). Artemis's iconography, attributes, and legends make it plain, as I show in what follows, that she was above all an independent goddess. Cybele, with whom she was sometimes identified, did have a consort, Attis, but he was, as Guthrie (1967, 60) emphasizes, "by no means on a level with her. He is only a youthful attendant who is passionately devoted to her service. Though a divinity, he is her servant and high priest rather than her compeer." I propose that Attis was a late and weak afterthought to the mythology of the self-sufficient, autogenetic Virgin Mother goddess.

Although Homer hints at Artemis's earlier amplified status in her title *Potnia Theron*, he otherwise depicts her in much diminished form as a young maiden hunter, daughter of Leto and Zeus, and twin sister of Apollo (e.g., *Odyssey* 6.100–109). Hesiod (*Theogony* 14, 918) and the Homeric *Hymns to Artemis* (9, 27, 28) do the same. Farnell ([1896–1909] 1977, 2:427) affirms that the Homeric view of Artemis reflects a late-stage transformation of the goddess from a once-powerful mother goddess of Minoan-Mycenaean religion into a mere nymph inhabiting the wilds of the mountain.[6] Given that Apollo does not appear in association with Artemis in her more primitive aspects, it is likely that the appending of Apollo to her mythology was a late development (Cook 1914–40, 3.1:501; Farnell [1896–1909] 1977, 2:465).

Artemis and Her Mother, Leto

An analysis of the relationship of Artemis to her mother, Leto, is, as was the case with Athena to Metis, important in that it reveals a matriarchal state of affairs that also may have involved parthenogenetic conception. In the Hesiodic genealogy (*Theogony* 404–8), Leto (Latin: Latona) was the granddaughter of Ge/Gaia. Her parents were the Titans Phoebe and Coeus, and her siblings were Asteria and Hecate.[7] Hesiod (*Theogony* 918) and Homer (*Iliad* 1.9; *Odyssey* 11.317) refer to her as the mother of the twins Artemis and Apollo by Zeus, to whom she was married before Hera. Later writers make her merely Zeus's concubine, persecuted during her pregnancy by Hera.[8]

A variety of attributes, symbols, and stories associated with Leto suggest that in her pre-Greek form she, too, was understood to be parthenogenetic. One of the most striking is her connection with weaving, a symbol of parthenogenesis associated, as I have shown, with both Neith and Athena. Pindar (*Nemean Ode* 6.35b; Threnoi/Dirges 3 [1997, 361 ed. and trans. Race]) calls Leto "goddess of the golden spindle" and "goddess of the golden distaff." This recalls, in particular, the Palladium statue, in which Pallas Athena, that representation of Amazonian virginity, was portrayed with a spindle and distaff in one hand. Another parthenogenetic symbol associated with Leto was the *ichneumon*, or "tracker," an Egyptian weasel-like animal that hunted crocodile eggs. According to Aelian (*On Animals* 10.47), the *ichneumon* was thought to be "both male and female in the same individual, partaking of both sexes, and nature [had] enabled each single same animal both to procreate and to give birth" (Aelian 1959, 2:343, trans. Scholfield). He reports that in Heraclepolis, this creature was sacred both to Leto and Eileithyia. The perceived hermaphroditic element of this animal in association with Leto and Eileithyia (who, again, was identified with Artemis) suggests an ancient conception that these two goddesses themselves possessed the attributes of this animal— that is, they were parthenogenetic in nature.

Some Greek legends separate Leto's birth of Artemis in both time and place from that of Apollo. This supports the argument that the Apollonian element was a later insertion into what was originally a pre-Greek story depicting matriarchal consciousness. According to the Homeric *Hymn 3 to Apollo* (15–16) and the Orphic *Hymn 34 to Leto*, Leto gave birth to Artemis on the island of Ortygia,[9] located along the coast of Ephesus in ancient Anatolia, while she gave birth to Apollo on Delos.[10] The Ortygia locale first of all emphasizes Artemis's Ephesian aspect. Athenaeus (1.31d) points to a tradition that attributed an Eastern origin to Leto, as well, noting that a mountain village near Ephesus was formerly called *Letous*, "Leto's Village," but was renamed *Latoreia* after "an Amazon of that name." This not only points to ancient worship of Leto in Anatolia, but also connects Leto with both Artemis and the Amazons, which will become more significant later in the chapter. Aristophanes (*Women at the Thesmophoria* 120) similarly hints at an Eastern connection for Leto when he has his character Agathon utter in the same breath praises to Artemis, Leto, and "the tones of the Asiatic lyre, which wed so well with the dances of the Phrygian Graces" (Oates and O'Neill 1938, 2:873, trans. anon.). This eastern geographical setting also points to Artemis's Ephesian aspect, which represented the goddess in her oldest form as creatrix, and which, as I argued earlier, was most likely parthenogenetic. Thus, if their stories should be connected in mother-daughter fashion at all,[11] Leto, as mother of the parthenogenetic Artemis, would, by logic, herself have to have been parthenogenetic. The story of Artemis's "birth" from Leto therefore seems to reference a condition of pure parthenogenesis, and, thus, I would argue that the story of Zeus's impregnation of Leto was a patriarchal intrusion into this mythology.

The more popular legend in later times held that Artemis was born on Delos along with Apollo. Even in this case, however, Apollodorus (1.4.1) relates that Leto was said to have given birth first to Artemis, who thereupon helped her mother deliver Apollo. Again, this detail points to both Artemis and Leto as "older" goddesses in relation to Apollo. It also emphasizes the closeness of their mother-daughter bond, which is suggestive of the matriarchal condition. Indeed, Artemis is rendered as having been quite fierce, even risking death, in defending her mother. One ancient legend, for example, says that she shot Tityus dead for attempting to rape Leto.[12] Leto is depicted as reciprocating her daughter's affection. Homer (*Iliad* 21.502–4) describes her as lovingly collecting Artemis's scattered arrows on an occasion when the latter was assaulted by Hera.

Moreover, in Callimachus (*Hymn 3 to Artemis* 21–22), we hear Artemis declare that, because her own mother gave birth to her without pain, she was forever after rendered by the Moerae, or Fates, a helper to women in childbirth. Thus, Artemis's loyalty to her motherline extended more widely to womankind, in general, which again points to her roots in matriarchal tradition. In the Orphic *Hymn to Prothyraea*, Artemis is identified with Eileithyia, the one who allayed labor pangs, eased pain as the child came through the mother's vagina, cared for infants, and guarded

the race of humans. In the Orphic *Hymn to Diana* (Artemis), she is identified as one who similarly assisted with births, despite what the hymn
pointedly refers to as the goddess's own virginity. Again, Artemis's aspect
as helper to women in childbirth is not at odds with her virginal aspect if
we consider her as originally having been a Virgin Mother herself.

Artemis's Connection with Athena/Neith

Although it is generally agreed that Artemis probably derived her identity
from a number of deities foreign to Greek soil, Artemis's resemblances to
Neith and Athena have not been explored in any detail in the extant literature. It is to this topic that I now turn my attention, as a consideration
of Artemis's possible connections to these deities reveals information that
may help to resolve many of the seemingly contradictory aspects of her
myth, iconography, and cult. The resultant data also lends support to my
argument that Artemis was originally a parthenogenetic goddess.

Artemis resembled the Libyan Neith in a number of ways. Like Neith,
her principle attributes were the bow, quiver, and arrows or a spear.[13] She
was the paragon of the huntress; ancient legends are filled with stories of
her love of slaying wild beasts and episodes of her engaging in, or resting from, hunting expeditions.[14] She was even called *parthenos iocheaira*,
"Virgin of Profuse Arrows" (Homeric *Hymn 9 to Artemis* 2), which further calls to mind Neith as both virgin ("no one has lifted my *peplos*")
and "Mistress of the Bow and Ruler of the Arrows." Guthrie (1967, 102)
confirms that Artemis's huntress aspect was indeed pre-Greek, suggesting it was one of her most archaic characteristics. Farnell ([1896–1909]
1977, 2:427) further posits that Artemis probably reflected quite ancient
totemistic ideas of hunting and fishing tribes in which women held particular status.

Artemis also shared with Neith and the Greek Athena a warrior aspect.
Callimachus gives a great deal of detail in this regard (*Hymn 3 to Artemis*
110, 120–24, 225–58) and depicts her as "shooting at the city of unjust
men" (122). In the *Greek Elegiac Theognis* (1.11), a petitioner calls on
Artemis to "ward off the evil Keres [Death Spirits]." These images call to
mind Neith's shooting at the "enemies" of the deceased soul in the otherworld. In Laodicea, coins displayed a striking figure of Artemis bearing an
uplifted shield and battle axe (Farnell [1896–1909] 1977, 2:527). A bronze
statue of Artemis bearing arms stood in Messene (Pausanias 4.13.1).

Various legends speak of Artemis requiring the sacrifice of Agamemnon's
daughter Iphigeneia in order to make conditions favorable for the Greeks
in the Trojan war.[15] In Callimachus (*Hymn 3 to Artemis* 225–29), we hear
that Agamemnon dedicated the rudder of his ship to the goddess in this

war, and that Neleus, son of Codrus, the latter of whom founded Miletus, called on Artemis to guide his ships out of Attica. The Spartans are said to have called on Artemis's powers before battle by sacrificing a goat to her (Plutarch *Lycurgus* 22.4; Xenophon *Hellenica* 4.2.20). Thanksgiving sacrifices were typically offered to Artemis after successful battles, as well, such as the five hundred goats that were sacrificed annually after the battle of Marathon (Xenophon *Anabasis* 3.2.12). The festival of the victory of Salamis in Cyprus commemorated the goddess having shone her full glory on the Greeks in that battle (Plutarch *Malice of Herodotus* 869). An inscription on slabs of white marble located in the ancient Artemision in northern Euboia was similarly laid down in honor of Artemis to commemorate the destruction of the Medes (Persians) (Plutarch *Themistocles* 8.1–2). Moreover, like Athena, Artemis was depicted as defeating the Titans in their war to regain supremacy over Zeus (Hyginus *Fabulae* 150). She also slew Gration in the great battle between the Giants and the gods, as well as the Aloads in their war against the gods (Apollodorus 1.6.2, 1.7.4).

Artemis also came to be honored as the goddess of the moon (Farnell [1896–1909] 1977, 2:457–61), another characteristic that links her with what may have been the earliest form of Neith in North Africa as the goddess Nyame/Atoapoma, as discussed in chapter 2. At Munychia in Attica, at full moon in the month of Munychion (April–May), large round loaves or cakes, decked all around with lights that symbolized the moon, were borne in procession and presented to Artemis. An ancient shrine of the moon goddess at Brauron in Attica also came to be associated with Artemis. There, one of her most famous festivals in the ancient world was held, the Brauronia. As the moon, Artemis was identified with Selene and Hecate (e.g., Plutarch *Table-Talk* 658F; Farnell 2:457). Her lunar aspect was emphasized particularly during the Roman period, when she was known as Diana (Cicero *De Natura Deorum* 2.27).[16]

Could these resemblances suggest that Artemis, like Athena, had roots in North Africa, and even "split off" from the Neith complex at some period? The idea is conjectural, and it is beyond the scope of this work to trace any such possible trajectory. It is nevertheless valid to ponder whether this may have been the case, and whether Athena may have absorbed Neith's warrior aspect, whereas Artemis took on primarily her huntress aspect. In the following sections, I offer further data that reveal additional convergences between these two goddesses that may point in the direction of Africa.

Artemis and the Amazons

Like Neith, Artemis was a patron goddess of Amazons. Greek writings identified two sets of legendary Amazons: one in Libya, and one whose homeland was variously posited as western Anatolia (contemporary Turkey) or northeastern Anatolia along the Black Sea (Bennett 1967, 12). The latter, in particular, was the location of the legendary Thermadon River and the Amazon-founded city of Themiscyra. Hence, this group of warrior women is frequently referred to as the Thermadon Amazons. It is this group that legend and iconography, including that of the Parthenon, mentioned in chapter 2, record as having unsuccessfully marched on Athens and been vanquished by the Greeks.[17] I argue in what follows that both sets of Amazons may have originated in Libya, where, as I posited in the previous chapter, Neith was most likely the primary Amazonian deity.

First, let us see what is said about Artemis in relation to the Amazons. Callimachus (*Hymn 3 to Artemis* 237–47) relates that in Ephesus, Amazons set up a statue to Artemis under a large oak tree.[18] There, their queen, Hippo, performed a holy rite in the goddess's honor. This included the warrior women enacting a war dance in shields and armor, which involved the stomping of feet and the loud rattling of quivers to the shrill accompaniment of pipes. The warriors concluded their ritual by arraying themselves in a circle to sing. It was at this location, the poet says, that the famous Ephesian temple to Artemis, mentioned earlier, was later erected. The Homeric *Hymn 9 to Artemis* (4) depicts Artemis as driving her golden chariot through the city of Smyrna, a town, as we will see, said to have been founded by Amazons. This may be a further indicator of her mythological association with Amazon culture.

Just as Diodorus treated the Libyan Amazons as historical women, as discussed in chapter 2, so various writers describe actual locations where the legendary Thermadon Amazons were said to have had a presence.[19] Writing about places of interest of his time, Pausanias (2.32.9) relates that Celenderis, for example, was the location of Theseus's defeat of the Amazons. In 2.31.4, he mentions that in Troezen, *Lycea*, or "Wolfish," was a surname of Artemis among the Amazons, and that a temple to Artemis Lycea stood there. Elsewhere (3.25.3), he reports that in Pyrrichos, a village in Lacedaemonia, a sanctuary was dedicated to Artemis Astrateia, so named because the Amazons were said to have stayed their advance (*strateia*) here. These "women of Thermadon," he says, dedicated a wooden image of the goddess in the shrine, and another to Apollo Amazonius. On the island of Patmos, lying southwest of Samos, was a place called the Amazonium, suggesting an Amazon presence there, as well (Bennett 1967, 9). Herodotus (4.105–19) relates that when the Thermadon Amazons were defeated in their war against the Greeks (an event dated to after the Trojan war), they eventually settled at the foot of the Caucasus Mountains between the Black and Caspian Seas.

There they interbred with the Scythians and became the Sauromatians, a people of his day whose women were warriors and hunters, whom he describes at length. Recent archaeological evidence by Davis-Kimball (2002) has confirmed the presence of warrior women in this part of the world in the Iron Age, lending weight to the possibility that the accounts such as Herodotus's attesting to Amazon-like tribes in the region were indeed historical in nature.

A train of associations connecting Artemis and Neith relates to the city names *Myrina*, *Smyrna*, and *Ephesus*, all named after Amazons (Strabo 11.5.4). *Myrina* designated two separate cities, one on Lemnos and another on the coast of Mysia (Pliny *Natural History* 4.12). *Myrina* was also the name of an Amazon of the Trojan period whose tomb was thought to be near the ancient city of Troy (Strabo 12.8.6; Homer *Iliad* 2.811–15). Heinrich Schliemann ([1881] 1968, 147), the excavator of Troy, notes that the name *Smyrna* may have been a transposition of *Myrina*. He further notes that *Smyrna* was the ancient name for Ephesus, one given to it by an Amazon whom Strabo (11.5.4, 14.1.4) says "took possession" of the city (see also Justin 2.4). These correspondences indicate that Ephesus, Smyrna, and Myrina were all considered Amazon-founded cities that shared a cultic identification.

This is highly significant, as *Myrina* was the name not only of the Amazon said to have been entombed at Troy, but also of the most important queen of the Amazons in Libya. According to Diodorus Siculus (3.52–55), the Libyan Myrina was a historical woman (and contemporary of the Amazon queen Medusa) who led her female warriors to colonize much of the Mediterranean, including the coast of Anatolia. On Samothrace, she set up rites to the "Mother of the Gods," indicating that she was a priestess as well as a warrior commander. Given Myrina's Libyan origins, I contend that this "Mother of the Gods" must have been Neith.

We thus see that Ephesus, where the Amazons took possession and set up worship to Artemis, was originally named *Smyrna/Myrina*, presumably after either the "Trojan-era" Myrina or the great Libyan Amazon queen. As we will recall, Callimachus says that it was "Hippo," specifically, who founded Ephesus and set up rites to Artemis there. This Hippo therefore must be the same Amazon to whom Strabo refers as having "taken possession" of the city and named it. Again, following Strabo, that city name originally must have been *Smyrna (Myrina)*. Clearly, Hippo's bestowing this name on the city must have been an act to commemorate one of the Myrinas. Diodorus says that the Libyan Myrina and her Amazons existed "many generations before the Trojan War," that is, presumably before Hippo's era. However, that both the Libyan and the "Trojan" Myrinas possessed the same name suggests that they may in fact have been the same person. If not, at least it seems likely that the "Trojan" Myrina was a direct descendant of the Libyan Myrina and was given the name in honor of her ancestor. That Hippo thus named Ephesus *Smyrna*—that is, a form of *Myrina*—similarly suggests she was commemorating this ancient African heritage. From this train of associations, then, I suggest that the ancestors of Hippo—and, by extension, of all Thermadon Amazons—were the Libyan Amazons of Africa.

I further propose that "Hippo" likely still worshipped the same deity as Myrina had, which in Callimachus's account is identified as "Artemis," but which may originally have had an older, African identity. In short, the goddess that Hippo established at Ephesus in Anatolia may have been Neith, goddess of the bow, arrow, and totality of creation. This idea is further supported by the fact that the Anatolian Artemis/Cybele indeed had the same warlike aspect as Neith (Bennett 1967, 22). Moreover, on Lemnos, an island that the Libyan Amazons are also said to have inhabited and where the city of Myrina stood, the Amazonian goddess Bendis had a clear similarity with Neith: She was conceived as a fierce huntress whose symbol was two spears (26), which recalls the icon that belonged to Neith in Africa. Bennett asserts that when Bendis first entered the Greek pantheon, she did so as the Thracian Artemis, thus confirming that Bendis/Artemis was a very ancient goddess. Thus, we have in Bendis the seeming union of Artemis and Neith. At Ephesus and elsewhere, Artemis shared Bendis's general characteristics, and was depicted as the armed goddess of battle (24–27; 43–44; 47–49).[20]

Significantly, on the Black Sea and in Thrace, the archaic Artemis as war goddess also appeared under the name *Parthenos* (Kerenyi 1978, 20). An armed figure, her name is significant in that it stresses the virgin/parthenogenetic aspect of the goddess. That she was an archaic goddess also indicates that her virginal aspect was "not the product of a relatively late and exclusively Greek development" (20). The virgin element unites her particularly with Athena, who also held the title *Parthenos*. In fact, this Thracian Parthenos was specifically identified with Athena on the island of Lemnos and on the Bosphorus, where she was also known as *Chryse* (20). Thus, in the goddess Parthenos of Thrace we have perhaps the clearest link demonstrating the convergence and fundamental unity between Artemis and Athena/Neith in their most ancient forms in Greece and Anatolia.

That Artemis loved "thrilling cries" (Homeric *Hymn 5 to Aphrodite* 19) may also connect her both to Athena/Neith and to Libya. The "thrilling cry," wherever it is referenced in ancient texts, is, in Greek, the onomatopoeic *ololugê*, a high-pitched utterance made by women that had numerous purposes. Herodotus (4.189.2) says that the Greek women learned how to make this cry from the "Libyan women," who emitted the sound ceremonially during religious rituals. It is what is known in North Africa today as the *zagharit* (sometimes transliterated as *zaghareet* and commonly referred to in English as "ululating"). It was, and still is, accomplished by rapidly moving the tongue back and forth against the teeth or top lip while uttering a high-pitched, single-toned sound.[21] Today the cry is used by the Berbers/Imazighen in North Africa in the way that it was used by the Libyan women in antiquity: to mark events such as births and deaths, the reception of startling or happy news, the entry of a notable person into a camp or village, and so forth (Bates 1970, 154n2). In discussing the tribes of Libya, particularly the Auses, Herodotus implies that such ritual vocalizing was done in honor of Neith/Athena, and one may not unreasonably assume that it was used during the combat ritual among the Ause maidens he describes, discussed in chapter 2. Thus, I suggest that, in addition to it having been a cry of exultation, triumph, grief, or surprise, it may have been a form of ritualized war cry to invoke Athena/ Neith and frighten enemies during battle.[22]

The connection of the *ololugê* with Athena can be found in Pindar (*Olympian Ode* 7.35), where the goddess is depicted as emerging from Zeus's head making this very utterance.[23] Moreover, in the *Iliad* (6.269–311), women worshippers and their priestess Theano utter the *ololugê* in praise of Athena while presenting her with a ceremonial *peplos*. In the *Odyssey* (4.759–67), Penelope makes the very same cry as part of a prayer to the goddess that her son Telemachus will return home safely. In a fragment of Euripides (351, in Dillon 2001, 242), women of Athens are called upon to make the *ololugê* so that Athena will come to the aid of the city. Thus, that Artemis was fond of this "cry" connects her to Athena and, once again, suggests possible origins for her in Libya, where Herodotus implies that this form of vocalizing first emerged.

Furthermore, Artemis's festival at Patrae contained reminiscences of the maidenhood combat ritual among the Auses in Libya. At Patrae, a virgin officiating as priestess rode in procession in a car yoked to deer (Pausanias 7.18.12). This calls to mind the Ause maiden who took the honored role among all other virgins and was paraded around Lake Tritonis in a chariot. Just as the Ause maiden may have served as the representative of Athena, so the Patraean maiden likely represented Artemis herself, who was frequently depicted as riding in her deer-borne chariot (see, e.g., Apollonius Rhodius *Argonautica* 3.878–79). Once again, we have the *parthenos* as a proxy for the goddess in a quasi-militaristic scenario, suggesting an affinity between the cults of Artemis and Athena as they related to warrior virgins.

Artemis as *Parthenos*

Ultimately, what unites Athena and Artemis, and what may support the idea of a possible common root for both goddesses in the Libyan Neith, is their mutual status as *Parthenos*, Virgin. As mentioned, in Homeric *Hymn 9 to Artemis* (2), Artemis is called *parthenos iocheaira*, "Virgin of Profuse Arrows." In *Hymn* 27 (2) she is called *parthenon aidoîên*, "Revered Virgin." Apollodorus (1.4.1) affirms that Artemis remained a stalwart virgin, and Diodorus Siculus (5.3.4) specifically says "she made the same choice of maidenhood" as had Kore [Persephone] and Athena. According to this tradition, all three goddesses were even "raised" together, again suggesting an archaic identification between Artemis and Athena. As I discuss in *CDB*, virginity was a highly important requirement for the women who served in Artemis's legendary retinue, and violation of their virginity was a cause for punishment by death meted out by the goddess (Rigoglioso 2009, 92–106).

As with Athena, much has been made of the seemingly contradictory fact of Artemis's having been a virgin yet, originally, an "All-mother" (Guthrie 1967, 101); a fierce guardian of her followers' chasteness, yet protector of those who gave birth. But, as Guthrie (1967, 103) notes, the "childlessness" of Artemis that was characteristic of her in classical times and later was not "original." Her identification with Eileithyia, the goddess of childbirth, he says, "is a strong indication that she was once...a patron of women's life in all its phases and was therefore supposed to have experienced them all herself." All, I suggest, except for sexual union. As with Athena, who was similarly a virgin and preferred the virginity of her followers, the paradoxical aspects of Artemis's own sexual status are resolved if we consider the possibility that Artemis was originally a parthenogenetic goddess, at once virgin and generative.

In addition to the generativity implied in Artemis's title "Mistress of the Animals" and in her iconography as the Great Mother goddess of Ephesus, discussed previously, one piece of data supporting the possibility that she was at once virgin and mother is the fact that one animal named as particularly sacred to her was the partridge (Aelian *On Animals* 10.35), a creature believed to have parthenogenetic capacity. Pliny (10.51), echoing Aristotle (*History of Animals* 5.5.25), specifically tells us that the female could be impregnated either by standing opposite a male while the wind blew from him toward her or simply by his flying over her head or, often, merely by hearing his voice. Athenaeus (9.389e) says that the sight of the male was enough to instigate conception.

Another indicator of Artemis's parthenogenetic nature—as well as her possible association with Neith—was the symbol of the bee associated with her in several cult locations. As I mentioned in chapter 2, the bee was a parthenogenetic totem that also belonged to Neith. Found among the ruins of the celebrated Artemisium at Ephesus, dating to the eighth or seventh century B.C.E., for example, was a gold decorative pin head in the form of a bee and three small plaques composed of flowers or leaves alternating with bees' bodies. The bee figured prominently on Artemis's famous "many-breasted" statue at Ephesus, as well as on Ephesian coins, some of which feature the goddess's other sacred symbol, the stag, on the obverse (Ransome [1937] 2004, 57–60, pls. V, VI, VII). At Camirus in Rhodes, in connection with the worship of Artemis Ephesia, was found a series of seven gold plaques, on each of which is a winged bee-like figure of the goddess with a lion on each side. Several other examples of this winged Artemis with lions were found, as were gold plaques on which she is represented not only with insect wings, but also with the body of the bee. In a grave on Thera, pieces of jewelry were found depicting a female head on a bee's body, very similar to those of Camirus, which were probably also associated with the worship of Artemis (pl. VI).

A further important point in this regard is that priestesses of Cybele, with whom Artemis was related, were known as *Melissai*, or "Bees" (Lactantius *Divine Institutes* 1.22; Porphyry *Cave of the Nymphs* 18). Although there is no documented use of the title specifically for Artemis at Ephesus, Aeschylus (*Priestesses* frag. 87, in Cook 1914–40, 1:443) speaks of the "bee keepers" who opened the temple gates of Artemis, which may possibly be a reference to bee priestesses at that sacred precinct. Moreover, male officials connected with the worship of Artemis there were known as *Essenes*, "King Bees" (Suda, s.v. *essên*). This suggests that the female title *Melissa* was indeed used in parallel for the priestesses at Ephesus. Pausanias (8.13.1) notes that the Essenes served for a year and were bound to observe chastity, and Strabo (14.1.23) comments that the priestesses of Ephesus were virgins also. Putting these associations together, it is likely that these "virgins" were *Melissai*, "Bee Priestesses."

Again, in *CDB*, I present a thorough analysis of the parthenogenetic aspects of the bee and of the prominence of *Melissa* as a priestess title (Rigoglioso 2009, 192–202). I also return to this discussion in chapter 5, where I note the title among Demeter's priestesses. I have proposed that the title *Melissa* designated what was originally a parthenogenetic priestess. The idea that Artemis's priestesses at Ephesus and elsewhere may have been women who attempted virgin motherhood resolves the seeming paradox of Artemis's embrace of women's birthing process but rejection of their sexual activity. I thus propose that the Artemisian cult embraced both motherhood and virginity, not as opposites, but as part of a specific practice with a specific purpose.

Artemis's "Great Mother" aspect was, on the whole, more fully retained than Athena's, and it may have been because her cult was able to take root in the land of Anatolia, where conditions were possibly more favorable for the retention of matriarchy. In Greece, however, she was transformed from the virgin creatrix to the virgin dedicated to a life uncomplicated by heterosexual sexuality and passion. Thus, her trajectory parallels that which I have theorized for Neith/Athena.

CHAPTER 4

HERA: VIRGIN QUEEN OF HEAVEN, EARTH, AND THE UNDERWORLD

Hera is the third of the Greek goddesses to have borne the title *Parthenos*. Legends and cultic activities concerning this Olympian Queen of the Gods indicate that, in her earliest form, she, like Athena/Neith and Artemis, was considered a great virgin creatrix. In this chapter, I explore legends and iconography indicating that, in pre-Greek antiquity, Hera was a goddess of the sky, earth, and underworld who had no male consort. Signs pointing to her earlier status as a Great Goddess include her titles "Queen of the Gods" and "Female Origin of All Things"; the numerous animals and plants that were sacred to her; her province over the winds and heavenly aspects; and stories portraying her as the mother or nurse of various chthonic beasts, such as the Sphinx, the Nemean lion, and her half-serpent son Typhon.

I present evidence from Hera's two oldest religious centers, Samos and Argos, affirming that this goddess was indeed seen in her earliest cult as a Virgin Mother. At Samos, her purported birth and ritual "tying" to the willow at Samos, a tree whose leaves served as an anaphrodisiac (desire queller) and emmenagogue (menstrual stimulant), reflected a schema in which the paradox of her simultaneous *partheneia,* or "virginity," and "motherhood" were resolved. I argue that the tree represented not only virginity and the regulation of the menstrual cycle, but also parthenogenetic fertility itself. The annually enacted "abduction" of her statue, I propose, may have represented the original drama of the advent of the Zeusian cult and the mythological "yoking" of Hera in marriage. At Argos, the mystery of Hera's annually restoring her virginity in the Canathus spring, which also may have been enacted with her cult statue, similarly may have reflected a felt need for Hera to be regularly restored to her status as a Virgin Mother.

Nowhere is Hera's original parthenogenetic capacity more dramatically expressed than in the myths of her miraculous conceptions of the gods Ares and Hephaestus, and the serpent-being Typhon. These stories relate the original parthenogenetic status of the goddess, the threat that her parthenogenetic capability posed to the Masculine, and Feminine rage in response to the "appropriation" of parthenogenetic power by the male sphere. I show that Hera's links with Delphi, where Typhon had a significant mythological role, suggest the existence of an entire network of relationships dedicated to the protection of female parthenogenetic power after the advent of Olympian religion.

Mythological motifs also speak of Hera's rebellion in other ways against Zeusian rule and the violation of female parthenogenetic mysteries, exemplified in her negative treatment of Zeus's son Heracles. Many of Heracles' labors represent what I argue were attempts to disrupt the matriarchy, in particular the divine birth priestesshoods associated with Hera and Artemis. Heracles' vanquishing of the parthenogenetic hydra is perhaps the most vivid symbol in this regard. Another is his stealing of the apples of the Hesperides, which, I argue, were originally, like Hera's attribute of the pomegranate, symbols of the perceived ability of the female to procreate without the need of a male partner. Under patriarchy, I posit, the apple migrated to the realm of Aphrodite, a phenomenon recorded in the so-called Judgment of Paris, where it became forever fixed as a symbol of heterosexual eroticism and fertility.

Mythological Evidence for Hera as a Great Goddess

In the Hesiodic genealogy, Hera was the eldest daughter[1] of the Titans Cronus and Rhea. As such, she was a granddaughter of Ge/Gaia and a cousin to Leto. Like her siblings Hestia, Demeter, Hades, and Poseidon, she was initially swallowed by her father Cronus before her youngest brother Zeus solicited Metis for advice on how the children could be disgorged (*Theogony* 453–500; Apollodorus 1.2.1).

In Homeric and Hesiodic tradition, Hera was not only the older sister but also the wife of Zeus. In the *Iliad* (14.295–96), she is said to have become Zeus's wife without her parents' knowledge. One tradition relates that Zeus seduced her by transforming himself into a cuckoo, which Hera caught to be her pet (Pausanias 2.17.4). The marriage of these two deities was referred to as the *hieros gamos*, "sacred marriage" (*Lexicon Rhetoricum Cantabrigiense*, s.v. *hieros gamos*, in Kerenyi 1975, 106). As a result of her being the only truly betrothed goddess in the Olympian pantheon, Hera came to be known as the "goddess of marriage."[2] Various locations claimed to have been the scene of her union with Zeus, among them Euboia, Samos, Cnossus in Crete, and Mt. Thornax in the south of Argolis.[3]

The consensus among classicists is that Hera's "marriage" with Zeus was the mythical representation of the (probably forced) merging of the pre-Olympian Hera cult with that of the Olympian pantheon.[4] Hera's legends, iconography, and cult clearly indicate that she was a goddess of pre-Greek antiquity. Indeed, as I show in *CDB*, at the primitive oracle of Dodona it was the goddess Dione who was Zeus's consort, not Hera (Rigoglioso 2009, 140–41). This points to a period of theological flux before Hera's position became fixed in the Olympian cult (Harrison [1903] 1957, 316). Hera's various aspects suggest that she was originally an earth goddess, Mistress of the "Animals," and Queen of Heaven, indicating that she was once a Great Goddess of the sky, earth, and underworld. Vestiges of her earlier, enlarged identity can be seen, for example, in her Homeric title "Queen of the Gods" and her command over the seasons, earthquakes, the atmosphere, rain, wind, the moon, and the stars (rendering her a Queen of Heaven).[5] That she was connected with the abundance of the earth and nature more broadly can be seen in her association with various trees, plants, and fruits including the willow (*lygos*), asterion, lily, pomegranate, and wheat.[6]

Hera was also, like the more archaic form of Artemis, a "Mistress of the Animals." Birds were sacred to her, including the peacock, the hawk, and the dove.[7] That one of Hera's most sacred animals was the cow is indicated by a number of literary and cultic references. One of her primary epithets, for example, was "cow-eyed mistress," *boôpis potnia* (Homer *Iliad* 1.551, 568; 14.159). Her sanctuary at Argos was located on the side of the hill called *Euboia*, "Rich in Oxen" (Cook 1914–40, 1:445–46). Cows were sacrificed to her (Pausanias 5.16.3, 9.2.8), and bovines were the oldest votives attested at her cult sanctuary at Samos (O'Brien 1993, 49). Various legends relate cattle to her worship. Herodotus (1.31) tells the story of the Argive brothers Cleobis and Biton, who, when their oxen did not return from the fields in time, took the yoke upon their own shoulders and conveyed a wagon carrying their mother to the annual festival of Hera at Argos. Suidas (s.v. *Kroisos*) adds that this woman was a priestess of Hera named Theano or Cydippe and that her son's actions allowed her to lead the traditional procession associated with the festival as far as the temple of Hera.[8]

Hera was also associated with the lion. At Samos, a lion's mask was consistently depicted on her silver coins, and, at Delos, her enthroned statuette depicted a lion in her lap. In Carthage, she was worshipped as a virgin who was carried through heaven by a lion (Apuleius *Golden*

Ass 6.4). Such leonine imagery calls to mind Cybele, who, as we saw in chapter 3, was also associated with Artemis (O'Brien 1993, 49).

Hera's chthonic and underworldly associations were expressed in mythological stories in which she was either the mother or nurse of various beasts and monsters, as I discuss further later. One such figure was the Sphinx, whom she is said to have sent to Thebes as a man-eating plague until someone could solve its famous riddle about the three ages of humanity (Apollodorus 3.5.7–8). Although Herodotus (2.50) states that Hera was one of the few deities who was not introduced into Greece from Egypt, such a motif suggests that this goddess indeed may have had integral connections in Africa. Another indicator of her possible association with Africa is the mythical placement of her paradisiacal "garden" near Mt. Atlas, frequently a reference to North Africa. One legend also relates that among the *Pygmaioi*, the Pygmies of Africa, a woman named either *Oinoe* or *Gerana* refused to give honor to Artemis and Hera (in one tradition also Aphrodite and Athena). As a result, Hera turned her into a crane that attacked its own people.[9] This legend, although late, suggests that Hera (or an African equivalent) was worshipped deep in the African continent. Certainly an African provenance for this goddess would best explain Hera's association with the cow, which naturally calls to mind the Egyptian Neith, Hathor, and Isis, all of whom had bovine epiphanies. As Cook (1914–40, 1:444) notes, Hera's epithet *boôpis*, "cow-eyed, cow-faced, of cowlike aspect," must have come down to Homer "from a distant past . . . and presupposed the primitive conception of Hera as a cow." A connection between Hera and these Egyptian goddesses would also be congruent with the parthenogenetic nature of Neith (chapter 2) and Isis, in particular, and with the tradition of divine birth in Egypt in which Hathor played a major role (see Rigoglioso 2007, 70–75, 79–80).

Of the two earliest chroniclers of Olympian theogony, Hesiod and Homer, Hesiod seems to preserve more of Hera's ancient chthonic character. He simultaneously refers to her as the "illustrious wife of Zeus" and the "nurse" of the savage Nemean lion who was a "plague" to humanity (*Theogony* 327–29). As O'Brien (1993, 173) points out, the poet seems "little concerned with the inconsistency inherent in an 'illustrious' wife . . . nursing a 'plague.' " Homer, on the other hand, reconfigures Hera more fully along Olympian lines. He demotes her from a goddess of life and death into a scheming, jealous, and rageful wife (Burkert 1985, 132). It is this image of Hera that has persisted down through the ages. However, Hera's older aspect as Queen of the great totality of Heaven, Earth, and the Underworld suggests that, like Athena/Neith and Artemis, she was originally conceived as a parthenogenetic mother who had no consort. On the authority of Eusebius, Plutarch (*Moralia* 15.157) in fact equates Hera with Ge/Gaia, the Earth herself. I submit this is because both goddesses were understood to possess the same self-generating capacity.

Evidence at Samos for Hera as a Virgin Mother

Strong indicators that Hera was originally conceived as a parthenogenetic goddess can be found in association with her cult on the island of Samos, located off the coast of ancient Anatolia (Turkey). On Samos, one of the primary and earliest seats of her worship, she was known as *Hera Parthenia*, "Hera the Virgin" (Callimachus, in scholiast on Apollonius Rhodius 1.87; cf. scholiast on Pindar's *Olympian Odes* 6.149). Such a title was apparently not uncommon in association with this goddess; in Hermione, located on the east coast of Argolis, and on the island of Euboia, she was similarly worshipped as *Parthenos* (Stephanus of Byzantium, s.v. *Hermion*; scholiast on Pindar's *Olympian Odes* 6.149e). Pindar (*Olympian Ode* 6.88) also refers to her with this epithet. According to some writers, the ancient name for Samos itself was *Parthenia*.[10] Some say this name derived from the name of the river Parthenios because the goddess Hera had been brought up there as a virgin.[11] That the epithet of the goddess and the name of the entire island that was sacred to her were both *Virgin* indicates the primacy of this characteristic in relation to her when she first emerged in Greek cult.

From mythological and cultic evidence, it is clear that Hera at Samos was also a creatrix; thus, I propose that she was considered a Virgin Mother. Lore and archaeological finds associated with the island, including votives in the shape of sphinxes, griffins, lions, and other animals confirm that Hera was a generative "Mistress of the Animals" not originally linked with Zeus or other Olympian deities (O'Brien 1993, 45–54). Moreover, the peristyle of her Samian temple may have been a reminder of a goddess worshipped in column or, earlier, tree form (Burkert 1985, 130). As such, she represented the "tree of life," the ancient symbol of (parthenogenetic) female generativity.[12] The idea of Hera's virgin motherhood is contained in a title at Lesbos that has been attributed to her: "(Female) Origin of All Things" (*genethlê pantôn*) (Alcaeus frag. 129, in O'Brien 106 and n52). In examining cultic evidence on the island, O'Brien (6, 71–74) concludes that Hera came to be viewed as the wife of Zeus in the Samian cult only with the imposition of Olympian mythology, perhaps as late as the late seventh century B.C.E. Even then, evidence suggests that Zeus's influence on her cult at Samos was minimal.

An inscribed stone block found at Samos, which possessed Hera's old-est and largest temple, dated to 1000 B.C.E. (O'Brien 1993, 11), may similarly hint at Hera's status as a parthenogenetic mother. The block was found buried in one of the ancient courses of the Parthenios River, later known as the Imbrasos (Callimachus frag. 599, trans. Trypanis 1975, 269). It bears an inscription of greeting to three holy persons: "Holy Imbrasos, Holy Parthenia, and Holy Parthenios" (*Imbrasos hieros Parthenié hieré Parthenios hieros*). As Kerenyi (1975, 160) notes, the first name refers to the river god, and the second refers to Hera herself. The third, how-ever, cannot be Imbrasos again, as the river has already been named. Kerenyi conjectures that *Parthenios* here is Zeus, but he does not provide any evidence to support such a possibility. I propose instead that the iden-tity of this third figure can be found in the very meaning of *parthenios* itself: "of a virgin" or, as used in the *Iliad*, "the son of an unmarried girl" (Liddell and Scott, 7th ed., s.v. *parthenios*).[13] Thus, it seems that *Parthenios* could be an archaic reference to a parthenogenetically produced offspring of Hera. As I discuss further later in the chapter, Hera was indeed associ-ated with specific parthenogenetic children in myth: Ares, Typhon, and Hephaestus.

The Samians held that Hera was born on their island by the side of the river Parthenios/Imbrasos under a willow hedge. Hera's tem-ple, the Heraion, was built around the willow, which could be seen in Pausanias's day and was considered the oldest extant tree in Greece (Pausanias 7.4.4, 8.23.5). The presence of the willow supports the argument that Hera was a Virgin Mother whose priestesses may have attempted parthenogenetic birth. For, in Greek, the willow was known as the *lygos* (*lugos*), and, in Latin, the *agnus castus*, or "chaste lamb," so named because it had an important reputation as a hedge whose leaves quelled sexual desire and stimulated menstruation, according to the ancient writers.[14] That Hera is said to have been "born" under this "chaste" hedge emphasizes the goddess's virginal aspect as core to her earliest identity. Moreover, at Samos the *lygos* had a central role in ritu-als associated with her, as I discuss shortly. The importance of the *lygos* to the Heraian cult and the fact that it was an anaphrodisiac bring up the question as to whether it may have been used by priestesses of Hera to help them maintain the virginity thought necessary for the task of pure parthenogenetic conception, or to regulate their menstrual cycle for divine conception through *hieros gamos*. I elaborate on this possibil-ity in *CDB*, where I show what I believe is evidence for a cult of divine birth in association with Hera (Rigoglioso 2009, 127–38). I also discuss the use of this plant at the Thesmophoria in connection with partheno-genesis in chapter 5.

The foundational myth of the tenth century B.C.E. Heraion at Samos centered on Admete, daughter of the Mycenaean hero Eurystheus. The legend relates that Admete, a priestess of Hera, fled from Argos to Samos for an unnamed reason. She subsequently saw Hera in a vision, and, wishing to thank the goddess for her safe arrival, undertook the care of the goddess's temple there. The Argolids convinced Tyrrhenian pirates to steal Hera's sacred icon so the Samians would punish Admete for negligence. When the thieves could not launch their ship from its place on the beach, however, they superstitiously abandoned the image there and offered it sacrificial cakes instead. The Carians of Samos found the statue the next day, set it by the *lygos* hedge, and tied it there with branches so that it would not stray. Admete freed the goddess, bathed her, and put her back on her pedestal in the temple (Menodotus, in Athenaeus [15.672a–72e]).

That Hera's priestess in the myth was named Admete—literally, "Untamed"—suggests that she was unmarried, a virgin of the pre-Zeus cult. As O'Brien (1993, 59) notes, her name is suggestive of a pre-Greek epoch, before marriage came to be understood as the domestication and yoking of young women. Perhaps Admete's "fleeing" Argos was a result of her rebellion against restrictions imposed on her priestesshood there. It may be that those restrictions specifically related to the attempted infiltration of the older Heraian cult by the Zeusian cult.

If we assume that, as the "foundational" myth for the establishment of the temple to Hera, Admete's arrival corresponded with the archaeologically attested date of 1000 B.C.E., the foregoing possibilities are supported through coordination of the story with another myth. A Samian legend held that when Zeus and Hera initially united, they made love for 300 years (Callimachus *Aetia* frag. 48, 1975, 41; scholiast on *Iliad* 1.609, in Kerenyi 1975, 129n70). Could this suggest a 300-year period over which the two cults assimilated on the island? That indeed would correspond roughly with O'Brien's (1993, 17) conjecture of a seventh century B.C.E. time frame in which Zeus's cult appears firmly planted in association with Hera's. Perhaps the attempt of the Argolids to disrupt Admete's priestesshood on Samos thus marked an initial attempt to impose the Zeusian cult over the Heraian cult on the island, an act symbolized by the "stealing" of Hera's statue. Indeed, the motif of stealing the statue could be seen to correspond with the ancient custom of bride abduction as a method of forcing marriage.[15] Thus, the Argolids' "abduction" of the statue could have symbolically served as the "abduction" of Hera for marriage with Zeus on the part of the patriarchal cult. Seen in this light, the story of the Carians' binding Hera's statue to the *lygos*, the tree of her birth, speaks to what

I posit was a felt need on the part of worshippers to "pin" their goddess back to her birthplace, to her virginal "origins" as a consortless
goddess who, like her priestess, would remain untamed, unyoked to a
male god.

Athenaeus (15.672–73) offers the additional interesting detail that the
oracle of Apollo at Hybla made the Carians "atone" for the tethering of
the goddess's image to the *lygos* by ordering them to wear wreaths of willow twigs, whereas only Hera's "true worshippers" could wear wreaths
of laurel. This motif points to the tie between the Carians, the island's
native peoples, with the earlier aspect of the cult, symbolized by the willow. Because the laurel was appropriated as a symbol of Apollo, son of
the "most high" Zeus (see Rigoglioso 2009, 185–86), I propose it represented religious allegiance to the patriarchal, Olympian schema. In fact,
the "true," earlier symbol of worship for Hera would have remained the
willow. Therefore, casting the donning of the willow wreath as "atonement" may have been an attempt by the patriarchy to denigrate and
diminish the Carians, who probably retained the original understanding
of Hera as a Virgin Mother. Keeping her "tied" to her virginity was, no
doubt, seen as a subversive form of resistance to the Zeusian cult.

That the myth of Admete and of the binding of Hera was tremendously important to the Samians is reflected in the fact that it was annually re-enacted in the Tonaia, or "Tight Pulling," festival conducted in
honor of the goddess. Again, according to Athenaeus (15.672–73), this
involved the annual procession of the goddess's cult statue to the sea and
its purification and "feeding" with barley-cake offerings there. Athenaeus
quotes the epic poet Nicaenetus as commenting that a (possibly related)
rite involved participants feasting near the willow tree in the sanctuary
on willow bedding. Thus, it seems that the ritual concluded with the
statue of the goddess being brought back to her temple, where an ancient
willow grew that was sacred to her. O'Brien (1993, 17–18, 54–58) suggests the Tonaia was a ritual ensuring new vegetation and the blessings
of human fertility through the annual "arrival" of Hera as Mistress of
the Animals. That at Samos in earliest times the cult statue was a primitive aniconic wooden board (Callimachus *Aetia* frag. 100, trans. Trypanis
1975, 75), a proxy for the "tree" itself, underscores the great antiquity
of the worship of Hera there and supports the idea that the ritual was
probably originally one of cyclical renewal. O'Brien believes it was only
during a later stage that the rite came to represent the marriage of Hera
and Zeus,[16] with the goddess now confined by the "subordinating bonds
of Greek wedlock."

O'Brien further conjectures (38–39, 61–62) that the rite depicted
Hera as an early earth goddess who united with the local river god. Kipp

(1974, 107, 204) speculates that the willow itself functioned as a god with whom the cult statue was believed to have had intercourse. However, such arguments are strained and unconvincing, and seem to be based on an unfounded a priori assumption that a creatrix goddess would necessarily have required a partner.[17] The information I have presented thus far indicates that evidence for the early Hera having had a consort is simply lacking.

I propose, again, that, as in the associated myth, Hera's being ritually "purified" and returned to the *lygos* symbolized a yearly return to her own origins as a Virgin Mother. Such an act served as a reminder of Hera's parthenogenetic capacity even in the Zeusian epoch. Moreover, the rite has analogs with rituals that speak to the parthenogenetic power of another goddess: Athena/Neith. The "transporting" of the goddess to the sea during the Tonaia festival echoes the Ausean maiden ritual in which the goddess Athena/Neith (represented by her priestess) was paraded around Lake Tritonis, the place of her "birth," which I discussed in chapter 2.

The motif of revelers banqueting on top of willow bedding also connects Hera's festival with that of two other goddesses who had parthenogenetic aspects: Demeter and Persephone. That rite was the Thesmophoria, a women-only festival conducted in honor of the mother/daughter (twin/parthenogenetic) goddesses. During the Thesmophoria, women similarly strewed *lygos* branches on their seating during days of the ritual when they were required to be sexually abstinent (Aelian *On Animals* 9.26). This may have had the effect not only of checking the sexual urge, but also of initiating a group menstruation, for *lygos* was known to stimulate women's menses.[18] I argue in chapter 5 that the Thesmophoria was a rite to celebrate the original pure parthenogenetic nature of Demeter and Persephone, as well as to commemorate the tragic disruption of that ability through rape by a male god. Given the motifs discussed in association with the Tonaia, it is reasonable to propose that this Heraian rite also originally may have been a celebration of parthenogenetic conception and birth—one, I would argue, that was originally led exclusively by women.

The Tonaia on Samos also suggests analogies with an aspect of another Virgin Mother: Artemis. In Sparta, Artemis was known as *Lygodesma*, "She Who Is Bound with *Lygos*." This epithet was explained by the legend that the image of the goddess was found in a *lygos* bush where her statue stood bound with the branches of the plant (Pausanias 3.16.10). In the Anatolian city of Erythraea, a sitting image was bound because it was believed that the images of gods were unsettled and often moved from one place to the other (Polemon in scholiast on Pindar's

Olympian Ode 7.95a, in Kerenyi 1975, 163). Here, we have a clear demonstration of the purpose of "binding": to assuage worshippers' anxiety that the deity could be taken or moved. We also have the *lygos*, the symbol of virginity. Thus, the virgin-related aspects of Hera's cult had correspondences with those of the parthenogenetic goddesses Demeter, Persephone, Athena, and Artemis, affirming a deep unity among these goddesses. Certainly, the affinities and the geographical proximity and overlap between Hera and Artemis, in particular, including the fact that cult statues of both in some areas wore the *polos* crown (Burkert 1985, 131), suggest that they may have been one and the same Mistress of the Animals in the Bronze Age or earlier, before they were broken up into separate goddesses with specialized spheres of influence (O'Brien 1993, 60–61).

Evidence at Argos for Hera as a Virgin Mother

At Hera's other main cult center of Argos, the goddess also had roots in the pre-Olympian Bronze Age and retained vestiges of her original parthenogenetic identity. Her eighth century B.C.E. sanctuary was located a few miles outside the city of Argos on the side of the hill called *Euboia*, "Rich in Oxen," a region that was inhabited from Neolithic times (O'Brien 1993, 120–24). Kerenyi (1975, 132) assigns the beginnings of the cult of Hera there to 2000 B.C.E., which indicates that Argos may have been her oldest cult site in Greece.[19] O'Brien (124) affirms that remains found in Mycenaean-era tombs there are suggestive of Heraian iconography.

Hera's archaic-period sanctuary stood in a narrow plain between the Bronze Age palaces of Mycenae and Tiryns, and the shield citadel of Argos, near the hero tombs of Prosymna. It is possible that the goddess, or at least her name, was brought to Argos by an early wave of Greek invaders, but, as Guthrie (1967, 72) notes, "It is likely that the Greeks found there a powerful goddess of the original inhabitants and recognized her greatness by uniting with her their own chief god [Zeus]." Zeus had few ties to the early Argolid; as on Samos, the existence of his cult there was initially separate from and secondary to that of Hera. Moreover, Homeric references to him as "spouse of Hera," *posis Hêrês* (e.g., *Iliad* 10.5), suggest the existence of pre-Olympian myths in which Hera, and not Zeus, was the region's dominant deity (O'Brien 1993, 3–4, 121–22). Legends also indicate that, like Athena's cult at Athens, Hera's cult at Argos may have encountered a rival in the religion dedicated to Poseidon. According to the ancient story, King Phoroneus, in collaboration with the river gods Cephisus, Asterion, and Inachus, proclaimed Argos sacred to Hera, rather than Poseidon, which caused the sea god to dry up the waterways of the region in anger (Pausanias 2.15.4).

That a consortless goddess seems to have dominated the entire region is supported by the fact that, at the nearby Bronze Age palace at Mycenae, no real evidence for male gods has been found. There, the primary deities were goddesses of trees and cultivation, war, and family life, all of whom may have reflected aspects of one Great Goddess. A goddess depicted aniconically at Mycenae as a column was probably Hera herself, given that at Argos the seated statue of the goddess also rested on a column or pillar. Since columns were made of tree trunks, it is likely that the columns and trees at Mycenae, as well as in the temple structure and related ritual motifs of Argos and Samos, were considered variations on the "tree of life" (O'Brien 1993, 125–28, 142).

What is particularly noteworthy about the Argive cult to Hera as regards parthenogenesis was its myth that the goddess annually bathed to restore her virginity in the Canathus spring at Nauplia (Hesychius and *Etymologicum Magnum*, s.v. *Heresedes*; scholiast on Pindar's *Olympian Ode* 6.149b, g). Pausanias (2.38.3) adds that the story was told as a "holy secret" at the mysteries celebrated in the goddess's honor. This myth once again underscores the importance of virginity in relationship to Hera and implies that *partheneia*, "virginity," represented her original state. I propose that the "holy secret" was none other than the fact that Hera's virginity was also generative. I further propose that the motif of the "restoration" of her virginity, like the "binding-to-the-*lygos*" motif in Samos, represented a felt need for Hera to be returned regularly to her original state as Holy *Parthenos*, her condition under the oldest stratum of the cult. At Argos, as at Samos, this was perceived as necessary, I suggest, precisely because of the imposition of the Zeus cult over hers and her forced "marriage" with the god, a relationship that was, on some level, understood to be unnatural for her.

The story may have been ritually enacted in an annual bathing of Hera's statue at Argos in the Inachus River, as we saw with her statue at Samos (Kerenyi 1975, 119; Cook 1914–40, 3.1:749). Guthrie (1967, 103) notes that the myth also calls to mind the festival of the Plynteria at Athens, in which two *parthenoi* took the old wooden image of Athena and washed it in the sea, while another washed her *peplos* (see Rigoglioso 2009, 70). Moreover, it relates to a rite at Ephesus, where the statue of Artemis was similarly taken out of the temple down to the seashore, laid on top of celery and other plants, offered food, and purified with salt (*Etymologicum Magnum*, s.v. *Daitis*, in Dillon 2001, 135). Dillon (132) notes that the "secrecy" around the mystery of Hera's "bath" implies that any ritual statue cleansing may well have been in the hands of women and Hera's priestesses only.

It is documented that at Argos a New Year festival was held in Hera's honor. Whether it was at this rite that her image may have been washed is unknown, but this festival, named successively the *Hekatomboia*, the *Heraia*, and the *Aspis*, did involve a cult statue (Burkert 1983, 165–68). It was dressed in a newly woven robe, a motif that brings to mind Athena's Panathenaia celebration, during which the *peplos*, which I intimated in chapter 1 and discuss more fully in *CDB* was a symbol of virginity/parthenogenesis (Rigoglioso 2009, 60–61, 70), was presented to the goddess (O'Brien 1993, 143). The Argive New Year festival also involved the priestess of Hera driving to the sanctuary in an ox-drawn wagon as boys processed carrying shields. Here, too, we have echoes of the priestess of Artemis at Patrae, who was drawn in a deer-led chariot, and of the Ausean virgin priestess of Athena/Neith, who was paraded around Lake Tritonis.

Hera's Parthenogenetic Birth of Ares, Hephaestus, and Typhon

That Hera was understood to possess parthenogenetic ability is clearly demonstrated even in Olympian myth. The first indication in this regard is the pure daughter-bearing parthenogenetic relationship that is hinted at in her relationship with her daughter Hebe. Hesiod (*Theogony* 922) reports that Hebe was Hera's daughter by Zeus. However, that the names *Hera* and *Hebe* are probably semantically related, being derived from two different extensions of the same Indo-European root (D. O. Adams 1987, 176), suggests that the two goddesses can be seen as "doubles" of one another. Moreover, that *Hebe* means "Youth" emphasizes the idea that Hebe was the "younger version" of Hera, who herself was honored at Stymphalus with the triple titles *Pais*, *Teleia*, and *Chero*, or "Maiden, Grown-up (Mother), and Widow (Crone)" (Pausanias 8.22.2). Thus, Hera and Hebe were possibly early Argolic mother-daughter deities of the earth's cyclical renewal, as were Demeter and Persephone elsewhere (O'Brien 1993, 118). In such a matriarchal schema, the daughter is the parthenogenetic offspring of the mother, an idea that I have explored regarding Metis and Athena (chapter 2), and Artemis and Leto (chapter 3), and that I will explore in the case of Demeter and Persephone (chapter 5).

Interestingly, in the *Iliad* (5.720–32) Hera and Hebe appear together fitting a chariot with wheels and yoking horses to it to help the Argives in the battle of Troy. Such mother-daughter martial activity echoes that of Metis fitting her daughter Athena with armor while they are both still in the belly of Zeus (Hesiod *Theogony* 925, ed. Lattimore). Hera is further imbued with a warrior aspect throughout the *Iliad*. In 5.718–813, she functions as a warrior goddess who is "furious for hate and battle" (732), arouses the Argives to renew their fighting with the Trojans, and rides the chariot herself. In 21.470–95, she physically attacks Artemis and sends the huntress goddess scurrying in distress and humiliation. Although it is likely that this martial aspect was a reshaping of Hera from her original form as earth goddess (O'Brien 1993, 79), it does point to yet another possible affinity with the parthenogenetic goddesses Athena and Artemis.

Like these two goddesses, Hera seems to have had a cultic connection with the Amazons. In front of the temple of Hera Anthea was a grave of women who, according to Pausanias (2.22.1), were killed in battle against the Argives under Perseus. These women had come from the Aegean islands to help the god Dionysus (possibly a reference to a political faction that venerated him?) in war. Such women who served Dionysus in battle are specifically referenced as Libyan Amazons by Diodorus Siculus (3.68–71). That they were buried in front of a temple to Hera indicates their cultic affinity with her. I propose this may have been the case precisely because she, like Artemis and Athena, was anciently considered to have been a parthenogenetic goddess and, thus, of particular interest to such matriarchal warriors.

The more direct and striking evidence for Hera as a pure parthenogenetic goddess can been found in the miraculous birth stories of Ares, Typhon, and Hephaestus. According to Hesiod (*Theogony* 922), Hera conceived Ares (like Hebe and Eileithyia) by Zeus, but Ovid (*Fasti* 193–260) reports a legend that she conceived the war god parthenogenetically. According to the story, Hera, unhappy that Zeus had become the father of Athena "without the use of a wife," claimed that she would try "all the drugs in the wide world" (*omnia temtabo latis medicamina terris*) to find a way to conceive without the use of a husband. It was the "nymph" Flora/Chloris who provided her with the means of doing so. Flora/Chloris had received from the fields of Olenus a special flower brought to her by a mysterious male individual who told her that the blossom would make pregnant any female touched by it. The "nymph" correspondingly touched Hera's bosom with the plant, and immediately the goddess conceived Ares.

I suggest the story records a much older belief that Hera herself was a parthenogenetic creatrix. Moreover, the motif of the "magical flower" affirms that plants and herbs were thought to have the power to facilitate conception without the need of a male, probably through their chemical absorption into the body.[20] The myth further indicates that the possession of knowledge for how to induce birth miraculously was specifically thought to be the province of "nymphs." This supports the argument I develop in *CDB* that "nymphs" were in fact priestesses of divine birth (see Rigoglioso 2009, 88–92).

Another legend relates that Hera parthenogenetically bore Hephaestus, the heavenly smith, in retaliation for Zeus having produced Athena from his head.[21] Hephaestus is variously depicted as having had either a cordial or an antagonistic relationship with his mother. In one story, he attempted to free Hera from chains in which Zeus had hung her because of a storm she had set on Heracles as he was sailing back from his conquest of Troy. For his attempt to rescue his mother, Hephaestus was thrown down from Olympus by the angry god and landed on Lemnos, crippled in both legs (Apollodorus 1.3.5). In another story, however, Hephaestus was born with a shriveled foot, which rendered him a source of disgrace for his mother (*Hymn to Apollo* 315–20). The goddess cast her son out of heaven; in revenge, he sent her a gift of a golden chair with invisible fetters. When Hera sat down in it, she was immediately held fast by the contraption, and Hephaestus refused to help until Dionysus persuaded him to free his mother (Pausanias 1.20.3).

These stories, I propose, are indicators of the patriarchal order's discomfort with the parthenogenetic capacity of goddesses. That the legend depicting the camaraderie between mother and son probably was the older tale is suggested by the fact that it includes the motif of Hera's rebellion against Zeus's favored son, Heracles. This, again, likely represents the early resistance of the Heraian cult to that of the invading Olympians. I propose that the theme of the antagonism between Hera and Hephaestus served as an attempt on the part of the systematizers of myth to de-emphasize Hera's parthenogenetic power. Zeus's unnatural and appropriated "parthenogenetic" birthing of Athena was theologically "allowed" to result in a normal child, whereas Hera's genuine pure parthenogenetic spawning of Hephaestus was made to produce a deformed offspring of which she was ashamed. The religious message conveyed was that female parthenogenetic capacity had become transgressive and worthy of punishment (i.e., through the birth of an imperfect child). In chapter 6, Angeleen Campra discusses how this same phenomenon befell the Gnostic Sophia.

The *Hymn to Apollo* (311–24) depicts Hera as railing to the rest of the deities at the injustice of what had happened to female parthenogenetic capacity, implying that Zeus was to blame:

> For [Zeus] has made me his wife—a dutiful one—and now he has given
> birth without me to steely eyed Athena, who stands out among the blessed

immortals, while my son has turned out a weakling among the gods, Hephaestus of the withered legs, whom I myself bore.... You cunning wretch [Zeus], what will you devise next? How could you bring yourself to father steely eyed Athena on your own? (Trans. West 2003b, 95.)

The segment gives voice to the female complaint against the demotion of goddesses from autogenic/parthenogenetic Great Mothers to lesser beings dependent on consorts for creation. Hera's producing a lame son could be read as the "laming" and "withering" of the goddess's own self-productive capacity. Her trajectory from Great Goddess to whining wife represents the most dramatic transformation in this regard of all of the Greek goddesses, the rest of whom managed to maintain some element of their independent status. Although Hera's domestication was the most complete of all, her plots against Zeus and his extramarital progeny, such as Heracles, can be seen as the refusal of the goddess and her cult to cooperate fully with the imposition of the yoke of marriage and the subordinate position in the cult (Harrison [1903] 1957, 316).

Hera's inherent resistance to Zeus is more clearly expressed in the story of her other parthenogenetic child, Typhon. In this story, vividly conveyed in the Homeric *Hymn to Apollo* (300–364),[22] Hera called on the powers of Ge/Gaia (Earth), Uranus (Sky), and the Titans of Tartarus (Underworld) to help her conceive a son who would be as superior to Zeus as Zeus had been to his father Cronus. That is, she was aiming to rid the cosmos of this new god of "father rule" before he had a chance to ascend fully to his heavenly throne. Given that Earth, Sky, and the Underworld were the realms "from whom," as Hera declared, were "sprung both gods and men," she perceived them to be particularly fitting for her request. In concluding her prayer, Hera beat the ground with her hand and felt the earth move, which she took as a sign that her request would be fulfilled.

After completing the time of her pregnancy, during which she stayed away from Zeus's bed, she gave birth to "one neither like gods nor mortal men." Her child was "the dreadful and problematic" Typhon,[23] who would be "an affliction to the gods." On Hera's request, the female serpent Python, who guarded the oracle of Ge/Gaia at Delphi, took in Typhon and raised him. Python fiercely protected both Hera's son and the oracle such that "whoever encountered her was carried off by his day of doom" (trans. West 2003b, 99).

Typhon was the greatest monster of them all and Zeus's most formidable enemy. He is variously depicted as having a hundred snake heads, out of whose eyes shot fire, or as serpentine from the waist down and anthropomorphic and winged from the waist up, with 100 serpents projecting from his hands. As the embodiment of the force of stormy wet winds, Typhon engaged in a battle with Zeus for the dominant position over gods and men but was defeated by his adversary in a great battle.[24] With that, Zeus's way was fully cleared to become ruler of the cosmos.

According to O'Brien (1993, 98), the legend of Typhon potently preserves an early tradition in which Hera was an ally of the rebel Titans in antecedent myths.[25] Indeed, a scholiast on the *Iliad* (in O'Brien, 99) relates a legend that Hera once approached Cronus for help against Zeus. The elder god gave her two eggs smeared with his own semen and told her to bury them underground, as the creature born of them would dethrone Zeus. After Hera buried them under Mt. Arimon, Typhon came forth. Even Homer, who disconnects Hera from the more primal Typhon legend,[26] directly expresses the theme of Hera's rebellion against Zeus in the *Iliad*. He briefly alludes (*Iliad* 1.399–400) to an episode in which the goddess joined in (eventually unsuccessful) efforts by Poseidon and Athena to keep Zeus in shackles after his initial victory over Cronus. According to Valerius Flaccus (*Argonautica* 2.82), Zeus retaliated by shackling Hera and hanging her above the doom of the abyss.[27]

Thus, the story of Typhon seems to have emerged from a time period in which Hera was in full possession of her parthenogenetic powers and used them to attempt to reimpose matriarchal order. Her invoking of Ge/Gaia, Uranus, and Tartarus demonstrates the regions in which she was at home, all of them pre-Zeusian abodes of power. It is particularly significant that it was the moment when she slapped the earth, and the earth responded by moving, that Hera knew she would conceive. For, as I have argued, Ge/Gaia herself was parthenogenetic. The detail serves to emphasize the identification of the two goddesses, precisely in their parthenogenetic capacity.

That Hera set Typhon under the care of the other serpent being, Python, protectress of the oracle of Delphi, means she essentially doubled guardianship of the oracle, which was originally under the tutelage of Ge/Gaia (Pausanias 10.5.5). As I argue in *CDB*, the oracle of Delphi was also likely a location of a divine birth priestesshood (see Rigoglioso 2009, 180–204). We begin to see in the story of Hera and Typhon the emergence of a network of relationships in service to the protection of female parthenogenetic power, which was considered an attribute of both divine and mortal women. This is further emphasized by the fact that Python was also known as *hêrôis*, or "mistress/heroine," which is another form of the name *Hera* (Fontenrose 1959, 119, 377–78). These terms suggest an identification of Hera and Python as parthenogenetic mothers. It may even be that Hera herself was originally conceived in serpent form, as Harrison ([1903] 1957, 232–36, 321) intimates, noting that scattered evidence of earlier animal forms of the goddess as bird and snake can be found throughout Crete and Greece.[28] Moreover, *hêrôis*, or "heroine," is also found in Pindar (*Pythian Ode* 11.7) and is generally taken to be the earliest female equivalent of hero (*hêrôs*). This connects Hera and Python with the concept of the human heroine more broadly, which supports the argument I made in *CDB* that *heroine*, like *nymph*, was a marker for the priestess of divine birth (see Rigoglioso 2009, 35–37).

Hera's intimate relationship with Python and Delphi allows her actions regarding Leto to be interpreted in a new light, as well. Ancient writers speak of Hera's efforts to thwart Leto in giving birth to Apollo, as well as Python's quest to kill Leto for the same purpose.[29] It is Apollo who would fulfill prophecy and slay Python, thereby installing himself as the oracular authority at Delphi and taking control of the priestesshood there. Given all of the associations previously discussed, one could read Hera's/Python's actions as the attempt by the parthenogenetic Mistress to prevent the arrival of one who would claim power over her dominion and her parthenogenetic women.

Hera as a Guardian of Parthenogenetic Secrets

One of Hera's grandchildren by Typhon, born of his union with the female serpent-being Echidna, was the legendary Sphinx (Apollodorus 3.5.8). The Sphinx had the face of a woman, the breast, feet, and tail of a lion, and the wings of a bird. Given Hera's own associations with lions and birds, we may read the Sphinx as another archaic, chthonic version of the goddess herself. According to Apollodorus (3.5.8), Hera sent the Sphinx to Mt. Phicium, where it propounded to the Thebans the riddle it had learned from the Muses: "What is that which has one voice and yet becomes four-footed and two-footed and three-footed?" (Apollodorus 1967, 1: 348–49, trans. Frazer). An oracle informed the Thebans that they would be rid of the Sphinx only when they solved the riddle. Each time they met to discuss the answer and could not decipher it, however, the creature killed and ate one of their citizenry. It was only Oedipus who came up with the solution: The riddle referred to the human being, who walked on four limbs as a baby, two as an adult, and three (with a cane) as an elder. The Sphinx thereupon threw itself from the citadel, ending the Thebans' period of misery.

The Sphinx apparently had the last laugh, however, as, in exchange for his cleverness, Oedipus was unwittingly given his mother as a bride. The

Sphinx, then, was a creature of "riddles"; that is, it guarded the secrets of the mysteries from the prying eyes of the uninitiated. It also seems to have punished violations of social code, in this case the incest taboo. The overwhelmingly female form of this creature suggests that the original mysteries it protected were likely those of women.

Support for this idea can be found in the meanings associated with the Sphinx in Egypt, where the sculptural image of the head of a woman and body of a lion appeared as a discernible sculptural genre during the Middle Kingdom (c. 2133 B.C.E.). During this period, it was used in reference to the king's daughter. With the additional feature of wings, the Sphinx was associated with the cow goddess Hathor. It was, moreover, a symbol related to queenship (Troy 1986, 64–65). Like Hathor, Hera was both "cow" and conveyer of immortality to the parthenogenetically born male through her breast milk, as I elaborate later in this chapter when I discuss Heracles' imbibing of her milk.[30] These associations suggest that the real "secret" of the Sphinx was parthenogenesis. One wonders, then, whether Hera's having sent the Sphinx to prey on the Thebans might have been a punishment for a cultic transgression against her divine birth priestesshood.[31] Perhaps the motif of Oedipus "uniting with his mother" was somehow related to this.

Another interesting legend that may relate to the violation of women's sacred mysteries concerns an episode in the life of the seer Tiresias. A variant of the story involving Hera is told by a number of ancient writers.[32] The composite of the tale includes the following elements. Tiresias beheld two snakes coupling on Mt. Cyllene in Arcadia (or Mt. Cithaeron in Boeotia), and killed or wounded the female. Upon doing so, he was turned into a woman and remained so for seven years. At the end of this period, he again saw a pair of snakes mating and killed the male, after which he was turned back into a man. On one occasion when Hera and Zeus were arguing about which gender enjoyed sex more fully, they put the question to Tiresias because of his intimate knowledge of both. Siding with Zeus, he said that women enjoyed it significantly more than men. In anger, Hera blinded him, but Zeus gave him the power of prophecy.

The implication in the story is that somehow Tiresias grew to "know too much" about women's sexuality. What seems to be indicated is that he came to possess privileged information not about their sexuality in general, but about their sexual "secrets" in particular. It is important to bring in here a variant of the legend as it relates to Athena, where this element is perhaps clearer. In that story, Tiresias, the son of the "nymph" Chariclo, accidentally came upon the goddess Athena while she was bathing in a mountain stream. As punishment for seeing her naked, Athena took away his sight but, in response to Chariclo's distress, bestowed him with the gift of prophecy (Apollodorus 3.6.7; Callimachus *Hymn 5, Bath of Pallas* 73–130). That Chariclo was a priestess of Athena is suggested by references to her being "dear to" (*prosphilê*) the goddess (Apollodorus 3.6.7). As a priestess, she was no doubt privy to the goddess's mysteries, including, I suggest, those regarding parthenogenesis. Indeed, her "nymph" epithet may be a signal that she herself was a parthenogenetic priestess, as I have mentioned. Additionally, she is said to have been a member of the family of Udaeus, one of the men who sprang from the "dragon's teeth" sown by Cadmus on the advice of Athena (Apollodorus 3.4.1). This itself is a parthenogenetic reference, emphasizing that the idea of parthenogenetic birth was deep in her lineage. Although Tiresias is said to have been the product of Chariclo's union with a certain personage briefly named by Apollodorus (3.6.7) as Everes, could he have been understood to be the product of his mother's own parthenogenetic conception?

Whatever the case, I suggest that his seeing Athena's "nakedness" refers to his happening upon or actively pursuing the information to which his mother was privy regarding the female parthenogenetic mysteries. This idea is strengthened by Apollodorus's mention that, according to some accounts, the reason for Tiresias's blinding by the gods was that "he revealed their secrets to men." The episode of his blinding by Athena may also refer to efforts, perhaps on the part of Athena's priesateshood, to prevent Tiresias from making such knowledge public.

In this variant about Athena, the idea that Tiresias came to know "too much" about women's sexual secrets is expressed in the motif of his seeing the naked or exposed body of the Holy *Parthenos* herself. In the variant with Hera, it is conveyed by the motif of his own transformation into a woman so that he could have a first-hand experience of female sexual nature. As in the case of Athena, the story suggests that Tiresias possessed his prophetic skills *before* the episode in question; his "transformation" into a woman likely refers to an episode of shape-shifting— that is, his literal adoption of female identity and consciousness in trance state.[33]

The motif of his interrupting snakes engaged in coitus suggests that such a journey was undertaken with the express purpose of understanding female sexual anatomy and processes. It is particularly important to note in this regard that snakes couple by winding around one another, a fact observed in antiquity (Aelian *On Animals* 1.24). In doing so, they create the double helix, a symbol that appeared on Hermes' caduceus as an insignia of the mysteries of life and death (Cook 1914–40, 1:398). I propose that the symbol referenced what we now understand to be DNA, pointing to the mystery of incarnation of spirit into matter.[34] Thus, Tiresias's experience could be read as one in which he peered into and attempted to "break apart" and tease out the mystery of female conception. Significantly, this was made possible only by his doing violence to the female (snake). As in the case of his "spying" the naked Athena, I again suggest that the mystery he was trying to understand was that of women's parthenogenetic ability. Hera's association with the story emphasizes this, given that she, like Athena, was a Virgin Mother. Interpreted in this way, the motif of Hera's blinding of Tiresias can be understood not as a capricious response to her having lost an argument but as an act symbolizing the punishment of violent male transgression into women's parthenogenetic mysteries. Thus, I contend that the Athena and Hera variants of the story express the same theme.

Hera, the Hesperides, and the Apples of Parthenogenesis

An important legend that I posit also alludes to Hera's parthenogenetic capabilities is that of the golden apples of the Hesperides. In one version of the myth, Ge/Gaia gave to Hera an orchard of golden apple trees as a present for her marriage to Zeus. The apples were guarded by an immortal serpent, as well as "nymphs," known as the Hesperides, whose names were Aegle, Erythia, Hesperia, and Arethusa (Apollodorus 2.5.11).[35] In another version, Ge/Gaia gave the goddess branches with golden apples, which Hera requested be planted in her own gardens "near distant Mt. Atlas." When the Hesperides, Atlas's daughters, kept picking the apples from the trees, Hera installed the serpent there as a guardian. After Heracles killed the serpent, Hera placed it among the stars as the constellation *Draco*, or "Serpent" (Hyginus *Poetic Astronomy* 2.3).

Both versions of the myth redound with parthenogenetic references. First is the mythologem of Ge/Gaia's gift of the golden apples. As I showed in chapter 1, Ge/Gaia was, at her deepest level, a parthenogenetic goddess. Her initial possession of the apple orchard or branches symbolizes her ownership of all of the earth's life by virtue of being its parthenogenetic creator. Moreover, as I discussed earlier, the tree was an early epiphany of female deity as the parthenogenetic "Tree of Life." Ge/Gaia's "passing on" of the apple to Hera thus suggests an interchangeability between the two goddesses, once again pointing to their identification, which I propose was based on their mutual parthenogenetic nature. I thus argue that the tree of the golden apples was, ultimately, a symbol of female parthenogenetic ability. In essence, the myth only serves to underscore the identification between the two goddesses, as we have seen that Hera already possessed the "Tree of Life" in its various forms as willow and pomegranate. I propose, then, that the motif of Ge/Gaia's granting of the apple tree was not so much a gift to honor Hera's yoking to the male element, but, rather, a pointed reminder of her original parthenogenetic nature. Hera's self-generative capacities would persist, despite her marriage, as evidenced by her parthenogenetic birth of Ares, Hephaestus, and Typhon.

My suggestion about the true meaning of the gift of the apple tree is further supported by the fact that the other inhabitants of this paradisiacal garden were similarly associated with parthenogenesis. The Hesperides themselves were, in Hesiodic theogony, parthenogenetically born daughters of the goddess Nyx (*Theogony* 270).[36] That Hesiod (*Theogony* 214–15) identifies them as "nymphs," keepers of the golden apples and fruit-bearing trees, and that Diodorus Siculus (4.27.1–2) identifies these female figures as historical women further suggests that they were in fact ancient parthenogenetic priestesses, according to my argument about the meaning of the "nymph" title. According to one tradition, their father was Atlas (Diodorus Siculus 4.26.2, Pherecydes, in Hyginus *Astronomica* 2.3), which, moreover, rendered them half-sisters of the Pleiades. As I show in *CDB*, the Pleiades, all but one of whom engaged in *hieros gamos* unions with gods, were also likely priestesses of virgin birth (Rigoglioso 2009, 161–69). Moreover, various legends place the location of the garden of the Hesperides in Africa,[37] and Hesiod (*Theogony* 270) makes a point of locating them near the Gorgons and Medusa. As I argued in *CDB*, the Gorgons were probably historical Libyan Amazons whose queen, Medusa, was, like Queen Myrina, probably a parthenogenetic priestess of Athena/Neith (Rigoglioso 2009, 71–74). Such tribes were, moreover, most likely ancestors of the Libyan Auses, whom I similarly argued in chapter 1 may have practiced parthenogenetic conception. Thus, it appears that what is being described in the myth of the Hesperides is a North African precinct that was part of a larger culture of parthenogenetic religious activity.

The guardian serpent, too, has parthenogenetic associations. As I discussed in chapter 1, the Greeks believed that serpents were parthenogenetically born of Ge/Gaia. In fact, Apollonius Rhodius (*Argonautica* 4.1396) specifically calls the snake that guarded the apples a "son of Ge/Gaia." The poet also gives him a name: Ladon. Elsewhere, Ladon is named as an offspring of none other than Hera's parthenogenetically born son Typhon (Apollodorus 2.5.11; Hyginus *Fabulae* 151). These associations again point to an identification between Hera and Ge/Gaia as parthenogenetic beings.

Moreover, in the garden of the Hesperides, we have a replication of the situation at Delphi: a precinct originally sacred to Ge/Gaia, guarded by her parthenogenetic serpent progeny, associated with Hera's son Typhon, and administered by nymph/priestesses. As I noted, Delphi, the site of an oracular priesthood, was also likely the location of a parthenogenetic cult. That the Hesperides are said to have possessed the power of "sweet song" (Hesiod *Theogony* 518; Apollonius Rhodius 4.1399) suggests that, like the Delphic priestesses, they possessed powers of inspiration and prophecy. Thus, the myth of the Hesperides' garden seems to be referencing a parthenogenetic, oracular precinct in association with Ge/Gaia and Hera.

I suggest that although Ge/Gaia's gift of the golden apples was meant to remind Hera of her own parthenogenetic nature, this meaning was lost over time under patriarchy, and the apple came to be misinterpreted as a symbol of heterosexual eroticism and resulting fertility. Henceforth, the apple was used in both myth and ritual to celebrate weddings, and it also appeared as a mythological motif associated with the bringing about of a desired marriage or the saving of a faltering one.[38]

Some cross-cultural comparisons may be useful here to indicate how the apple retained its parthenogenetic symbolism underneath the heterosexual erotic overlay in numerous mythologies of different time periods. A manuscript from the sixteenth century, for example, relates that the mother of the Irish St. Molasius of Devenish dreamt of seven fragrant apples, the last of which was, to her, "lovelier than gold." The dream presaged the saint's birth and, as Hartland (1909–10, 1:10) notes, "we can hardly doubt that as the story was originally told Molasius was the direct result of his mother's eating an apple." That is, his birth was likely considered to have been a parthenogenetic one.

Indeed, given that, as Hartland (1909–10, 1:31) observes, frequently stories of conception via miraculous means "imply, if we are not told in so many words, that the origin of the child afterwards born is not the semen received in the act of coition, but the drug or magical potency of the ceremony or the incantation," several other customs regarding the use of apples to "cause" pregnancy are worth noting. In nineteenth-century Florence, for example, a woman who desired offspring might go to a priest and obtain a blessed apple, after which she would repair to St. Anne and repeat a prayer or spell over it (Leland 1892, 246). St. Anne, the mother of the Virgin Mary, was probably identified with the Roman Lucina, who was Hera herself (Apuleius *Golden Ass* 6.4; Kerenyi 1975, 173). St. Anne was associated with this goddess because the saint is said to have given birth miraculously to Mary in her old age. Thus, we have, in this Florentine tradition, what I propose is a memory of the direct association of the apple with both Hera and parthenogenetic birth.

A tradition of the Schokaz in Hungary to promote pregnancy in a barren woman involved a woman who had borne children looking for a stone that had been thrown at an apple tree and had remained on the tree. The woman was to take the stone down, put it in a vessel with an egg, pour water over both on the new moon, and give the water to a barren woman to drink. The fertile woman was then to take the other's bridal shift and wear it for nine weeks (Hartland 1909–10, 1:60). Among the Kara Kirghiz, rolling or wallowing beneath a solitary apple tree was seen as a method for obtaining pregnancy. An old custom of the southern Slavs was to unveil a bride beneath an apple tree and sometimes hang her veil on the tree (113). A Manchu bride, on reaching the bridegroom's house, was sometimes required to step over an apple placed on the threshold (134). These and other such stories point to a primal understanding of women's reproductive connection to the apple tree. Again, although some are suggestive of ordinary means to obtain conception, they all point to an underlying belief that the apple tree was symbolic of nonordinary, miraculous birth.

As Faraone (1990, 219) notes, in ancient Greek the word for apple, *mêlon*, was also used for pomegranates and other fruit. Thus, I suggest that the apple and pomegranate were analogs for one another from the religious perspective. That would mean, according to my argument, that the pomegranate was also a symbol of parthenogenesis.[39] It is for this reason, I suggest, that the pomegranate abounded as a votive to Hera. Philostratus (*Life of Apollonius of Tyana* 4.28) says the pomegranate was the only fruit grown in honor of the goddess. In the early period of her important sanctuary at Samos, real pomegranates, as well as those of clay and ivory, were brought as offerings to her, and no other Greek site of the early Archaic period was as rich in clay pomegranate votives as this particular Heraion (O'Brien 1993, 63–64). At Argos, as we will recall, Hera's Classical period cult statue held a pomegranate in one hand. About it, Pausanias (2.17.3) was constrained from commenting further because of its meaning being "something of a holy mystery." This is the same rationale he uses to avoid discussing the legend of Hera's bath to "renew" her virginity. Again, I propose that both mysteries could not be spoken about because both had to do with the capacity to conceive in virgin fashion attributed to Hera and her holy priestesses.

That the pomegranate was originally not a symbol of marriage, or of fertility arising from sexual union, is further suggested by the fact that, after around 600 B.C.E., the rich offerings of pomegranates at Hera's cult center at Samos suddenly stopped. O'Brien (1993, 63–66) contends that this corresponds with the time period in which Hera probably came to be viewed as Zeus's wife. As O'Brien explains, the pomegranate was dropped as a votive during this time probably because, as "the earth's votive *par excellence*," it was no longer seen as an appropriate symbol for a goddess who was not an Earth Mother. Elsewhere in Hera's cult, in time, the pomegranate contracted into a bridal symbol to commemorate her marriage with Zeus. Pomegranates could be found among her votives at Argos, Delos, and Paestum in Italy, and, at Archaic Paestum, her figurines held pomegranates in their hands. The fruit also came to be used as a gift for brides (63, 66). Again, I propose that the transformation of the pomegranate into a nuptial symbol occurred as the original memory of its meaning was forgotten. I return to a discussion of the pomegranate's parthenogenetic associations in chapter 5, where I discuss its role in Persephone's story.

"Judgment of Paris" as Loss of Parthenogenetic Power

Interpreting the golden apples of the Hesperides as symbols of parthenogenesis allows us to interpret another famous legend in a new light, the so-called Judgment of Paris. The episode that triggered what has been billed as the most famous "beauty contest" of all times—as well as the Trojan War itself—took place at the wedding of Thetis. Thetis was the most prominent of the Nereids, those sea goddess daughters of Nereus and granddaughters of Ge/Gaia and Pontus (Hesiod *Theogony* 233–43). According to one tradition, Zeus wished to marry Thetis, but she rejected the offer because she did not wish to betray Hera, who had brought her up (Homer *Iliad* 24.59–61; Apollonius Rhodius 4.793–95). In anger, Zeus decreed that Thetis should marry a mortal. Peleus ended up winning the Nereid,[40] and the couple's wedding was attended by all the gods (Homer *Iliad* 24.62). Thetis thereafter became the mother of the hero Achilles.[41]

It was at Thetis's wedding party that Eris, the goddess of strife, angry over not having been invited, is said to have tossed one of the golden apples of the Hesperides (Colluthus *Rape of Helen* 59–63), challenging the fairest to take it. When the goddesses Athena, Hera, and Aphrodite began to dispute among themselves as to which of them was the fairest, Zeus commanded them to be judged by Paris on Mt. Ida. The youth chose Aphrodite because she promised that the most beautiful mortal in the world, Helen, would be his wife. These events led to the start of the Trojan War, with Athena and Hera, in anger over Paris's decision, allying with the Greeks against the Trojans.[42]

The story recounts a struggle over which goddess should possess the "golden apple"—that is, the fruit guarded by the Hesperides and Ladon. If we interpret this apple to be a symbol of parthenogenesis, as I have argued, then the "Judgment of Paris" becomes symbolic of the loss of status of the parthenogenetic goddesses Hera and Athena—indeed, possibly of the loss of their parthenogenetic ability itself. By virtue of the fact that Hera possessed the golden apple trees, the apple already "belonged" to her. That the apple was "awarded" to Aphrodite rather than to its rightful parthenogenetic owner can be read as reflective of the shift in the meaning of the apple from parthenogenetic to heterosexual erotic symbol that I posited earlier. Furthermore, the judgment as to who should possess this symbol of female sexual and reproductive power was now in the hands of men (Paris as proxy for Zeus).[43]

Heracles as Foe of Parthenogenesis

To understand the nature of Hera's relationship with Heracles, it is first important to discuss the goddess's relationship with Greek heroes more generally. Hera's name is etymologically linked to "hero" (*hêrôs*) and to "season" (*hôrâ*); thus, "hero" would have meant "he who belonged to the goddess of the season/Hera" (O'Brien 1993, 3–5, 116–17). Hera was considered the protector of citadels and heroes more generally, particularly those of Argos, as suggested by her surname *Argeia*, "of Argos." Homeric passages show her as protectress of the Achaean heroes Agamemnon, Jason, and Achilles, in particular (*Iliad* 1.208–9; *Odyssey* 4.513, 12.72).

The important point about Greek heroes in this context is that, as I show in *CDB*, they were frequently sons of gods either by heroines or "nymphs" (Rigoglioso 2009, 30–31). That is, they were understood to be *parthenioi*, children of holy virgins. Thus, Hera's "protectorship" over heroes underscores the idea that a close relationship must have existed between this goddess and the institution of the divine birth priestesshood thought to have bred such children. Even Homer (*Iliad* 18.59) has Zeus declare "from [Hera] were born the long-haired Achaeans" (*seio ex autês egenonto karê komonôntes Achaioi*). This seems to refer to an earlier mythological stratum in which it was Hera who was considered the mother of Achaean heroes who fought at Troy (O'Brien 1993, 164). The inference, I suggest, is that the goddess produced these heroes parthenogenetically, an idea that is strengthened if we recall that Ge/Gaia was also credited with having parthenogenetically spawned human beings. Thus, Homer's oblique reference seems to allude to a time when Hera was indeed considered the parthenogenetic creatrix of heroes. I propose that this is a hint that she once was thought to supersede even Zeus in his role as father of such "divine" humans. That the Dorian Argives built their sanctuary to Hera near Mycenaean hero tombs on the hill called Prosymna also suggests that the Argives understood Hera as the goddess who regulated the hero's short lifespan by returning him to the earth (168). If we consider that priestesses served as doubles or proxies for their goddesses (see Rigoglioso 2009, 62; Connelly 2007, 83, 104–15), we could read this complex of cultic and mythical material as indicating that it was in fact Hera's *priestesses* who were credited with bringing forth the heroes of Mycenae and Argos.

As I argue throughout *CDB*, in the condition of divine birth through *hieros gamos*, divinization of what was thought to be a child of a holy *parthenos* was granted to those who agreed to submit themselves to a ritualized sacrificial death (see, particularly, Rigoglioso 2009, 20). Nowhere was such self-sacrifice made easier than on the battlefield. This is why, I suggest, the great theater of Bronze Age warfare served as a particularly prolific source of heroes for cultic worship.[44] Despite a possible earlier role ascribed to Hera for the production of divine individuals, however, with Zeus assuming "fatherhood" of many of Greece's finest sons, the worship of local heroes became an extension of the worship of Zeus. Hero worship was thus a means of keeping in place the new Olympian order (O'Brien 1993, 118).

Yet the cult of the hero—and Olympian religion itself—was originally dependent on the goddess and her priestesses for its very existence. For one primary way in which a hero was thought to come onto the earthly plane was through his mother's sexual liaison with a god.[45] And, as we will see with Heracles, it was only through "imbibing the milk or ambrosia of Hera" that the hero could achieve apotheosis as a full-fledged god in his own right. Thus, just as I have suggested that Athena was appropriated to support the patriarchal Greek military machine, so I propose that Hera was appropriated, as well. Correspondingly, as we see in *CDB* with Hera's priestess Io and the legendary priestesses and "nymphs" associated with Athena and Artemis, it is likely that the Heraian priesthood was conscripted into what was believed to have been the birthing of heroes via gods, those men necessary to fuel the patriarchy (see Rigoglioso 2009, 71–81, 92–106, 130–33). I suggest that although priestesses may have derived power from such a role, they may not have been entirely happy with this new male-dominant state of affairs.

Nowhere do we see the distortions resulting from this situation more strongly than in the story of Hera's relationship with Heracles, Zeus's son by Alcmene. Heracles was arguably Greece's most famous hero. More so than even Theseus, Perseus, and Cadmus, he is credited with having introduced Olympian ways to Greece. Given that he was one of Zeus's favorite sons by a mortal and his role in establishing patriarchy in Greece, it is perhaps not surprising that Heracles was Hera's most hated "stepson."

Heracles' mother was Alcmene, a granddaughter of the legendary Mycenaean king Perseus. As such, she was a descendant of Io.[46] Given her genealogical relationship to Io, herself a priestess of Hera, and given the fact that Hera's wrath toward Alcmene was particularly virulent, I suggest that Alcmene was originally a priestess of Hera. According to Hesiod (*Shield of Hercles* 1–26), Zeus visited Alcmene's bed and impregnated her with Heracles. That same night, her husband Amphitryon returned and made love with her, also impregnating her with another child. In another tradition recorded by Apollodorus (2.4.3–5), Zeus engaged with Alcmene "in the likeness" of her husband.[47] Taken together, these stories suggest an instance of *hieros gamos* with a god via a human male surrogate akin to that reported for the Egyptian Queens Mutemwia and Ahmose (see Rigoglioso 2007, 74–85; 2009, 24). They also recall an episode in which Athena's priestess Aethra was said to have been visited by Zeus and King Pelcus "on the same night," indicating that the god was understood to have come to her through the body of the king. Thus, I propose that the legend of Alcmene refers to a ritual intercourse she engaged in with Amphitryon to engender a hero.[48]

According to legend, the day on which Heracles was to be born, Zeus declared his son would rule over the entire race of Perseus—that is, he would become the king of Mycenae. When Hera made Zeus swear that the descendant of Perseus born that day would indeed rule, she sped to Argos and there hastened the birth of Eurystheus, another child in line to the throne, while delaying the confinement of Alcmene. Unable to go back on his word, the enraged god was forced to concede the empire to Eurystheus. However, he persuaded Hera to agree that if Heracles executed twelve labors in the service of Eurystheus, he should become immortal. Eurystheus's assumption of the kingship of Mycenae at the bidding of Hera, again, likely represents a Bronze Age political conflict that took place between worshippers of the pre-Olympian and Olympian cults (O'Brien 1993, 4).

It is at this point in the story that the Hera's "milk" becomes important. As Pseudo-Eratosthenes (*Constellations* 44) reports, it was not possible for the sons of Zeus to share in heavenly honor before one of them had been nursed by this goddess. For this reason, Hermes brought Heracles shortly after his birth to the breast of Hera, without revealing the child's identity. The goddess unknowingly nursed the future hero, some say while she slept. When, however, she realized what was happening, she pushed the baby away, and the milk that was spilled produced the Milky Way.[49] This mythologem again ties the legend to Egyptian beliefs and rituals regarding divine kingship. After Egyptian kings were born, they were thought to be suckled by the cow goddess Hathor as a means of completing the divinizing process (Rigoglioso 2007, 79–80). Such a connection strongly points to Egyptian influence in Greece regarding the cult of divine birth and further supports the idea that Alcmene and Amphitryon's union was ritually engineered.[50]

The degree to which Hera wished to do away with Heracles can be seen in the legends of her relentless pursuit of the hero throughout his life. When Heracles was only a few months old, for example, Hera is said to have sent two serpents into his room to kill him. The infant strangled them with his own hands, however (Pindar *Nemean Ode* 1.39–47; Apollodorus 2.4.8). Later, when Heracles was grown and married, Hera visited him with madness such that he murdered his own children (Apollodorus 2.4.12).[51] Hera's attitude can perhaps be read as a protest on the part of the older matriarchal order to the continued imposition of the Olympian religion, now into its second and even more violent "generation." For of the twelve labors that Heracles completed in order to obtain his immortality, seven involved what I argue were attempts to dismantle or disrupt the earlier religion, in a number of cases particularly as it related to the cult of divine birth.[52]

The Lernaean Hydra

One of the labors involved the conquering of the Hydra of Lerna. The Lernaean Hydra, said to have been a snake-like monster with nine heads, the middle one of which was immortal, was Hera's grandson by Typhon and his half-viper wife Echidna. It ravaged the countryside of Lerna near Argos and dwelt in a swamp near the well of Amymone. When Heracles attempted to cut off its heads, two new ones grew forth in the place of each one that was cut. With the assistance of his servant Iolaus, he eventually demolished the creature by burning away its heads and burying the immortal one under a huge rock.[53]

As O'Brien notes (1993, 99), the genealogy involved here, which includes Hera's parthenogenetically produced son Typhon, likely references an older version of Hera whose regional roots clashed with her "new" role as sister and wife of Zeus in the Olympian family. Moreover, it is significant that, in the realm of biology, the hydra is an actual living organism that, like its mythical counterpart, lives in water, can have multiple heads, and possesses the capacity not only to survive amputations, but also to be dissolved into a single-cell solution, from which it will reconstitute itself over a period of weeks. Its amputated fragments will, furthermore, proceed to grow back as so many new little hydras. In adverse conditions, it resorts to sexual reproduction, but ordinarily it is able to multiply itself indefinitely through a process of asexual budding. The hydra is unique among even self-regenerating animals in that it never loses this extreme regenerative power. Moreover, it is literally immortal in that it is continually regenerated through stem cells that never stop proliferating and migrating throughout the body to replace other cells as they age.[54] In short, the hydra is the paragon of parthenogenesis.

The biological reality of the hydra only serves to underscore what is conveyed in its purely mythological description—that it was a symbol of parthenogenesis, and parthenogenesis particularly as it related to "immortality," expressed in the motif of the creature's divine middle head. Hera's "nursing" of the Lernaean Hydra may thus be seen as her caretaking the realm of parthenogenetic reproduction of divine humans, which, in the original form of this cult practice, was understood to involve a completely pure or asexual process akin to the reproductive activities of the hydra itself. Such capacity on the part of women would indeed no doubt have been seen as an impediment to the ascension of the male political and theological establishment, which lacked the necessary biology to carry out such holy and generative feats without taking control of the associated priestesses. The creature's many heads could be seen as representing the multiplicity of priestesses who were thought to have been involved in such a process (and suggests perhaps there were nine such holy colleges?). It stands to reason that Heracles, as the ultimate symbol of patriarchy, would have needed to dismantle that priestesshood (kill the hydra) in order to attain his own lordship (immortality) in the new political schema.

The Nemean Lion

Another creature Heracles pursued was the Nemean lion, which also has interesting associations with Hera. By one account, the lion was the son of Echidna and was raised by Hera, who set the animal free in the hills of Nemea to be a plague to humankind (Hesiod *Theogony* 326–29). By another account, however, the lion was, like the Lernaean Hydra, parthenogenetically born. According to Aelian (*On Animals* 12.7), the lion of Nemea "fell from the moon [Selene]." Aelian quotes Epimenides as saying that the lion was "sprung from fair-tressed Selene the Moon, who in a fearful shudder shook off the savage [beast], and brought him forth at the bidding of Queen Hera."[55] As we have seen, Hera herself had associations with the moon. This description, in fact, resembles that of the Heraian priestess Io's parthenogenetic conception of Epaphus by a "ray of light coming from the moon," a motif I discuss in *CDB* (Rigoglioso 2009, 132). Thus, the moon had powerful resonances in connection with parthenogenesis. Moreover, we know, as discussed earlier, that the lion was one of the animals identified with

Hera. This story, therefore, like that of the Lernaean Hydra, seems to be referencing a creature from the realm of Hera that was partheno-genetically born. Again, Heracles' killing of the Nemean lion could be seen as an attack on female parthenogenetic capacity and its related priestesshood.

The Ceryneian Stag

Another labor on the part of Heracles involved capturing the stag of Ceryneia. This animal, which had golden antlers and brazen feet, was the deer that Hera had allowed to escape Artemis's capture and dwell in the Ceryneian hills (Callimachus *Hymn 3 to Artemis* 100–109). According to one tradition, the stag had been dedicated to Artemis as a holy offering by the Pleiad Taygete in thanks for the goddess having turned her into a stag when she sought to elude Zeus's embrace (Euripides *Helen* 381–83; Pindar *Olympian Ode* 3.25–30). Heracles wounded the stag with an arrow and carried it away on his shoulders to Mycenae.[56]

Once again, with the Ceryneian stag we have motifs suggestive of par-thenogenesis. First, the animal was sacred to Artemis, a Virgin Mother. Second, the hind was made as a gift to the goddess specifically by one of the seven Pleiades sisters in thanks for Artemis having rescued the maiden from a *hieros gamos* encounter with Zeus by turning her into one such ani-mal.[57] Thus, the stag represents Taygete's original commitment to pure parthenogenesis. The capture of this creature, therefore, also seems to symbolize the despoiling of the divine birth priestesshood.

The Oxen of Geryones and Stymphalian Birds

In a subsequent labor, Heracles captured another set of animals sacred to Hera, the oxen of Geryones in Erytheia (Apollodorus 2.5.10). He also slew a group of creatures sacred to Artemis: the man-eating Stymphalian birds (Apollodorus 2.5.6). As we saw in chapter 3, these birds were depicted in carvings at Artemis's sanctuary at Stymphalus in Arcadia, behind which also stood marble statues of maidens with the legs of birds (Pausanias 8.22.4–7). These details suggest a connection between the birds and Artemis's priestesses, whom I have argued may at one point have been in service to parthenogenesis.

The Belt of Hippolyte

Heracles' labors also involved stealing the belt of the Amazon Hippolyte. According to one tradition, Hippolyte is said initially to have offered him her belt upon his arrival in the Thermadon region by the Black Sea. But Hera, in the guise of an Amazon woman, went through the crowd saying that the new arrivals were robbing or kidnapping the queen. The women thereupon armed themselves and rode down to the ships on horses. When Heracles saw they were armed, he feared a trap, and so killed Hippolyte and took the belt (Apollodorus 2.5.9; Plutarch *Theseus* 26.1). Diodorus (4.16.2–4), however, relates that Hippolyte refused to relinquish the belt, and that the Amazons, led by Melanippa, engaged in fierce battle with Heracles, who cut down the most renowned of them one by one and slaughtered most of the rest as they fled, so that their race was utterly exterminated.

Although in some Greek texts the belt is portrayed as an accoutrement of warfare,[58] more often, as the *zônê*, it is portrayed as a symbol of maidenhood or virginity. This can be seen in its having been a dedicatory offering to Athena (Rigoglioso 2009, 77). In some cases, it was also a possession of Aphrodite and, as such, a symbol of women's sexuality. This is expressed, for example, in a legend in which Hera once borrowed Aphrodite's belt to seduce Zeus (Homer *Iliad* 14.214–21). Thus, the belt had multiple resonances as a symbol of warfare, virginity, and female sexuality. This complex of attributes calls to mind those that comprise the totality of Athena/Neith and Artemis themselves: warrior virgins who were also once goddesses of generativity. Both of these goddesses, I have shown, were also sacred to the Amazons. Moreover, as I suggested was possibly the case with Queen Medusa, Amazon queens, at least those of the Libyans, may have attempted to practice parthenogenetic birth in association with their goddess. Thus one could argue that the "belt" of Hippolyte was a symbol of what was understood as the priestess's parthenogenetic capability. Hera's attempt to rouse up the Amazon women in one version of the myth could thus be read as an effort (by an oracular priestess representing her?) to prevent women's parthenogenetic capacity from being stolen and put in service to the patriarchy. Indeed, Diodorus's account indicates that Hippolyte in fact never intended to give up the belt and that the labor referenced Heracles' attack on the Amazons more broadly.

A detail Apollodorus (2.5.9) relates, that Heracles was sent to obtain the belt at the behest of Admete, is also worth exploring. As we will recall, Admete, the daughter of the Mycenaean king Eurystheus, was a priestess of Hera who eventually fled Argos and established the formal sanctuary to Hera on Samos. If my argument that the belt was a symbol of parthenogenesis has any merit at all, we can read this detail about Admete in several ways: We can see it as a spurious addition to the story that is unrelated to the meaning of the labor. We can see it as an attempt on the part of the systematizers of myth to divert responsibility for the violent act away from Heracles. We can interpret it at face value as reflecting Admete's frivolous desire to obtain a curiosity piece. Or we may read it as an expression of Admete's need to "repossess" her own power and status as a parthenogenetic priestess of Hera. We know from myth that Admete fled from Argos for reasons that are not stated and that, "under Hera's protection," she arrived safely on Samos. Perhaps her coveting another woman's symbol of power corresponded with her own diminishment under the male-run regimes of Argos and, later, Samos.

The Apples of the Hesperides

One last labor on the part of Heracles also must be mentioned. This was his ultimately successful attempt to steal the golden apples of the Hesperides from Hera's garden in Africa.[59] Given my earlier argument that these apples represented the parthenogenetic capability of Ge/Gaia and Hera, no further commentary is needed here to demonstrate how the theft of such apples (and, by some accounts, Heracles' killing of the guardian snake Ladon) represented yet another instance of the patriarchal incursion into women's sacred parthenogenetic mysteries.

Hera continued to plague Heracles after he concluded his twelve labors. As he was sailing away from Troy following its sacking, for example, she sent a raging storm upon his ship. Heracles was forced to land on Cos, where he was almost killed—an episode, as we saw, that roused Zeus's own murderous rage against his wife (Apollodorus 1.3.5, 2.7.1). Yet, ultimately, it was a mortal woman, Heracles' own wife Deianeira, who succeeded in hastening his demise by poisoning him out of jealousy. Like any divine son with ambitions of godhood, however, Heracles must have realized that anything but a ritual death would have prevented him from achieving full apotheosis. Thus as the poison coursed through his body he ascended Mt. Oeia, raised a pile of wood, climbed on top of it, and ordered that it be set on fire. Myths recount that as he was dying, he was carried off to Olympus, where he was honored with immortality (Apollodorus 2.7.7). Curiously, Pindar (*Nemean Ode* 1.72–73, 10.18; *Isthmian Ode* 4.59–60) assigns to Heracles a posthumous marriage to Hebe, Hera's daughter. Apollodorus (2.7.7) adds that the event followed Hera's "reconciliation" with the apotheosized hero. On earth, Heracles was subsequently worshipped throughout Greece and Rome as both a god and a hero (e.g., Diodorus 4.39.1; Herodotus 2.44.1). In Rome, however, women were not allowed to take part in his worship; Plutarch (*Roman Questions* 60, *Oracles at Delphi* 20) says this injunction was a consequence of his having been poisoned by his wife. In Phocis, Heracles' surname was *Mysogynist*, "Woman Hater" (Plutarch *Oracles at Delphi* 20). The existence of such a shrine seems to cement the general program of misogyny that Heracles helped usher in.

In closing this chapter, one last comment should be made regarding Heracles' name. At some point prior to his labors, he visited the Delphic oracle, where he was for the first time given the name *Heracles* by the Pythia. Previously, he had been named *Alcides* or *Alcaeus* (Apollodorus 2.4.12). *Heracles*, in fact, means "he who wins ancestral fame or glory (*kleos*) from Hera" (O'Brien 1993, 116n9). His very name points to an older relationship with the goddess whereby it was under her auspices that immortality was offered. As the stories of Greek Heracles reveal, however, that fame was ultimately won not on the goddess's terms, but at her *expense*. For Heracles' heroic exploits are symbolic of the further entrenchment of an Olympian religion that spelled the end of the old Heraian cult in its original form.

CHAPTER 5

DEMETER AND PERSEPHONE: DOUBLE
GODDESSES OF PARTHENOGENESIS

In the Olympian conception, Demeter was the goddess of the grain; Kore or Persephone was her daughter, the maiden goddess of the springtime and the underworld. Much of our knowledge about these two deities derives from the Homeric *Hymn to Demeter*.[1] Probably composed between 650 and 550 B.C.E., the *Hymn* tells the story of Persephone's abduction by her uncle Hades, god of the underworld and brother of Zeus, and of Demeter's quest to have her returned. Demeter roams the earth, coming to Eleusis, where, disguised as an old woman, she unsuccessfully attempts to immortalize the child of the local king and, in anger over the loss of her daughter, creates a famine on earth to pressure the gods to return the girl. The gods comply, but, given that Persephone has eaten of the pomegranate in the underworld, she is constrained to return there as its queen for one-third of the year. The *Hymn* closes with Demeter founding the Eleusinian Mysteries.

As Richardson (1974, 12) notes, there is general agreement that the *Hymn* represents a relatively developed stage in the history of the cult of the two goddesses and that it most likely "adapted some features of the myth" and served as "a compromise between local beliefs and the rather artificial synthesis found in the epics" (17). The Orphic versions, attributed to Orpheus, Musaeus, and Eumolpus, he argues (85), may contain older and more genuine traditions.[2] To tease out the original myth and cult, Richardson contends (13), one must turn to other versions, testimony of later writers, archaeology, and accounts of similar religious phenomena in other societies. That is precisely what I do in this chapter, hermeneutically applying my theory of the existence of a divine birth cult in Greece to the material, as well. As I have done throughout this book, I present plentiful evidence that Demeter and Persephone, too, were originally conceived as Virgin Mothers. I further show that Persephone was, in the most esoteric reckoning of these goddesses, understood to be the parthenogenetic daughter, the "double," of her mother. I argue that Persephone herself was destined to be a parthenogntentic mother but was interrupted in her task by the advent of a male god who willfully and without permission used her to create his own "double." This event, I contend, marked a tragic moment for matriarchy and ushered in the era of patriarchy. In the immortal realms, as well as on the earthly plane, it signaled the usurping of the parthenogenetic power of the female in service to the birthing of the "sons of gods."

This understanding of Persephone as the paradigmatic case of the Raped Holy Virgin allows for a new interpretation of the two most important rites dedicated to the two goddesses, the Thesmophoria and the Eleusinian Mysteries. Indeed, it allows us to see both rituals as rooted in divine birth practices. Moreover, it permits us to understand the Thesmophoria as a matriarchal rite that originally celebrated pure parthenogenesis, and to discern that the Mysteries were a later development over which the practice of *hieros gamos* was placed for the purpose of generating what were believed to be living divine kings. Under this schema, previously puzzling elements of the rites become clear and paradoxical elements are resolved.

Older Roots for Demeter as Great Goddess

Digging beneath the Homeric *Hymn*, we immediately see signs that Demeter was once an older universal mother. In ancient times, she was sometimes seen as the equivalent of Ge/Gaia, the "Mother of All."[3] Certain texts indicate that Demeter was also possibly one and the same with Rhea. Rhea was the Olympian "Mother of the Gods," having given birth to the entire divine pantheon—Demeter and her siblings Zeus, Poseidon, Hades, Hestia, and Hera. In Euripides' play *Helen* (1301–7), Rhea is conflated with Demeter when the chorus identifies the "Mother of the Gods" (who, as Kerenyi affirms [1967, 132], "can only be Rhea") as the mother of the *arrhêtos koura,* the "ineffable maiden" (who can only be Kore/Persephone). Such conflation of these two monumental goddesses can also be seen in the Orphic tradition, where in one strain Rhea is identified as the mother of Persephone, whereas in another Demeter is (133). The names of Rhea and Demeter similarly alternate in the Orphic myth of Dionysus as Persephone's son (Orphic frags. 58 and 36, in Kerenyi 133n67; Diodorus Siculus 3.62.7). The latest version of the Orphic theogony (frag. 145, in Guthrie [1952] 1993, 139) reports blatantly the transmutation from one goddess to the other, stating, "After becoming the mother of Zeus, she who had formerly been Rhea became Demeter." Kerenyi (133) writes, "Thus the great Mother Goddess of an older, in part pre-Greek world was not forgotten behind that figure of Demeter the grain mother."

We see hints of links between Demeter and Rhea even in the Homeric *Hymn*, in the motif of Rhea's descending from Olympus to bring her daughter and granddaughter, Demeter and Persephone, to new honors there. As Foley (1994, 131–32) notes, Rhea's unusual role of messenger here, one usually held by Hermes or Iris, "seems to stress a reconstituting of intergenerational bonds between mother and daughter." I suggest that it is specifically an allusion to the more matriarchal condition in which all three originated.

Moreover, as I have shown was the case with Athena, Demeter appears to have been a goddess with roots in North Africa. Regarding "the mysterious rites of Demeter, which the Greeks call Thesmophoria," celebrated at Eleusis, which I discuss later in the chapter, the Greek historian Herodotus (2.171.2–3) writes, "it was the daughters of Danaus who brought this ceremony from Egypt and instructed the Pelasgian [Greek] women in it." The root of *Danaus* and of the term anciently used to refer to his daughters, *Danaids,* is *don-u/dan-u*. This root also appeared in names for rivers in areas claimed as homelands of Indo-European speakers (e.g., Danube, Don, Dneister, etc.). According to Dexter (1980, 20–21; 1990, 41–46), the root may reflect a pre- or proto-Indo-European word for "stream" or "watery place," which may have eventually become personified as the goddess Danu, mother of the withholder of the waters. We know that, linguistically, Demeter's name can be broken into two words, the second being *mêtêr,* or "mother," and the first being *De,* or, in its older form, *Da.* Kerenyi (1967, 28) notes that Da "was a female deity whose succor and assistance were evoked in archaic formulas by the use of this syllable." The *Da* in Demeter's archaic name may also be related to the root *don-u/dan-u,* rendering her name "mother of Da" (Suter 2002, 160–61). Given that, as I show later in the chapter, the Danaids were strongly associated with the waters, I propose that Demeter's original name meant "mother of *the* Da"—that is, the peoples of North Africa who venerated her and brought her to Greek shores.

Various sources indicate that Demeter was also identified with the Egyptian goddess Isis (e.g., Diodorus, 4.69.1). That the Egyptians often called Isis by the name *Athena* (Plutarch *On Isis and Osiris* 62/376A) suggests an ancient equation between Demeter, Isis, and Athena. Indeed, we know that the Danaids from Egypt established rites not only to Demeter but also to Athena (Apollodorus 2.1.4). This supports the possibility that Athena and Demeter were originally closely related goddesses who hailed from ancient "Libya." Indeed, in one of her most ancient forms at Phigaleia, Demeter was known as *Melaina*, "Black" (Pausanias 8.42.1; Farnell [1896–1909] 1977, 3.50–51). This could well be a memory of her roots among the North Africans.

Who Was Persephone?

Scholars have discussed at length the possible origins of Demeter's daughter, known variously as Kore or Persephone.[4] What complicates the analysis is confusion over her very name. As Demeter's daughter, she was generally referred to by poets as *Kore*, that is, "Maiden" (Kerenyi 1967, 28). However, it is not clear that Kore was ever more than her title. Pausanias (8.37.9) tells us that Kore was not her real name; rather, it was Persephone, first written by Homer, and, allegedly, the hymn writer Pamphus before him. Suter (2002, 124) affirms that, in the Homeric *Hymn* at least, Persephone is referred to as a *kourê*, a "maiden," but that Kore is not, in fact, her name.[5]

Confusion over the identity of this goddess has also made exploring her roots difficult. As the maiden, she was associated with the planted seed and thus was considered to be absent during the Mediterranean winter, when seed was sown.[6] As Persephone, she was Queen of the Underworld. Were these two figures, maiden and queen, originally the same goddess? Zuntz (1971, 75–83) argues that Kore, whose name is Greek, was a possible agricultural deity, whereas Persephone was a goddess of the underworld not of Greek origin (at least as far as her name goes). Suter (2002, 121) maintains that Persephone was indeed once independent from Demeter as a manifestation of a Bronze Age goddess of fertility and the underworld who governed the cycle of seasonal growth, death, and rebirth. This goddess, argues Suter, came be associated in many places with the later Greek Demeter, who held similar attributes, and eventually was put under her control by mythographers as her daughter. Richardson (1974, 16) suggests that both figures—Kore and Persephone—originally possessed both agricultural and eschatological significance. What these studies accurately assess, I contend, is that Persephone indeed was a fully formed goddess in her own right. However, as I argue in what follows, this does not preclude her ancient, primal connection to a mother figure, as well.

It is also important to note that, whereas in the Homeric *Hymn* Kore/Persephone becomes associated with the underworld by virtue of her abduction there, pre-Olympian stories of "the descent to the underworld" undertaken by goddesses such as the Egyptian Isis and the Sumerian Inanna contain no mention of "rape" or "abduction" as a part of their journeying to the nether realms. Spretnak (1981 [1978], 105–7), therefore, posits that an early Greek version of the myth probably existed in which Persephone, like these earlier goddesses, willingly and freely passed to and from the underworld as a means of acquiring wisdom. The element of the abduction by Hades, she argues, was probably a later revision to the story by the Indo-Europeans. I discuss my own interpretation of this shift, which includes consideration of the meaning of *korê* and the identity of Persephone in relationship to Demeter, throughout the rest of the chapter.

Signs of Parthenogenesis in the Demeter/Persephone Mythologem

Textual evidence suggests Demeter was originally considered to be a Virgin Mother. We recall her identification with Rhea, noted above. Rhea was anciently a goddess of totality—of heaven, earth, and sea (*Hymn of Epidaurus*, in Kerenyi 1967, 148). Even more striking, for the Pythagoreans, Rhea as Primordial Mother *was duality itself* (148n129). If we equate her with Demeter, as the aforementioned textual fragments suggest, this conception indicates a profound esoteric understanding of Demeter/Rhea as a deity of first principle and a prime mover. As both primordial mother and duality, she necessarily would have been understood to *incorporate totality within herself and birth it from herself*. That is, she would have been considered parthenogenetic. As mentioned earlier, Demeter's ancient identification with Ge/Gaia is significant, as well, in that, as I argued in chapter 1, the Earth Mother was also understood to be self-generative.

Harrison ([1903] 1957, 272) posits, in fact, that Demeter and Persephone both may have emerged from this earth deity: "It was mainly in connection with agriculture, it would seem, that the Earth-goddess developed her double form as Mother and Maid. The ancient 'Lady of the Wild Things' is both in one or perhaps not consciously either, but at Eleusis the two figures are clearly outlined; Demeter and Kore are two persons through one god." Farnell ([1896–1909] 1977, 3.114, 119) similarly argues that in Demeter and Kore "the single personality of the earth-goddess is dualized in two distinct and clearly correlated personalities," which are "pre-Homeric offshoots of Gaia." I suggest that interpreting Demeter and Persephone as having been intimately related in this way, "two persons through one deity," is the most fruitful approach when considering their origins. This view is the one most consistent with what the Greeks discerned about these deities. It also corresponds with earlier imagery that may represent such goddesses in their pre-Greek incarnations, as I elaborate in what follows.

At Eleusis, Demeter and Persephone were famously known to the public as "the two deities"—that is, the "two goddesses" (Kerenyi 1967, 28). I contend that the Greeks placed them together in this way based on the understanding that they were ultimately inseparable. Corradini (1997, 83) cogently ascertains that the "mother-daughter dualism" we see in the myth complex of Demeter and Persephone is based on a primordial identity that is conceived as a *doubling*. This arrangement reflects the vital cycle of birth–growth–death–rebirth. More to the point, Corradini notes, it reflects the condition of the goddess's parthenogenetic reproduction of herself.

Like Harrison, Kerenyi came close to this idea decades ago in intimating the possibility that the two goddesses were, in fact, part of a "Great Mother": "a single figure which was *at once* Mother and Daughter." He elaborates, "As mistress of all living creatures on land and sea she could reach up from the underworld to heaven" (1967, 32). The "duplication" of the goddesses can be seen in various attributes, stories, and iconography in which they seem to possess identical or nearly identical aspects and undergo similar experiences. In the Homeric *Hymn*, we see Persephone granted governance over heaven, earth, and sea (365–69), which may reflect her earlier totality. Such attributes remind us of Rhea/Demeter, who, as explained, also had provenance over such realms. Demeter was the grain; as mentioned earlier, Kore/Persephone was understood to be the planted seed. Although Persephone was known as Queen of the Underworld, Demeter, too, was once the ward of the dead (Plutarch *Face on the Moon* 28/943B) and possessed the title *Chthonia*, "Of the Underworld" (Harrison ([1903] 1957, 275–76). An inscription at Delos affirms the unity of the two goddesses, calling her/them "Demeter the Eleusinian, maiden and woman" (Kerenyi 1967, 33).

Other textual evidence points to an identification between Demeter and Persephone in their experience of rape. Persephone was raped by Hades (*Hymn* 30) in the Homeric tradition and Zeus in the Orphic tradition.[7] Demeter was also raped. Clement of Alexandria (*Exhortation to the Greeks* 2.13) mentions her rape by none other than her "son" Zeus, which indicates that we are in the Orphic tradition in which Demeter was conflated with Rhea. In that story, it was Rhea, Zeus's mother, who was raped by the god (Janko 2001, 29n168). This overlap underscores the understanding of the "twinning" element of the goddesses, which also draws Rhea into the schema. In this Orphic configuration, Demeter/Rhea's rape engendered Persephone (Guthrie [1952] 1993, 82). Demeter was raped in Arcadia, as well, this time by Poseidon during her search for her daughter. Although she transformed herself into a mare to avoid him, the god shape-shifted into a stallion, begetting on her a mythical steed (Pausanias 8.25.7, 8.42.1–2). As Kerenyi (1967, 32) notes, "Was the Arcadian Persephone really different from her mother, who had also suffered the fate of the Kore?" In the Homeric *Hymn* (434), when the two goddesses joyously reunite after Persephone's abduction, they are described as being *homophrona*, "of one mind." This again emphasizes their underlying unity.

The "twinning" aspect is reflected in numerous ancient visual images, as well, in which, as other scholars have noted, it is nearly impossible to distinguish the two goddesses (e.g., Harrison ([1903] 1957, 273–74; Neumann 1963, 309). At Thelpousa, the double goddesses were subsumed into one identity, as can be seen by the fact that Demeter *alone* was represented with two statues (Kerenyi 1967, 32). Figures that may represent these two goddesses dating between the sixteenth and early fourteenth centuries B.C.E. were found at Mycenae. In one grouping, two women are seated close to one another; one's arm is over the other's shoulder, and a single shawl drapes them both. In front of them, a child leans against their knees. This has been interpreted possibly to be Demeter, Persephone, and Iacchus or Ploutus, two male figures associated with their myth as "sons," as I discuss later in the chapter. In a Mycenaean grave, a terracotta of two "Siamese twin" figures attached from the hip to the shoulders and carrying a small figure that seems to be female was found (Mylonas 1966, 155–56). Although there may not be evidence to indicate that these Mycenaean figures were associated with any sort of shrine (Mylonas 1961, 155–66), various interpretations have naturally gravitated toward the conjecture that they represented Demeter and Persephone (Suter 2002, 190).[8]

The "twin" iconography of Demeter and Persephone may have roots even farther back, in the "double-formed" goddess represented in Neolithic archaeological finds (see, e.g., Noble 2003). In ancient Çatalhöyük (situated in contemporary Turkey), a settlement dating back to the sixth millennium B.C.E., for example, we see two goddesses who already seem to appear as mother and daughter, the former of which is connected with the grain.[9] Such pre-Greek images suggest that these two goddesses may indeed be manifestations of very old deities who were always linked as "doubles."

Before proceeding further with the argument, it is important to underscore the female-centered nature of the Demeter/Persephone paradigm. Jung ([1963] 1973, 177) observes, "Demeter-Kore exists on the plane of mother-daughter experience, which is alien to the man and shuts him out. In fact, the psychology of the Demeter cult has all the features of a matriarchal order of society, where the man is an indispensable but on the whole disturbing factor." Indeed, Harrison

([1903] 1957], 273) asserts that the early Demeter and Persephone were "matriarchal" and "husbandless." Kerenyi (1967, 118–19) notes that at Alexandria, Egypt, where mystery rites dedicated to the two goddesses were also celebrated, the deities "were looked upon as the protectors of young women...whose loves were not sanctioned by the patriarchal bond of marriage." I suggest that this aspect of the Alexandrian cult is a survival from an archaic time when monogamous marriage did not exist. As I discuss in *CDB*, legend points to the possibility that the institution of marriage was not established in Greece until the reign of the first Attic king, Cecrops, a newcomer from Egypt who installed other patriarchal customs, as well, among them worship of Zeus as the "most high" god (Rigoglioso 2009, 66). I suggest that this characteristic of the Demetrian mystery complex in Egypt dedicated to the two goddesses recalls the matriarchal period under which women were independent, and Demeter was conceived in her original role as Virgin Mother. A hint that such a period indeed existed in North Africa lies in the stories of the Danaids, the priestesses of Demeter who brought the Thesmophoria to Greek soil. The motif that they escaped forced marriages in Egypt by murdering their would-be husbands indicates a possible previous state of affairs in which women were not yoked in marriage (Harrison [1903] 1957, 619). Moreover, there is ample evidence to suggest that the Thesmophoria was a matriarchal rite commemorating women's sexual independence from men. I further discuss the Danaids and this ritual later in the chapter.

In Demeter and Persephone, we have a female-only configuration of twinning. More than twinning, what we have is "doubling"—that is, reproduction. I thus emphasize that these deities represent the mystery of the goddess as One and Two. Again, they specifically reflect the mystery of parthenogenesis, of the Virgin Mother who is able to replicate herself without need of a male partner. Here, it may be useful to consider biological parthenogenesis in the animal and insect world. Given that progeny conceived without male sperm share the same genetic material as their mothers, such offspring are generally female.[10] Biologically, a female egg that replicates in such a way produces a child that has the mother's exact genetic makeup. Although this child is not, technically, an identical genetic "clone" of the mother, given that some recombination of the mother's genes occurs during the process of egg division,[11] she is symbolically considered such because no outside genetic material has gone into her making. Theoretically, were a human mother to be able to reproduce parthenognetically,[12] on a strictly biological basis her child would be female, and, given the close genetic tie, her daughter would no doubt resemble her closely. Here, we have the "twinning" motif that we see in the Demeter/Persephone complex. The birth, death, and rebirth of the grain, of which Demeter was the patron, was understood to encompass the same parthenogenetic mystery. As mentioned in chapter 1, in Plato's *Menexenus* (237A–38A), a funeral oration that Socrates puts in the mouth of Aspasia tells us of the ancient Greek understanding that Ge/Gaia, the earth, had *spontaneously* brought forth the wheat and barley, just as she had given birth to humans. In this, the confluence of themes is clear: the mystery of the grain, parthenogenesis, and the female godhead are all part of one religious schema.

This parthenogenetic mystery, I contend, predated the two goddesses' absorption into the Olympic pantheon, where Persephone was said to have been conceived through Demeter's union with Zeus. The antiquity of the earlier mystery is evident in all of the aforementioned associations between these two figures, as well as in the ancient epithet *monogenês*, "first born," attributed to both goddesses.[13] As discussed in chapter 2, this epithet was similarly applied to Athena (Orphic *Hymn to Pallas* 32.1). There, I noted the definition of the term not only as "only-begotten" (Liddell and Scott, 7th edition, s.v.), but also as "only born sole offspring," "unique in kind," and "singly born" (Long 1992, 49). Again, it connotes a self-born, self-created being, which corresponds perfectly with Athena's identification with the autogenetic Neith and the idea that Persephone was virgin-born of Demeter. Its use as a title for Demeter suggests a virgin-born origin for her, as well, from Rhea. That the rarely used term indeed was associated with virgin birth can be seen in its persistence as an epithet for Jesus (John 1:14), that famous parthenogenetically born son of Mary.

In this light, Persephone's resemblances to Rhea, noted earlier, become particularly significant. I propose that the conflation among Rhea, Demeter, and Persephone indicates that all three were understood to be one, a goddess who self-replicated in a potentially endless line of succession. Even Foley (1994, 42) approaches this in her observation that Demeter is twice called the "daughter of Rhea" in the *Hymn* (60, 75), "thus emphasizing the maternal (even matrilineal) links among the three generations of females that Zeus and Hades disrupt." This configuration also recalls the Neith/Metis/Athena and Leto/Artemis schemas, which, as I discussed in chapters 2 and 3, were also redolent of the flaring forth of the goddess in successive iterations of herself. As I argue in subsequent sections of this chapter, this original parthenogenetic mystery was not only at the heart of the Demeter and Persephone schema, but also served as the foundation for the mystery celebrations dedicated to them.

Reconstruction of the Demeter/Persephone Mythologem: Pure Parthenogenesis Interrupted

In the Olympian reckoning, Rhea's yoking to Cronus and Demeter's yoking to Zeus represented an intrusion into the parthenogenetic mysteries of the Virgin Mother goddess. I submit that, as the granddaughter of such a lineage, Persephone would have been the next in line to reproduce parthenogenetically. Yet what we see encoded particularly dramatically in the ancient stories is the disruption of her ambitions in this regard. As I elaborate in what follows, this cosmic disruption was interpreted by the early or pre-Greeks, and commemorated into Hellenistic times, as the greatest tragedy of the old matriarchal order, one that was experienced "above," in the heavens, as well as "below," on the human plane.

Persephone as Holy Parthenos

In this section, I establish that Persephone was indeed understood to be parthenogenetic in her own right. I propose that in the archaic conception she, in fact, served as the very paradigm for the Holy *Parthenos*, the great Maiden/Virgin Goddess who would give birth spontaneously. Her own capacity for virgin motherhood may be discerned in her connection with various motifs, all of which, as I show, were related to parthenogenesis.

Persephone's Connection with Virgin Mother Goddesses

One important motif linking Persephone with parthenogenesis is her mythological association with other virgin goddesses at the time of her abduction by Hades. Specifically, in the *Hymn* (417–24) and other versions of the myth, the powerful virgins Athena and Artemis are present as her playmates.[14] As noted in chapter 3, Diodorus Siculus (5.3.4) mentions Persephone as having "made the same choice of maidenhood" (i.e., virginity) as these two goddesses. He even follows the tradition that the three were "reared together" in Sicily. Herodotus (2.156.6), moreover, reports that the playwright Aeschylus called Artemis the "daughter" of Demeter, further solidifying the idea of an intimate relationship among these goddesses. In later versions of the myth, Athena and Artemis sometimes tried but failed to protect Persephone from being abducted.[15] As I showed in chapters 2 and 3, these two goddesses originally were virgin creatrixes associated with ancient Amazon warrior women. Their presence alongside Persephone in the various mythological renderings can thus be interpreted as a "cultural memory" of the earlier pre-Greek/matriarchal religion in which Persephone was one among several Virgin Mothers.

Persephone's Connection with Weaving

The weaving motif in various stories associated with Persephone further links her with parthenogenesis. In the *Rhapsodic Theogony*, her rape takes place while she is weaving a *peplos* (Richardson 1974, 84).[16] Porphyry affirms (*On the Cave of the Nymph* 14) that the loom was a symbol of the process of incarnation. He, too, connects the weaving function with Kore/Persephone, noting that she, whom he calls "the overseer of all things sown in the earth," was also depicted as a weaver. It is because of the ancient connection between "weaving" and "incarnating," no doubt, that Athena/Neith was the patron of weaving. As we recall from chapter 2, Neith was considered the Virgin Mother par excellence, whose parthenogenetic abilities were affirmed in the inscription "No one has lifted my *peplos*"—that is, no male entity had engaged with her sexually, despite the fact that she was the Mother of All. By linking Persephone with this great parthenogenetic/autogenetic creatrix, the weaving element suggests that she, too, was poised to replicate herself in a new generation. In Claudian (1.246 ff.), she weaves a robe for her mother on which the universe is portrayed. Here, we see weaving come into the parthenogenetic province of Demeter, in particular, as virginal creatrix of the universe. Apollodorus of Athens (*Die Fragmente der Griechischen Historiker* 244 F 89, Jacoby) echoes that Persephone was abducted when preparing herself for marriage by weaving clothes for her wedding and marital life, but adds one important detail: The maiden goddess was considered to be a "nymph." Given my argument that *nymph* was frequently a title for priestesses of miraculous conception, this affirms Persephone's status as a female agent of divine birth and, further, connects her with a long line of such women in the Greek record, some of whom were similarly associated with weaving (see, e.g., Rigoglioso 2009, 74–75, 107). Thus, we see Persephone serving as the cosmic paradigm for holy *parthenoi*, priestesses of virginal conception on earth.

Kalligeneia is also an important figure related to Persephone and the weaving function. Venerated at the Eleusinian Mysteries, in mythology she served as the nurse of both Demeter and Persephone.[17] In Nonnus (*Dionysiaca* 6.139–42), Kalligeneia is charged with Persephone's care by Demeter, overseeing the maiden in what are specifically characterized as "Athena's" tasks of spinning and weaving. Her name, which means "beautiful or well born," was a surname of Ge/Gaia or Demeter (Smith 1870, s.v. *Calligeneia*) and serves as the title for the culminating day of the Thesmophoria, one of the great rituals dedicated to the "two goddesses." I submit that the "beautiful birth" to which such a name alluded was understood to be nothing less than *miraculous* birth, which I discuss further when I consider the Thesmophoria. This meaning helps us understand why the name would have been associated with Ge/Gaia: It was a particularly fitting surname for a great virgin creatrix who herself was skilled in "beautifully" birthing living things out of her body. I propose that the motif of Kalligeneia "overseeing" Persephone's weaving refers to the maiden goddess's own "cosmic apprenticeship" in learning about parthenogenesis.

Persephone's Connection with the Bee

Another sign of Persephone's own parthenogenetic nature was her ancient title *Melitodes,* "Honey-Like" (Porphyry *On the Cave of the Nymphs* 18). This points to an identification of Persephone with the *melissa,* or "honey bee," which, as I discuss at length in *CDB,* was a creature associated with parthenogenetic birth in antiquity. Bees were thought to generate spontaneously from flowers, the carcasses of oxen and bulls, and the ashes of fig-tree wood. Never having been observed to engage in sexual intercourse, they were furthermore considered symbols of virginity. What I also argue was not lost on the ancients, despite the inability of male naturalists to understand the role of the queen bee, is the fact that the queen produces male drones spontaneously out of her body (see Rigoglioso 2009, 192–94).

The strong connection between Persephone and the bee persisted in the special title designating priestesses of Demeter and Persephone: *Melissai,* or "Bees."[18] Women who performed the ritual of the Thesmophoria in honor of Demeter and Persephone were also known by this title (Apollodorus of Athens, *Die Fragmente der Griechischen Historiker* 244 F 89, Jacoby), as were women initiated into Demeter's mysteries more generally (Hesychius, s.v. *Melissai*). This points to an entire female cult dedicated to these goddesses that was at one time dedicated to divine conception, a topic to which I return later in the chapter.

Persephone's Connection with the Pomegranate

Persephone has a close association with the pomegranate, which, as I discussed in chapter 4, was also a symbol of virgin birth. As I argued, the pomegranate was considered part of a "holy mystery" relating to Hera that had to do with the goddess's ability to produce life spontaneously. This fruit is linked with another great *Parthenos,* as well: Athena. Like Hera's statue, an archaic cultic image of Athena Nike held a pomegranate in the right hand.[19] Again, I contend this points to the great mystery of the goddess as originally possessing powers as a Virgin Mother.

The pomegranate's parthenogenetic associations abound in the story of Agdistis, a bisexual and primordial Great Goddess in Greek, Roman, and Anatolian mythology who was sometimes identified with Cybele (Hesychius, s.v. *Agdistis*). When this deity was emasculated, the pomegranate tree sprung from its blood—that is, the tree's birth was an instance of parthenogenesis. Another instance of spontaneous conception occurred when Nana, whose very name was one by which the Great Goddess was known, became pregnant simply by eating the tree's fruit (Kerenyi 1967, 136).[20] As daughter of the river god Sangarius, Nana was a "nymph," which, again, was likely a marker for her status as a priestess of divine birth. Thus, we have what I suggest is a priestess who, by virtue of her name doubling, was understood to be a human embodiment of the goddess,[21] conceiving miraculously with the pomegranate. The story implies that somehow the pomegranate could be used magically to instigate the conception of a divine child.

Persephone's connection with the parthenogenetic pomegranate is attested in text and iconography. In speaking directly about the Eleusinian Mysteries, Clement of Alexandria (*Exhortation to the Greeks* 2.16) informs us that the pomegranate tree was believed to have sprung from the drops of the blood of Dionysus, a god whom the Orphics say was born of Persephone's rape by Zeus (Guthrie [1952] 1993, 133–34). Ancient statues occasionally depict the goddess holding the fruit. Further, we have her famous association with the pomegranate in the Homeric *Hymn*, where we hear that she ate one of its seeds (371–74), which was forced on her by Hades (411–13). In the story, her eating of the seed apparently made it necessary for her to spend one-third of the year in the underworld even after she was rescued (398–400, 445–47).

I contend that Persephone's eating of the pomegranate was the magical action that instigated her ability to conceive parthenogenetically.[22] However, the *Hymn* shows us that because she ate it in the underworldly realm, the locus of Hades, she became bound to divine birth *in that realm with him*, under his conditions. That is, she became conscripted to *hieros gamos* with him, no longer free to engage in the matriarchal form of pure parthenogenesis. In discussing the pomegranate seed in Persephone's story, Richardson (1974, 276) affirms that, in folk belief in Greece and beyond, "eating and drinking ratify one's membership of a community." By eating the pomegranate seed in that deathly "community," Persephone became a permanent—and most illustrious—citizen of it. That the union between her and Hades was indeed consummated is suggested in 343–44, where she is presented as a reluctant spouse in the god's bed. That it resulted in progeny is something I argue later in the chapter by weaving together the Orphic, Homeric, and cultic elements associated with the story. Read one way, we may understand the myth to be revealing that instead of becoming the *Parthenos*, the queen of the realm of divine birth, Persephone became queen of the realm of "divine birth *in death.*" That is, she became Virgin Mother of Rebirth. Read another way, as I show later, she became the Virgin Mother of the Rebirth of the Male God.

Persephone's Connection with Flower Gathering

I submit that the motif of Persephone's abduction taking place while she was picking flowers in a meadow (*Hymn* 6) is a reference to a ritual prep-aration for engendering a state in which parthenogenetic conception was thought to be possible. To understand this idea, we must correlate it with examples of legendary human women who were similarly described as picking flowers at a critical moment in their lives, among them Creusa, Oreithyia, and Europa. What is key here is that, like Persephone, all of these female figures were picking flowers *just before they were sexually abducted and impregnated by male deities* (Foley 1994, 41–41; Ruck, in Wasson et al. 2008, 97n3). According to the theory I propose in *CDB*, given that all of these women were believed to have given birth to the sons of gods, they were considered holy *parthenoi*, priestesses of divine conception, as I detail in particular with Oreithyia and Europa (see Rigoglioso 2009, 70–71, 145–46). Thus, flower-picking was intimately associated with virgin birth in the ancient world. But what did it mean, more precisely?

First, it is important to bring forth the argument I support in *CDB* that entering a trance state was a necessary prerequisite for attempting what was believed to be divine conception. Part of that ritual preparation involved imbibing or absorbing some kind of psychotropic substance, or entheogen,[23] so as to contact the "otherworldly" realms (Rigoglioso 2009, 16–18). I propose that the story of Persephone affirms this idea in the detail that it was her reaching out for a *magical narcissus* with one hundred heads (*Hymn* 12) that precipitated her abduction into the under-world. Speaking about this motif in the *Hymn*, Richardson (1974, 144) affirms that, in folk stories, "the magic flower is the key that opens the earth, revealing the underworld, and its hidden treasures." To anyone educated about the use of plants in shamanic work, the "magic flower" is clearly a reference to an entheogenic plant. Indeed, we learn that the Greeks understood the narcissus to be narcotic in nature (Plutarch *Table-Talk* 3.1.3/647B; see also Pseudo-Dioscorides, *de Materia Medica* 4.158). I thus propose that "flower-picking" was a means of gathering plants whose consuming opened priestesses to the altered state of consciousness required to conduct a divine conception ritual.

Indeed, the detail of "picking" the flower, I contend, was a code for the moment of "entry" into the trance. As I show in *CDB*, it is in an entheogen-induced state that the female agent attempting partheno-genesis during the patriarchal stage of the cult of divine birth suddenly encountered the aggressive sexual presence of the god. Such an encoun-ter was believed to result in an impregnation with the divine child (see Rigoglioso 2009, 16–18, 21–23, 97–100). In her "entheogen picking" and subsequent entry into the underworld, *Persephone thus served as the divine template for human priestesses of virgin birth who entered into the subtle realms to do their work.* The story seems to imply that deities themselves had to undergo events, practices, and ordeals that, to the Western mind, had a particularly "human" flavor. It also implies that humans were required to imitate the deities in attempting any kind of sacred rite. The rela-tionship between divinities and humans was parallel, circular, reciprocal, and relational. Indeed, as I discuss later in the chapter, communication between the earthly and immortal realms was understood to be at the very heart of the Demeter/Persephone mystery.

The narcissus's "hundred-headed" aspect is particularly important to this argument. Intriguingly, the interpolator of Dioscorides refers to a white flower whose synonyms were *leukos* (white), "hundred-headed," and *moly* (Lindsay 1970, 85). I contend that the magical nar-cissus of Persephone was understood to be none other than this plant. The "hundred-headed" reference is the first and clearest clue in this regard. Second, the plant was white, like the narcissus. Third, its iden-tification with *moly* affirms that, as I suggested of the narcissus, it was an entheogenic plant, given that *moly* was widely understood to be such in antiquity (Scarborough 1991, 138–74). Forth, like the narcissus, this plant had remarkable associations with women, sex and conception ritu-als, and female divinization, some of which strikingly call to mind the Persephone story. From Psellus (7.478, in Lindsay 1970, 85), for example, we learn that it grew mostly under earth, but that it popped up to watch if a girl mated nearby. This echoes the very events involving Persephone, for whom the narcissus "popped" up from the earth just before she was about to go "under the earth" and "mate."

Even more remarkable, this flower appears in Martianus Capella's *The Marriage of Mercury and Philology*, a medieval compendium on Roman learning in the seven liberal arts set within a tale of courtship and mar-riage among the pagan gods. The beginning of the volume recounts the *hieros gamos* of Philology with Mercury/Hermes. It details how as a result of achieving her union with the god, the "virgin" Philology achieves full apotheosis, or divinization. As I argue extensively in *CDB*, the end result of a woman achieving what was believed to be divine conception was indeed her apotheosis (see, e.g., Rigoglioso 2009, 36, 88–90, 133). Thus, the story of Philology, while supposedly "allegorical," seems to detail elements of what was required for a maiden's sacred marriage and subsequent immortalization. Here, according to Lindsay (1970, 83), we find the very "hundred-headed flower" mentioned earlier. Philology uses the plant to create an unguent that she smears on her body as part of her ritual to enter the otherworldly realms. In another passage, she is immortalized, raised to the level of her divine husband, after being crowned with what may well be this same flower. Such details support the position that Persephone's plant was indeed an entheogen connected with virginal conception aimed at the ultimate achievement of divinization.

It is clear from the myth that Hades' entry into Persephone's realm was unbidden and unwanted. Indeed, I contend that, in entering her magical state, Persephone was readying for parthenogenetic self-replication, not conception through a *hieros gamos* encounter. This argument is supported if we examine the symbolic meaning of the narcissus. This flower was an emblem of "narcissism," or self-love, by virtue of its connection to the mythological youth named Narcissus, who fell in love with his own image reflected in a well. Having perished with longing for himself, he metamorphosed into the flower, which was thereafter named for him (Ovid *Metamorphoses* 3.339–509; Pausanias 9.31.7–9). I propose that this element encoded in the narcissus underscores the idea that Persephone's ritual state was originally intended to allow her to conceive through "self-loving"—that is, *parthenogenetically*. We see the element of self-desiring associated with parthenogenesis in one Gnostic passage that contains a stunning reference to pure parthenogenesis in a religious context. The passage appears in *The Revelation [or Apocalypse] of Adam*, the last tractate of Nag Hammadi Codex V. It describes one of the means by which "the illuminator of knowledge," the salvific figure known as Seth (of whom Jesus was considered by some to be a manifestation), was thought to have been brought to humanity:

> [F]rom the nine muses one separated. She came to a high mountain and spent some time seated there, so that she desired her own body in order to become androgynous. She fulfilled her desire and became pregnant from her desire. He [the illuminator] was born. The angels who were over the desire nourished him. And he received glory there and power. (In Barnstone and Meyer 2003, 186–87.)

The text, ascribed to the end of the first or beginning of the second centuries C.E. (Meyer 2007, 345), affirms the method involved in divine conception: "sitting on a mountain" for some time—that is, entering a trance state—and engaging in a kind of inner sexual tantra involving profound narcissistic desire. The identification of the female as a "muse" suggests a priestly connection to the Greek tradition, where muses and nymphs, as I explain throughout *CDB*, were related figures frequently associated with divine birth stories. Although the child believed to have arisen from this particular miraculous conception is male, it is not unreasonable to suggest that such a self-generative mechanism would have been considered a valid method of producing a female child, as well—especially given, as noted earlier, that the production of a daughter would be a more likely result from a strictly biological perspective.

That Persephone would have preferred to undergo what we might term "a narcissistic tantric encounter" rather than a *hieros gamos* with Hades is further suggested in lines 343–44 of the *Hymn*, where she is presented as a resistant spouse in the god's bed. Tellingly, the lines relate that she was full of "desire" for her mother. The word used, *pothos*, often has sexual overtones (Foley 1994, 131). I propose this reflects that fact that Persephone was still erotically longing for the older, inward, matriarchal sexual method by which divine conception could be accomplished. Again, I contend that these various elements related to Persephone's "narcissus" support the idea that her original intention in entering into "magical space" was to reproduce herself parthenogenetically in the type of self-loving moment of creation that we see in the Gnostic excerpt. In doing so, this great Divine Virgin would have repeated what her mother and grandmother had done before her. However, the entry of Hades into her proceedings dramatically changed the course of her destiny—and of the entire cosmos and its earthly microcosm.

Persephone's Parthenogenetically Related Title

Persephone was the only goddess to have been given the epithet *arrhêtos koura*, by which she was venerated in the secret rites of Eleusis.[24] *Arrhêtos* means "ineffable, not to be divulged," and, conventionally understood, *koura,* or *kourê/korê,* means "maiden," or "virgin." Thus, the title ostensibly meant "virgin of the holy secret not to be spoken" or "ineffable virgin." Given all of the aforementioned evidence pointing to Persephone as a parthenogenetic creatrix, however, I propose that *koura/kourê/korê* was a deliberate title meaning "holy virgin of divine birth." As I argue was the case with the related and similarly ambiguous terms *parthenos* and *nymph* (Rigoglioso 2009, 39–43, 88–92), this definition resolves the seeming contradiction of Persephone being a "virgin" as well as a "mother"—of Dionysus, Aeon, and possibly other figures in the Eleusinian complex, discussed later in the chapter. I suggest she was so paradigmatic in this role, in fact, that *Korê* came to be used for her more or less as a proper name. That it was technically a title signifying her rank and function as a Virgin Mother, however, is, I posit, what has been missed, leading to confusion as to her real name. It is not so much that Persephone *was* Kore; rather, correctly understood, she was *the* Kore, *the* Holy Virgin Mother.

The argument that *Korê/Kourê/Koura* is a specific title related to the female divine birthing function is strengthened if we consider that this is the very designation Hesiod uses to describe the Oceanids, those daughters of Oceanus and Tethys who were Persephone's companions while gathering flowers before her abduction. As I noted in chapter 2, the ancient poet (*Theogony* 346–48) specifically calls these female figures "a holy race of *Kourai* who on earth raise youths to manhood, with Lord Apollo and the Rivers" (Hesiod 1987, 48, trans. Caldwell). We will recall my argument that what Hesiod implies here is these holy *Kourai*—that is, "maidens" or, more to the point, "virgins"—either took earthly form or had human counterparts; in either case, the task of the holy daughters was to rear boys. I suggested that their charges were not just *any* boys, but the progeny of male deities such as Zeus and Apollo. I have suggested that the *Kourai* were tasked not only with raising these boys (serving as what were known in the Greek tradition as *kourotrophoi*, "nurses"), but also with mating with the gods so as bring such boys onto the earth plane to begin with.[25] For, again, what is particularly significant is that quite a number of these *Kourai* are identical with those female figures who, as I show in *CDB*, were depicted in myth as being associated with divine birth or with parthenogenetic goddesses.

As Richardson (1974, 140) emphasizes, these Oceanids "are the *kourai par excellence,* and Persephone is their leader." Their being *kourai* refers not only to their maidenhood and their virginity, but also to their specific role as birthers and caretakers of divine children. Again, we can see from the foregoing the strong indication that the term was a specific title in this regard. Persephone's role as nothing less than the "leader" of these female figures underscores her own connection with virginity and the simultaneous birthing of divinity, as well as the centrality of this complex to her identity. Indeed, what we discern in this is that she was, again, *the Korê, the* Holy *Parthenos, the* Virgin Maiden writ large in the cosmic scheme. Although other goddesses had gone before her as creatrixes, including her own mother and grandmother, it was Persephone who was cosmically designated the sole *arrhêtos koura,* the ineffable virgin of divine parthenogenesis. This exclusive title concealed a "forbidden sacred tale," says Kerenyi (1967, 26). I contend that it points to a particular, unique role that Persephone had in the cosmic drama, which I elaborate as the chapter progresses.

Persephone as the Paradigmatic Raped Virgin Mother

What we see in Persephone's story is a cosmic case of the parthenoge-netic maiden whose aspirations to self-replicate in the manner of her mother and grandmother before her were grossly and tragically inter-rupted. Indeed, the fact of her being the only goddess granted the epithet *arrhêtos koura* reveals an esoteric understanding that the deities themselves saw her as *the* cosmic case of the virgin goddess of parthenogenesis. This great universal event of her rape, I posit, marked the moment in which the Great Goddess's parthenogenetic ability was usurped in service to the male gods. Here, in the circular and overlapping tradition of the myth themselves, we must eschew any attempt to look at the ancient stories in "linear" fashion; we must refrain from getting bogged down in notions such as "but Persephone came *after* goddesses were already cavorting with male gods." A demand for linearity will only make us miss the very great point. What is important is that Persephone's story is *emblematic* of *the* key moment in the cosmic order: the transition from matriarchy and pure parthenogenesis to patriarchy and divine birth through *hieros gamos*—both in the "above" realm, the domain of the deities, and the "below" realm, the domain of humankind. She was the divinely ordained "chosen one" who carried the banner for this most cursed and blessed story, as evidenced by her singular title *arrhêtos koura*.

I contend that the entire story and its associated rituals turn around this great event, which was experienced as a tragedy of monumental pro-portions from the perspective of the divine and earthly matriarchies. I suggest that this insight, this much-avoided recognition in contemporary times of the *matriarchal* drama involved—a drama that I maintain was evi-dent to the Greeks—is the key to unlocking the mythologem of the two goddesses and the mystery rites dedicated to them. As I argue in what follows, initiates into the mysteries of Demeter and Persephone were required to recognize and endure this divine truth—that the Matriarchy had been broken—as the very means, the very password, by which they were able to enter into divine knowledge of the realm of the deities under the patriarchal epoch. By embracing this nightmare, this great hell descent of the Feminine, initiates were given an opening into *female* spiritual reality, which centered on the profound truths and tragedies of the Virgin Mother, the Great Cosmic Creatrix, as elaborated later. It involved, as I show, nothing less than becoming a raped and grieving woman—whether one was a male or female.

I emphasize that, in addition to the refusal by many contemporary observers to acknowledge this matriarchal theme fully, or at all, what has obscured a complete understanding of these goddesses and their rites is the inability to see the *divine birth* element woven into the very fiber of their stories and cults. This "sight" requires, I propose, and as I have been explicating throughout this book and in *CDB*, an acknowledgement that the ancients apprehended what they saw as the ontologically ordained parthenogenetic ability of the female on the divine level. It also requires recognition that the ancients understood the relationship between the human and divine realms to be extremely porous (see Rigoglioso 2009, 29–31). Indeed, this understanding was part and parcel of the very myth and rites of these two goddesses themselves, in which divinities could appear on earth and humans could be transported to other realms. The ancients believed that humans could traffic in the production of deities on earth *through the bodies of specially trained women*. In short, they held that specialized priestesses could be made to cultivate the very miraculous abilities to give birth that the goddess possessed herself. An understanding of this entire complex is, as I show in the rest of the chapter, what allows us to grasp the nature of Demeter and Persephone's drama fully as it related to humankind. It is also what allows the obscure shards of memory recorded by ancient writers about the Thesmophoria and Eleusinian Mysteries to pop into relief, revealing in startling and dramatic ways just what the ancient Greeks believed and did in service to their goddesses— and their own souls.

One concept that is encoded in the story of Persephone involves quite an interesting notion indeed: Although the goddesses were originally able to reproduce parthenogenetically, the male gods were not—at least, not without swallowing such goddesses, as we see in the case of Zeus's absorption of Metis, for example. Alternatively—and this is key to the Demeter and Persephone story—the gods could not reproduce without using the goddesses' bodies "sexually," whatever that may have meant in the cosmic realms, and I think it is important not to assume that such a concept is a hopelessly naïve and projected anthropomorphization. Given the resistance of the matriarchal divine order to such appropriation of immortal female "bodies," that usually meant raping them.

It is this key understanding that allows us to see precisely why the Persephone story was so heinous from the perspective of the matriarchal order. It represented the paradigmatic case of the male god reproducing himself on the ontologically cosmic level, rather than allowing himself to be birthed, in due time and due order, through the will, beneficence, and direction of the goddess of which he was an emanation. It represented the patriarchal will to power, the desire to populate the cosmos with male beings. It had its analogue on earth, as I propose in *CDB*, with the appropriation of the parthenogenetic priestesshoods to bring the sons of the gods to the earth plane (again, one must acknowledge the ancient notion of the veils between the realms being thin to allow for this understanding). Further, it had its analogue on earth with the advancement of the patriarchal ethos that numerous such sons of gods brought with them, as we saw, for example, in the case of Heracles in chapter 4.

Thus, Persephone was the paradigmatic case of the Holy *Parthenos*, the *Korê/Kourê/Koura*, the Virgin Mother, who was raped *for the purpose of the god willfully replicating himself*. She was, by extension, the paradigmatic case of the virgin priestess who was forced to switch from pure parthenogenesis designed to bring in female avatars, female representations of the divine, to divine birth through *hieros gamos* in order to conceive the gods' sons. I show in the remainder of this section just what gods it was to whom Persephone was thought to have given birth in this way.

Persephone as Virgin Mother of the God's "Double"

As I have indicated in the foregoing analysis of Persephone's connection with various parthenogenetic attributes, what becomes apparent in her stories is that she was interrupted in her attempt at pure self-replication by the advent of a sexually predatory male god. Who was Persephone's rapist? According to the Homeric *Hymn*, it was Hades. According to the Orphic tradition, it was Zeus, her Olympian "father," who approached her in one of his common manifestations as a snake (Clement of Alexandria *Exhortation to the Greeks* 2.14).[26] Given that Zeus was also sometimes portrayed as having an incarnation in the underworld that was closely identified with Hades (Foley 1994, 110n97), we can read here that Zeus and Hades were essentially two representations of the same god. Thus, Persephone's abductor was what I will term Zeus/Hades.

Working from this assumption, it becomes clear that although the *Hymn* does not state a child was born out of Persephone's union with Hades, such a concept was implied and understood in antiquity. In the Orphic tradition, Persephone definitively gave birth, as a result of her rape by Zeus, to Dionysus.[27] In commenting on this, Clement of Alexandria (*Exhortation to the Greeks* 2.14) notes the Dionysian *symbolon* current in antiquity: "The bull is father of the serpent, and the serpent father of the bull." He decodes it by explaining that Zeus, in the form of the bull, had intercourse with Demeter and produced Persephone; subsequently, in the form of a serpent, he had intercourse with Persephone and produced Dionysus, who had an epiphany as a bull. Elsewhere, we hear that Persephone produced with Zeus the chthonic nymph Melinoë (Orphic *Hymn to Melinoë* 71.2–3), or Tritopatreus and Eubouleus (Cicero *De Natura Deorum* 3.53). Another tradition relates that, with Hades, she produced the chthonic Eumenides (Orphic frags. 197 and 360, in Foley 1994, 110n97).

Yet other possibilities as to Persephone's offspring may be encoded in the mythological complex involving the two goddesses. We can look first to Ploutus, Demeter's son by Iasion (Hesiod *Theogony* 969–74; Homer *Odyssey* 5.125–30). Kerenyi (1967, 31) notes the similarities between the names *Ploutus* and *Plouton*, the latter of which was another name for Hades. Working with the notion of Demeter and Persephone as essentially being "one" goddess, he allows for the possibility that Demeter's child was also Persephone's child. In support of this, he points to several vase paintings of the Eleusinian goddesses depicting the child being handed to Demeter by a goddess rising out of the earth, noting that the boy seems to emerge from "the realm to which Kore had been carried away." We can also turn to Brimos, a child whose birth from the "great virgin" Brimo was announced at the end of the Eleusinian Mysteries, as I discuss later in the chapter. Brimos is sometimes thought to be Persephone's son, sometimes the son or Demeter or another goddess (Foley 1994 110). Again, given what I have established to be the essential "twin" nature of the two goddesses, on the esoteric level, a child of Demeter would have been considered a child of Persephone also. Moreover, given that the Mysteries were so closely focused on these deities, it unlikely likely that Brimo was anything other than the child of one or the other of them.

Yet another level of complexity is evident in the identification not only of Zeus with Hades, but of both figures with Dionysus. The ancient writer Heracleitus blatantly declares "Hades is the same as Dionysus" (frag. 15 Diels, in Kerenyi 1967, 40). Kerenyi (1967, 34) sees the presence of Dionysus behind Hades in the Homeric *Hymn* in the mention of the "Nysan Plain," the location of Persephone's abduction, given that "Nysa" was regarded as the birthplace and first home of the wine god. He also points to a vase painting in which Persephone, with Demeter nearby, seems to be "marrying" not Hades, but Dionysus, as evidenced by the grapevine that is depicted by his side. Moreover, Ruck (in Wasson et al. 2008, 98) notes Dionysus's connection with Zeus, stating that his name "was etymologically the Zeus or Dios [god] of Nysa, the form that the celestial god assumed when he became corporeal in conspiracy with his nether sibling [Hades]." Thus, Zeus, Hades, and Dionysus may be seen as analogs for one another in this broader story encompassing Orphic and Olympian elements.

The idea that Hades equals Dionysus, and that this dual god impregnated Persephone in the Eleusinian tradition, therefore, is in perfect accord with the story that Zeus impregnated her with Dionysus in Orphic myth, given that Hades equals Zeus, as well. Moreover, what we see from this esoteric complex is that, in seeding Persephone, Zeus/Hades/Dionysus created what Kerenyi (1967, 93, 133) perceptively calls "a second, a little

Dionysus," a "subterranean Zeus." This insight, taken in the context of the parthenogenetic theory I have put forth here, allows for a sudden and striking realization: The male godhead used Persephone as a means not just to procreate, but to *self-replicate*, to double himself in the way the goddess could do on her own. Because he lacked the power ascribed to the goddess alone—parthenogenetic ability—he could only turn to the body of the goddess to emit the next generation of himself. He did so willfully and without permission. This complex also explains why Dionysus came to be so closely association with the Eleusinian Mysteries, as I elaborate later in the chapter.

To understand the wine god's presence in the rites of Demeter and Persephone more fully, we must grasp a mystery encoded in Greek religion: Through the bodies of divine and human females, the god could keep replicating himself in successive incarnations, some of which were believed to have walked the earth. In his second and third books of *De Natura Deorum*, Cicero alludes to this concept in his discussion of ancient beliefs that there was "more than one version" of many of the deities. We see this phenomenon in relationship to Dionysus particularly clearly in the works of Diodorus Siculus (3.62–64) and Nonnus (48.951ff.), for example. Reporting bits of Orphic theogony, Nonnus says the first incarnation of the god was Zagreus, born of Persephone; the second was Bromius, son of Semele; the third was Iacchus, who was received with dance and song by the "nymphs" of Eleusis (see also Cook 1914–30, 2:1031). The idea that this god could continue to be reborn in successive human bodies was, I contend, one of the central mysteries laid over those of the two goddesses at Eleusis.

Persephone as Virgin Mother of (the) Aeon

A late reference about a rite conducted at the temple to Kore, the Koreion, in Alexandria, Egypt, tells us that Persephone was the mother of yet another figure. According to the fourth-century Church father Epiphanius (*Panarion* 51.22.13, in Cook 1914–40, 3:913), on the pagan festival of Epiphany on January 5, locals spent the night in the temple singing to the accompaniment of flutes. Torchbearers entered the underground chamber and brought up a naked wooden idol, which was placed in a litter and carried around the inner temple seven times. We learn that a stranger inquiring about the meaning of such rites was told, "Today, at this hour, the Kore, that is, the virgin, gave birth to Aeon."

In Homer, *aeon* (or, in transliteration from the Greek, *aion*) typically refers to "life" or "lifespan," but in Hesiod it can refer to "ages" or "generations." In short, to the Greek mind it meant an extended period of cosmic time, an age or epoch.[28] In Gnostic theology, various emanations of God were known as *Aeons*, including the male/female pairs known as "syzygies" in Valentinian cosmology, which Angeleen Campra discusses in chapter 6 of the present volume. Although in the *exoteric* understanding of the Alexandrian rite the divinely born Aeon referred to the beginning of the new year, I propose the name was in fact an *esoteric* reference to these older meanings, implying that Kore/Persephone gave birth to the "male deity who governed an epoch." I further propose that the similarity of the Alexandrian declaration to the statement at the conclusion of the Eleusinian rites about the Holy Virgin's birth of Brimos indicates both were expressing the same mystery. Moreover, a comment about the Eleusinian rites by the Attic orator Isocrates (*Panegyric on Athens* 4.28) that those who took part in the Mysteries "possess[ed] better hopes in regard to the end of life and in regard to the whole *aion*" shows that the concept of the *aeon/aion* was part of the Eleusinian religious schema. Thus, I contend that the Alexandrian symbolon had its roots in the Eleusinian Mysteries.

I propose, then, that the *aeon* to which Persephone was thought to give birth was understood to be a particular one, indeed: nothing less than the "epoch of the male godhead"—that is, patriarchy. Once again, encoded in this allusion is the ancient understanding that her rape by a god marked a shift in divine and earthly affairs. In the immortal realms, it meant the commencement of the age of the patriarchs of the Olympian pantheon; on earth, it meant the start of the hero epoch. In both, it meant the advent of warfare, domination, and the propagation of "male god-centered" adoration. However, we can read in Isocrates an indication that initiates to the Mysteries of Demeter/Persephone were also given to understand the *aeon* was not eternal; it, too, would pass. Meanwhile, his remark seems to suggest, coming into possession of *gnosis,* deep knowledge, about the secrets of the immortal realms, which was the result of being initiated into the Eleusinian Mysteries, would make enduring that *aeon* more bearable. I return to a larger discussion related to this idea at the conclusion of the chapter.

As Above, So Below: The Appropriation of Divine Birth Priestesshoods

As I have argued, Persephone's situation marked a major transition in the virgin birth pristesshoods. One perhaps must consult *The Cult of Divine Birth in Ancient Greece* to gain a fuller appreciation for what I am suggesting here, as the evidence that such priestesshoods existed is carefully laid out in that volume. Nevertheless, I will reiterate the main point I have been making thus far, which extends the argument presented in *CDB:* With the back of the cosmic and earthly Matriarchy broken through the rape of Persephone, holy virgins dedicated to miraculous conception became increasingly beleaguered in their parthenogenetic attempts to bring forth the daughters of the goddess, female avatars. They were, instead, conscripted into having sexual encounters in the trance state with male gods. That is, they were forced or coerced into becoming conduits for what were believed to be the gods' children. Frequently, such children were male warrior heroes bent on further eroding the Matriarchy, as I noted in chapter 4 in my discussion of Heracles' actions to dismantle the divine birth cult itself.

I must emphasize that to understand the Greek mindset in this regard, we may need to bracket some of our own contemporary assumptions. The suggestion that the Holy Virgin Persephone's rape opened the door to the patriarchal usurping of human virgins dedicated to divine birth may seem an outlandish assertion by today's standards on a number of counts. It flies in the face of our own beliefs about human capacities, the nature of divinity, and, indeed, the nature of reality itself. I am suggesting that to understand anything about the Mysteries as they related to Demeter and Persephone, one must be open to the possibility that a significant cadre of Greeks embraced a worldview that was very foreign to our own. This does not mean we must embrace such a view. It does mean, however, that we must be willing to see things as they may have been, *on their own terms*, regardless of how strange they may appear to us.[29]

It is my hope that the reader will find in what follows persuasive groundwork to support the assertion that the very complex of the Thesmophoria and Eleusinian Mysteries commemorated and marked the transition from pure parthenogenesis to divine birth through *hieros gamos*. In the sections below, I attempt to show that this phenomenon was encoded in all of the stories and rites associated with these goddesses and their great ceremonies. If nothing else, one will find the sheer proliferation of signs of divine birth in this greater myth complex to be so remarkable as to require some sort of attention at long last.

Daughters of Danaus as Divine Birth Priestesses

As mentioned earlier, according to Herodotus (2.171) the Thesmophoria was brought to Greece by the daughters of King Danaus of Libya. Their story was significant to the Greeks; Aeschylus used it as the basis for an early trilogy, of which we still have *The Suppliants* and which probably included the lost plays *The Egyptians* and *The Daughters of Danaus* (Zeitlin 1996, 164 and n109). The mythological version is told most comprehensively by Apollodorus (2.1.4ff.). Danaus and his twin brother, King Aegyptus of Egypt, quarreled over their inheritance after their father's death. As a conciliatory gesture, Aegyptus proposed a mass marriage between his own fifty sons and Danaus's fifty daughters, all of them children by many wives. When an oracle confirmed Danaus's fears that Aegyptus planned to kill his daughters, however, the Libyan king fled with them to Greece under guidance from Athena. At Rhodes, he set up an image of this goddess, and thence went on to Argos. With the country in a drought, his daughters sought water. One of them, Amymone, engaged in sexual intercourse with Poseidon, who showed her the springs at Lerna. The incumbent king abdicated, Danaus became the leader, and the inhabitants subsequently became known as the *Danaoi*.

When Aegyptus thereafter laid siege on Argos, Danaus agreed to the mass wedding of his daughters in order for the siege to be lifted. At the wedding feast, however, he gave the maidens daggers, with which they slew their bridegrooms as they slept. The Danaid Hypermnestra did not kill her husband, Lynceus, however, because he respected her virginity; her father subsequently imprisoned her. The rest of the daughters buried the heads of their bridegrooms at Lerna. There they performed funeral rites and purified themselves of the murders. Danaus afterward united Hypermnestra to Lynceus and bestowed his other daughters on victors in an athletic contest. In another tradition, the Danaids were punished for their murderous actions by being forced to carry water endlessly in sieved containers in Hades (scholiast on Aristides *Orationes* 2, in Harrison [1903] 1957, 622).

Cook (1914–40, 3:354) speaks of a historical Graeco-Libyan tribe known as the Daanau of Danauna, which attacked the kingdom of Ramses III shortly after 1200 B.C.E. and which may be identified with the Danaoi of Homer. He asserts that they, in turn, are probably related to their eponym, Danaus, or his daughters, the Danaids. Cook further discusses archaeological evidence that may affirm their arrival in Greece, which also would have coincided with the founding of Mycenae by Perseus (see Pausanias 2.15.4). He thus suggests (3:362–63) that the Danaids were in fact the historical Danauna, immigrants from Egypt who came by sea via Rhodes and settled in Argos. Strabo (8.6.8), and probably Hesiod before him (frag. 47, in Cook 3:361n8), affirm that the Danaids made Argos "well watered"; hence their ancient characterization as "water carriers" (Pseudo-Plato *Axiochus* 573E, in Harrison [1903] 1957, 615). Noting modern parallels among Russian peasants, Buddhist monks, and others, Cook conjectures (3:336) that an ancient Greek method for conjuring rain involved pouring water through a sieve. Indeed, in the town of Acanthus in Hellenistic Egypt, each day a different priest emptied water from the Nile into a jar with a hole in it (Diodorus Siculus 1.97.1). He thus suggests (3:339, 362–63) that the Danaids' water-carrying and rainmaking ability was considered a sacred activity akin to such customs. He goes so far as to posit that it was their ability to find water that forced the abdication of the reigning Argive king during the drought that was ravaging the land when they arrived.

Bernal (1987–2006, 1:90) notes that the Danaids are explicitly described as black-skinned in *The Suppliants* (1.154–55; "a dark, sun-burned race") and that, in a fragment of the playwright's lost epic *Daughters of Danaus*, they armed themselves by the bank of the Nile. Arguing for their historicity, as well, he posits that they were fifty black daughters of King Danaus who were involved in a Bronze Age (or earlier) political power struggle in Egypt. These women murdered male adversaries and fled to Greece, where they may have settled in Argos. Along the way, he suggests, they not only brought the Thesmophoria, as Herodotus stated, but also established a temple to Athena at Rhodes.

Agreeing with the idea that the Danaids were historical women, I would add that their connection with Athena and their "arming" themselves (whether on the Nile or with daggers on their so-called wedding night) further suggest they may have been the Amazonian priestesses of North Africa dedicated to Neith/Athena, whom I discussed in chapter 2. Indeed, in *The Suppliants* (280–89), King Pelasgus pointedly states that so greatly did they resemble "the women of Libya" that, were they to have been armed with the bow, he would have mistaken them for Amazons. The fact that these women were dedicated to Demeter and Persephone further underscores their Amazonian identity. The Demeter/Persephone religion, in which the mother-daughter relationship was central, would have been a logical sacred expression of an Amazonian culture in which the mother-daughter relationship was, by definition, the primary social relationship. Not necessarily arguing for their historicity, Harrison ([1903] 1957, 619) affirms that the Danaides were "of the old matriarchal order."

Given what I have discussed throughout this book as well as in *CDB*, the Danaids' associations with the Virgin Mother goddesses Athena and Demeter/Persephone, as well as with the Libyan Amazons, already provide strong hints that they may have been priestesses of divine birth. This argument becomes even stronger as we begin to sift through their lineage and analyze various motifs in their story.

First, it seems clear the Danaids were priestesses. The fact that they brought the Thesmophoria to Greece suggests as much, as does their position as princesses. As I demonstrate in *CDB*, many, if not all royal women had a sacerdotal role (e.g., Rigoglioso 2009, 62, 75–78, 130–31). That Herodotus affirms (2.182) that the Danaids themselves (and not just their father) set up worship to Athena at Rhodes suggests they were priestesses of this goddess, as well as of Demeter. Their priestess status is further suggested by their remarkable ability to locate water: They were likely divining its sources, perhaps dowsing, or performing rain ceremonies using perforated jars, as in the Egyptian tradition discussed earlier. From a practical standpoint, this also suggests that they were involved in agriculture, given that rain was particularly important to crop cultivation. This would correspond to their veneration of Demeter. Thus, we are drawn again to the conjunction of women, crop growing, sacred rain making, and specific goddesses that was always considered a magical combination in the ancient mind.

The detail in Apollodorus that Hympermnestra did not kill her bridegroom because he preserved her virginity hints that virgin status was probably extremely important to all of the Danaids. *The Suppliants,* which chronicles part of their story in dramatic form, makes this point even more strongly: They pray (143–45) to remain *adamatos*—that is, not simply "unwedded," but also "unconquered, untamed" (Liddell and Scott, s.v. *adamatos*). They call on Athena for help in their plight, noting the aptness of invoking "a virgin to a virgin's aid" (149). I posit that this desire to retain their virginity reflected not a moralistic notion of "purity" but, rather, something far more profound. As mentioned earlier, the story that the Danaid Amymone had sexual relations with Poseidon and was subsequently granted the location of springs tells us that with these fifty daughters we are in the realm of priestesses who engage with gods sexually. This emphasizes that they were virgins, given that virginity was always a requirement for such activity (Rigoglioso 2009, 39–43). Moreover, in *The Suppliants* (223–24), they assert their dismay at being hunted down by their Egyptian suitors, as "doves" by "hawks." As I show in *CDB*, the dove was a longstanding ancient symbol of the holy virgin who achieved divine conception (Rigoglioso 2009, 147–51). Hence, the metaphor here is likely no idle allusion.

Indeed, divine birth is firmly entrenched in the Danaids' lineage. Apollodorus (2.1.5) lists their mothers as "Queen" Europa, Elephantis, "Hamadryad nymphs" such as Atlantia and Phoebe, the "Naiad nymph" Polyxo, Piera, Herse, Crino, and an unnamed "Ethiopian woman." Thus among their mothers were queens and "nymphs." Again, as I have argued, "nymph" was likely a marker for "priestess of virgin birth." Moreover, the "Queen" Europa named here is probably none other than the legendary woman who was known throughout the ancient world for having conceived by Zeus important legendary kings (Rigoglioso 2009, 145–46). This shows that the Danaids were directly descended from priestesses of divine birth in the generation immediately preceding them. They were also descendents of one of the most famous divine birth priestesses of all times: Io, whom I discuss in detail in *CDB*, and for whose historicity compelling evidence exists (see Rigoglioso 2009, 130–33). In *The Suppliants,* Aeschylus emphasizes that Io was said to have mated with Zeus on the banks of the Nile and that she founded the Danaids' lineage through her son of that union, Epaphus. Furthermore, the Danaids' own descendent was Danaë, another famous priestess, who was impregnated with the hero Perseus by Zeus in the form of a "shower of gold" (Apollodorus 2.4.1). This indicates that she, too, was a priestess of divine birth. Thus, I contend the Danaids wished to preserve their virginity to the point that they would kill men who took it because they themselves were divine birth priestesses in this lineage. As I show in *CDB, partheneia,* or virginity, was a bio-spiritual condition thought necessary to engage in any kind of divine birth practice (Rigoglioso 2009, 39–43). For the Danaids, then, virginity was their most precious commodity, their highest spiritual calling card.

I agree with Zeitlin, who discerns in *The Suppliants* the assimilation of Zeus as they relate to the Dainaids to the Egyptian Amun-Re. As I show elsewhere, Zeus was, indeed, identified with this god as Zeus-Amun (Rigoglioso 2009, 141). What is particularly significant is that Amun-Re was believed to have impregnated virgin queens with the next generation of pharaohs through divine birth rituals (141; Rigoglioso 2007, 74–94) Zeitlin (1996, 124–25) comes close to discerning the Danaids' function in this regard: "[They] are ... curious hybrids. By reason of their unusual lineage (*genos*), they are related to two very different cultures (Egypt and Argos), and ... they are associated too with divinity." Elsewhere (125), she says, "In their attachment to the myth of Io, these women seem also to be identified with the past rather than with the historical present, with the worlds of gods and the sacred rather than with the secular concerns of men." Quite so, I would say, and that is precisely because they were priestesses dedicated to attempting divine conception.

Were the Danaids specifically priestesses engaged in *hieros gamos* with Zeus, then? Zeitlin (1996, 154–56) indeed discerns in *The Suppliants* (86–96) signs of an erotic relationship they already have or are about to have with Zeus/Amun-Re. However, their attitude toward this god is unclear. They speak of Zeus's desire (*Dios himeros*) as being "difficult to hunt down" (*ouk euthêratos*), "for in shadowy thickets stretch the ways of his mind, unperceivable to the sight." Zeitlin notes the ambiguity in the Greek: *Dios himeros* may either mean "desire of Zeus" or "desire for Zeus." If "desire *of* Zeus" is intended, I propose that the playwright is having the Danaids say they find it difficult to know when Zeus may be upon them with his desire. This would correspond with my argument that holy *parthenoi* in the period after Persephone's rape were likely to be visited in unwanted fashion by a sexually aggressive male god in their trance state while trying to attempt parthenogenetic conception. The entry was "shadowy" and "unperceivable"—that is, furtive and unpredictable. If "desire *for* Zeus" is meant, however, the playwright may be having them say that that intentionally engaging with the god sexually through trance was not an easy feat for a priestess, as carefully locating and uniting with the god took great spiritual prowess. This latter case would position them as priestesses of divine birth through *hieros gamos*, most likely without a male surrogate.

One way or another, in the Greek rendering, the Danaids were priestesses already operating in a milieu in which *hieros gamos* was in force. Indeed, we see that Amymone supposedly had sexual relations with Poseidon. Perhaps they were indeed virgins in service to Zeus-Amun. Sex with the sons of Aegyptus meant the loss of their "virginity"— that is, the loss of their status as divine birth priestesses. However, I submit that their links with Athena and Demeter/Persephone, as well as their Amazonian nature, are too strong here to admit the possibility that these priestesses would have willingly engaged in sexual union with the very god who raped Persephone (Zeus/Hades/Dionysus). Recalling Harrison's analysis that they represented "the old matriarchal ways," I propose, instead, that the Greek rendition of their story was a gloss over an older one in which these virgins adhered to the form of divine birth that would have corresponded with matriarchy: pure parthenogenesis. Indeed, even Io before them, a divine birth priestess dedicated to Hera, had attempted to resist her unbidden sexual encounter with Zeus, albeit unsuccessfully. Moreover, as I show later in the chapter, to the Greeks, the Danaids' Thesmophoria was a fiercely matriarchal affair. What is key here is that it placed the participants themselves in the role of chaste virgins who were at the same time stimulated to a heightened sexual state, suggesting the "narcissistic tantra" condition that I explicated earlier in relation to Persephone. Moreover, at least in the historical period, the rite commemorated Demeter's grief over Persephone's rape. It was not a rite that celebrated union with the masculine—in any form. It was a rite that lamented it.

The motif that the Danaids were condemned to carry water in a sieve in "Hades" as punishment for having murdered their bridegrooms is also significant to this argument. Harrison writes ([1903] 1957, 620), "Of old the Danaides carried water because they were well-nymphs; the new order has made them criminals, and it makes of their fruitful water-carrying a fruitless punishment—an atonement for murder." Their crime, she emphasizes, was not just murder, but also the rejection of marriage. What is critical here is that *carrying water in a sieve was an ancient test of virginity*; Valerius Maximus (8.1.5) reports that it was used to verify that the Vestal Virgin Tuccia had remained chaste. Thus, again, the Danaids' "rejection of marriage" was actually a rejection that was far more threatening to the patriarchy: It represented resistance to the forcing of holy *parthenoi* into sexual engagement with male gods. The women's reaction against the imposition on their priesieshood was Amazonian—armed rebellion and murder for the taking of their virginity. Indeed, we may read the detail that they cut off their bridegrooms' "heads" as a euphemism for castration.[30] Apollodorus underplays this matriarchal strain, reporting that they carried out their actions merely at the bidding of their father and noting that, in the end, they were married off to other suitors anyway. The ultimate fate they were assigned in myth, however, suggests a level of patriarchal rage and retaliation against these priestesses that in fact reveals a deeper understanding of their matriarchal nature. Their punishment was particularly sadistic: For refusing to cooperate with patriarchy, the virgin Danaids were eternally condemned to the underworld to "carry water in a sieve"—that is, to prove their virginity and work their agricultural rain magic where it would yield no results.

A curious ancient Greek custom may represent an embedded memory of these African holy priestesses who established a religion dedicated to their parthenogenetic goddess(es) of virgin birth and death. Women who died unmarried had black pitchers called "Libyans" set upon their tombs (Cook 1914–40 3.372; Harrison [1903] 1957, 621). This custom incorporates the elements of "virginity," "pitchers," "black skin," and "Libyan" identity that were associated with the Danaids. I thus contend that the practice was a means of honoring virgins as symbolic representatives of these ancient Libyan divine birth ancestresses. An obscure phrase of Aeschylus (*Suppliants* 151) may also preserve the Danaids' original grandeur: The playwright calls them *"a holy seed"* (*sperma semnas*) of their ancestress Io. Indeed, as migrating priestesses of the Virgin Mothers Demeter and Persephone, these holy daughters dispersed their mysteries of virgin birth, seeding them on new soil. As priestesses of water and rain magic, they perhaps dispersed agricultural knowledge to the Greeks from Africa. Hereafter, they may persist in our memory as holy *parthenoi*, women who once pledged to use their "seed" to conceive parthenogenetically and incarnate female avatars of the Great Virgin.

The Melissai of Paros as Divine Birth Priestesses

Another group of women had strong associations with Demeter, Persephone, and the Thesmophoria, as well: the legendary *Melissai* of

Paros. As mentioned earlier, Apollodorus of Athens relates a tradition in which Persephone as "nymph" was abducted while weaving clothes for her wedding. The ancient writer reports that, after Persephone's disappearance, Demeter brought the maiden's *kalathos*, the sacred workbasket in which the clothes had been stored, to the nymphs. She then took the clothes to the island of Paros, where she was hosted by King Melisseus, whose name means "King of the Bees." After her stay, Demeter expressed her thanks by giving the bridal dress, the *kalathos*, and the loom of Persephone to the king's "sixty maiden daughters." She also taught them the secret rituals of the Thesmophoria, as a result of which all of them become "nymphs." From that time on, says Apollodorus, all participants of the Thesmophoria came to be known as *Melissai* in honor of these first maiden daughters who performed it.

By now, we should be stunned by the remarkable panoply of parthenogenetic motifs in this story, as well as the striking resemblance of these *Melissai* to the Danaids. Using the interpretations developed thus far, we can decode the story as follows: It seems to recount an arrival of the Thesmophoria on Greek soil, specifically Paros, one of the Cycladic islands in the central Aegean Sea. Could it refer to a stop by the Danaids along their flight from Libya to Rhodes, and thence Argos? Might the "Demeter" in the story be the Danaids themselves, or one of their number who embodied the goddess as her priestess? Whether or not we can take the argument that far, the story affirms the depiction of Persephone's "preparation for divine conception as involving "weaving," which emphasizes that this activity was a metaphor for the magical creative process.[31] I contend that the detail of her weaving being "interrupted" by the abduction supports the idea that she was in the process of reproducing herself parthenognetically when the god forced himself upon her. Her "wedding" garment, therefore, originally would have been intended to commemorate her "union" with herself, the very type of "narcissistic tantra" in which we saw the "muse on the mountain" engage, as reported by the Gnostic text discussed earlier. We will recall here Athena's *peplos*, or sacred dress, which, as I showed in chapter 2, was a strong symbol of Athena/Neith's parthenogenetic ability. The garment also formed the centerpiece of the Panathenaia, a ritual honoring the virgin goddess's "birthday," which I also argue centered on parthenogenesis (Rigoglioso 2009, 60–62). Thus, I contend that the "wedding dress" that Persephone was weaving in this case originally was her own *peplos*. We see affirmation of this idea in other stories of her weaving mentioned earlier, in which the garment was, indeed, a *peplos* of one kind or another.

Indeed, with the conflation of the "weaving function," the *peplos*/dress of the goddess, and the "bee" in this story about Persephone, we seem to be firmly in the territory of Athena/Neith, the Virgin Mother goddess of weaving whose African symbol was also the parthenogenetic bee, as I noted in chapter 2. In fact, King Melisseus's name calls to mind Egyptian royal titles, which included the hieroglyph inscription *nesu-bity,* "he of the sedge [plant] and the bee," translated as "King of Upper and Lower Egypt." It was used as a prefix to the throne name (prenomen) of the pharaoh (Allen 2000, 31–32, 42, 434, 461). We recall that the Danaids were likely priestesses of *both* Athena and Demeter/Persephone. Thus, this entire story seems to reference an African complex of rituals, leaders, and sacred personnel, which was in the process of migrating to Greece. That the Greek title *Melissa* thereafter became the official name of Demeter's priestesses marks, I propose, a key moment in the Greeks' appropriation of this ritual complex.

In its "origin story" aspect, the myth recounted by Apollodorus of Athens seems to affirm the Thesmophoria as the oldest ritual associated with Demeter and Persephone, a topic to which I return later when I discuss that great rite more fully. In its combined motifs of the daughters "weaving," "learning the mysteries of the Thesmophoria," and "becoming nymphs" as a result of gaining mystical understanding imparted by the goddess, it speaks of the transfer of knowledge of parthenogenesis to a new group of priestesses who subsequently become holy *parthenoi.* It also provides a telling detail: The *kalathos,* Persephone's sacred "work basket," was a significant ritual object in this regard.[32] This becomes highly significant later in the chapter, when I discuss the Eleusinian Mysteries. The central part of that rite involved the initiates conducting some kind of ritual activity with a *kalathos*—as well as with a *kiste,* "chest." Apollodorus thus hints that the *kalathos* was intimately associated with Persephone's reproductive aspirations. I contend that it was a symbol for her very "womb," in which her "woven garment"—her miraculously conceived child—was "stored." I elaborate on this womb symbolism as it relates to initiates' activities in the Mysteries later.

Another pure parthenogenetic story in relation to Demeter, Persephone, their *Melissai,* and the "bee" can be found in the following myth: As Servius (in Virgil's *Aeneid* 1.430) recounts, an elderly priestess of Demeter named Melissa (again, "Bee"), who lived on the Isthmus of Corinth, was said to have been initiated into the mysteries by the goddess Demeter herself. When this Melissa refused to reveal the secrets of these mysteries to the neighborhood women, they tore her to pieces in anger. In retaliation, Demeter sent a plague and caused bees to emerge from Melissa's corpse. This story could be interpreted as an incident in which a "bee" priestess remained steadfast in keeping the secret of parthenogenesis from the uninitiated or the unworthy. The motif of the bees spontaneously emerging from her body is an important clue, given, as I mentioned earlier, the ancient belief that bees were parthenogenetically born of the carcasses of bulls.

Metanaera of Eleusis as a Basilinna

I now turn to legendary figures named in the Homeric *Hymn to Demeter* to elucidate further the degree to which divine birth was woven into the Demeter and Persephone myth, as well as the foundation of the Thesemophoria and Eleusinian Mysteries. I first analyze key female figures in the *Hymn*, Metanaera and her daughters, to make the case that these women were priestesses of divine birth of the later period, when *hieros gamos* practices were in force. Indeed, I show that their story is indicative of the very power struggle regarding divine birth practices that ensued as patriarchy encroached on the Mysteries of Demeter and Persephone and their virgin birth cult.

I start by looking at the figure of Metanaera, who, according to the *Hymn*, was queen of Eleusis when Demeter arrived in search of her daughter. There are numerous indications that Metanaera was a priestess of miraculous conception via *hieros gamos*. The first is the special title held by her husband Celeus, *basileus* (103, 215, 473). We know that *basileus* was the title of a corresponding historical functionary in classical Athens who held a position of religious authority. More or less meaning "king archon," the title may have been a remnant of the days when the official was an actual king who held both political and religious power (see, e.g., Kerenyi 1975, 44–45; Dillon 2001, 101). I propose that Celeus hailed from a time when the original political kingship behind the title was intact, for the *Hymn* affirms that he was among the men who had power (*kratos*) at Eleusis (150) and administered the law (473). What is significant is that, in Athens, the wife of the *basileus* was known as the *basilinna*, a figure attested in the historical records of the classical period to have engaged in a sacred sexual ritual with the god Dionysus. Although no child of that union is reported in ancient texts for that period, in *CDB* I make the case that the original intention of the *basilinna's* sexual union with the god was most likely to engender his child (Rigoglioso 2009, 46–50). I propose that at Eleusis, Celeus, as *basileus*, also would have had a *basilinna* as his consort, and that Metanaera would have fulfilled that role. As I suggest in *CDB*, the Athenian *basilinna* may have engaged with Dionysus directly, not in a *hieros gamos* with the *basileus* as the god's stand-in. That may have been the case with Metanaera, as well. It could also be that, by the time of the events recounted by the *Hymn,* the rite had degenerated into the late-stage *hieros gamos* by surrogate.

Either way, the argument that Metanaera was a *basilinna,* a priestess of divine birth, is supported by an analysis of the strange events that concern her son, Demophoön. The generally accepted scholarly view is that Demophoön was himself specifically identified with Iacchus/Dionysus and that he was considered a form of the divine child whose birth was announced at the climax of the Mysteries (Richardson 1974, 24, 27; see also 233). This notion corresponds perfectly with my claim that Metanaera would have conceived Demophoön in a divine birth ritual with the wine god in order to engender his "double" on earth. The hermeneutical application of the theory that her actions reflected her participation in a cult of divine birth renders the entire story behind Metanaera, Celeus, and their children suddenly coherent and understandable.

Seen from the perspective that Demophoön was the divinely born son of Metanaera's union with Dionysus, the meaning of Demeter's attempts to "immortalize" the child by passing him through fire, a motif whose true significance has puzzled scholars for some time, becomes clear, for example. In the *Hymn* (160–67), Metanaera and her daughters invite Demeter to live in the women's quarters of the palace and serve as Demophoön's nurse. There, secretly at night, the goddess buries the boy like a brand in the fire as a means of making him immortal (239). I propose that the goddess's actions reflect an integral part of the divine birth cult: the subjecting of the miraculously born child to a ritual early in his life to help "seal" his divine status. I noted in chapter 4 possible evidence for such rituals expressed mythologically as the need to have the child "imbibe the breast milk" of Hera or, in Egypt, of Hathor. In *CDB*, I speak of Athena's "immortalization" of Erichthonius, the divinely born first king of Athens, by enclosing him in a wooden chest and giving it to the care of the daughters of King Cecrops (Rigoglioso 2009, 62–65).[33] Cook (1914–40, 1:676–79) notes other myths and practices in Thrace and Phrygia suggesting that at one time being "boiled in milk" was a ritual to achieve immortality. Richardson (1974, 233) acknowledges the accepted view that an alternate form of fire, exposure to Zeus's thunderbolt (e.g., lightning?), was also a method for apotheosis, which we see specifically in the case of Asclepius, another divinized child of a miraculous union (see Rigoglioso 2009, 31, 106). He also points to stories of the "burning away or purging of the mortal parts" in the birth or death tales of various heroes and gods (240), as well as immersion in water—the purpose of which, similarly, was "union with a magical or divine power" (232).[34] As I discussed in chapter 4, it is likely that Heracles threw himself on a funeral pyre rather than die by poison because he understood that he would achieve full apotheosis only by a ritual self-sacrifice through fire.

I thus propose a further theoretical enhancement to my work in *CDB*, which will help us decode the story of Demophoön. Specifically, I posit that we find in the ancient stories related to the cult of divine birth at least three stages of divinization. The first involved the child's miraculous conception via the mother's sexual union with a god. The second involved a rite to "seal" the child's divine status early on, through a fire or "milk-imbibing" ritual. Anointing and water-immersion rites also may have played a role.[35] The third involved the divinely born individual's ritual sacrificial death as an adult—again, by fire, exposure to lightning, boiling in a cauldron, or other means.[36] This template allows us to see the actions of the goddess regarding Demophoön as part of an entire divine birth program. As I posit later, the motif of "Demeter" conducting the rite may be read neo-euhemeristically as a reference to the ministering of the proceedings by one of her priestesses. According to the *Hymn*, Demophoön's immortalization was in fact interrupted (242–67), meaning that it was a failed rite. I discuss the full meaning of this motif later in the chapter.

Other details about Demophoön seem to affirm his divine status. The first is his name, which may mean either "giver of light or illumination to the people/*dêmos*" (as *Dêmo-phaôn*; Foley 1994, 52), or "slayer of the people" (*as Dêmo-phontês*; Kerenyi 1967, 126).[37] "Light giver," would correspond precisely with what I show in *CDB* was the most elevated type of role for the divinely born child: that of spiritual teacher, of bringer of greater knowledge and consciousness to humanity. "Slayer" suggests the role of the divinely born child under a degenerated patriarchy: that of the warrior hero, as I discussed in some depth in chapter 4. The second affirmation of Demophoön's divine status is the fact that he received honors and had a hero cult at Eleusis (Richardson 1974, 24), a phenomenon whose meaning in relationship to the cult of divine birth I also discussed in that chapter.

Metanaera's Daughters as Divine Birth Priestesses

In addition to Demophoön, Metanaera had several daughters. The *Hymn* (109) lists them as four: Callidice, Cleisidice, Demo, and Callithoe. Pasuanias (1.38.3), attributing his information to the pre-Homeric hymn writer Pamphus as well as Homer, lists them as three and offers different names: Diogenia, Pammerope, and Saesara. The geographer further affirms these girls were legendary priestesses by telling us they performed sacred rites with Eumolpus, the first hierophant, or priest, of the Eleusinian Mysteries. This suggests, in particular, that they were considered the first priestesses of the Mysteries themselves (Richardson

1974, 189). Indeed, the daughters' role in the *Hymn* as "the first witnesses to the miracles of Demeter and host[s to] the disguised goddess during her stay on earth" (Foley 1994, 80) suggests that they formed the inner female sanctum of the goddess's mysteries. Richardson posits (1974, 201) that the image in the *Hymn* (170–81) of the girls running down the road and leading Demeter to Eleusus may reflect actual ceremonies at the Mysteries involving a procession or ritual dance led by priestesses, of whom the daughters of Metanaera "may be the prototype." These legendary maidens may also have served as the prototype for the priestesses who carried the *kistai*, or chests containing sacred objects, from Eleusis to Athens in the rite (Richardson, 235). Their other activities in the *Hymn*, such as seating Demeter on a stool covered with fleece and having her breaking her fast by drinking a mixture known as the *kykeon*, similarly suggest elements from the Lesser and Greater Mysteries, as well (Foley 1994, 138). I discuss the importance of the *kykeon* at Eleusis later in the chapter.

Whether the daughters of Metanaera were considered divinely born in the manner of their brother is unclear. One possible clue in this direction is their comparison in the *Hymn* (108) to "goddesses" (*theai*). As I have noted, children miraculously conceived were considered divine, as was the case with the girls' brother. At the very least, there are several signs that they were destined to birth children miraculously in the manner of their mother. One is that they are referred to as *kourai* (108), which, as I argued earlier, was likely a specific title for Persephone as Virgin Mother, one that was extended to priestesses dedicated to divine birth. Callidice is specifically called a *parthenos* (145), another term that I argue in *CDB* was a deliberate title in this regard. Thus, the girls' comparison to "goddesses" may be a reflection of the fact that, as virgin birth priestesses, they were seen as Demeter and Persephone's hypostases, their earthly "doubles," female considered capable of conceiving miraculously, like these deities. This idea is supported by the fact that the name of one of the daughters in the *Hymn*, Demo, was used elsewhere for Demeter herself (Foley 1994, 41), indicating the close identification of the girl with the goddess.

Another sign of the daughters' status is the motif in the *Hymn* (99) of their encountering the grieving Demeter at the Parthenion, the "Well of the *Parthenos*," or "Virgin's Well." This underscores their association with the *parthenos* title, "virginity," and Persephone-as-Virgin,[38] all of which further point to their own relationship with divine birth. Another name for the well, Anthion, "Flower Well" (Pausanias 1.38.6, 39.1), suggests an association between the girls and the motif of Persephone gathering flowers at the time of her abduction, a ritual action I argued was a key part of the goddess's parthenogenetic activity. The *Hymn's* comparing the girls to "flowers" (108) may also point to this connection. Indeed, the Parthenion/Anthion may have been directly connected with the worship of Persephone (Richardson 1974 18–19). Furthermore, by situating the daughters of Metanaera at a well, the *Hymn* characterizes them as water carriers. This may be an allusion to their kinship with the Danaids, those famous water bearers and holy *parthenoi* who brought the Thesmophoria to the Greeks.

A more direct indication that Metanaera's daughters were priestesses of divine birth may also be found in the *Hymn* in lines 145–55. Immediately after Demeter, in her guise as an old woman, wishes the girls good fortune in finding husbands and bearing children (135–36), Callidice steps in as though to set the record straight. She tells the goddess, "Good mother, we mortals are forced, though it hurts us, to bear the gifts of the gods; for they are far stronger" (*Maia theôn men dôra kai achnumenoi per anankê tetlamen anthrôpoi. dê gar polu ferteroi eisin.*). I propose Callidice is explaining here that she and her sisters are destined to bear particular "gifts" of the gods, indeed: their divine sons. This is supported in part by the fact that she is specifically called a *parthenos admês* (146). *Admês* has the connotation of "untamed" (O'Brien 1993, 59) and, in fact, served as the basis for the name of a priestess of Hera, Admete, at Samos, where I argue in *CDB* there is strong evidence that Hera's priestesses were involved in divine birth in imitation of their originally "unmarried," "untamed," "undomesticated" goddess (Rigoglioso 2009, 127–28). As we recall, a related form of the word is used by the Danaids in *The Supplants* (143–45), where they pray that, like their ancestress, the divine birth priestess Io, they will remain *adamatos*, "unwedded, unconquered, untamed" (Liddell and Scott, s.v.). In short, I suggest, the use of *admês* in the *Hymn* indicates that Callidice is a girl who will *never* marry in the conventional sense, thus underscoring the meaning of *parthenos* here as priestess of divine birth.

The idea that Callidice has revealed to Demeter that she and her sisters are holy *parthenoi* is also supported by the fact that she immediately says she will "explain these things clearly and name the men to whom great power and honor belong here" (*tauta de toi safeôs hupothêsomai êd'onomênô aneras hoisin epesti mega kratos enthade timês*). She then launches into a list of the kings of the land. Although three of the figures are obscure, the three others may be readily identified: Triptolemus, Eumolpus, and Celeus, the girls' father. As I explain further below, a great deal of mythological and cultic evidence suggests that Triptolemus, who figures largely in the cult of Demeter and Persephone, was considered divinely born. Indeed, he was sometimes conflated with Demophoön. Eumolpus, the first heirophant of Demeter, was considered divinely born, as well, as I also explicate shortly. Furthermore, Callidice's description of their father as being "lordly" (*patros agênoros*) hints that he, too, may have had a divine pedigree.

The maiden's using the list of the local kings to explain her statement to Demeter that "mortals are forced to bear the gifts of the gods" really only makes sense as an "explanation" (from *hupotithêmi*, "to instruct, demonstrate") if we understand her list to be a local catalogue of these very "gifts of the gods": their divinely born sons. Where there is a divinely born son, there is always a mother who conceived him miraculously. I propose that Callidice is therefore thanking Demeter for her good wishes regarding their marriages but telling the goddess that she and her sisters will not be involved in conventional unions, as they are destined for something greater. Callidice's comment that bearing the gifts of the gods "hurts" mortals but is something they have been "forced" to do through the will of those gods is also indicates some resistance to this destiny. Hers is a lament. This, I posit, places the events of the *Hymn* firmly in a time when the priesthoods have been conscripted into divine birth via *hieros gamos* and are perhaps not happy about it.

That Metanaera's daughters may be the prototype for the priestesses who carried the chests containing sacred objects on their heads from Eleusis to Athens may also connect them with the karyatids of the Erechtheion on the Acropolis at Athens. Those statues of maidens bearing elaborate baskets on their heads likely immortalize priestesses who took part in the Panathenaia, that sacred rite celebrating Athena's "birthday." Here, again, we are in the territory of divine birth. As I posit in *CDB*, the karyatids may have depicted holy priestesses of virgin birth in connection with the Athena cult (Rigoglioso 2009, 70). The similarities between the daughters of Metanaera/Celeus and the daughters of King Cecrops in Athens are also significant in this light. As I argue at length in *CDB* (62–66), the latter were royal princesses who were also holy *parthenoi*, in their case, in service to Athena. Both the daughters of Cecrops and the daughters of Celeus, along with their mother Metanaera, had tombs and received honors at Eleusis (Clement *Exhortation to the Greeks* 3.39). Again, this corresponds with the divinizing of divine birth priestesses that I describe in *CDB*. What all of this suggests, then, is the presence of a complex of princesses in the Athenian environs who were dedicated to miraculous conception.

We may also discern in the ancient texts older, more matriarchal roots for the daughters of Metanaera, as for the Athenian daughters of Cecrops. The Suda (s.v. *Eumolpos*) states that Demeter communicated the Mysteries directly to these women. This indicates women's precedence in presiding over aspects of the rites founded at Eleusis. This textual hint of women's original leadership at Eleusis is congruent with the argument

I make later in the chapter that the Mysteries likely emerged out of the women-only Thesmophoria. In this regard, it is particularly significant, as mentioned earlier, that one of Celeus's daughters was named *Saesara*. For we hear elsewhere that *Saesara* was the original name for Eleusis itself (Hesychius, s.v.). Hyginus (*Fabulae* 147) says that it was Triptolemus who changed the town's name to Eleusus in a political struggle with Celeus. Although the mythographer does not tell us the original name of the locale, it is reasonable to assume that it was Saesara. This earlier name indicates that the town and its early rites centered on a foundational female ancestress. Whether she predated the figures in the *Hymn* or was in fact Metanaera's daughter cannot be determined. Whatever the case, the name points once again to the original precedence of women at this holy precinct. That this particular "foundress" Saesara served as the eponym of the town would not be at odds with the possibility that she was a priestess involved in divine birth. As I show throughout *CDB*, many of the towns, cities, and topographical features of Greece were named after such women or their divine children (see, e.g., Rigoglioso 2009, 23, 97–99; 112, 127, 133, 145–46, 185–92).

"Divine" Genealogies of Legendary Founders: The Advent of Dionysus and Hieros Gamos *in the Eleusinian Tradition*

As I have shown, divine birth forms the foundation of the Mysteries of Demeter and Persephone at Eleusis in the genealogies of that locale's mythical male ancestors. I have already noted the generally accepted scholarly view that Demophoön was himself specifically identified with Iacchus/ Dionysus, and I argued this was a sign of his miraculous conception. I also suggested the possibility that Celeus was considered to be a divine son.

I now turn to another figure mentioned earlier, Triptolemus. In the Attic tradition, he was the oldest son of Metanaera and Celeus, and the brother of Demophoön (Apollodorus 1.5.1; Pausanias 1.14.2).[39] Eventually, he came to supplant Demophoön as the child Demeter attempted to make immortal (see Richardson 1974, 195–96). In the Homeric *Hymn* (473–78), Triptolemus is one of the leaders Demeter instructs in her sacred worship, as well. In the popular Athenian tradition, he received the gift of the grain from Demeter and became the teacher of agriculture.[40] We see in this conflation of details affirmations of Triptolemus's status as a divinely born son who became a king/religious leader—in short, what was probably a *basileus*. This is affirmed by the myth that King Celeus, identified earlier as the *basileus* of Eleusis, was obliged to give up his country to Triptolemus, who thereafter established rites to Demeter (Hyginus *Fabulae* 147).[41] That is, Triptolemus became the new *basileus*.

Clement of Alexandria's (*Exhortation to the Greeks* 2.17) report that Triptolemus was a cowherd may refer to this figure's origins in the pre-agriculture period. As Kerenyi (1967, 128) notes, "[T]here is no doubt that the myth of Triptolemos leads us back to early archaic times, preceding the existence of the Homeric hymn." His being credited with "bringing the gift of agriculture" would be in alignment with my theory that the divinely born child was always thought to be specially endowed in some way.[42] That he also had a cult at Eleusis and Athens, complete with temples and statues,[43] would further be in congruence with the theory in *CDB* that miraculously born individuals were worshipped after death as some form of divine spirit. It is noteworthy that, in talking about Triptolemus's lineage and story, Pausanias (1.14.3) says he was warned in a dream not to say more. This most likely indicates that the geographer had bordered into the realm of the taboo regarding the Eleusinian Mysteries, about which initiates were required to maintain grave secrecy. His remark tells us that Triptolemus's origins and relationship to the Mysteries contained esoteric meanings, underscoring the mystical and divine associations attributed to him.

Yet another significant figure connected to the Mysteries was Eubouleus. According to Argive and Orphic traditions, he was Triptolemus's brother (Pausanias 1.14.2). In one story, he was the swineherd who saw his pigs swallowed into the earth with Hades' chariot when the god abducted Persephone (Clement *Exhortation to the Greeks* 2.14). In the Orphic Hymns, Eubouleus is equated with Plouton (Hades) (18.12) or is a son of Demeter (41.6, 8) or Persephone (29.8). His name, which means "Good Counselor," after the Greek *euboulos,* occurs also as a surname of Zeus, Hades, and Dionysus.[44] Like Triptolemus, Eubouleus received offerings and honors at Eleusis (Richardson 1974, 84; Mylonas 1961, 198 ff.). His characterization as the "son" of either Demeter or Persephone, his blatant identification with Zeus/Hades/Dionysus, and his posthumous veneration indicate, once again, that he was considered another of the divinely born kings of Eleusis.

The two founding hierophants of the Mysteries have perhaps more obvious divine lineages. Keryx, whose name means "Herald," was the eponymous ancestor of one of the two major families from which priests had to claim lineage, the Kerykes. According to the most accepted genealogy, he was the son of Hermes, the messenger god, and of Aglaurus, daughter of King Cecrops of Athens (Pausanias 1.38.3). This tells us that his royal line was descended from the founding family of Athens, which had established Athena as the resident goddess there. In *CDB*, I detail Aglaurus's role as a divine birth priestess dedicated to that goddess; she, along with at least one of her sisters, was conscripted into *hieros gamos* practices (Rigoglioso 2009, 62–71). The legendary attribution of her conception of Keryx to union with the god Hermes affirms the argument I make there. It also indicates the degree to which Athenian patriarchs inserted themselves into the religious affairs of Eleusis. Indeed, as a son of the royal princess/priestess of Athens, Keryx was not indigenous to Eleusis but, rather, a new arrival. We begin to suspect, therefore, a possible imposition of *hieros gamos* practices over a female-centered cult whose ancestress was the aforementioned Saesara.

Eumolpus, whose name means "Beautiful Singer," was the eponymous ancestor of the other family from whom the hierophants were descended, the Eumolpidai. Legend relates that he, too, was divinely born, the son of the sea god Poseidon and Chione. An Athenian lineage is also embedded here, in that Chione was the daughter of Oreithyia, another priestess of Athena at Athens, who was impregnated by the Boreas, or North Wind (Pausanias 1.38.2). As I argue in *CDB*, the notion of "wind impregnation" may well be a reference to pure parthenogenetic conception on Oreithyia's part (Rigoglioso 2009, 38–39, 70–71). As the female child of such a mother, Chione was herself indeed in the lineage of divine birth priestesses, as I have shown was the case with the Danaids and other women discussed in *CDB*. What we see in this story is that Chione was conscripted for *hieros gamos* with Athena's great rival, Poseidon. That she was unhappy with the situation is affirmed by the detail that she threw Eumolpus into the sea. Poseidon rescued him and took him to Ethiopia, where he became ruler of Thrace (Euripides *Erechtheus* fr. 39, in Richardson 1974, 198).[45]

As a Thracian, Eumolpus was accompanied by his countrymen in the Eleusinian war against the Athenian king Erechtheus. Legend records that, although Athens won, Eleusus retained its own religious authority (Harrison [1903] 1957, 554). Again, according to Pausanias (1.38.3), Eumolpus was the first to perform the "holy rites" at Eleusis with the three daughters of King Celeus. Harrison (553–63) argues on the basis of legend and iconography that Eumolpus may have brought the "Dionysian element" to the Mysteries. This "Dionysian element" included the very *hieros gamos*-related motifs that I have been discussing throughout this chapter and explicate further when I hermeneutically reconstruct the Eleusinian Mysteries. That Celeus was in power at Eleusis when Demeter stopped there in her search for Persephone indicates, I suggest, that the *Hymn* commemorates the very moment of transition from pure parthenogenesis to divine birth *hieros gamos* in the mystery practices of Demeter. The holy *Korê/Kourê/Koura* on the cosmic level—Persephone—was abducted or conscripted, whereas, on earth, the male divine child (Demophoön) was "immortalized," and the "holy rites" were instituted by another divinely born son (Eumolpus). The program reveals a massive shift in proceedings angled toward the masculine.

Reviewing these lineages, what we see most strikingly in the stories of Demophoön, Triptolemus, and Eubouleus in particular, is their identification with the child said to have been born at the conclusion of the mysteries: Brimo/Iacchus/Dionysus. I thus propose that *these individuals were among some of the early children considered divinely conceived during the very Mystery celebrations themselves in the Dionysian period*. As I show later, certain Christian fathers reveal, with anti-pagan horror, that the priestess of the Mysteries enacted a *hieros gamos*. I contend that this was not done simply for the sake of "sympathetic magic" to bolster the fertility of the fields, as is sometimes suggested, but to accomplish precisely what sexual intercourse is intended to do: create a baby. In short, I submit that the *hieros gamos* was ritually enacted at the Mysteries to engender what was believed to be the living Zeus/Hades/Dionysus, the man who would serve as a future divine leader of the land. In a rite originally dedicated to the matriarchal parthenogenetic goddesses Demeter and Persephone, this no doubt was a later development. Indeed, as I argue in what follows, it was an unwelcome intrusion from the perspective of the goddesses, one that had to be propitiated.

Degeneration of Esoteric Knowledge: Demophoön's Failed Immortalization

As noted earlier, in the Homeric *Hymn*, Demeter passes Demophoön through fire. Before this event takes place, in line 220, Metanaera asks the goddess to raise her child, whom the gods (*athanatoi*) provided her. While this could be read as a normal statement revealing beliefs that children come from the gods, it could well be an indicator that Demophoön was indeed a gift of Dionysus, in particular, the product of Metanaera's union with the deity. This is supported in 216–17, where the queen repeats to Demeter the very words her daughter Callidice has uttered earlier: "We mortals are forced, though it may hurt us, to bear the gifts of the gods." Again, I submit that, like Callidice, Metanaera is telling the mysterious woman before her that she is a priestess of divine birth, and that, in fact, she has on her hands a son miraculously conceived through a (not entirely consensual) *hieros gamos*. In the very next lines, she asks Demeter to rear the boy. Demophoön's position here in the text affirms his identification with the (divine) kings of Eleusis enumerated by Callidice immediately after making the same comment. Like them, Demophoön is a "gift of the gods" that Metanaera has suffered to bear.

We also see in Metanaera's request the hint of something else: She feels inadequate to the task of rearing such a child. Yet she discerns in this female figure a holy woman who might know how to do it properly. Earlier, in lines 188–90, Metanaera has witnessed Demeter's divine light (*selaos theioio*) and has become filled with awe and reverence for her. She praises her for being noble (*agathon*) (215). "Now that you have come here," she tells Demeter, "all that's mine will be yours" (218). In short, I propose that she is relieved to see that a holy woman of this stature has arrived. Now she may have the proper help in preparing this divine child for his destiny. To this queen, no price is too great in compensation for such services; she will pay the woman handsomely. Read neo-euhemeristically, the story may on one level be an account of a priestess of Demeter who made her way to Eleusis. Perhaps, in fact, she was one of the very parthenogenetically born female avatars of the goddess about whom I have theorized throughout this work and in *CDB*. This would not be inconsistent with the observation of Foley (1994, 83) that the entire story revolves around "the intersection between divine and mortal experience." What seems to be suggested is the advent of a female hypostasis of the goddess in the earth realm.

Other details are significant here. Just before Metanaera requests that Demeter raise her son, we see the characters engage in a sequence of activities (195–210) that may reflect ritual actions conducted in the Mysteries themselves.[46] Another female figure, Iambe, sets out a stool for Demeter and casts over it a silvery fleece. The goddess draws a veil before her face and sits on the stool for some time in grief, in a period of fasting. Then, Iambe jokes and provokes her to laughter. Metanaera offers Demeter wine, but she refuses, instructing them to concoct for her another drink, the *kykeon*. With this holy woman before her thusly "juiced," Metanaera praises her and asks for her great benefaction for her son.

I connect several of these motifs to the Mysteries later in the chapter, but for now I will focus briefly on one: Demeter's refusal of the wine and instructions for mixing the *kykeon*. I propose that her rejection of the wine reflects the tension between two cults: the older, matriarchal one dedicated exclusively to Demeter, Persephone, and parthenogenesis and the newer, patriarchal one that had incorporated Dionysus and divine birth by *hieros gamos*. The clue in this regard is Demeter's statement that to partake of the wine (the very symbol of Dionysus) would be contrary to *themis*. Themis means "law" and was related to another term, *thesmos,* which was the basis for one of the goddess's very titles, *Thesmophoros,* "Law Giver." Thus, I propose that Demeter is complaining here about the violation of the "law" of matriarchy that has taken place through the insertion of Zeus/Hades/Dionysus into Persephone's reproductive plans. She is, by extension, complaining about the degeneration of divine birth into an affair with male gods, as well. It seems clear from the ancient texts that the "wine" of Dionysus was an entheogen used to reach ecstatic states of oneness with the god. This can be seen, for example, in the foundational myth of the Haloa festival of Demeter and Kore held at Eleusis in December/January: Dionysus gave wine to Icarus, who was killed by shepherds crazed by its effects (scholiast to Lucian's *Dialogue of the Courtesans,* in Brumfield 1981, 108–9).[47] Clearly, this wine was no ordinary table drink, but rather a powerful psychotropic substance. Additionally, as I argue in *CDB*, this special wine was used by Dionysus's female followers, the *mainades*, as a means of uniting with the god sexually (Rigoglioso 2009, 97–98). I thus propose that Demeter's refusal of the wine signifies a rejection of the entheogen that would lead to Dionysian worship and *hieros gamos* with a male god, particularly the god implicated in Persephone's rape.[48] Demeter instead offers her own intoxicating recipe (*Hymn* 208), one in which her staple plant, barley, is a main ingredient: the *kykeon*. I discuss evidence for the hallucinogenic nature of the *kykeon* used in the Mysteries later in the chapter.

I propose that this section of the *Hymn* describes ritual preparations that were part of the Mysteries and also intimately related to divinization rituals. What may be discerned is that Demeter has drunk a hallucinogenic potion. Like Persephone, who was gathering enthogenic flowers, she is thus in the requisite trance state to engage in a magical ritual. Indeed, the *Hymn* states (210) that "almighty Deo [Demeter] received [the *kykeon*] for the sake of the rite" (*dexamenê d' hosiês heneken polupotnia Dêô*), indicating that the foregoing was part of a ritual enactment. In short, the goddess was sacramentally prepared for something. The lines immediately following (228–40) tell us what that is: the immortalization of Demophoön.

The process involves Demeter in several activities: administering a plant as a charm (*hulotomos*), nursing the child at her breast, anointing him with *ambrosia*, breathing on him, and burying him like a brand in a fire at night. "Ambrosia" is a general ancient term for entheogens (Hillman 2008, 89–93). What we may read here neo-euhemeristically is that the ritual, as conducted by a priestess, required her to 1) enter a deep trance via a psychotropic substance; 2) perform magical spells over the child that involved plants; 3) feed him an entheogen as a means of opening and training his own awareness to divine realms; 4) nurse him with magical intent (which would further dispense a drug to him, given that she herself had the *kykeon* running through her bloodstream); and 5) ritually immerse him in fire. We will recall here that "divine nursing" was also a component of the divinization of Egyptian pharaohs and of the sons of Zeus, as we saw in the case of Heracles. The *Hymn* also indicates that there was a time element involved: The rite was done repeatedly over days, weeks, or months.

The comparison between Demeter's immortalizing of Demophoön and Athena's immortalizing of Erichthonius is instructive here. Like Demophoön, Erichthonius was a divinely born child destined for king-ship—in his case, over neighboring Athens. The latter's conception was a result of an unsuccessful attempt on the part of the smith god, Hephaestus, to rape Athena.[49] In both stories, goddesses agree to immortalize divinely born children despite the fact that they are Virgin Mothers and want nothing to do with procreation by male gods—and despite the fact that their wishes in this regard have been violated through rape. I draw from this an insight: To Athena and Demeter, to the matriarchy, a fully divinized king was better than a mere human king. I propose that these stories represent a time of divine and priestessly compromise: Although the birth of a king via a god was undesirable from the perspective of the matriarchy, a king possessed of divine consciousness was better than one who lacked such awareness. A divinely endowed king was more apt to make wise decisions. Moreover, he was more likely to keep the channels open between the human and divine realms (and, thus, keep offerings flowing to the deities) than a king steeped in worldly consciousness. In short, a "divine" patriarchy was better than a degenerated "human" one. In this respect, the perspective of Demeter and Athena apparently differed from that of Hera, who would have refused to divinize Heracles had she not been tricked into offering him her breast milk. Given the choice, she would have preferred to let patriarchy stew in its own juices.

Demeter does, however, eventually give up on the cause, as detailed in lines 242–333 of the *Hymn*. One night, Metanaera eavesdrops on the god-dess's doings, and, horrified at seeing her son in the fire, begins shrieking and lamenting. An angry Demeter dashes the child to the ground, rag-ing at Metanaera about the ignorance and foolishness of humankind and their inability to discern destiny and the gods' will. She tells the queen that her ignorance will now prevent the child from being fully immor-talized, although he will still garner honors. Instead, she prophecies, throughout his life the sons of Eleusis will continue to wage war on one another. At that moment, Demeter reveals her identity as a goddess, leav-ing Metanaera speechless and on her knees. She commands that the peo-ple build her a great temple and declares she will institute rites that will propitiate her. Hearing the cries of their brother, the daughters rush to the scene, pick the boy up, and try to soothe both him and their mother. They then spend the entire night attempting to appease the goddess. At dawn, they tell their father what has happened, and the king immediately calls an assembly to begin the building of the goddess's temple. Demeter, however, is still grieving for Persephone and ordains a famine upon the earth until her daughter is returned to her.

As Richardson (1974, 241) notes, the rite was probably something done in secret, and its secrecy was transgressed. The interruption of the immortalization ritual rendered it null and void. Demophoön would not become a divinity. I contend that these events represented something that had gone deeply wrong in the ritual life of the people, a spiritual travesty. Again, recalling Foley's words (1994, 83), I underscore that such a travesty had to do with "the intersection between divine and mortal experience." As I have intimated throughout this chapter, it is likely that Demeter's "living presence" among the people of Eleusis in the *Hymn* harks back to a time when it was thought possible that a goddess could be incarnated through the body of a holy virgin priestess. What the *Hymn* seems to relate is a period when the veils between the divine and human realms have become thicker—to the dismay of the deities and the detriment of humankind. Not only have divine birth practices degenerated from matriarchal parthenogenesis to patriarchal *hieros gamos,* but the participants also no longer possess full knowledge about the corresponding rites. Metanaera does not know how to conduct a divinization ritual herself, presumably something in which a divine birth priestess would have been schooled when the cult was strong. Her ignorance is so great that she even lacks the wisdom to stay out of secret proceedings—or at least to stay calm when she witnesses these dangerous and uncanny rites pitting life against death.[50] She represents a humanity that has lost the knowledge of the Old Ways. Humans can no longer conduct magical rites properly in a manner that would preserve their connection with the divine realms. The goddess's prophecy is clear: Chronic warfare will be the result of this travesty. The patriarchy will degenerate into an ever greater mass of suffering.

It is at this point that Demeter puts her foot down. Matriarchy will not be totally vanquished. The goddess must be propitiated and her daughter must be returned to her, or humanity will perish and the gods will no longer have "the glorious honor of their gifts" (311), the offerings and sacrifices of humanity, which, for the immortals, amount to real sustenance. The gods have miscalculated the will and power of the Virgin Mother. As the rest of the *Hymn* details, they must compromise and return the *arrhêtos koura* to Demeter for two-thirds of the year.

Read neo-euhemeristically, Demeter's "decree" may have been ascertained through Metanaera's daughters during their night-long vigil to appease the goddess. It would not be unreasonable to suggest that they used customary means of divination to determine the wishes of the goddess, notice of which they delivered to their father, the king of the land, in the morning. Indeed, the transgressing of a sacrosanct rite to prepare the next divine king for leadership must have been something the royal family and their people viewed with extreme horror. It was not to be taken lightly. They would do whatever the priestesses of the goddess had discerned was necessary to right relations between the human and divine realms once more.

The Great Beneficence of Demeter: Making the Best of a Patriarchal Situation

As I noted at the beginning of this chapter, there is general agreement that the Homeric *Hymn* represents a relatively late stage in the history of the cult, and that it most likely was an amalgam of, and compromise between, various mythical traditions and local beliefs (Richardson 1974, 12, 17). It is important, therefore, to bear in mind that the *Hymn* represents competing cultic elements. This understanding allows for further hermeneutical analysis that does not rely on a linear untangling of the *Hymn's* themes. Indeed, we must understand the *Hymn* to be the product of layerings that reflect contradictions, conflicts, and non-linear sequencing. I propose that only by embracing such paradoxes and oddities may we fully mine the story for what it may tell us about Demeter, Persephone, and their cult. It is with this approach that I conclude this section of the chapter, establishing the foundation for what is to come. The points I make here are particularly critical to my reconstruction of the Thesemophoria and the rites at Eleusis later.

One theme in which we see a confusion of timelines in the *Hymn* is that of Demeter's famous gift to humanity: the knowledge of grain growing. In Orphic versions of the myth, mortals are still hunter-gatherers who have not yet learned how to cultivate the land. In some of these stories, Demeter grants mortals the knowledge of agriculture after she learns Persephone's whereabouts from them (see Richardson 1974, 77–86). We also have the reports of Pausanias and Apollodorus that it was Triptolemus who first sowed grain for cultivation. Yet the *Hymn* says nothing of this, telling us only that Triptolemus is one of the leaders to whom the goddess dispenses knowledge of her Mysteries and their associated rites. Moreover, the description of oxen dragging plows in vain after Demeter has refused to let the barley grow (305–8) implies that agriculture is already in effect at the time of the *Hymn's* events. Scholars generally agree, however, that the presence of Triptolemus in the *Hymn* serves as a vestige of this earlier story line (e.g., Kerenyi 1967, 128; Richardson 1974, 17, 259–60, 301).

Similarly, we see in the *Hymn* what I propose is a confused time-line regarding another great event: Persephone's rape. As I have argued throughout the chapter, the abduction of Persephone was the paradigm for the initiation of *hieros gamos* divine birth among the earthly priestess-hoods. In the *Hymn,* however, it seems that *hieros gamos* is already function-ing at Eleusis at the time of Demeter's search for her daughter, given what I have argued were the divine pedigrees of Demophoön, Triptolemus, Eumolpus, and possibly Celeus. Thus, I suggest that the *Hymn* represents a manipulation regarding the central importance of female-only parthe-nogenesis in the Demeter/Persephone mythologem. It at once "hints at" and "veils" this parthenogenetic mystery, to use the words of Kerenyi (1978, 39) in describing how myth motifs often functioned in ancient Greece. It reveals such a mystery by showing clearly that the rape of Persephone was considered a grave violation from the standpoint of the divine Matriarchy and by intimating that Persephone felt "desire" for the old way of self-replication, as discussed earlier. However, it conceals the mystery by placing the advent of divinely born kings antecedent to the rape and by characterizing Demeter as willing to participate in the divinization of one such king.

Demeter's command that the Eleusinians build her a temple and her declaration that she will lay down the associated rites (270–74) are gen-erally taken to be the *aition,* the causal story, for the establishment of the Eleusinian Mysteries. Following the argument I have been developing throughout this chapter, I propose that the Homeric *Hymn to Demeter* represents a theological *justification* for the inclusion of divine birth through *hieros gamos* in these Mysteries. Indeed, I suggest that the "estab-lishment of the Mysteries" by Demeter at the end of the *Hymn* (473–79) represents a key development in the cult at Eleusis: *the imposition of* hieros gamos *practices to produce male kings (Persephone/Dionysus) over what were originally women-only parthenogenetic rites to produce female avatars (Demeter/ Persephone).* I discuss parts of the rites reflective of this development later in the chapter, including ancient testimony that the Eleusinian priestess performed a sacred sexual rite during the proceedings. We will also recall here the formulaic cry at the conclusion of the ceremonies—"Brimo has given birth to Brimos"—which, as has long been established, refers to the divine birth of a male child.

Thus, I contend that the "Mysteries" being "founded" in the *Hymn* are not entirely Demeter's original rites, which, as I argue below, con-sisted of the Thesmophoria brought by the Danaids from Africa. They are Mysteries that males could now get their hands on—and, indeed, the rites were, in contrast to the Thesmophoria, famously co-ed. Eumolpus was installed as the "first hierophant" of these newly revised celebrations, with the daughters of Metanaera now in tow, as we hear from Pausanias. We see in this configuration the establishment of the divinely born son as head priest alongside the holy *parthenoi* who were, after their mother, next in line to unite sexually with Dionysus as *basilinnai*. We must remember, however, that one of those daughters was named after Saesara, the original the queen of the realm. We may read from this that Eleusis was once a female-run religious precinct dedicated to the two goddesses. We see a further historical vestige of this matriarchal condition in the possible presence of a very archaic virgin priestesshood at Eleusis, the *hiereiai panageis*, as I discuss later.

The *Hymn* thus carries within itself a deep contradiction. Although it attempts to justify the entry of a new form of divine birth into a female-centered cult, it cannot escape *the* central fact: *The Virgin Mother is not happy about the state of affairs in which* hieros gamos *has arisen and is being perpetuated*. Through her own beneficence, she, like Athena, is willing to bend in support of a divine king born in this way—but only so far. When humans reveal the depth of their ignorance about the immortal realms by foiling even her compromised attempt to help them, she snaps.

This is where the *Hymn* reveals something central about Demeter, an essential element that is also a key to unlocking the Thesmophoria and the Eleusinian Mysteries. This is also where an oblique, non-linear approach to the material is required. What we see in the *Hymn* and related Orphic fragments is that, despite the transgression of the male gods against the feminine and the corresponding folly of humankind, the goddess grants humans a gift. This gift consists of rites that, according to the *Hymn* (*Hymn* 480–82), render mortals "blessed" and give them a better lot after death. As Foley (1994, 87) expresses it, the goddess establishes "a permanent and beneficial modification of the relation between divinity and humankind." In short, as I discuss later in the chapter, the Mysteries provide humans with a means by which they may once again remember their true relationship to, and destiny in, the divine cosmos. These ministrations, therefore, serve as a powerful aid to the reopening of human consciousness in an era of esoteric degeneration. They are a means of revivifying the old ways of the matriarchy, even while a new, increasingly "rational" patriarchal epoch is upon humanity.

Although in granting this generous benefaction Demeter justifies the claim that she is "the greatest source of help and joy to mortals and immortals" (*hê te megiston athanatois thnêtoisi t'onear kai charma tetuktai*) (268–69), she is at the same time demanding. In order for humans to access the divine under these new, patriarchal conditions, they must pay a price. That price is the offering of their very lives. As we shall see, initiates to the Eleusinian Mysteries underwent what may be interpreted as a profound experience of death, entry into the underworld/otherworld, and, eventually, re-emergence. More to the point, initiates who wished to gain access to the divine knowledge of Demeter and Persephone, in particular, had to experience directly what the Feminine had undergone. As I explicate later, whether initiates were male or female, to acquire the *gnosis*, or deep knowing, of the realm of the Virgin Mother, they had to experience nothing less than the rape and grief of the two goddesses. It was no metaphorical encounter. It was a visceral and frightening ordeal. Ultimately, it was also ecstatic; participants eventually experienced the unification of the two goddesses: their resolution back into their original, parthenogenetic whole. In short, the human actors experienced their own reunification with their goddess-given origins.

The Eleusinian Mysteries were, therefore, at once redemptive and propitiatory. The *Hymn* emphasizes the latter in Demeter's declaration (274) that in performing her rites participants would "propitiate" (*hilaskoisthe*) her. Thus, the enactment of the Mysteries served as an ongoing form of appeasement to the two goddesses for the great violation they had endured at the hands of the gods and men. It was a violation in which humans continued to be implicated by virtue of their cooperation with the machinations of patriarchy. Indeed, by layering the *hieros gamos* element over what was originally a mystery celebrating the parthenogenetic creative capacity of the feminine, as I discuss more fully later, humans continued to violate the Matriarchy while at the same time making amends to it. It was an uneasy coexistence that amounted to a paradoxical feat of magic. We see parallels here to other rites that I show in *CDB* were propitiations to Virgin Mothers in acknowledgement of violations of their pure parthenogenetic cults, such as the mysterious basket-carrying ritual held the nights before the Skira and Panathenaia of Athena at Athens, and the Arkteia of Artemis (see Rigoglioso 2009, 67–71, 100–103). Humans were constrained to offer recompense for their sacrileges regarding the Great Goddess and the old matriarchal order.

I propose that the other "great gift" of the goddess as indicated in the Orphic tradition—agriculture—also reflects a "moment of change" in cultic practices devoted to Demeter and Persephone. As Richardson (1974, 259ff., 301ff.) intimates, humanity learned to engage in agriculture as a result of Persephone's rape. We recall here that the goddesses' original mystery rite, the Thesmophoria, came to Greece with the Danaids. The ability of those priestesses to locate sources of water and conjure rain, directly and indirectly indicated in the ancient stories, also suggests that they may have been part of a tribe of early horticulturalists, those living by simple, small-scale farming techniques. Indeed, the very connection of grain to Demeter and Persephone suggests that growing crops was originally a female affair, an idea that has enjoyed support from the field of archaeology (Ehrenberg 1989, 77–78). Thus, the idea that agricultural knowledge "began" with Triptolemus should by now raise another flag. What the Orphic stories speak of, more appropriately, is the *transfer* of agricultural knowledge from Demeter and Persephone to Triptolemus. This motif could indicate that the Eleusinian rites also served as a marker for the *male appropriation of women's agricultural mysteries.* Certainly, this would be in congruence with what I have posited was the *male appropriation of women's parthenogenetic mysteries.* As I discussed earlier in the chapter, grain growing was indeed understood to be a parthenogenetic process in the ancient mind.

Thus, the "two gifts" of Demeter both had to do with seed: the parthenogenetic seed of the female womb, and the parthenogenetic seed of Ge/Gaia. The great tragedy of Demeter and Persephone, encoded in their stories and rites, then, seems to be the cosmic and earthly appropriation by the male principle of the female "seed" on all levels and in all forms. The establishment of the Eleusinian Mysteries may therefore mark the transfer of the "secrets" of the seed as both plant and ovum to the male for the purposes of large-scale sowing (a move from horticulture to agriculture) and the production of divine kings (a move from parthenogenesis to *hieros gamos* practices).[51] In granting humans access to divine knowledge, the goddesses perhaps were making the best of a bad situation, hoping to "(re)cultivate" and "(re)civilize" a humanity that was growing increasingly savage and disrespectful of the harmonizing *themis/thesmos* of the Virgin Mother.

The Thesmophoria: Known Fragments

I now discuss one of the two most famous rites associated with Demeter and Persephone: the Thesmophoria.[52] In this section, I summarize what is known about that rite from the ancient texts, analyze that evidence, and argue that the Thesmophoria originally commemorated the two goddesses' parthenogenetic ability, a capacity that the ancients believed their holiest virgin priestesses could also cultivate.

The Thesmophoria is considered to be a very early women-exclusive ritual that predated the Eleusinian Mysteries and may even have been its precursor (Foley 1994, 103n74). The rite was secret, related to the myth of Demeter and Persephone, and dedicated to human and agricultural fertility (scholiast to Lucian's *Dialogue of the Courtesans,* in Brumfield 1981, 73–74).[53] According to Lucian (*Dialogue of the Courtesans* 2.1), mothers and daughters celebrated it together. The fierce exclusion of men from the rite is reflected in myths about severe punishments inflicted on males who transgressed into its proceedings, as well as comedic depictions of the Thesmophoria as representing nothing less than a separate society of women.[54] Indeed, the female participants possessed an exceptional degree of autonomy not permitted to them in ordinary Greek life.

In Attica,[55] the Thesmophoria, including the preliminary Stenia festival that at some point became part of the same ritual complex, lasted for five days at the time of the autumn sowing, from the ninth to the thirteenth of the month of Pyanopsion (October/November) (Brumfield 1981, 79–80). Women apparently camped out during the entire period in special huts they erected (Aritsophanes *Women at the Thesmophoria* 624; Stehle 2007, 168). The proceedings involved a day known as the *Anados,* "Going Up" (or sometimes the *Kathados,* "Going Down").[56] The second day was called the *Nestia,* "Fast," or the *Mesê,* "Middle Day" (Athenaeus 307F, in Brumfield 1981, 83n51). On that day, the women fasted while seated on the ground on palettes strewn with anaphrodisiac plants such as the *agnus castus.*[57] The third day was known as the *Kalligeneia,* "Beautiful Birth" and was likely a time of feasting.[58]

The women at the festival were said to imitate the "ancient way of life" before the discovery of civilization and to commemorate Persephone's descent into Hades.[59] Clement of Alexandria (*Exhortation to the Greeks* 2.14) notes that the women cast swine into sacred caverns in recognition of the fact that the swine of Eubouleus were swallowed up along with Persephone when Hades seized the maiden and the earth opened up. We further hear from the scholiast on Lucian's *Dialogues of the Courtesans* (in Brumfield 1981, 73–74) that women also threw pine branches, representative of fertility, and wheat cakes in the shape of snakes and phalli into these caverns, or *megara.* Special women who had abstained from sexual intercourse for three days known as *antlêtriai,* "bailers," descended into the *megara* amidst clapping and shouting to frighten away the snakes said to live there, and gather the rotted remains of pigs. The remains were then mixed with seed about to be planted in order to assure a good crop.

Participants in the Thesmophoria remained celibate during the festival.[60] Part of the Attic rite even may have involved a procession of virgins to Eleusis. The scholiast on Theocritus's *Idylls* 4.25C (in Harrison [1903] 1957, 136–37) says that at the festival "women who are virgins and have lived a holy life, on the day of the feast, place certain customary and holy books on their heads, and as though to perform a liturgy they go to Eleusis." At the same time, the women at the festival engaged in *skommata* or *aischrologia*—that is, ritual abuse, jesting, and bawdy language.[61] Speaking of the Sicilian Thesmophoria, Diodorus Siculus (5.4.7) notes that the practice supposedly derived from Demeter's laughter at crude jokes when she was grieving for her daughter. One mythical source for this custom is given in the Homeric *Hymn* (203), where Iambe causes Demeter to laugh with her jesting. In the Orphic tradition, where the bawdy nature of her actions is made more explicit, that figure is named Baubo. Theodoretos of Cyrrhus (*Greacarum Affectionum Curatio* 3.84, in Brumfield 1981, 80n37) tells us that the women also worshipped representations of male and female genitalia. Athenaeus (14.647A) says that in Sicily sesame cakes were fashioned as the female vulva and carried around in honor of the goddesses.

Ancient texts provide other details regarding women's attire, diet, and activities during the festival. Those attending were not to wear flower crowns, because Persephone had been gathering flowers when she was captured (scholiast on Sophocles' *Oedipus at Colonus* 681, in Brumfield 1981, 84n63). They also ate pomegranate seeds but were forbidden to eat those that had fallen on the ground (Clement of Alexandria *Exhortation to the Greeks* 2.16). At one point, the women beat each other with a basket of woven bark known as the *morroton* as a form of fertility rite (Hesychius, s.v. *morotton*). They also offered a sacrifice called "the penalty" (Hesychius s.v. *zêmia*) and enacted a rite known as "the Chalcidian pursuit" (Hesychius, s.v. *diôgma*; Suda, s.v. *Chalkidikon diôgma*).

Thesmophoria as Commemoration of Pure Parthenogenesis

We see the first clue as to the locus of the Thesmophoria in divine birth in Herodotus's report that the rite was brought to Greece by the daughters of Danaus, who, as I have argued, were likely holy *parthenoi* dedicated to miraculous conception in honor of Demeter and Persephone. We also recall the *Melissai*, the "Bee Priestesses," of Paros, who received the Thesmophoric teachings of Demeter. Those teachings, as noted earlier, involved "weaving" and the women "becoming nymphs" as a result of gaining mystical understanding imparted by the goddess. The story also reveals that that all women celebrating the Thesmophoria became known as *Melissai*. Given that weaving and the bee were African symbols of parthenogenetic activity and that *nymph* designated a priestess of virgin birth, the story hints that the original Thesmophoria was the product of an African matriarchal society that centered on knowledge of parthenogenesis in the context of veneration of Demeter and Persephone as Virgin Mothers. We recall the discussion of the Ause girls of Libya in chapter 2, who I argued were similarly part of a North African matriarchy dedicated to parthenogenesis, in their case in association with Athena. Evidence for the idea that the Thesmophoria was rooted in parthenogenesis may be discerned in the forementioned fragmentary details about this ancient festival, as I demonstrate in what follows. Indeed, as I show, various scholars have already intuited that the Thesmophoria was a parthenogenetic affair. The hermeneutical application of the theory that a cult of divine birth existed in ancient Greece allows us at last to make sense of this element fully.

Matriarchal, Amazonian Elements in the Rite

It is, first, important to note that scholars generally agree the Thesmophoria was a ritual stressing women's power. As Burkert (1985, 245) states, through this rite, women demonstrated "their independence, their responsibility, and their importance for the fertility of the community and the land. The...festival emphasize[d] the creation of solidarity in the role of the woman." Zeitlin (1982, 142) elaborates,

> The authority of women on the Acropolis [at the Thesmophoria] is perfectly commensurate with the ritual recreation of the "matriarchal" conditions of the time which preceded the advent of culture, ushered in by the gifts of Demeter [i.e. agriculture]. The society of women...is...a mimesis of the time before Erichthonius [the founder of Athens] when women still had the franchise in the local Athenian version of the "myth of matriarchy." The building of temporary huts, the use of acts of woven osier for sleeping on the ground, the curing of meat in the sun instead of roasting it with fire...and the inclusion of foods which "predate" those of the grain culture...all point to a primitive stage of development consonant with the myth of time when women were in charge.

This matriarchal tone is particularly emphasized in the Roman festival of Ceres (Demeter), a later version of the Thesmophoria: even the use of the word *pater* (father) was forbidden (Servius on Virgil's *Aeneid* 4.57, in Zeitlin 1996, 165n112).

The ferocity with which Greek women protected the ritual from the eyes of men is also significant. Men were kept away by the threat of punishments (Suda, s.vv. *Sphaktriai*, *Thesmophoros*; Aristophanes, *Women of the Thesmophoria* 1150–51). Tellingly, Versnel (1992, 41) notes that participants at the Thesmophoria, "mirror[ed] the disruptive imagery of the Amazons." In one myth, women in Cyrene castrated a man who came to spy on them at the festival. This man was none other than Battus, king of the land (Aelian frag. 44 Hercher, in Goff 2004, 136). Pausanias (4.171) writes that when Aristomenes of Messenia approached the celebration too closely, he was seized and assaulted with knives, spits, and torches. Such legendary stories suggest that the rite was steeped in a tradition of female warriorhood, which is consonant with my argument that its originators, the Danaids, were North African Amazons.

The Centrality of Chastity/Virginity

Another key element of the rite was chastity and the control of women's reproductive affairs. As we saw, the scholiast on Theocritus's *Idylls* describes a cadre of virgins associated with the Thesmophoria who were charged with processing holy books to Eleusis at the beginning of the festivities. This suggests the existence of a longstanding virgin priestess-hood connected to the tradition; perhaps the women were a vestige of the holy *parthenoi* dedicated to divine birth in association with Demeter and Persephone. Their serving as custodians of "holy books" suggests that they were responsible for religious writings that may have preserved the secrets of the mysteries of the two goddesses. Another group of women with an important role in the proceedings, the "bailers," were required to enter a ritual state of chastity several days before the event. Additionally, as we saw, days of sexual abstinence were ordained at the Thesmophoria for all participants, who strewed branches of the *agnus castus* (*lygos,* in Greek), or "willow," on their seating. As noted in chapter 4, the *agnus castus,* literally translated from the Latin as the "chaste lamb" tree, had an important reputation for quelling sexual desire, according to the ancient medical writers. It also stimulated women's menstrual bleeding.[62] This may have had the effect not only of checking the sexual urge, but also initiating group menstruation (Kerenyi 1975, 157).

Analyzing this emphasis on chastity, Goff (2004, 133) writes of the matrons who participated in the Thesmophoria, "Do they not resemble to some extent the virgin girls, the daughters, that they once were?" Further, she intuits, do they not resemble the virgin daughter Persephone? Working along these same lines, Versnel (1992, 42) comments on the fact that participants were referred to as *Melissai,* noting, "Bees are often regarded as preserving their virginity throughout their life-time, being notable for their asexual manner of reproduction." He asserts (43) that during the Thesmophoria "the matrons were temporarily reduced to the status of *numphai* [nymphs]. They became *melissai,* in the sense of virginal and sexually abstinent maiden-bees." He further remarks that bees represent "the ideal virgin mothers" (42). With such observations, Versnel indirectly provides support for the argument I am making here: that the Thesmophoria recalled a time when holy *parthenoi* were the living representatives of the parthenogenetic goddesses they served. Zeitlin's comments (1982, 146) are uncannily apt here, as well:

> Inherent in this harnessing of the powers of female fecundity which necessitates an active, even violent, role for women, is the anxiety which surrounds the giving of power to women, power *that is as close to parthenogenesis as possible.*... [C]ultic chastity...seems to separate sexuality

and fertility.... [T]he *agunus castus* plant upon which the women sat is emblematic of this division, for while it was thought to possess antaphrodisiac qualities, it was also believed to stimulate fertility in women by encouraging menstruation and lactation.... This threat recalls the continuing Greek fantasy, *the Amazon complex*, one might say, which envisions a city, a society, an alternate structure, composed only of women and innately hostile to men. (Italics mine.)

I agree with Zeitlin's cogent point that the mysteries of the Thesmophoria revolved around the symbol of parthenogenesis. I would add, however, that, if we understand the focus of the rite to have been "virgin motherhood," we realize that there was no contradiction in participants using a plant that both quelled desire and stimulated fertility. I submit that the "quelling of desire" rendered participants like their ancestral virgin birth priestesses, women who were required to resist sex with human males. The stimulating of their reproductive functions was symbolic of "readying for motherhood under sexless conditions"— that is, parthenogenesis. The *agnus castus* was thus the perfect symbol of "chaste fertility," of virgin motherhood. Moreover, its inclusion in the rite supports the idea that Demeter's parthenogenetic mysteries originally involved an intimate working with plant substances. As I suggested earlier when discussing the narcissus of Persephone, careful regulation of women's menstrual cycles may have been necessary in the divine birth cult. The *agnus castus*, considered in chapter 4, was similarly associated with Hera, whom I argue in *CDB* also had a divine priestesshood (Rigoglioso 2009, 127–38).

Bawdy Joking and Inner Tantra

We may also discern from the ancient testimony that sexual stimulation was not, in fact, absent at the Thesmophoria. It was merely, I propose, redirected. We recall that, at some point during the rite, the women beat each other with a basket of woven bark known as the *morroton* as a form of fertility rite. I contend that this was a mock method of stirring up sexual energies. The *aischrologia*, or bawdy talk in which they engaged, I propose, was done with the same intent. As noted earlier, such jesting had mythological origins in the bawdy actions of Iambe/Baubo. Any woman who has participated in such illicit banter knows that doing so stimulates sexual arousal. Stehle's observation (2007, 171–72) about the meaning of this activity in the rite is particularly fitting: "It is as though sexual speech could replace intercourse and form an autonomous female form of fecundation. Intimacy now takes the turn of seeking imaginative sexual pleasure among women, including the goddess." Stehle, like Zeitlin, comes close to identifying what I suggest was at the heart of the Thesmophoria: the knowledge that female parthenogenesis was a manifestation of the generative power of both the goddess and her holy women. The female-focused sexual pleasure elicited at the rite, I propose, put participants in the state of autoerotic arousal in which I argued Persephone herself had been when she was abducted and raped. It also put them in the state that presumably would have been required of their ancestral virgin birth priestesses—the "narcissistic tantric" condition necessary to generate the spontaneous division of their ova. Again, we recall here the erotic description in the Gnostic text discussed earlier in the chapter, in which a "muse" desires herself to the point of conceiving a holy being.

Friendliness toward the Pomegranate

At the Thesmophoria, the women ate pomegranate seeds, at least on one of the days of fasting. However, they were forbidden to eat any seeds that fell on the ground, supposedly because the pomegranate tree was believed to have sprung from the drops of Dionysus's blood (Clement of Alexandria *Exhortation to the Greeks* 2.16). In contrast, the pomegranate was prohibited altogether, along with the apple, at the Eleusinian Mysteries, as well as at the Haloa, a winter festival for women held in honor of Demeter, Kore, and Dionysus. At the these rites, such fruits were forbidden presumably because of the gloomy memories they invoked regarding Persephone's abduction (scholiast on Lucian's *Dialogue of the Courtesans* 6.4, in Kerenyi 1967, 138).

As I discussed earlier in this chapter and in chapter 4 in relation to Hera, the pomegranate and, by extension, the apple were symbols of parthenogenesis. I thus propose that the original relationship of women to the pomegranate can be seen in the older festival, the Thesmophoria. There, the women were strongly connected to this fruit, I argue, because the rite maintained its roots in divine parthenogenetic birth more strongly than the later celebrations did. As I showed earlier in the chapter, eating the pomegranate was a magical invocation of divine birth originally unconnected with Hades. The fruit was also a birth control agent. Thus, I propose that the women's eating of its seeds served to honor the magical reproductive knowledge of their ancestral holy *parthenoi*, whom they had symbolically "become" through their enforced celibacy for the rite. In contrast, the fruit was prohibited at the Eleusinian Mysteries precisely because of its association with female-only parthenogenesis and the old matriarchy, as *hieros gamos* had become the Mysteries' rite of central importance.

I propose that the prohibition at the Thesmophoria against eating the seeds that fell to the ground was related to an understanding encoded in the story of Nana, discussed earlier: The pomegranate could also be used magically to instigate the conception of a holy male who was destined to become a full-fledged deity upon his ritual murder. We have already seen that Dionysus was a late arrival to the Demetrian Mysteries, one whose advent marked the transition from pure parthenogenesis to *hieros gamos* in the divine birth cults. Indeed, he was implicated as the very god who impregnated Persephone (as Zeus/Hades/Dionysus) and was subsequently reborn of her. Moreover, as mentioned, and as discussed more fully later in the chapter, the divine child announced at the conclusion of the Mysteries was apparently considered a manifestation of this god. We also hear of Dionysus's earthly birth through the priestess Semele and his death through dismemberment (e.g., Hesiod *Theogony* 940 43; Clement of Alexandria *Exhortation to the Greeks* 2.15ff.). Semele's conception of the god represented, according to Diodorus Siculus and Nonnus, as noted earlier, what was thought to be one of the god's first incarnations on earth. The "dismemberment" motif may have referred to a ritual means whereby he was fully apotheosized. Thus, I suggest that the injunction against eating the "fallen" seeds that could be associated with his birth/ death/rebirth was akin to Demeter's refusal of the wine in the *Hymn*: It was a sign of resistance toward Dionysian *hieros gamos* on the part of a religious complex originally dedicated to the pure parthenogenetic mystery of the two goddesses.

It is also interesting to note that the story of the pomegranate tree emerging from Dionysus's blood may have had its origins in a parthenogenetic myth originally focused on women. In Boeotia and elsewhere, the pomegranate was called *side* (Kerenyi 1967, 139). *Side* was also the name of various legendary women whose stories are significant in this context. One such Side committed suicide on her mother's grave because her father wanted to seduce her; from her blood the earth caused the pomegranate tree to grow (Dionysius *De Aucupio* 7, in Kerenyi 1967, 139). In the motif of the parthenogenetic creation of Side/the pomegranate from Ge/Gaia, we have an indication that the story refers to a priestess of virgin birth. Her refusal to have sexual intercourse with the "father"—that is, the symbolic patriarch—and her preference to die "on the grave of the mother" could be read as her resistance to *hieros gamos* practices and loyalty to the old method of divine conception. Another Side was none other than a daughter of Danaus, one who was said to have had a city named after her (Pausanias 3.22.11). I have shown that the daughters of Danaus were also priestesses of divine birth and that serving as an eponym was frequently a sign of divinization associated with such practice. Yet a third Side was a wife of Orion the hunter and was sent to the underworld by Hera for having rivaled herself in beauty with the goddess (Apollodorus 1.4.3). Kerenyi (139) conjectures that the addition of Hera to the story was late and superficial and that the real legend probably concerned a woman who undertook a descent to the underworld for the benefit of the community. That, as we learn elsewhere, Orion was not a friend to holy *parthenoi* may be related to this. For example, he sexually preyed on the virgin birth priestesses known as the Pleiades, as well as on a legendary female named Opis, who I argue in *CDB* was a divine birth priestess of Artemis (Apollodorus 1.3.5; Rigoglioso 2009, 92, 94, 152). The real reason for this particular Side's "descent to the underworld," then, may have had something to do, once again, with male disruption of female virginity or divine birth practices. Thus, in this conflation of Sides, we have the name of the parthenogenetically related pomegranate bestowed on holy *parthenoi* who resisted the disruption of their mysteries and were pressed to descend to the underworld. The parallels to Persephone should, by now, be obvious. Such stories emphasize why the pomegranate would have been embraced by the women at the Thesmophoria—unless the seeds touched the ground, whereby they became a symbol of the interloper into their mysteries.

Entering an Altered State of Consciousness

We see at the Thesmophoria possible evidence for women's use of plants not only to regulate their fertility, but also to enter an altered state of consciousness. As I argued earlier, and as I discuss more fully later in the chapter, the *kykeon* was likely a substance used to put initiates at the Eleusinian Mysteries into the trance required for their descent to the underworld. Demeter's drinking of the *kykeon* in the *Hymn* (208–10) may indicate that participants of the Thesmophoria also used it. For the fact that she imbibes it after (the bawdy) Iambe makes her laugh could be a reference to the *aischrologia* that was a part of the women's rite. Based on an analysis of the very name of the festival, I propose that the *kykeon* may *originally* have belonged to the Thesmophoria.[63] We will recall in the *Hymn* that Demeter rejects the wine (of Dionysus), stating that its use violates *themis*, or her law, in favor of a potion more suited to her own mysteries. The word *Thesmophoria* seems to have derived from *thesmoi*, meaning old, traditional, divine laws, or even a rite.[64] The term is, thus, related conceptually to *themis*.[65] Again, Demeter herself was popularly known as *Thesmophoros*, "Divine Lawgiver" (scholiast on Lucian's *Dialogues of the Courtesans*, in Brumfield 1981, 74). The name of the festival, therefore, may be translated as "The Bearing of the Holy *Themis/Thesmos* (Law) of Demeter." I propose that this "law" was Demeter and Persephone's great matriarchal law, with its attendant notions of respect for the feminine cycles inherent in a cosmos governed by a Virgin Mother. Part of that "law," as I have been attempting to demonstrate, involved entering into the goddess's mysteries—including, in their most holy and advanced form, generating a divine daughter parthenogenetically. This would have entailed a woman's using particular plant medicines, which meant drinking the *kykeon* into which such medicines were mixed.

A number of scholars agree that the *kykeon* was indeed entheogenic, although the precise psychotropic substance it included has been debated.[66] The word means a mixed or stirred drink. In the *Hymn*, it is a potion of barley groats and water, mixed with *glêchon,* a form of pennyroyal (Kerenyi 1967, 177, 179). Kerenyi notes that an oil derived of this plant, poley, can induce "delirium" and "spasms"—that is, it is hallucinogenic. A plant of the same family found in Mexico, *salvia divinorum,* similarly induces visions. Kerenyi (179) quotes Albert Hoffman: "The volatile oils contained in poley oil (*Oelium pulegii*) might very well, added to the alcoholic content of the *kykeon,* have produced hallucinations in persons whose sensibility was heightened by fasting." In Plutarch (*Moralia* 511C), we hear of the use of the Eleusinian *kykeon* by Heracleitus: When asked by the Ephesians his opinion on the subject of political concord, he downed a cup and left the speaker's stand in silence. Plutarch comments that this was a lesson on keeping peace by using what was at hand, rather than expensive things (perhaps alluding to the fact that peace was generally cemented with libations of wine). I would assert that the enigmatic Heracleitus was most likely reminding his audience of the visionary aspect of the drink at Eleusis, one that, as we will see later, allowed for the transcendence of petty human concerns and conflicts.

Interestingly, Riddle (1992, 53–54) reports that pennyroyal was also used as an emmenagogue and abortifacient, which would put it in the same category as the narcissus. As we saw, that plant was similarly used both to address female reproductive issues and to induce an altered state of consciousness. Pennyroyal was also linked to female sexuality in Greek comedy; in Aristophanes (*Peace* 712), a drink with pennyroyal is offered as a cure for too much sexual intercourse. Thus, that the entheogenic brew of the goddess Demeter may have been associated specifically with the regulation of female fertility supports the idea that we are once again firmly in the realm of female reproductive mysteries, both human and divine. It is not surprising, then, that an ancient text indicates it was women who presided over the mixing of the *kykeon* in vessels called *kernoi* at the Mysteries of Eleusis (Pollux 4.103, in Wasson et al. 2008, 93).

Altered-State Ascents and Descents

Entheogenic medicines have long been used in ritual the world over to stimulate journeys to the "otherworld" in a trance state. We see signs in the ancient texts that participants at the Thesmophoria engaged in such a journey. Evidence lies, first, in the very names given to one of the days of the Thesmophoria (or possibly the Stenia held prior to but considered part of it): *Anados,* "Upgoing," or *Kathados,* "Downgoing." Photius's assertion (s.v. *Stênia,* in Brumfield 1981, 80n34) about the meaning of the term *Anados* is important here: He says it referred to the "ascent of Demeter." A related word, *katabasis,* referred to a ritual descent into a cave, frequently for the purpose of entering the realm of the underworld. Pythagoras, for example, was reported to have undergone one such *katabasis,* subsequently regaling his students with dramatic tales of his experiences in Hades (Diogenes Laertius *Pythagoras* 8.41). Putting these ideas together, we can see that, as Foley (1994, 72) intuits, *Anados* and *Kathados* referred to the goddesses' traversing from one sphere of the universe to another. Because we know from the ancient fragments that women at the Thesmophoria commemorated Persephone's descent, I maintain that these terms indicate that participants themselves journeyed to the upper and lower worlds to communicate with their goddesses, whose province, as I discussed at the beginning of this chapter, included both realms.[67] The psychoactive nature of the *kykeon* allowed them to enter these worlds.

We find further evidence for an entheogenic journey of this nature in the scholiast to Lucian's statement that the chaste women known as "bailers" made ritual "ascents and descents" into the *megara,* or chasms. These *megara* are elsewhere described as underground chambers where sacrifice was made to the two goddesses who dwelt there and where the *hiera,* or sacred objects, were kept.[68] The fact that no evidence for such chambers has been found in Demeter's temples at Athens or Eleusis (see Brumfield 1981, 100n53) lends support to the idea that the scholiast is in fact describing "descents" and "ascents" conducted not literally in space/time, but inwardly in the trance state. The idea that the goddesses "dwelt" in the *megara* also affirms the idea the term refers to a reality in the "subtle worlds." Brumfield (238–39) offers helpful insights here:

> Clearly the underground realm, though it is the tomb of the dead, can also be viewed as the womb of Ge, from which new vegetative birth springs up. Descent to the *megara,* and return from them, is an action heavy with symbolic meanings. The celebrant dies and is reborn; she visits for a while the ultimate secret place, to deposit or retrieve *arrêta* [holy, secret things]; she mimics the actions of Kore, whose death and sexual awakening took

place on her descent to underworld realms, where the secrets of life and death are to be learned.

I agree with Brumfield that the *Kathados* involved a ritual descent to the "underground realm" that rendered the participant one with Kore. What is particularly significant is the implication encoded in the ancient understanding of the term *megara* that the place of death/rebirth and sexual knowledge was not the male "Hades-type" underworld of the later Eleusinian Mysteries, but rather a "female-type" underworld: the womb of Ge/Gaia and Demeter/Persephone. Perhaps it refers to a cosmic time/space when Persephone was ruler of the underworld and death, before Hades claimed dominion over this realm (see Spretnak 1978, 106). Furthermore, Brumfield's apt characterization of this "womb-like" underworld as the place where "new vegetative birth springs up" is in consonance with ancient Greek beliefs that Ge/Gaia was the *parthenogenetic* source of life, as I showed in chapter 1. Thus, I propose that the original intention of the *Kathados* associated with the Thesmophoria was to bring the participant to the mystical realm where knowledge of parthenogenetic conception was rendered plain and where the act was made possible. This very trance journey, as I discern in *CDB*, was a necessary part of any divine birth priestess's work. In this ancient rite, the women entered the subtle realms in which the holy *parthenoi* were thought to conceive the divine daughters of the goddess. Although their journey to this place as common citizen women was probably not intended to result in their own pregnancies, it served as a means by which they could symbolically reconnect with the core essence of the Matriarchal Mystery of the Two Goddesses: the parthenogenetic birth of the female out of the female, in both human and divine realms. It rendered them one with their goddesses and the female ancestral priestesses before them who had attempted this practice. It is no surprise, then, that the rites were guarded from male intrusion with such ferocity.

Following on the idea that *megara* were the "realms of the parthenogenetic goddesses Ge/Gaia, Demeter, and Persephone," rather than of the male Hades, we may conjecture that *the commemoration of Persephone's descent as abduction was not a part of the rite until the advent of patriarchy.* Even then, I suggest that the means of dealing with it in the Thesmophoria was very different from what took place during the Eleusinian Mysteries. As I have mentioned, and as I detail later in the chapter, during the latter rites the abduction was something participants had to experience directly *as a rape.* In the Thesmophoria, in contrast, all indications are that the rape was mourned but not experienced. The women's sitting on the ground and fasting may have represented the mourning of Demeter, who, in the

Hymn, refuses food because she is grieving (197–201). I propose that for the old matriarchal order, entry to the otherworld/underworld for the purposes of encountering the goddesses and acquiring their wisdom did not require violation.

I contend that this aspect is encoded in details provided in the ancient sources that various elements of the rite were intended to protect the ritual space from "snakes." Snakes had various meanings to the ancient Greeks. On one hand, they were believed to serve as "protectors" of sacred precincts often associated with goddesses or female oracular ability (see, e.g., Rigoglioso 2009, 122–23). Indeed, we see them depicted as such by the scholiast on Lucian's *Dialogues of the Courtesans* (in Brumfield 1982, 73–74) in describing their presence in the *megara* of the Thesmophoria. On the other hand, however, the snake was clearly a symbol of the male god or phallus. We recall that, in the Orphic story, Zeus rapes Persephone in his form as a serpent, impregnating her with Dionysus. Furthermore, Lucian's scholiast mentions that the bailers "descended" to the *megara* to carry up "snakes and representations of male members" (*drakontôn kai andreiôn schêmatôn*).[69] Here, we see the identification of the snake and the phallus, specifically in the Thesmophorian context.

I agree with Stehle (2007, 173), who discerns that the snakes in the *megara* "are an underworld motif." If we agree that the "descent to the *megara*" indeed was a ritual journey to the otherworld enacted by the participants of the Thesmophoria, then the various motifs described by the scholiast on Lucian's *Dialogues of the Courtesans* can be read in a new light. He tells us that the "bailers" who have purified themselves for three days—that is, they have abstained from sexual intercourse—descended into the *megara* to carry up the remains of pigs that had been thrown there as an offering to Demeter. They also carried up representations of snakes and phalli that were scattered along with the pigs. In going down, the women had to make noise, so as to frighten snakes away from eating the pigs. The scholiast affirms that the pig was a symbol of fertility, and elsewhere we hear that pig (*choiros*) was an idiomatic name for the female genitalia (Athanis, *Fragmente der Griechischen Historiker* 562 F1, in Georgopoulos et al. 2003, n14).

Thus, I propose what the scholiast is describing in prosaic terms as a rite related to the promotion of human and agricultural fertility was in fact something deeply esoteric about which he and the source from which he derived his information had little understanding. Indeed, both of them being men, they had probably discerned or been given only the superficial outlines of this female–only secret proceeding.[70] Specifically, I suggest that the scholiast is unknowingly describing an initial entry into the otherworld by women who first had to frighten the "snake/phallus"

from "eating/penetrating" the "pig/vagina." Their noisemaking probably refers to standard practices among shamans, where clapping, rattling,
and other forms of sound are used to dislodge negative spirits. The bailers, then, served as a "first guard" to render the space purified of male
energies so that the rest of the women could enter the "dwelling" of the
goddess and offer their "pig/genitals" up to the mystery of pure parthenogenesis. As I have noted throughout this chapter and in *CDB*, one of
the greatest dangers for a virgin attempting parthenogenesis in the trance
state was the unbidden advent of the god who wished to impregnate her.
Thus, the bailers rendered the space clear of unwanted male intrusion/
snakes. I suggest, then, that it is no accident that these women fashioned
themselves as "virgins" for this activity by refraining from sexual intercourse for three days prior to the rite. In becoming even more "virginal"
than the participants, who remained chaste only for the duration of the
celebration, they took on the role of the most honored representatives of
the holy *parthenoi* of old, the ancestresses who had descended in trance to
the realm of the pure generative capacity of the female.

Interestingly, we also see the idea that snakes had to be "banished"
from the proceedings in Aelian (*History of Animals* 9.26). The ancient
naturalist reports that the women at the Thesmophoria sat on *agnus castus*
because *it was believed to ward off snakes*, to the attacks of which the women
in their temporary huts were especially exposed. The danger may have
been practical, but, given the meaning of the snakes in the *megara* I posited
above, it was also, once again, probably magical. The fact that *agnus castus*
quelled sexual desire, meant, symbolically, that it helped the women ban-
ish "snakes" of the male persuasion.[71] This small detail affirms the argument that for the women to engage the realm of pure parthenogenesis,
they had to dispel the serpents/phalli that would be wont to disrupt their
activity and impregnate them with male spirit.

The bailers also managed the snakes in another capacity. They were
exclusively charged with "bringing up" from the *megara* the representations rendered in dough of serpents and phalli. Versnel (1992, 40) notes,
"overtly sexual symbols are handled by a group of women who have
strict instructions to preserve a state of purity." Indeed, I suggest that
it was only these women, serving as the most honored representatives
of the holy *parthenoi* of old, who would have been qualified to handle
the intrusive male element with impunity. They are the ones, too, who,
according to the scholiast, brought up the "pig remains" that were then
mixed with seed to fertilize it for a good harvest. Thus, it may be that
literal pigs and phallic representations were used as tools in the descent/
ascent journey, and were handled only by these specialized ritual agents.
As Stehle (2007, 172–73) explains, they "bring the humus to birth, as it

were, in a completely female cycle" that echoes the women "spur[ring] Demeter to reproductive energy without male input." In short, I propose that they were the leaders in a schema of virginal reproduction, one in which women's parthenogenetic fertility (pig/vagina) was symbolically and literally brought into identification with the parthenogenetic fertility of the grain/Demeter/Gaia.

Pursuit, Penalty, and Beautiful Birth

Several other details whose meaning has generally baffled scholars may be rendered sensible when seen in the context of the Thesmophoria as a rite celebrating daughter-bearing parthenogenesis, as well. One is the women's engagement in what was called the "Chalcidian pursuit." Hesychius (s.v. *diogma*) says the origin of this rite was an occasion on which women in the city prayed for the enemy to be routed, whence the enemy fled to Chalcis. It stands to reason that the practice must have had something to do with Demeter and Persephone more closely, however. In light of the theory of divine birth I have been applying here, I suggest that the activity was an expression of women's power in fending off spiritual attack. In this sense, I propose, it was similar to the ritual motif of the bailers making noise to frighten "snakes" away: It affirmed that women were capable of focusing their spiritual intention to ward off danger in the subtle as well as the phenomenal realms. The "enemy" here, once again, must have been understood as the male run amok. Indeed, the distorted masculine had proven to be an "enemy" of the Virgin Mother goddesses by raping them, as well as an enemy to parthenogenesis by pressing holy virgins into *hieros gamos* unions with gods. Thus, I read the Chalcidian pursuit as an activity that symbolically reaffirmed and restored women's ability to protect themselves and maintain their matriarchal secrets despite living in a male-dominated and oppressive world. It also may have represented their collective attempt to "reverse" Persephone's rape in the patriarchal period through the symbolic fending off of the "enemy" Zeus/Hades/Dionysus. It was, thus, quite possibly a remnant of the original Amazonian prowess of their goddesses and their founding ancestral priestesses.

Another obscure part of the Thesmophoria was an activity known as the "penalty" (*zēmia*). According to Hesychius (s.v. *zēmia*), this was "a sacrifice offered on account of the things done at the Thesmophoria." The implication here seems to be that it was a form of recompense for something carried out that was considered transgressive in nature. We have seen that many aspects of the rite were blatantly subversive from the perspective of the patriarchy; indeed, women almost completely overturned social norms. The Thesmophoria restored power and sacrality to activities considered ritually "polluting" in ancient Greece—female sexuality and bawdiness, "rotting" substances (the "humus" of Stehle), death, and birth. As Stehle (2007, 174) writes, "Contact with death is contact with the goddess. Demeter...delights in [women's] exposing of their hidden, 'shameful' sexual knowledge and parts." Moreover, the rite affirmed women's sovereignty and spiritual power and even endorsed female aggression in this regard. Perhaps, then, the "penalty" was a ritual nod during the patriarchal era to the forces and gods who were temporarily being disregarded, even dismissed, in favor of goddesses who promoted the "old ways" of Amazonian, parthenogenetic matriarchy. Alternatively, the "transgression" may have been toward the matriarchy itself: The allowance of phallic elements and the acknowledgment of Persephone's rape in the patriarchal later period may have been considered necessary compromises that had to be ritually propitiated in a matriarchal queendom.

The final puzzling detail that becomes clear in light of the argument being made here is the name of the last day of the festival: *Kalligeneia*, or "Beautiful Birth." We recall that *Kalligeneia* was a surname of Ge/Gaia and also the name of the nurse who taught Persephone how to "weave." In both cases, we see her connection to parthenogenesis, as has been discussed throughout the chapter. It should be clear in the context of this discussion that the "beautiful birth" to which the title attached to this day refers must have been none other than that of the Holy Daughter who had emerged parthenogenetically from the Virgin Mother. In contrast to the male "Brimos" emerging from the "Brimo" of the Eleusinian Mysteries, the child of the Thesmophorian birth, be she of the goddess or her human virgin priestess, was always female. This conception represented the culmination of the Demetrian matriarchal mystery with whose contours the women reacquainted themselves yearly through their ritual descent to the dwelling place of the two goddesses.

In summation, the women of the Thesmophoria recalled the original state of *partheneia* (virginity) of both the goddesses and their virgin priestesses. They returned to the "old ways" as mothers and daughters, free from the constraints of marriage. They re-entered a matriarchal world in which they were able to speak, eat, and drink in ways not permitted in patriarchal Greek culture. They honored Persephone's parthenogenetic generation from Demeter, grieved the disruption of pure parthenogenesis cosmically and terrestrially, and registered resistance against the appropriation of the Great Virgin and her earthly *parthenoi* to produce the sons of the Olympian gods. Finally, in remembering that women once had the capacity to give birth to divine female avatars in service to the matriarchy, they perhaps affirmed that such a capacity might be restored in future. The Thesmophoria continued to be celebrated alongside the Eleusinian Mysteries. Preserving the old ways in the women's minds, it allowed them, as Stehle (2007, 179) says, to continue to develop "their own ideas about what their intimacy with Demeter meant to their lives and fates."

The Eleusinian Mysteries: Known Fragments

I conclude this monumental chapter with an analysis of the second major festival that celebrated the rites of Demeter and Persephone: the Eleusinian Mysteries. As I did with the Thesmophoria, I first offer a summation of the extant information about this most famous ritual of the ancient world. I then follow with an analysis to show that these mysteries had as their foundation the practice of divine birth through *hieros gamos*. Moreover, I offer a new interpretation of what may have transpired during the Greater Mysteries, one that renders the proceedings suddenly clear, comprehensible, and part of a coherent philosophical whole.

The Eleusinian Mysteries were the most prominent of the mystery cults of antiquity and, according to Pausanias (10.31.11), were considered by the earlier Greeks to have been the most important of all religious rituals. In the historical period, the Mysteries were open to both men and women of all ages, slave or free, who spoke Greek and had not committed murder. Archaeological evidence suggests that the cult site at Eleusis dates at least as far back as the Mycenaean period (fifteenth century B.C.E.), although the bulk of the remains date to the eighth century B.C.E. (Mylonas 1961, 33ff., 57 ff.).[72] As mentioned, in Pausanias we learn that Eleusis was incorporated into the Attic state during the prehistoric period but that the town was allowed to retain control of the rites. The fact that the *Hymn* does not mention Athens is taken to indicate that it refers to the Eleusinian cult before Athens began involving itself in the Mysteries, a development that is generally dated to the mid-sixth century B.C.E (Richardson 1974, 6, 85). The Goths probably destroyed the sanctuary around 395 C.E., and imperial decrees of 390–91 C.E. prohibiting the celebration of pagan cults assured the demise of the cult of Demeter and Persephone (Foley 1994, 65 and n2).

The Lesser Mysteries

The great rite involved a preliminary stage known as the Lesser Mysteries, which took place in the month of Anthesterion (February/March). Held in Agrai near the Illissos River, a short distance outside Athens, the Lesser Mysteries were required as preparation for those who wished to experience the Greater Mysteries in fall (Scholiast on Aristophanes' *Ploutus*, in Harrison [1903] 1957, 559). The Lesser Mysteries were known as "the Mysteries of Persephone."[73] According to tradition, they were founded later than the Greater Myseries so that Heracles, who was not admitted because he was a stranger, could be initiated at the latter.[74] They were also said to have been an imitation of "what happened to Dionysus," which included his *hieros gamos* with the queen archon of Athens, the *basilinna* (Stephen of Byzantium, s.v. *Agra kai Agrai*; Kerenyi 1967, 51–52). Given that initiates learned of the marriage of Persephone, although we do not know in what form (Kerenyi 52), the overlap between Hades and Dionysus in this role must have been felt. Thus, we have in the Lesser Mysteries the strong theme of *hieros gamos* divine birth, with an implied connection between Persephone and Dionysus. The god appears to have had a double role here: In his somewhat veiled identification with Hades, he was the ravisher of Persephone.

The Greater Mysteries

The Greater Mysteries were held once a year for nine days in the month of Boedromion (September/October), just before the plowing and sowing in the autumn (Diodorus Siculus 5.4.7). Every fourth year, they were celebrated with special splendor in what was known as the *penteteris* (Mylonas 1961, 243). Each day of the festival centered on a different activity: the processing of sacred objects from Eleusis to Athens and back; bathing; animal sacrifice; the honoring of Asclepius and Iacchus/Dionysus; fasting; prayer; and ritual jesting, which may have included bawdy content (see, e.g., Brumfield 1981, 194–96). On the third day of the festival, a libation was offered to "Iacchus," a "double" of Dionysus; on the fourth, initiates carried his statue in the procession from Athens to Eleusis.[75] Priestesses also carried the "sacred objects" in "mystical baskets" on their heads (Plutarch *Phocion* 28.2; *IG* ii² 81.10, in Kerenyi 1967, 63). Priests and priestesses who descended from particular families were in charge of the proceedings. As noted earlier, the chief priests, or hierophants, hailed from the Eumolpidai and the Kerykes. The chief priestess of Demeter and Kore was generally a member of the Philleidai family and lived at the sanctuary (Clinton 1974, 76).[76]

At the Greater Mysteries, the first stage of initiation was known as the *myêsis* (Suda, s.v. *epoptai; IG* i².6B.4ff., in Richardson 1974, 20), after *myein*, "to close." The *mystês* (pl. *mystai*) was the initiate who closed his or her eyes and mouth to engage in the experience (Plutarch *Alcibiades* 22.3). Those who allowed a year to pass after their *myêsis* were permitted to return for the *epopteia* (Suda, s.v. *epoptai;* Plutarch *Demetrius* 26.2–3);

the *epoptês* was one who "saw." Initiates were individually sponsored and guided by *mystagogai*, or leaders of the *mystai*, and were permitted to return to the festival more than once.

The central part of the Mysteries, conducted within the hall of initiation (Telesterion), seems to have been divided into the *dromena* (things done), *deiknumena* (things shown), and *legomena* (things said).[77] The *orgia* (*Hymn* 273), or deepest part of the rite, was held as a strict secret. However, testimony from late Christian writers indicates that a sacred drama was enacted, in which initiates participated.[78] Clement of Alexandria (*Exhortation to the Greeks* 2.13–18) says that the rites commemorated what appear in his narrative to be a conflation of Orphic and Homeric elements, most likely reflecting the overlapping of practices at Eleusis at the time of his writing (second century C.E.). The Orphic aspects include Demeter's rape by her "son" Zeus (the goddess here being conflated with Rhea); her wrath (on account of which Clement says she received the name "Brimo"[79]); the "penance" or "supplications" of Zeus; the drink of "bile"; the tearing out of victims' hearts; "unspeakable obscenities" (*arrêtourgiai*); the birth of Kore; Kore's rape by a serpentine Zeus and conception of a bovine Dionysus; and the appearance of Baubo, who makes the goddess laugh by exposing her genitals. The Homeric elements of Clement's description include the abduction of Persephone by Hades as she picked flowers, Demeter's sorrow and search for her daughter, and the grain mother's refusal of wine. In Proclus, we hear that "sacred lamentations" were a part of the rites, as well (Richardson 1974, 25).

Clement also notes (2.18) that the *synthema*, or formulaic password, of the Mysteries was "I fasted, I drank the *kykeon*, I took (it?) from the chest (*kiste*), I did something (with it?), and deposited (it?) in the basket (*kalathos*) and from the basket into the chest" (*enêsteusa, epion ton kukeôna, elabon ek kistês, ergasamenos apethemên eis kalathon, kai ek kalathou eis kistên*) (trans. Brumfield 1981, 200). The Christian writer hints disapprovingly (2.19) that the objects used were of a sexual nature, perhaps representations of genitalia. He reports that they included images of serpents as the mystic sign of Dionysus, fennel stalks,[80] pyramidal cakes (probably symbolizing the female pubis), cakes with navels, and a woman's comb, which he blatantly says was a euphemistic symbol of the vulva.

Interestingly, in the same writing, Clement (2.14) also gives an alternative description of Eleusinian *synthema*. He may be conflating the tasks with those in the cult to Cybele and Attis, but the list is so similar to that of 2.18 that one may assume he is describing more or less the same phenomena in both.[81] As Harrison ([1903] 1957, 158) notes, "Demeter and Cybele were but local forms of the Great Mother worshipped under diverse names all over Greece." Thus, Clement's addition here of one activity performed—the "stealing into a bridal chamber" (*pastos*)—is instructive for what it may suggests about what transpired during the Greater Mysteries. This last is, as Harrison ([1903] 1957, 535) asserts, "a manifest avowal of a Sacred Marriage."[82] This idea that the hierophant and priestess literally may have enacted a *hieros gamos* is indeed asserted by Asterius, bishop of Amaseia at the turn of the fifth century, who, in writing that the entire mystery religion at Alexandria had its source in the Eleusinian Mysteries, declares, "Is there not there the dark subterranean passage (*katabasion to skoteinon*), and is it not there that occur the sacrosanct encounters of the hierophant with the priestess, of a man with a woman alone? Are the lights not extinguished? And does the multitude not believe that they achieve salvation (*sôteria*) through what the two of them do in the darkness?" (*Homilia 10 in S.S. Martyres*, in Kerenyi 1967, 117).[83] Lucian (*Alexander* 38), in describing the false prophet Alexander's parody of the rites of Eleusis, affirms the Mysteries' inclusion of a sacred marriage, as well as the birth of a god. Tertullian (*Ad Nationes* 2.7) may be echoing this idea in his rhetorical question "Why is the priestess of Demeter ravished if this is not what happened to Demeter?" His statement indicates that the sacred marriage enacted had a "rape" element, which becomes significant to my argument later.

At a critical moment in the proceedings, the *mystai* may have had some sort of vision of Persephone, possibly timed with the gong of the hierophant, the opening of an inner chamber, and the shining forth of fire or a great light (for ancient references, see Foley 1994, 68–69; Richardson 1974, 25). Accompanied by this light, the hierophant announced, "The Great Virgin/Maiden/Kore has given birth to a Divine Child; Brimo has given birth to Brimos!" (*hieron eteke Potnia Kouron, Brimô Brimon*) (Hippolytus *Refutation of All Heresies* 5.3). Again, the child may have been identified with Iacchus/Dionysus, who was either the son of Persephone (in the Orphic version) or the son of Demeter.[84] He also may have been identified with Ploutus (Wealth), the son of Demeter (Richardson 1974, 320). Among the very final moments was the *epopteia*, a vision, which apparently was induced by the hierophant raising up a sprig of wheat in silence (Hippolytus *Refutation of All Heresies* 5.3).

The last day of the Greater Mysteries was devoted to the *plemochoai*, the "pourings of plenty." This involved the overturning of two vessels filled with an unidentified liquid into a cleft in the earth. One was set up in the West, the other in the East (Athenaeus 9.496B). Looking skyward, an officiant cried out "Hye!"; looking toward the ground he cried "Kye!"[85] These words may be respectively translated as "Flow!" (or "Rain!") and "Conceive!"

The Eleusinian Mysteries as Cosmic Rape and Birth of the God

Foley asserts (1994, 139) that "the Mysteries emerge[d] from the private and even secret world of female experience." That female experience, as I have shown throughout this chapter, centered specifically on the mystery of virgin motherhood. However, as I have noted already, the famous rites at Eleusis represented a later stage in which that mystery was "interrupted" on the divine and human levels. I culminate this chapter by offering a new interpretation of the Eleusinian Mysteries as a propitiation to the two goddesses for the rape of Persephone, a mystical enactment of the divine birth of the male rather than the holy female, and a means by which initiates could re-establish their connection with a matriarchal cosmos.

Female Origins of the Rite

The feminine roots of the Mysteries may be discerned in the prominence and nature of the female leadership at Eleusis. Noting a comment by Dionysius of Halicarnassus (*Roman Antiquities*) that women, in particular, performed rites at Demeter's temple in Arcadia, Harrison ([1903] 1957, 146–47, 150) posits that the Mysteries were probably at first controlled by women. We see one sign of women's precedence in the fact that, on the night initiates arrived at the sacred precinct, women occupied the Telesterion for a ritual of dancing and singing known as the *pannychis* (Euripides *Ion* 1074f; Aristophanes *Frogs* 445–46). We see another sign in the title of the most important female official: *Priestess of Demeter and Persephone*. As Clinton (1974, 76) asserts, the fact that her title specifically refers to the individual names of the goddesses indicates that her role was "probably attached to the sanctuary at an earlier date than the hierophant." Moreover, although the dominant actor in the Mysteries, the hierophant, was male, for the rites he "emasculated" himself by means of imbibing hemlock (Hippolytus *Refutation of All Heresies* 5.3; Origen *Contra Celsum* 7.48), rendering himself, symbolically, female. This ritual act seems an acknowledgement of both the original power of the feminine in the Demetrian cult and the necessity of maintaining the feminine energy as central to the successful execution of related rites. His act reflects the very tone of the entire Mystery celebration as being steeped in "the secret world of female experience," to refer to Foley's comment earlier. I argue later that all male initiates symbolically had to become "women," as well, to the point of being sexually penetrated by the phallus of the god in imitation of Persephone's rape.

Stehle (2007, 177–79) argues that the Mysteries were a downgraded version of the Thesmophoria in which women's practice was disguised. The Mysteries, she contends, were "co-opted and adapted" by men, who continued elaborating them with "more overtly political community content." Agreeing with this, I would emphasize that the primary element disguised in the Mysteries was the origin of the Demeter/Persephone cult in pure parthenogenetic practice. As I posited earlier, the "elaborations" made to transform the Thesmophoria into the Mysteries involved appropriating holy *parthenoi* for the purpose of bringing male avatars to the earth plane. This argument is lent support by the possible presence of a very ancient cult of virgin priestesses associated with Eleusis known as *hiereiai panageis* (all-holy priestesses), who may have helped carry the sacred objects to Athens and back in *kiste*, or chests, on their head. Also called *Melissai*, or "Bees," they were celibate (Hesychius s.v. *panageis*).[86] Their name tells us that they were part of Demeter's larger cult, in which priestesses were also known as *Melissai*.[87] Again, their virginity and relationship with the bee suggests that they were originally dedicated to attempting divine birth. Their possibly having carried objects on their heads also calls to mind the karyatids of the Erectheion in Athens, who I similarly posited were priestesses of divine birth. I propose, therefore, that the *hiereiai panageis* may in fact have been a holdover from the pre-patriarchal era at Eleusis, when divine birth was dedicated to parthenogenesis. It may be that Saesara was a significant ancestress of this period, as I discussed earlier.

Although we do not know precisely what items priestesses carried in the chests between Athens and Eleusis, Clement's description of the contents of the chests that initiates handled, mentioned above, suggests they probably included symbols of phalli (Kerenyi 1967, 66). This would be congruent with the later *hieros gamos* stage of divine birth to which the Mysteries were, I propose, devoted. As I discuss in *CDB*, priestesses probably used artificial phalli in *hieros gamos* rites to stimulate the sensation of sexual union with the god in the trance state (Rigoglioso 2009, 27). As I detail later, during the nights of the Mysteries, initiates probably also used such phalli for a similar purpose. That the phallus would have corresponded with a later stage of the Mysteries is corroborated by the generally accepted idea, noted earlier, that Dionysus was a late arrival to the various mystery celebrations of Demeter and Persephone (Harrison [1903] 1957, 146–47, 150).

Entering Altered-State Reality

As we recall, women's centrality in the Mysteries is also evidenced by the fact that they were in charge of mixing Demeter's special potion, the *kykeon,* which was a significant element in the celebration. Anyone initiated at Eleusis had to drink it. Although the hallucinogenic nature of the *kykeon* is more veiled in the ancient descriptions of the Thesmophoria, it becomes blatantly obvious in accounts of initiates' experience during and after the Mysteries. Plutarch's excerpt of a passage from Themistius's essay "On the Soul," for example, makes this clear. The passage describes how the soul at the point of death has the same experience as those initiated into the Greater Mysteries:

> At first one wearily hurries to and fro, and journeys with suspicion through the dark as one uninitiated: then come all the terrors before the final initiation, shuddering, trembling, sweating, amazement: then one is struck with a marvellous light, one is received into pure regions and meadows, with voices and dances and the majesty of holy sounds and shapes: among these he who has fulfilled initiation wanders free, and released and bearing his crown joins in the divine communion, and consorts with pure and holy men, beholding those who live here uninitiated, an uncleansed horde, trodden under foot of him and huddled together in mud and fog, abiding in their miseries through fear of death and mistrust of the blessings there. (Trans. in Mylonas 1961, 264–65.)[88]

To anyone who has worked with sacred plant compounds, it is plain that this dramatic experience of the Eleusinian *mystai,* undertaken on one of the final nights of the rite, could only have been instigated by the ingestion of a psychotropic substance.[89] Terror, trembling, sweating, and, finally, the experience of ecstatic communion with ancestors and beings in other realms are all classical aspects of trance journeys embarked upon with the use of entheogens. Clearly, initiates to the Mysteries encountered what shamans and other spiritual practitioners have experienced the world over: a symbolic death and rebirth that felt very real. As Aristotle observes (fr. 15, in Foley 1994, 69), the initiates did not learn (*mathein*) anything, but rather were made to suffer or experience (*pathein*) the Mysteries and thereby undergo a critical shift in consciousness. That what initiates undertook was no mere intellectual exercise, but a deeply felt, first-hand experience, is emphasized by Kerenyi (1967, 107) in his comments about the Mysteries: "Religion and cults that live a thousand years are not based on parables alone. *A religious experience* is a very different matter, and we must assume that such an experience was present at Eleusis, for this alone could have given the parable content and validity."

Moreover, I contend it is only an entheogen-induced state that could have provided the *mystai* with an experience dramatic enough to change their views on life and death to the degree reported by ancient commentators. The rhetorician Sopatros describes the experience at Eleusis as follows: "I came out of the mystery hall feeling like a stranger to myself" (*Rhetores Graeci* 8.114–15). Pindar claims (fr. 137, 1997, ed. Race) that, as a result of taking part in the Mysteries, the initiate no longer feared death, for he or she "knows the end of life and knows its...beginning." Isocrates (*Panegyrikos* 4.28) echoes that the *mystai* had "better hopes for the end of life and for all eternity." Similarly, Cicero (*On the Laws* 2.14.36) claims that the experience "gave a reason not only to live in joy but to die with better hope." The Homeric *Hymn to Demeter* declares (480–82), "Blessed is the mortal on earth who has seen these rites, but the uninitiate who has no share in them never has the same lot once dead in the dreary darkness" (trans. Foley 1994). Sophocles, putting the same idea into the mouth of a character in one of his plays, says, "Thrice blessed are those among men who, after beholding these rites, go down to Hades. Only for them is there life; all the rest will suffer an evil lot" (fr. 837, in Kerenyi 1967, 14).

Whatever the actual psychotropic element in the *kykeon*, the idea that it was entheogenic is strengthened by the detail that the initiates engaged in a prolonged period of restricted diet and fasting prior to imbibing it. Just as Demeter drank it after fasting (Hymn to Demeter 47), initiates of the Greater Mysteries likely did so, as well (Richardson 1974, 165). Fasting is common practice all over the world prior to the ingestion of entheogens; it is undertaken, in part, to prepare the body physically and energetically for the absorption of a psychoactive substance, which can typically cause nausea and other physical symptoms.[90] Indeed, Clement's description, noted earlier, of initiates imbibing a "drink of bile" may refer precisely to this aspect of the *kykeon*. Fasting often has the benefit of lessening the accompanying nausea and, certainly, reducing the amount of bile should a person indeed vomit. Eating little or nothing can also induce visionary states independently and, thus, may have functioned to heighten the effects of the *kykeon* (Kerenyi 1967, 179).

The argument that entheogens were used at Eleusis is, finally, the only sensible way to account for the fact that great numbers of initiates, as many as three thousand people at a time (Aristides *Panathenaic Oration* 373), could have had a similar experience in such cramped quarters. The restricted footage of the sanctuary, even the exterior grounds, would not have permitted enough space for a great dramatic spectacle (Richardson 1978, 25). It is likely, rather, that initiates simply sat on the tiered steps that lined the Telesterion and went inward. As noted, the word from which Mysteries derived, *myein*, means "to close." That "closing" most likely referred to the closing off from the exterior world and moving into the interior world that were part of such a journey. It may, at some points in the ceremony, have also involved the literal closing of the eyes (Kerenyi 1967, 96), an impulse that many practitioners experience under the influence of entheogens. The entheogen would have allowed for the "seeing" that, as we know from epigrammatic testimonies and a bas relief of human eyes found at Eleusis, was an essential part of the Mysteries (see, e.g., Kerenyi 1967, 97–98; Richardson 1974, 229). The emphasis on "seeing" is also evident in the title for the *mystês* who came for the experience more than once: the *epoptês*, "he/she who has seen." I propose that the entire inner journey was guided by the hierophant, priestess, and other personnel who, as discussed earlier, descended from special families. It seems reasonable to suggest that these families possessed and passed down the knowledge of how to navigate the underworld shaman-ically—and how to guide others in it—for the thousand-year period for which we have evidence that Eleusis operated. Seated on the steps of the Telesterion, then, and under the guidance of the sacred lineage holders, the *mystai* closed their eyes, became quiet, and experienced the vision of a lifetime.

Being Raped: The Dildo of Descent

It is likely that the initiate enacted the last three ritual steps of the *synthema* in a trance state under the influence of the *kykeon*: "I fasted, I drank the *kykeon*, I took (it?) from the chest (*kiste*), I did something (with it?), and deposited (it?) in the basket (*kalathos*) and from the basket into the chest." In such an altered state of consciousness, initiates would have experienced these activities far more profoundly than in an ordinary state. Indeed, I propose that it is only by means of the psychotropic potion that participants would have been able to enter into the proper mindset to experience the steps of the rite in a spiritually meaningful way. Thus, what we have is a picture of individuals in an entheogenic state enacting some kind of solemn ritual involving sacred objects. What were those objects, and what were the actions performed? Discerning the answer has occupied scholars for more than a century. I offer here an analysis based on the ideas put forth in this chapter about the meanings of the Demeter/Persephone mythologem and related cultic activity.

In developing this argument, I first explore the motifs of the *kalathos*, "little" basket, and the *kiste*, "big" chest, as they relate to the *synthema*. As we saw in the fragment by Apollodorus of Athens, Persephone was using a *kalathos* as a repository for her "weaving" at the time of her abduction. Kerenyi (1967, 66) thus intuits that the *kalathos* of the *mystai* was proba-bly an implement associated with Persephone. As to the *kiste*, on an urn depicting Heracles' initiation into the Lesser Mysteries is a snake twining around such a basket (see Kerenyi 1967, 57, fig. d). We recall that, in the Orphic tradition, Persephone was raped by her father Zeus in the form of a snake and that Zeus/Hades/Dionysus formed one divine complex, each god being understood as a manifestation of the same entity. Kerenyi thus posits (66) that the presence of the snake on the urn may be an allusion to Persephone's encounter with this male god complex. We recall that Demeter-as-Rhea was raped by Zeus, as well. On the urn, it is Demeter who sits on the *kiste mistica* around which the snake twines. The creature's upper half is depicted resting on and emerging, tellingly, from her lap.

As I proposed earlier, the *kalathos*/"little basket" was a symbol of the womb/vagina of Persephone. Again, this is suggested by the fact that it was the "repository" for her weaving; that is, it was the very womb in which she was magically creating a child—initially alone, and then through the intrusion of Zeus/Hades/Dionysus. I suggest that the *kiste mistica*/"big basket" was a complementary symbol of the womb/vagina of her mother, Demeter, who had also experienced rape. We see this depicted visually on the urn in the positioning of the goddess: She is sitting directly on it. That the *kiste* was understood to be a metaphor for the womb is evident in Aristophanes (*Lysistrata* 1182–84), where Lysistrata humorously says to the men, "Now keep yourselves nice and clean so that we women can then entertain you in the city with the contents of our *kistai*" (Burkert 1983, 271). As I have shown throughout this chapter, there was really no separation between Demeter and Persephone, one being the parthenogenetic twin of the other. Thus, the *kalalthos* and *kiste* were, taken together, the "womb of the Virgin Mother." The snake coiling about the *kiste mistica* and emerging from Demeter's lap, therefore, was symbolic of the phallus used to rape/impregnate this double goddess.

It is significant that, in this same image, the initiate blatantly caresses the head of the snake as it pokes out from Demeter's body (Harrison [1903] 1957, 546). Of this detail, Kerenyi (1967, 59) says, "To make friends with the snake was Dionysian." I propose that the image was specifically understood to be the phallus of the god Zeus/Hades/Dionysus. I further submit that the "caressing" or "making friends" with the serpent on the urn was a visual allusion to the initates' own encounter with the phallus during the Greater Mysteries, and possibly also the Lesser Mysteries, which, as we saw, were blatantly centered on the "marriage" of Persephone in a strongly Dionysian context. More to the point, I propose that this image refers to an artificial phallus taken from the *kiste* by the initiate and used in a sexually explicit way as part of enacting the *synthema*.

I am not the first to approach such an idea. Based on Clement's assertion (*Exhortation to the Greeks* 2.19) that the *kistai* contained reproductions of male and female genitalia, Albrecht Dieterich early on argued that the object taken from the *kiste* was a symbolic phallus. He proposed that the initiate took it and placed it on his or her breast as a means of unit-ing with the goddess and becoming her child. Otto Kern went so far as to assert that the initiate came into symbolic union with the goddess by manipulating "his" own genital organ in a symbol of the female vulva, the *kteis*. (This, of course, precludes consideration of what the female initiate would have done.) Charles Picard suggested that a manipulation between a symbolic phallus and *kteis* was enacted by each initiate as a means of achieving union with Demeter and Persephone.[91] I propose that these scholars were in the right neighborhood but had not quite found the right door. All of them ignore the fact that the Mystery celebration involved the initiate entering what was, as I have established, primarily a *female* experience. Thus, the androcentrism of their arguments leads us in the wrong direction.

I propose that enacting the *synthema* at the Greater Mysteries required the initiate to simulate Persephone's intercourse with the phallic god. More to the point, it required the individual to *be raped by the god, just has the goddess had been raped.* It is this rape, I assert, that instigated the partic-ipant's own descent into the underworld, just as it had Persephone's. The *willingness to experience the great drama of the goddesses* was the secret pass-word that gained the *mystai* entry into the mystical worlds of those dei-ties, where profound knowledge of the mysteries of life and death, and of the individual's own relationship to the divine realms, would be revealed. To know the Mysteries of the Virgin Mother, one had to be willing to become the Virgin and experience the cosmic violation of the Matriarchy by the Male. One had to be raped to death. By being "known" in this way, one would come to "know."

As we saw earlier, in describing the phallic objects in the chests asso-ciated with the Mysteries, Clement specifically identifies the serpent as a symbol of Dionysus. Elsewhere, it is affirmed that tools of the wine god's rites typically included phalli (Sophocles fr. 760, in Kerenyi 1967, 57n35). I propose, then, that the actions in the *synthema* of "taking from the big chest" and "putting in the little basket" were veiled references to the ini-tiate taking the artificial phallus of Dionysus from the womb of Demeter, the original cosmic source of the masculine, and inserting it into his/her womb/body-as-Persephone. Put blatantly, women would have inserted the phallus into their vaginas, men into their anuses. All male initiates were thus rendered symbolically "female," just as the hierophant became a "woman" by imbibing hemlock to make himself temporarily impo-tent. The degree to which males took on female identity in connection with the Mysteries can also be seen, for example, in coins of the Emperor Gallienus from 265–66 C.E.: They read "Gallienae Augustae" and depict him as a divinity wearing a wreath of Demeter's ears of wheat. The explanation as to why his name would be in the feminine form as well as the dative, meaning, "belonging to," is that he attached particular importance to his initiation at Eleusis (Kerenyi 1967, 145n122). He perceived himself to have become "emperor as goddess" and "emperor belonging *to* the goddess," that deity being Demeter/Persephone. It was understood that unless a man became "female," he could not enter into the queendom of the underworld. Thus, in this violent-erotic encounter of rape, male and female initiates were torn open to be miraculously impregnated with/by the god, the late-arrival Dionysus, who himself engendered cosmic knowing in humans through his own entheogen, wine.[92]

Although on the surface the idea that a dildo was used this explicitly may seem an absurd and shocking assertion, we need only turn to the Church fathers to affirm that initiates indeed enacted something so obscene as to prevent the men of god from describing the acts directly. Clement (*Exhortation to the Greeks* 2.13) says the Mysteries celebrated *arrêtourgiai,* "unspeakable, shameful, horrible things." Immediately after revealing the *synthema* (2.18), he exclaims, "Beautiful sights indeed, and fit for a goddess! Yet such rites are meet for the night and torch fires" (Clement, 1919, trans. Butterworth). Clearly he is asserting that initiates engaged in something salacious. A bit later (2.19), he alludes to this more pointedly: "[N]ight is for those being initiated a temptation to licentiousness . . . and the torch-fires convict unbridled passions." Presumably referring to the "great light" or "fire" shone at the end of the Mysteries, he adds, "Light convicts your Iacchus." Finally (2.19), he condemns the practitioners for worshipping "parts of the body, which, from a sense of shame, are truly too sacred to speak of." Again, among the items of the *kistai* of the initiates he lists "the serpent of Dionysus," which may refer precisely to a dildo. Thus, Clement affirms that the rites engaged the initiates in entering into a highly charged sexual state that involved obscene actions and symbols associated with the god Iacchus/Dionysus.

The idea that initiates inserted an artificial phallus into themselves may be further alluded to in another mysterious cry allegedly uttered by initiates: "Cross the bridge, O Kore, before it is time to begin the three-fold plowing."[93] This, I propose, may be a sexual reference to the "plowing of the orifice of Kore" that was part of the original cosmic drama. An ancient equation between agricultural "plowing" and sexual intercourse indeed can be seen in Hesiod (*Theogony* 969–74) and Homer (*Odyssey* 5.125–30), where the union of Demeter and Iasion takes place in a field, and "may reflect a mystery ritual of *hieros gamos*" (Richardson 1974, 317). In Aristophanes (*Lysistrata* 157ff.), males' bawdy jokes about "plowing" and "fertilizing" indicate a clear connection between these activities and sexual intercourse in the Greek mind. The reference to "threefold"

plowing in the Eleusinian exclamation, in particular, also may be an allusion to Triptolemus, whose name means "threefold warrior" and may be
linguistically associated with the *neios tripolos,* the "thrice-plowed field,"
as well (Kerenyi 1967, 126–27). This links the cry with what I have
argued was a figure thought to have been conceived through a *hieros
gamos.* These allusions, I contend, indicate that the cry of the initiates
served as a foreshadowing of their own taking on the role of the Kore as
Raped Virgin.

Extant information about another festival of Demeter, Kore, and
Dionysus, the Haloa, a female-only rite celebrated in mid-winter at
Eleusis, further affirms that artificial phalli were used in erotic and
"obscene" ways in relation to the story of Persephone's rape. A scholiast on Lucian's *Dialogue of the Courtesans* (6.1, in Brumfield 1981, 108–9)
reports that at the Haloa, images of male organs were displayed and "performed as a symbol of the procreation of men, since Dionysus, who gave
the wine, made it a potion which stimulates one to intercourse." The
origin of the practice is the legend that an oracle ordered shepherds to
make and dedicate clay phalli in recompense for having killed Icarus after
becoming crazed by Dionysus's wine. The scholiast says that women at
the Haloa were initiated by engaging in obscene talk and lewdly bran-
dishing replicas of male and female organs. Priestesses whispered in the
women's ear "unspeakable" (*aporrêton*) things concerning *klepsigamia.*
The latter means "rape" or "illicit love" and likely refers to the rape of
Persephone by Hades (Brumfield 1981, 113).

Thus, we have a rite in which the phallus and the rape of Persephone
were conjoined amidst sexual stimulation through *aischrologia.* We have
no further information about exactly how the phalli were used, but the
scholiast's statement that the images were "performed as a symbol of the
procreation of men" may intimate that the women at the Haloa indeed
used them as dildos. This may be further implied in his subsequent comment that such performance had to do with Dionysian wine, which
"stimulates one to intercourse." As I mentioned earlier, Dionysian wine
was likely an entheogen used by women to enter a trance state in which
they united with the god sexually. In *CDB,* I argue that the women's
engagement with Dionysus in this regard involved using artificial phalli.
I also show that the same was probably true of the *basilinna,* who engaged
in a yearly *hieros gamos* with the god in Athens. Among other women's
initiations elsewhere in the Mediterranean world, the "obscene" gesture
of *anasuromai,* the lifting of the skirts, was enacted by women who were
"otherwise the soul of propriety" (Lincoln 1981, 80). Thus, subversive
and seemingly shocking sexual elements were indeed a part of ritual in
antiquity, enacted by the most ordinary of citizens.

Baubo as Dildo

Further support for the assertion that initiates of the Mysteries triggered their descent to the underworld through the insertion of a dildo may be found in the figure of Baubo (Iambe of the *Hymn*). As mentioned briefly, Clement (*Exhortation to the Greeks* 2.18) reports a bit of Orphic theology in which Baubo succeeded in soliciting laughter from the grieving Demeter after lifting her skirts to display her vulva. Clement's passage has been translated in various ways; here I use Butterworth's (Clement 1919):

> [Baubo] drew aside her robes, and showed
> A sight of shame; child Iacchos was there,
> And laughing, plunged his hand below her breasts.

However, Arnobius (*Adversus Nationes* 5.24–26, in Georgopoulos et al. 2003) renders the story this way:

> [Baubo] at once drew up her garments from down below
> and revealed to the sight the form of her privy parts;
> which Baubo tossing with hollow hand—for their
> appearance was puerile—strikes, handles caressingly.

Georgopoulos et al. (2003) note that Arnobius elaborates in his explanatory remarks that Baubo's vulva had the shape of a *"nondum duri atque hystriculi pusionis"*; the form was like that of "a little boy's, not yet hard and rough with hair." "The sense," they observe, "must be that Baubo handled what appeared as a childlike *membrum virile* in her womb." Noting that parts of the Clementine text have been widely held to be corrupt, they amend it to read as follows: "and with *her* hand Baubo, laughing, tossed and jerked it (the *tupos* = Iacchus) under (her) womb." They conclude, "It was something like a little prepubertal phallus which layed [*sic*] encompassed between Baubo's external genitalia.... Her appearance was that of a female, while her external genitalia presented elements of both sexes, both a vulva and a juvenile phallus."

In other words, despite the gloss by most modern translators, the ancient texts tell us that what Baubo displayed to Demeter was a vulva that was hermaphroditic, at once female and male. As Georgopoulos et al. (2003) write,

> [Baubo's] ambiguous pudenda rendered explicit the unity of sexes: that the different formations characterizing the male and female nature are fundamentally the same. In the cosmic womb, the penetration is complete, to

the point of fusion....Differentiation is a tension within the same thing
that is bound to be resolved eventually into the re-affirmation of its underlying unity. In [this] context...we may understand Demeter's otherwise
miraculous emotional change at the sight of Baubo's genitalia.

What they aptly discern is that Baubo revealed herself to be a representation of the cosmic unity, the "Female that contains the Male." She was
mirroring back, reminding Demeter of her own ultimate female powers
as a parthenogenetic creatrix. It is this that caused the Great Goddess to
snap out of her grief for her raped daughter/self. She remembered that she
was a Virgin Mother, still powerful.

The image of the "hermaphroditic/phallic" Baubo renders sensible
something that has puzzled scholars for quite some time: the significance
of her strange name in the larger schema of the Eleusinian complex. As
Lincoln (1981, 80), notes, Baubo's name "literally means 'vagina' or a
'mock vagina,' counterpart to a dildo (*baubôn*)." Baubo was frequently
represented iconographically as a naked headless torso with her face
appearing in the abdomen and the vulva serving as her chin. Lincoln
(81) remarks on the "markedly phallic shape" of the figurines, which
renders them "reminiscent of Baubo's implied male counterpart, Baubon
(dildo)." What we see in this constellation of meanings and allusions is
this: Baubo *was* the dildo, the dildo that was at once phallic and vulvar.
A penis-within-a-vagina, a vagina-within-a-penis, she was, indeed, the
ultimate symbol of parthenogenetic reproduction in a mother-centered
universe.

I suggest the imagery and wordplay associated with Baubo as a central motif in the *aition* for the Mysteries further supports the argument
that initiates indeed used a dildo in conjunction with the *kykeon* to
stimulate their underworld journey. Certainly, these elements are consistent with such a notion. By grasping the various allusions, we may
more fully understand the meaning likely associated with the use of
the dildo in the rite: The initiate had to be "raped" by an implement
that was at once the god's phallus (Dionyus/Iacchus) and the goddess's
vagina (Demeter/Persephone). The Baubo/Baubôn thus incorporated
the mystery of both female parthenogenesis and *hieros gamos*, or male
parthenogenesis-through-rape. The initiate entered a realm in which
boundaries between male and female, life and death, this world and
otherworld, heavens and underworld, were dissolved. It was, nevertheless, still the realm of the feminine, the Virgin, where Persephone
was queen. Clement's assertion that Baubo appeared as part of the
Mystery rites thus may refer to the presence of the dildo-understood-
as-Baubo.

An image on a fifth-century *pelike* vase now in the British museum may also be relevant here. In this rendering, plants are depicted as phalluses growing from the ground. A woman stands sprinkling something over them from a small chest as though they are soon to be harvested. The attitude of the woman suggests that of a priestess, and the portrayal of the phalluses seems to allude to a connection with psychotropic plants that were an important part of Greek life.[94] This image seems to link the phallus/Baubo(n) with entheogens. Might it serve as a visual pun referring to the idea that the dildo used in the Eleusinian rite also served as a mortar that the initiate used to grind a portion of his or her own drugs? Although priestesses may be recorded as having prepared the *kykeon*, the notion that they could have provided enough extract to be sufficient for as many as three thousand participants seems questionable.

Support for the idea that *mystai* may have prepared their own psychotropic compounds using a pestle-as-phallus may be found in Aristophanes' *Plutus* (290ff.). Ruck (in Wasson et al. 2008, 131n5) interprets the scene in this way: "[A]s the chorus dances the obscene accompaniment to [Dionysus's] visit, the phallus is employed as a mortar [*sic*] for preparing the *kykeon* and then becomes the intoxicant, wine without water, for them to lick like goats." At Eleusis, then, the *kalathos* may have been the "mortar" in which the ingredients of the *kykeon* were ground. Still, the ultimate *kalathos* would have been the orafice of the initiate, who may have inserted the herb-covered pestle-as-Baubo/god's phallus as a means of absorbing the entheogen into the bloodstream. Perhaps the initate was already under the influence of a *kykeon* that had been drunk and was now taking on another dose in this way to intensify the journey. It may be significant in this regard that one of the main ingredients of the *kykeon*, *glêchon* or *blêchon* (again, pennyroyal) was also used as a bawdy metaphor for a woman's pubic hair (Aristophanes *Lysistrata* 87–89). In Greek herbalism it also connoted illicit sexuality, given that perfumes and ungents were made of it (Ruck, in Wasson et al. 2008 110–11). In the secret rite of the Greater Mysteries as I have deciphered it, the *kykeon* indeed would have been associated with a sexuality so illicit that it has taken us nearly two thousand years to uncover it.

Grieving for the Matriarchy

As the ancient writings indicate, Persephone's abduction was not the only drama that initiates experienced first-hand during the Mysteries—they also experienced the grief of Demeter.[95] Like Demeter, who the *Hymn* relates engages in a mournful, nine-day fast while searching for her daughter, so the initiates fasted, perhaps also in part to experience the goddess's sorrow directly (Richardson 1974, 165). Moreover, as part of the rite, men and women "sought out" Persephone (Lactantius *Epitome of the Divine Institutes* 18 [23].7), further enacting the role of Demeter.

Thus, it seems that initiates experienced both the rape of the Feminine, as well as the grieving of the Feminine over the great cosmic travesty. Given that the story they encountered was, as Foley (1994, 105) observes, "a conflict between genders," it seems reasonable to assume that the *mystai* would have entered into a deeper appreciation of this gender war than ever before. As I have demonstrated throughout this chapter, this war marked the cosmic moment in which the Masculine overpowered the Feminine. That is, it was the moment at which the great cosmic Matriarchy, governed by a Virgin Mother, received the blow from which it never fully recovered. I contend that the influence of mind-altering medicines would have rendered this grief particularly acute and real for the initiates. Just as they were required to experience the rape of Persephone to be permitted into the halls of wisdom, so they had to know, deeply, what Demeter, the Great Virgin Mother of All, had suffered. They were constrained to feel the longing for the lost daughter, to engage in a profound inner search to find her. Further, as Kerenyi (1967, 145) observes, they became the goddess looking for *herself* in her daughter. This means, too, that they were searching for a lost part of themselves. I contend that, in their otherworldly journey, they were searching for the lost female power that had once been inherent in cosmic, as well as human, matriarchy.

Thinking along these lines, Neumann (1963, 323–24) discerns that the Mysteries offered the male initiate, in particular, the opportunity to come into connection with his own feminine, pre-patriarchal aspect. It is no wonder, then, that an initiate of the stature of Emperor Gallienus was thereafter willing to take on a female identity in his public image. The Mysteries required both men and women to acknowledge what Kerenyi (1967, xxxiii) calls "the *feminine source of life*." Here, we also recall from chapter 4 Hera's title as Virgin Mother, "(female) origin of all things." I would emphasize that this feminine source was specifically understood to be *parthenogenetic* in nature. Even though males were living under—and in many cases promoting—patriarchy, the Mysteries forced them to "switch" rather than "fight," at least temporarily, to embrace the goddesshead in her still-to-be-reckoned-with capacity as Virgin Creatrix. The masculine was tempered and transformed in its passage through the mysteries of the Virgin Mother, just as Zeus/Hades had been tempered and transformed by passing through the alchemical chamber of the *arrhêtos koura* to be reborn. Indeed, Dionysus was famous for being a gentler, more effeminate rendering of masculine deity. It is clear from the great honor accorded the Mysteries that, to the ancients, the two goddesses still retained power over the realms of death and human-otherworldly communication, power that even Zeus and the male gods of the patriarchal *aeon* could not fully eradicate or control. In short, even well into the Christian era, Demeter and Persephone still "had it."

Witnessing the Divine Birth

As the Demetrian myth and Mysteries reveal, matriarchy remained something that the patriarchalized populace had to contend with. Not being able to erase it entirely, they had to work with—and around—it. As I mentioned earlier, although the Mysteries served to "propitiate" Demeter and Persephone—to atone for the grave violation of the Feminine—they simultaneously, and perhaps perversely, served to perpetuate customs that continued to violate the matriarchy and the cosmic reality of the Virgin Mother. Namely, they turned the acknowledgment of Persephone's rape (as found also in the later version of the Thesmophoria) into a formal ritual incorporation of *hieros gamos* intended to engender a male holy child. Harrison ([1903] 1957, 563), too, recognizes that the central mystery at Eleusis was the sacred marriage and birth of the holy child, culminating ritual acts by which union with the divine was achieved for the initiates.

As mentioned earlier, I propose that this divine birth was understood to be no mere metaphorical event, but, at least in the earliest days of the rite, was believed to have resulted in a *literal* conception of a divine son or king. Indeed, I have proposed that the Mysteries were founded precisely to insert the production of the male Zeus/Hades/Dionysus avatar into the older (Thesmophoric) proceedings intended to engender the female Demeter/Persephone avatar. They turned what was once a strictly parthenogenetic affair into a tool to populate the patriarchy with the sons of god(s). This understanding resolves the paradox long discerned about the Mysteries that Brumfield (1981, 204) articulates: "The divine child [whose birth is announced at the Eleusinian Mysteries] remains a problem, because it is difficult to explain the ritual emphasis on the birth of a (male) child, when the myth is concerned almost entirely with the regaining (rebirth?) of a female child." There is no real contradiction if we understand that the Mysteries were, in a sense, the Thesmophoria (Demeter→Persephone) overlain by *hieros gamos* (Persephone→Dionysus). The Eleusinian rite raised the sacred marriage ritual, more privately practiced in other quarters of the divine birth cult, to the level of public festival, albeit one enshrouded in secrecy.

In support of this argument are ancient textual references, mentioned earlier, that the priestess and hierophant engaged in a *hieros gamos* rite at some point during the Mysteries celebration. If we accept that the hiero-phant indeed made himself temporarily impotent by ingesting hemlock, we see that such a ritual could not have involved his physical union with the priestess. This need not render the idea of a sacred marriage rite implausible. Rather, according the taxonomy of divine birth practices that I posit in *CDB* and note in the introduction to the present book, it would place the rite in the penultimate slot, as *hieros gamos* of the priest-ess directly with the god in trance state, without the participation of a human male surrogate embodying the god. Again, as I also propose in *CDB*, such a rite most likely involved the use of an artificial phallus. This would certainly be congruent with the important role of the Baubo/ *baubôn*/dildo in Eleusinian lore. Thus, I propose that the hierophant's role at the Mysteries was merely to ritually oversee the priestess's sex act with Zeus/Hades/Dionsyus via the dildo. As we will recall, Tertullian's comment indicates that the priestess's experience simulated the rape of Demeter/Persephone, which would further be consistent with the entire schema I am proposing here—the male participant in her rite would have been the god himself, not the hierophant. The hierophant's ritual cry, "Brimo has given birth to Brimos!" was likely an announcement that the priestess had concluded her sex ritual, which was conducted apart from the initiates in secrecy. It may be that the rite was not intended to result in a pregnancy every year, but rather at specified intervals. We recall that the Mysteries were celebrated with extra verve every four years as the "Great Eleusina"; perhaps it was only at this "great" time that the divine conception was attempted in full force.

Uniting (with) the Ineffable

Reading between the lines of the ancient testimonies, we may discern that the Eleusinian Mystery experience was multivalent, multilayered, neither solely one thing nor another, and sometimes two opposite things at once. The theme of divine birth through violation/*hieros gamos* was at the core, but so was the theme of the unification of the Mother and Daughter. We see this thread in the Homeric *Hymn to Demeter* and in a famous relief from Eleusis depicting Demeter and Persephone bent toward one another in an attitude of pleasant connection. We also see it in ancient testimonies hinting that in experiencing the underworld, the initiates, like Demeter, "sought out" Persephone. Finally, we see it in reports that, like Demeter, they eventually "found" her.

To "call the goddess" at the right moment, toward the end of the mys-tery rite, the hierophant beat the *echeion*, a kind of gong used in the Greek theater to simulate thunder, probably borrowed from an archaic cult of the dead (scholiast on Theocritus 2.35–36b, in Richardson 1974, 25). The resulting experience for participants was more than just intellectual. They were believed literally to "see" the goddess (Kerenyi 1967, 94). To the more mystically inclined Greeks, it was indeed possible to see deities and non-corporeal entities. Psellus (*Ad Johannem Climacum*, in Kerenyi 1967, 114) describes the phenomenon of *autopsia*, a term for divine apparition, which Iamblichus (*On the Mysteries* 2.4, 7.3) reports could be induced by magical ceremonies. In the *Phaedrus* (250BC), Plato has Socrates confirm that visions were seen in the Eleusinian Telesterion in his statements that "the souls beheld the beatific spectacle and vision and were perfected in the mystery of mysteries" and that the "initiates...were allowed to see perfect and simple, still and happy Phantoms (*phasmata*)" (in Kerenyi 1967, 98). Plutarch (*On the Perfection of Virtue* 81DE) intimates that initiates also witnessed "a great light," as, again, does Plato (Phaedrus 250BC): "[P]urer was the light that shone around [the initiates]" (in Kerenyi 1967, 98). If we accept that the *kykeon* was psychotropic in nature, we may understand how it was that initiates "saw" the Ineffable Virgin, the *arrhêtos koura*. For travelers working in altered states of consciousness, the direct and very real experience of deities "appearing" on the inner planes is claimed to be a frequent occurrence, particularly if specific divinities are consciously invoked.

As noted earlier, the phenomenon of Persephone's "appearance" seems to have been aided by the blazing up of fire. Fire is a tremendously powerful element that facilitates the envisioning of non-corporeal beings; dancing flames seem to embody specters and phantasms in startlingly uncanny ways, particularly when one is in the special state of "seeing" brought about by trance. Moreover, it is common for participants working in groups to enter a mutual telepathic state in which similar thoughts, ideas, and visions are experienced. I propose, therefore, that the appearance of the fire at Eleusis was the moment at which initiates opened their eyes. Looking into the blazing flames, they witnessed together shapes and specters that struck awe: visions of Persephone herself at a culminating moment of glory. We recall here the "fire" through which Demeter, in the Homeric *Hymn*, passed the child Demophoön to seal his immortality. Thus, with the "fiery," "light-filled" culmination of the Mysteries, we are fully in the territory of divine birth and divine death/immortality. It is highly relevant in this regard that, as I show in *CDB*, ancient texts hint that the miraculous conceptions of the divine birth priestesses likely occurred through the effect of "a ray of light" (Rigoglioso 2009, 132).

The appearance of Persephone amidst fire and light suggests that she herself was seen as an exalted being of light for having achieving her divine task of conceiving the god's double. It seems clear that the hierophant's proclamation in a loud (possibly singing) voice, "The Great Virgin/Maiden/Kore has given birth to a Divine Child; Brimo has given birth to Brimos!" reflected the divine conception by Persephone, as well as by the earthly priestess who enacted the goddess's ravagement in a secret chamber during the Mysteries. This is supported by the fact that *Brimo* was indeed an epithet for Persephone as queen of the realm of the dead, as well as for Demeter; the name meant "angry" or "terrifying."[96] Moreover, the scholiast on Apollonius (in Smith 1870, s.v. *Brimo*) offers an alternate derivation of the name from *Bromos,* saying it referred to the crackling of the fire, given that Hecate, the underworldly goddess of the crossroads, was conceived bearing a torch. It is attested that Persephone herself was conceived as the goddess of fire (Euripides *Phaethon* 59–60, in Kerenyi 1967, 101). We see from the foregoing that *Brimo* was at once Persephone and Demeter. This identification, I propose, referred to their original nature as a single parthenogenetic being, as I discussed at the beginning of the chapter. Drawing these associations together, we may read that the epithet *Brimo* referred to the Great Goddess who was raped, was enraged over that rape, conceived, and was eventually lauded amidst the cracking fire of Hecate/hell/Hades as the *arrhêtos koura,* the Ineffable Virgin Mother who became the Terrifying Underworld Queen. We recall that the child of Persephone was "Dionysus/Iacchus/Brimos." In death, from the underworld, the divine child was born. Amidst the flames of hell, the holy son was conceived. I contend that initiates perceived these divine mysteries as part of their profound journey.

As mentioned, another manifestation of the holy child of Demeter/Persephone was Ploutus, whose name means "Riches." The "wealth" here was surely that obtained by journeying the underworld—namely, wisdom. Thus, "Brimo has given birth to Brimos!" also reflected another divine "conception": that of the initiates' rebirth of self. By undergoing the "rape" of the goddess, the *mystai* were granted the knowledge of the nether realms, which included the realization, as evidenced by the ancient testimonies offered earlier, that they would never truly die. What was "rich" about this knowledge was that, once again, it was no mere intellectual concept. It was an understanding that *mystai* thereafter possessed deeply and unequivocally *because they had been to the land of death, and they had come back.* They had seen their Dread Queen. They had been *united with her.*

In this, initiates experienced not only unification *with* the Feminine but also something even deeper: the unification *of* the Feminine. They experienced Persephone's return to the Mother. It was, as Kerenyi discerns (1967, 147), the rejoining of the goddess to herself, to her "double" aspect. In the language of the theory I have brought forth in this chapter, that "rejoining" was the rendering whole of the Virgin Mother who had been torn asunder by the intrusion of the Masculine. It was the restoration of the parthenogenetic Matriarchy.

There are perhaps no better words to express the profound levels of paradox and meaning encoded in this aspect of the Eleusinian Mystery experience than those of Georgopoulos, Vagenakis, and Pierris (2003):

> What has been separated reunites in coition. By the same token chthonic darkness and celestial light come ultimately to the same reality, as do death and life. Death is (re)birth. Universal cyclicity ensures eternity. Kore lives for ever, eternally reconstituted in her Virginity through never-ceasing copulation, remaining in actuality unraped by Malehood and Death in the midst of total rape. Even more, malehood emerges from the womb of Ur-femininity. Similarly, death is a modification of life, not the other way around. One pole in the pair of opposites enjoys a certain priority, in that it better expresses the original unity. Demeter has no reason to grieve anymore for the loss of her daughter. Truth came to her in a flash from Baubo's [hermaphroditic] genitalia.
>
> Harmony reigns supreme amidst the apparent chaos of discord and disorder.

We see in this stunningly insightful analysis that, in the heart of each initiate, the Eleusinian Mysteries effected a kind of healing of the "gender war" that had raged in the cosmos and the psyches of humans. The experience allowed participants to see that the Great Rape was a horrific event that, like any travail understood from a higher perspective, cracked open the universal soul—a feminine reality—to a greater understanding of itself. It enabled them to understand that, as Brumfield (1981, 228) notes, "Kore....was the first to achieve what is made available to all through the Mysteries." It inspired them to honor her as the Great Sacrifice, the being who surrendered pure parthenogenesis to conceive the male god's double for the benefit of expanding knowledge/wisdom itself. At the same time, it permitted them to grieve a heinous act that *never should have happened and was profoundy unnecessary for the expansion of knowledge/ wisdom.*[97] Finally, it assisted them in resolving this excruciating paradox in the understanding that, ultimately, the Feminine Universe remained intact as the core out of which the Masculine emerged. This is what may have helped them endure the ultimate understanding: Undergoing this wisdom-provoking ordeal may, on the most exalted level, have been Persephone's choice.

In engaging the Mysteries, initates themselves made the same choice: to allow themselves to be raped. They allowed it, sensing the "hard-won benefits" that would be granted them as a result of their self-sacrifice into the realm of horror. They took the road to Eleusis, the road less traveled, to partake of the great gift that the Two Goddesses, who they understood to be ultimately One, had granted humanity upon the advent of the Masculine violation. As Foley (1994, 82) expresses it, "Persephone's role in what has been called 'the traffic in women' creates a new relation between earth, Olympus (heaven), and Hades (the world of the dead below) by linking them for the first time in her own person. [She]...thus makes possible the promises offered to the initiates in the Mysteries." I would agree, with one amendation: The Mysteries were likely not the *first* introduction of human beings to the realms "above" and "below" under the auspices of Persephone. As I argued, the Thesmophoria had probably involved women in the *Anados* and *Kathados* for a long time prior. Rather, I propose, the Mysteries now allowed *males*, in particular, to "go up" and "go down" into the hidden female realms. The rites also may have served to revivify humanity's connection to the land of the immortals in an epoch in which the esoteric knowledge for doing so was fading under the influence of the hyper-masculine patriarchy.

We have seen that both *hieros gamos* and the reconstitution of the Feminine were celebrated at the Eleusinian Mysteries. I propose it is in the final moment inside the Telesterion that the rite returned to its origins in the pure—mother/daughter—parthenogenetic reality: The hierophant, in profound silence, held up a sprig of wheat. According to the source of this claim, Hippolytus (*Refutation of all Heresies* 5.3), a Christian commentator, this was "the mighty and wonderful and most perfect mystery for an *epopt*." As I argued earlier, it was also the original mystery associated with the Thesmophoria: the parthenogenetic birth of the "grain" out of the "grain," the Daughter out of the Grain Mother. That in Greek plant shoots were called *korai* (Porphyry, in Eusebius *Praeparatio Evangelica* 3.11), the title of Persephone as parthenogenetic virgin, further attests to the ancient understanding of the cyclicity of the plants as a female affair, one of generation and regeneration in parthenogenetic perpetuation.

The "pourings of plenty" enacted on the last day of the Greater Mysteries may also have been a reference to the rite's older matriarchal origins. As we will recall, this ritual act involved the overturning of two vessels accompanied by the skyward cry "*Hye!*" ("Flow!" or "Rain!") and the earthbound cry "*Kye!*" ("Conceive!"). Proclus (*In Timaeum* 293C) interprets these utterances as invocations of humanity's paternal and maternal origins. This may be the case, but, as Kerenyi (1967, 141) notes, Proclus "lived too late to have witnessed the normal, traditional functioning of the Mysteries." What seems apparent is that the invocations relate to "conception" on the part of the earth. As I discussed in chapter 1, that conception was originally seen a parthenogenetic act. Ge/Gaia was understood to have generated numerous plants and animals—even humans—out of her own body. Moreover, as I discussed at the beginning of this chapter, in her original form Demeter was identified with Ge/Gaia. Thus, the concluding invocation of the rites at Eleusis, too, may have been a reference to the original mystery of pure parthenogenetic birth, once again bringing the initiate full circle to realm of the matriarchal reality of the Virgin Mother.

Speaking of other mystery rites at Samothrace, Diodorus (5.49.6) says initiates were thought to become "more pious, more just, and better in everything." We may assume the same was true of the *mystai* of Eleusis. Indeed, it would be hard to imagine that one could encounter the deities and see the beginning and end of life without having one's sense of morality completely transformed. At Eleusis, I contend, this was owing to the tempering effect of the "Ur-feminine," the Virgin Mother as Supreme Being. Having crossed the boundaries to the netherworld, suffered the Great Violation, propitiated Demeter/Persephone with their very lives for their continued part in the travesty, witnessed the goddesses' sacrifice and miracles, and been graced by the Terrifying Cosmic Womb to which they would eventually return, they could live with more heart, soul, and equanimity. This was the gift granted humanity by the Virgin Mother, the double goddess of parthenogenesis who "remained unraped by Malehood and Death in the midst of total rape."

CHAPTER 6

THE GNOSTIC SOPHIA: DIVINE GENERATIVE VIRGIN

Angeleen Campra

This chapter presents Sophia of the Gnostic texts as one manifestation of the long line of powerful female deities discussed previously. Sophia, the Virgin, is divine generative force, fundamental life energy that manifests as the generation of life through the cycles of birth, death, and rebirth; as the wisdom inherent in the expression and order of the universe.

This divine female authority, long unacknowledged in the West, is firmly situated within historical Jewish and Christian traditions. She is present as *Hochma*—literally, "Wisdom"—in the Hebrew wisdom litera-ture of the fifth to first centuries B.C.E., predating the Hellenized *Sophia*, also "Wisdom," of later Greek translations and texts. This latter manifes-tation, in turn, predates the anglicized *Wisdom* of later English transla-tions of these texts. Sophia's story is central to the Hellenized Valentinian Gnostic creation myth of the first century C.E., and her strong voice in *The Thunder: Perfect Mind* establishes her authority through her connec-tions to a long line of ancient deities.

When I speak of Sophia as divine generative force, I am referring to that numinous energy of Source that humans call "divine" and that manifests as the intelligent generation and continuation of life through the cycles of birth, death, and rebirth. Sophia and various other female deities, some of whom have been discussed in this book, are manifes-tations of that deep underlying energy that for millennia has been associated with generativity, fecundity, life, death, decay, order, and wisdom. That is, they are emblems of the "wisdom" inherent in that generative progression of life and order. In her early Hebrew manifestation as *Hochma*/Wisdom, Sophia was there, before all creation, "from the beginning" (Proverbs 8:23, New Jerusalem Bible). The wisdom and order of the system existed before the system even manifested itself, much in the way a seed holds within it the entire potentiality of the plant that will grow from it. In examining the ancient texts, I have come to the conclusion that Sophia of the Gnostic tradition, as the exemplar of divine generative force, existed "when,"[1] in that liminal time before "the beginning," *before the starting point of our current creation stories*. I posit, in short, that she is, like Athena/Neith, a Prime Mover, an autogenetic goddess who created herself out of the All. In this chapter, I discuss evidence to support this image of the Gnostic Sophia as a primordial Virgin Mother.

Sophia as Bridge to an Older Paradigm

Much of the richness, as well as the tensions, in Sophia's Valentinian Gnostic story can be traced to her relationship with two ancient and differing worldviews. One posits a *generated universe*, in which the divine is immanent in what is manifested, and interconnection and unity of life are the norm. Another posits a *created universe*, in which the divine is separate and remote from creation, and separation and opposition are the norm. A generated universe, in which the connection between Source and creation is seen as fundamental, allows "differentiation" to exist without diminishment or devaluation. A created universe, on the other hand, in which Source and creation are seen as disconnected, encourages a hierarchically dualistic worldview based on opposition.

Sophia's story bridges these two cosmologies. In doing so, it reveals, in microcosm, how humans have conceived the divine image and how they have moved from materiality to abstraction, from Earth to Wisdom to the Word. When viewed through the ideology of a created universe, Sophia is an enigma full of paradox and contradiction. When seen from the more ancient perspective of a generated universe, however, she expresses complexity and wholeness.

Her story speaks of times of cultural change and upheaval (Cady, Ronan, and Taussig 1989, 50–53; Schroer 2000, 30–33). As the Gnostics redrew the heavens to attempt to better understand their earthly uncertainties, they expanded their image of the divine. Pagels (1979, 49) says of the Gnostic texts that, although "their language is...unmistakably related to a Jewish heritage, instead of describing a monistic and masculine God, many of these texts speak of God as a dyad who embraces both masculine and feminine elements." This expansion of the divine image to include a Mother/Father Source appears to express a void felt by the Gnostics during those uncertain times and a subsequent attempt to expand and refashion their spiritual and secular realities through the acknowledgment of a female divine image (Engelsman [1979] 1987, 74–75; Schroer 2000, 30). Sophia rose out of a patriarchal worldview, but I argue that both iterations—Hochma/Sophia of the Wisdom literature of the fifth to first centuries B.C.E. and Sophia of the Valentinian Gnostic myth of the first centuries C.E.—reveal the attributes of the more ancient Virgin Mother deities from the areas neighboring West Asia.

Sophia of the Valentinian Cosmogony

I begin with the Gnostic Sophia's portrayal in the Valentinian creation myth as recorded in *Against Heresies* (1.1–8) by Irenaeus, the second century Bishop of Lyons,[2] and in the work of Gnostic scholar Robert Grant (1961). The following plot line, greatly simplified, provides a brief overview to help the reader focus on the Sophia narrative while navigating the complexities of the myth. In the subsequent section, I present a more detailed amalgam of the story that follows Irenaeus more closely.

In the Valentinian cosmogony, Sophia is the last and youngest of the 30 *aeons*, 15 male and female pairs who, together, comprise the attributes of the divine. She, like her sister and brother *aeons*, had a burning desire to better know and reconnect with the Source whence they came. Unlike the others, however, she acted on that desire, even though it was against the rules: she acted without permission from the parents, and she acted without her consort, both of which were strictly forbidden. Therefore, according to this story, in creating parthenogenetically, as female by herself, she was able to generate only a "less-than-perfect" result, something weak and ugly Eventually, however, her overreaching was contained; she was purified, restored to her place, and became known as the Upper Sophia. The result of her "passion," the Lower Sophia, was banished to a lower realm and given form, and she was also redeemed. This Lower Sophia, with a consort, brought forth Ialdabaoth, the demiurge creator of the material world.

Summary of the Valentinian Creation Story

This story[3] begins not just "in the beginning," but "before the beginning"—in fact, "in the pre-beginning," when, alone before all, eternal, ungenerated, uncontainable, was the Source; the first pair; or the first parents: the male Forefather, Depth, or Pre-beginning and the female Thought, Grace, or Silence. Wanting to make themselves known, together they produced the first generated pair, or syzygy, the male Mind, or Only-begotten, and the female Truth.

These first four, Depth and Silence, Mind and Truth, were the root of all existence. The *aeons*, Mind and Truth, as the begotten or generated couple, understood their purpose to continue this generation. Together, they emitted Word/Logos and Life/Zoe, who, in turn, brought forth Man and Church. These third and fourth pairs of *aeons* each united so that they, too, could glorify the Parents with emanations of their own. Word and Life generated five additional pairs of *aeons*, and Man and Church emanated six. In total, including the original pre-beginning source couple Depth and Silence, there came to be fifteen pairs of *aeons*, male and female, thirty in all, of which Sophia/Wisdom and Theletos/Willed were the last. Together, these thirty represented the divine attributes and constitute the Pleroma,[4] *the fullness or all, the full expression of divine characteristics.*

Sophia and Willed were the final syzygy, the last emanation, the furthest from the Source, from the Pre-beginning Parents. This last pair of *aeons*, like all those who came after Mind and Truth, longed to know the Source, the root of their beginnings. Only Mind and Truth, the only-begotten pair who were generated directly from the Source, had this knowledge, which was forbidden to the others because "Silence, by the Father's will...wished to lead all of them to the thought and longing of seeking for their Forefather" (Grant 1961, 165). However, Sophia's longing for this knowledge and understanding, this connection, was so great that she acted without consent of the Parents "and experienced passion apart from the embrace of her consort Willed" (165).

Sophia was unable to reach the Parents, but her "thought" and action bore results: "She brought forth a shapeless being, a thing such as a female [by herself] can bear" (Grant 1961, 166). She had undertaken a task that was impossible within that system, and it was only her encounter with Limit or Cross, the consolidator or maintainer of boundaries, who was emanated specifically to contain her and limit the damage done to the Pleroma as a whole, that kept her from dissolving into the uncontainable vastness of the Source. Instead, her emanation or desire, that which she brought forth from herself, was separated from her. Sophia was made pure, reunited with her consort, and returned to her place in the Pleroma. There, she became known as Upper Sophia. Her emanation was banished from the Pleroma and became known as the Lower Sophia or Achamoth.

To prevent this passion and longing for knowledge that they knew to burn also within the breasts of the other *aeons* to cause another near catastrophe, the Parents, Depth and Silence, directed the Only-begotten couple, Mind and Truth, to bring forth yet another syzygy, Christ and Holy Spirit,[5] to instruct the aeons on "the nature of pairs" (Grant, 1961, 167) and the unknowable nature of the Parents, and to restore balance or rest. When all the *aeons* "became equal in form and mind" (167) and shared the same knowledge of the Parents, the previous inequities and turmoil were erased, and a state of perfect harmony existed. Out of this harmony, each pair contributed the best they had to offer and together emitted the most perfect fruit of the Pleroma: Jesus, also called Savior. Instead of a female consort, Jesus was emitted with a band of angels as companions and guardians.

When separated from the Pleroma by Limit, Achamoth, the "desire" or passion of Sophia, was considered "like some natural desire of an *aeon*, but it was shapeless and ugly because it comprehended nothing. Therefore it was a weak female fruit...like an abortion" (Grant 1961, 166–67, 170). Achamoth received shape and intelligence from Christ, who was extended down from the Pleroma through Limit or Cross to give her form and awaken in her a sense of her divine origins. Striving to disentangle herself from the passions and fear that were banished from the Pleroma with her, she turned toward the light that left with Christ when he returned to the Pleroma. Because of that act of conversion by Sophia—literally, a turning around—Christ sent the Savior Jesus to provide knowledge and healing for her. Freed of her passions, Achamoth "joyfully conceived the vision of the lights with him, [i.e., the angels with him] and in her longing became pregnant with fruits after their image, a spiritual embryo after the likeness of the guards of the Saviour [*sic*]" (172). Thus did Ialdabaoth, the Demiurge, come into being, the Craftsman, who created the material world A system mirroring the Pleroma was set into motion with Achamoth or Lower Sophia representing the invisible, unknowable Parents, the Demiurge as the Only-begotten Son, and the archangels and angels he subsequently created standing in for the other *aeons*.

Ialdabaoth created the seven heavens of the cosmos where he dwelt, and his mother, Sophia/Achamoth, dwelt above him in the eighth heaven, just below the Pleroma. Ialdabaoth was ignorant of the larger system, of the "pre-beginning," of the existence of his mother, and of the Pleroma above her. Thinking he was the sole lord and creator, he created out of ignorance, unaware of the role played by his mother, who removed herself from material creation but remained a bridge between it and the upper realm.

After creating the universe, the Demiurge made the first human, fashioning a body from liquid and matter, and was a conduit for breathing the spark of divinity into it, unknowingly acting as an instrument of his mother Achamoth. The Demiurge himself did not contain this spark of divinity and was as unaware of it in his human creations as he was unaware of the existence of the larger system of which he was a part. The universe, therefore, was created for the purpose of promoting transformation and shaping and instructing spiritual humans. As Grant (1961, 175) observes, "The end will come when all that is spiritual is shaped and perfected in knowledge." This implies the advent of awakened Gnostics "who have perfect knowledge about God and have been initiated in the mysteries of Achamoth" (175).

Parthenogenesis in Sophia's Story

In this elaborate cosmogony, Sophia plays a major—and parthenogenetic—role. The wisdom attribute of the divine source, the last emitted, she longs to know, reconnect with, and unite with her source, as do all the other *aeons* emitted after the Only-begotten couple. The Only-begotten indeed want to share this knowledge, but the Parents forbid it. Sophia acts on her passion and longing, against the proscription of the Parents and without her consort. Because Sophia is divine, her action or "thought" does produce results, but, in this story, because of her distance from the Source, because she acts alone, and because she is female, her divinity is not considered "great" enough to realize her goal; she does not produce "whole" or adequate results. Therefore, she is said to create a shapeless, formless thing, like an abortion, a weak fruit that becomes Achamoth or Lower Sophia.

The system of the Pleroma is based on syzygial pairs, female and male energies that, in most instances, work cooperatively and in combination. Parthenogenesis is forbidden—yet not when it comes to the male. Regarding the "Limit" or "Cross" mentioned in the narrative, Irenaeus (*Against Heresies* 1.4) tells us, "The Father afterwards produces, in his own image, by means of Monogenes [Mind or Only-begotten], the above-mentioned Horos [Limit], without conjunction masculo-feminine. For they [the Valentinians] maintain that sometimes the Father acts in conjunction with Sige, but that at other times he shows himself independent both of male and female." Thus, in this case, emanation is shown to happen outside the syzygial pairing that has been established as the norm. This act of parthenogenesis is both possible and productive of a viable, "good" result when it originates with the Father through Mind. However, when it originates with Sophia, it is considered "impossible" and results in an "imperfection." We note here the similarity to Hera, whose parthenogenetically produced children were either deformed or monstrous, as discussed in chapter 4. The emanation of Jesus without a female consort represents another significant departure from male/female syzygy as the norm—one, again, that is permitted to the male and not the female. Reviewing what has been presented throughout this book, we can understand that such departures mark a reversal of the older order in which the Sacred Female was a Virgin Mother. We see that, in the Gnostic story, although parthenogenesis produces a daughter, as in the matriarchal condition of Demeter/Persephone, we are firmly in the grip of a patriarchal paradigm.

As we continue to examine this story, we see that Sophia is the one female figure among the *aeons* who plays a significant individual part in the drama. She has been assigned the role that brings about the rupture of the Pleroma or divine order, represents the descent of the divine into the lower realms, and causes the creation of the material world. Herein lie the tensions inherent in her story. I posit that these tensions reveal Sophia's older role as a Great Mother/Virgin Mother. Although she is limited by the constraints of the role designated to her in this later, patriarchal tale, her actions indicate an inherent sense of limitlessness. Indeed, neither her innate divinity nor her generativity can be contained within the confines of this limiting role. I suggest that Sophia acts as pure wisdom, as all-knowing, as unlimited potentiality. She acts as wisdom-as-the-ability-to-create (see Vermaseren 1977, 9–11; Long 1993, 18), as expression of Source. Although this story reduces her to a "placeholder" for the divine female generatrix, apparently even the deeply patriarchal and monotheistic worldview that permeates it was unable to envision a creation story that did not contain this generative energy expressed by a female. While Sophia acted willfully, still, she acted without her consort, Willed. This foreordained act of disobedience resulted in the creation of the material world.

Creative powers are revealed in Lower Sophia, as well, who unites with Jesus and his angels as her consort. With them, she conceives Ialdabaoth,[6] who, despite all his powers to create the cosmos and the material world, remains ignorant of his mother and of the Pleroma above her. Lower Sophia breathes spirit into humans through her son, animating his creations that would otherwise remain lifeless (Ialdabaoth does not contain spirit and is unaware of his mother and her actions). Achamoth or Lower Sophia retires to a realm between the Pleroma and the universe. We see that this manifestation of Sophia, although "less" than those above her, is still linked to their authority in her role as mother of the creator of the cosmos and as a bridge between the worlds. It is she who contains the power to generate life, not the son, who is only capable of creating inert, material substance. Once again, the story points to an older generatrix role for Sophia, repeated in a lower "octave."

Sophia in *The Thunder: Perfect Mind*

I now focus on the hymn *The Thunder: Perfect Mind*, which I suggest carries the imprint of this generative female figure as a Virgin Mother. *Thunder* is a self-proclamatory hymn or poem by an unnamed female deity.[7] Although we have no way of knowing with certainty that it is a Gnostic text, contextual clues and the fact that the hymn was found with the Gnostic tractates buried at Nag Hammadi suggest that it should be understood in relationship to the Gnostic myths and scriptures. We also cannot be certain of the speaker's identity, but I believe that *Thunder* represents the energy of divine generative force and, therefore, can be identified *with*, if not strictly identified *as*, Sophia, as I argue in what follows.

There are several indicators pointing in this direction. One is the name of the hymn itself. In his introduction to *The Thunder: Perfect Mind*, Parrott (1988, 296) describes thunder as "the way in which the god makes his [*sic*] presence known on earth." Parrott associates thunder with "the highest god," and refers us to the Hebrew Bible and the Greek myths, noting in particular Zeus' title "The Thundering One." When we expand our historical view, we also find earlier examples of the association of thunder with the power of divinity in the Egyptian Isis, who declares, "I am the mistress of Thunder" (Arthur 1984, 161), and in the ancient Sumerian pantheon in one of the titles of Inanna, "Loud Thundering Storm" (Wolkstein and Kramer 1983, 95). Mesopotamian scholar Thorkild Jacobsen (1976, 73) tells us that a basic characteristic of fourth-millennium-B.C.E. Mesopotamia was "the worship of forces in nature." Before human forms replaced natural phenomena as representations of divinity, the numinous was understood as immanent, as "indwelling spirit, as power at the center of something that caused it to be and thrive and flourish" (6). In other words, thunder, wind, fire, and other powerful natural phenomena were themselves numinous or divine.[8] I suggest that it would be fitting for a hymn intended to honor the older energy of divine generation to reclaim "thunder" as a symbol, particularly when "thunder" as title or symbol of identity had been appropriated by male deities over the course of several millennia.

In discussing the second part of the title, "Perfect Mind," Parrott, although careful not to classify the hymn as belonging to the Stoic school of Greek philosophy, comments on his understanding of the use of "Perfect Mind" as "an extension of the divine into the world" and its similarity to "the Stoic notion of cosmic *Pneuma*, the active, intelligent element in all things...spanning all worldly divisions and dichotomies and at some level being responsible for everything that occurs" (1988, 296).

He also notes that this element, as "reason," is thought to give instruction to "those who listen about the way to true life," another similarity with the speaker of *Thunder*. This "active, intelligent element," this essence of "reason," I contend, is Sophia, the very manifestation of wisdom. McGuire (1994, 42) affirms that Wisdom/Sophia is indeed one of the divine images called to mind by the text.[9]

Thunder is in the tradition of other hymns of praise in the form of "I am" statements by deities, known as aretalogies, attributed to powerful female figures. Several of the most well-known are in honor of Isis of Egypt.[10] The speaker of *Thunder* opens with these various declarations:

> I was sent forth from [the] power,
> > and I have come to those who reflect upon me,
> > and I have been found among those who seek after me ... (13:1–5)
> Do not be ignorant of me anywhere or any time.
> > Be on your guard!
> Do not be ignorant of me.
> For I am the first and the last.
> I am the honored one and the scorned one.
> I am the whore and the holy one. (13:14–19)

Later, the speaker asserts,

> For I am knowledge and ignorance.
> I am shame and boldness. ...
> I am strength and I am fear.
> I am war and peace. (14:26–32)
> For I am the wisdom of the Greeks
> > and the knowledge of [the] barbarians.
> I am the judgment of [the] Greeks and of the barbarians. (16:4–7)

I agree with Arthur (1984, 164), who eliminates the possibility that Isis could be the speaker here, because there is no clear statement of identity as is found in her hymns: "I am Isis." Also, Isis texts are generally more praiseworthy and less conflicted. As these verses show, *Thunder* is rich in riddle and paradox. Many statements appear contradictory or antithetical. Indeed, they can be seen as separate and oppositional aspects—or they can be seen as an expression of wholeness. Given that the hymn addresses divine mystery, I suggest that it points to both unity and multiplicity, to the wholeness of the unity through its multiple parts. I propose that a perspective that encompasses both the "whore" *and* the "holy one" describes a female wholly grounded in her sexuality, for example, a sexuality that is sacred because it and she are divine. Further, I suggest the speaker, as encompassing the "whole" that is greater than the sum of her parts, is herself the "power" from which she was sent. She *is* divine generative energy. Moreover, the speaker states that she is "wisdom," particularly the wisdom "of the Greeks." This seems to be one of the clearest indications that she is indeed the *Sophia* known in the ancient Mediterranean world and beyond.

Assuming, then, that I have correctly identified the speaker of *Thunder* as Sophia, it is noteworthy to my argument that, in the hymn, she makes a direct assertion of her relationship to earlier deities:

> Do not separate me from the first ones whom you have [known]....
> I know the (first ones) and those after them [know] me. (18:1, 9)

Here, she claims an earlier status and place within a more ancient pantheon. It would appear that there were "first ones," and she was either one of them or, at least, close enough in the lineage to have either a direct connection with or knowledge of them, and there were others who came after her. Such "knowledge" of these others can be understood as an expression of her link with various manifestations of divine generative energy.

It is also significant that Sophia calls attention to the fact that a shift has taken place within her world, that things are different from what they once were:

> I am the one who has been hated everywhere
> and who has been loved everywhere.
> I am the one whom they call Life,
> and you have called Death.
> I am the one whom they call Law,
> and you have called Lawlessness. (16:10–16)

Sophia acknowledges that a significant cultural and spiritual transition is taking place. She is called "Life" by one group and "Death" by another. In an oppositional system, these elements are separate from one another, and no connection between them is possible. Seen from a different perspective, however, they can be interpreted to encompass the polarity that is held within the image of Sophia as totality, as one who is loved *and* hated, is life *and* death, is law *and* lawlessness. Returning to the distinction I made at the beginning of this chapter, I contend that, here, Sophia is harking back to the memory of a generated universe, one in which she is both Life and Death, rather than one or the other. An understanding of life as a generated universe encompasses both elements. The destruction of storms and natural cataclysms, the chain of sustenance in which one life form becomes food for another, and the death and rotting of all life forms are all part of the birth/death/rebirth cycle that is life as a whole. Within a created universe, on the other hand, the understanding of death is reflected in the context of chronic warfare of tribe against tribe, empire against empire, and humans against nature, the antithesis of the natural life/death/rebirth cycle. The anxiety expressed in the text, the implied dismay with the audience's insistence on duality, is already an acknowledgement that the holistic paradigm in which the divine generative energy that connected humans to their source is slipping away.

Thus, what we have in *Thunder* is an expression of Sophia as an original Great Goddess, one who encompassed contradiction, opposites, and paradox; one in whom the cosmos was contained. In this and in the verses that follow, *Thunder* also affirms Sophia's virgin motherhood.

Parthenogenetic References in Thunder

Consider the following lines in *Thunder*:

> I am the wife and the virgin
> I am the mother and the daughter.
> I am the members of my mother
> I am the barren one
>   and many are her [offspring]
> I am she whose wedding is great,
>   and I have not taken a husband.
> I am the midwife and she who does not bear,
> I am the solace of my labor pains.
> I am the bride and the bridegroom,
>   and it is my husband who begot me.
> I am the mother of my father
>   and the sister of my husband,
>   and he is my offspring
> I am the slave of him who prepared me.
> I am the ruler of my offspring.
>   But he is the one who begot me before the time
>   on a birthday.
>   And he is my offspring in due time. (13:20–14:4)

Not only does Sophia/Thunder proclaim her parthenogenetic authority in unambiguous terms, but she also uses ambiguity and paradox to express and claim the wholeness she represents. This amplifies her role as *Hochma/ Sophia/*Wisdom, as we saw earlier, who was "there" in Proverbs (8:23) "from the beginning," before all creation, and it extends her role forward by anthropomorphizing her in terms of human relationships. In both cases, hers is a declaration of power and authority that have been invested in images of Earth and Great Mother/Virgin Mother deities for millennia. As Vermaseren (1977, 9–10) explains, "In the civilizations of Asia Minor, Crete and the early Greek mainland the Goddess appeared everywhere in the form of the Great Mother.... The Earth Mother is the mysterious power that awakes everything to life.... Her authority did not reside in her power to command, but in her mysterious gift of being able continually to create new beings."

We see in Sophia's utterances expressing wholeness, paradox, and parthenogenetic capacity echoes of Egyptian Virgin Mothers, as well. Mut enjoyed titles such as "daughter-mother who made her creator"; "the mother of her maker, the daughter who made the mother"; and "mother of the mothers who bore every god, the splendid serpent who wrapped herself around her father Re, and gave him to the world as Khonsu" (Rigoglioso 2007, 75–76). As we saw in chapter 2, Neith was also depicted as having given birth to the god Re, who thereafter became her consort; she was simultaneously said to be born of Re. Hathor later absorbed these attributes as mother, wife, and daughter of the god.[11]

Sophia, both in her aspect in the Gnostic creation story and in her aspect as "Thunder," is claiming her connection to these more ancient deities. Through her exclamations in *Thunder* and her actions in the Gnostic creation story, she asserts her right and authority as a parthenogenetic force. What we see in the stated genealogical relationships of all such female divinities, however, is their demotion from "Mother of All" to "Daughter of the Father/Husband/Son," which reflects the erosion of their original parthenogenetic power. This power will later be ascribed to the male deities who first become their consorts and then, eventually, supplant them. As noted earlier, the Sophia we meet in *Thunder* acknowledges that this process is in play (I am the one whom they call Life/and you have called Death), whereas the Sophia of the Valentinian cosmogony has already been almost totally subsumed, although her initial parthenogenetic actions suggest that she does not accept that change.

Parthenogenetic References in Other Gnostic Texts

It is worth noting two other Gnostic texts for their parthenogenetic themes, as they show an enduring recognition of the importance of this female function to ancient creation stories of the Gnostic stream to which Sophia belongs. One is *On the Origin of the World,* a later Gnostic text probably from the fourth century C.E. (Bethge 1988, 170–71). It is an origin story that brings together a number of principal Gnostic ideas about creation and the nature of humans and draws on several Gnostic schools of thought, as well as non-Gnostic material. Given the variety of views and philosophical concepts traceable to Jewish, Manichaean, Greek, and Christian ideas, this text, like *Thunder*, most likely emerged from the cosmopolitan Hellenistic crossroads city of Alexandria (170). The following passage, an aretalogy attributed to the biblical Eve (Bethge, Layton, and Societas Coptica Hierosolymitana, trans., 1988, 181) parallels almost exactly the statements in *Thunder* quoted above:

> Now, Eve is the first virgin, the one who without a husband bore her
>   first offspring. It is she who served as her own midwife.
> For this reason she is held to have said:
> "It is I who am the part of my mother;
> And it is I who am the mother;
> It is I who am the wife;
> It is I who am the virgin;
> It is I who am pregnant;
> It is I who am the midwife;
> It is I who am the one that comforts pains of travail;
> It is my husband who bore me;
> And it is I who am his mother,
> And it is he who is my father and my lord;
> It is he who is my force;
> What he desires, he says with reason.
> I am in the process of becoming.
> Yet I have borne a man as lord. (114:5–15)

Arthur (1984, 162) notes that this text "is used to praise Eve's parthenogenic [*sic*] conception, illustrating a certain juxtaposition of Egyptian and Judaistic traditions." She concludes that its ultimate origin "seems to have been in an Egyptian aretalogy praising some Egyptian goddess who is hardly anything less than the universal woman personified" (164). Eve, as the personification of the universal woman, the first woman in Judaic and Christian texts, takes on these powerful words associated with the ancient lineage of divine females who were the acknowledged source of all life. The authors of this Gnostic text are explicit in the first line of their description as quoted above: "Eve is the first virgin, the one who without a husband bore her first offspring." This is an acknowledgment that human women share a connection to our oldest associations with divinity, to the Earth herself, as the source of the continuation of life. Being both the "mother" and "the part of my mother" renders her in the tradition of Demeter and Persephone, in particular, in which the mother gives birth to her daughter/self.

Rigoglioso's theory, detailed in *CDB* and noted throughout this volume, that certain holy women also attempted to mimic the parthenogenetic ability of the great Virgin Mothers, is also relevant here. *On the Origin of the World* posits Eve as the first holy *parthenos*, or priestess of divine birth. Eve's statement "I have born a man as a lord" is in congruence with Rigoglioso's argument that miraculously conceived children were themselves considered to be divine. Eve's seemingly paradoxical genealogy ("It is my husband who bore me/ And it is I who am his mother/ And it is he who is my father and my lord") harks back to the schema made most obvious in ancient Egypt. There, the queens who gave birth miraculously to the pharaohs were considered to be part of such a lineage. The queen's "father" was considered to be the creator god Amun-Re, who then became her "husband" in a divine conception rite. Impregnated by the god, the queen subsequently gave birth to what was believed to be his reincarnation as pharaoh (see Rigoglioso 2007, 70–92). That Eve was not only the first *virgin* but also the first *woman* is also interesting. The fact that in this story the first female is also parthenogenetic raises questions about early beliefs regarding human procreation.

Another text with a parthenogenetic theme is *The Hypostasis of the Archons*, also a part of the Nag Hammadi codex. It dates from approximately the same period as *On the Origin of the World* and is similar in that it, too, is a syncretic blending of Jewish, Christian, and Gnostic sources. According to Bullard (1988, 161), it is an esoteric teaching to the initiated, "the work of a gnostic teacher instructing a...self-conscious community which probably felt pressure from a Christian community that defined itself as orthodox and others as heretical." The relevant passage here is spoken by Adam to Eve the first time he sees her:

> And the spirit-endowed woman came to him and spoke with him saying, "Arise, Adam." And when he saw her, he said, "it is you who have given me life; you will be called 'Mother of the living.' For it is she who is my mother. It is she who is the physician, and the woman, and she who has given birth." (Layton, trans., 1988, 89:14–17)

In these accounts of creation, it is Eve who is created before Adam and who gives life to him. Again, in *On the Origin of the World* she is portrayed as the first virgin who gave birth without a man. Although not explicit in *The Hypostasis of the Archons*, her virginal conception of Adam is implied in his words "It is you who have given me life." The next line, "you will be called 'Mother of the living'" finds a close parallel in Genesis 3:20, which says "she was the mother of all those who live." Once again, these texts seem to be pointing to the important role of female deities—and human women—as Virgin Mothers. Indeed, as this portrayal of Eve as "Mother of the living" exemplifies, there is a strong indication of a very ancient belief that the human race owes its very existence to the parthenogenetic capacity of the female.

Wisdom as the Ability to Generate Life—Parthenogenetically

In our contemporary culture, wisdom is often associated with sagacity, insight, understanding, intelligence, and common sense but rarely with the deep *gnosis* of the universe that connects it with the alchemy of life and death, with the creative force. The latter concept, however, seems to have elicited a fundamental resonance with the ancients, as suggested by Bleeker (1983, 32): "According to the religious conceptions of antiquity, real wisdom consisted of insight into the mystery of life and death. This knowledge is creative; it evokes life from death." Long (1993, 18) makes the connection between *Sophia*/Wisdom and her generativity explicit: "Wisdom...means the ability to create life."

I suggest that the statement "Wisdom *is* the ability to *generate* life" would be even more accurate. Returning to my initial discussion distinguishing between notions of a generated and a created universe, I would stress that generation is an internal action, whereas creation is external. That is, generation is the manifestation or emanation of life from within and is, therefore, inherently parthenogenetic. As Vermaseren (1977, 9–11), Bleeker (1983, 32), and Long (1993, 18) have concluded from their independent research, and as the previous chapters in this book have shown, the authority of the ancient female deities rests in their association with generation.

The Legacy of the Loss of Female Parthenogenetic Power

In spite of the enduring symbols of female divine energy, even a brief review of the Western canon points to the notion of femaleness equated with deficiency. It is on this point, the deficiency of the female, that the plot of Sophia's story turns.

Parthenogenesis is a common motif in the Gnostic stories, from the beginning Source or Unbegotten to the later appearance of Limit in the Valentinian cosmogony, and in many other variations in other Gnostic stories not mentioned here. For Sophia, however, parthenogenesis was said to be wrong. She no longer had the power to complete her "thought" or express her "desire," to bring it to fruition, to fructify, to generate, to manifest from her being. The rules had been changed, and her actions, once the most natural possible, were now a crime against the existing order. She who was lawgiver now found herself outside the law. Therefore, when she did emanate from her being, she was said to bring forth something like "an abortion" or an "ugly fruit." Like all the Virgin Mother goddesses, Sophia was caught in the transition to patriarchy, divested of the power she once held. Her connection to "life as living unity" was acknowledged, but her authority as divine generative force was no longer honored. In this new worldview, what Sophia generated was no longer perceived as whole.

Parthenogenesis became problematic for all female deities under patriarchy. The journey from divine generatrix to deficient female happened gradually over a long period of time, but it was significant in the transition process that eventually ascribed the ability to create life to male deities. The womb, as the locus of generativity, was denigrated along with femaleness and gradually supplanted by the head, as was demonstrated in chapter 2 by Zeus's claim to have birthed Athena from his forehead. Also, the confusion of passion and thought in Sophia's story is a reflection of this shift in focus from womb to head and the subsequent devaluation of generated materiality in favor of created abstraction.

From the iconographic and textual evidence presented in this book, we can discern a recognizable progression in our relationship with the divine and our representation of sacrality: Earth (as representative of Nature and natural energies) → Great Mother → Mother/Daughter → Mother/Son-Lover → Sacred Marriage → Great Father → Heaven. In this lineage, the progression is from materiality to transcendence, as well as from female parthenogenetic generation to sexual intercourse to asexual creation with male as agent of creation. The radical difference between the beginning and ending positions, between Great Mother and Great Father, is well articulated by Baring and Cashford (1991, 274):

> Now a father god establishes a position of supremacy in relation to a mother goddess, and he is gradually transformed into the consortless god of the three patriarchal religions known to us today: Judaism, Christianity and Islam. The god is then the sole primal creator, where before the goddess had been the only source of life. But the god becomes the *maker* of heaven and earth, whereas the goddess *was* heaven and earth. The concept of "making" is radically different from "being," in the sense that what is made is not necessarily of the same substance as its maker, and may be conceived as inferior to him; while what emerges from the mother is necessarily part of her and she of it.

At the end of the progression is the newest representation of divinity, the symbol that is currently in the forefront of Western culture, as it has been for only approximately the past 4,000 years, as the sky gods of the Graeco-Roman pantheon and the monotheistic religions. Some of the early Great Fathers had female consorts, with whom they produced children. Those consorts were often the earlier Virgin Mother goddesses, whose power and authority were gradually appropriated in the transition to a patriarchal worldview. The Great Father creator of Judaism and Christianity is a monad who creates alone; he is above his creation, removed from the Earth and intimate connection, residing in the sky or Heaven. The Father Creator does not generate or manifest from himself but claims creation as his exclusive province.

Even still, as was intimated in the introduction to this book, the instances in myth that are the basis for this concept belie the claim of single parenthood and rely heavily on the obviously necessary but unacknowledged contribution of the female: "Yahweh God shaped man from the soil of the ground and blew the breath of life into his nostrils, and man became a living being" (Genesis 2:7). We have seen that Earth was held as parthenogentric creatrix for millennia in the ancient world; here, her inherent power is usurped and named differently. Earth becomes mere "soil" or "dust." It is the legacy of this usurping and desacralizing of the great Virgin Mothers with which we continue to struggle today, as we grapple with warfare, global warming, climate change, and a host of environmental and social ills as normative.

NOTES

Introduction

1. See, e.g., Guthrie (1967, 101–3), in the case of Artemis; Farnell ([1896–1909] 1977, 1:179–204), in the case of Hera.
2. See, e.g., Spretnak (1978), Dexter (1990), Baring and Cashford (1991), Sjöö and Mor (1991), Downing (1992), and O'Brien (1993).
3. See Rigoglioso (2009, xx) for a brief discussion of contradictory views regarding the utility of such an approach.
4. For the classical exposition of matriarchy (one that is interesting but in many ways problematic from a feminist viewpoint), see Bachofen ([1861] 1897), portions of which can be found in English translation in Bachofen (1973; [1861] 2005). For a recent critique of theories of matriarchy, see Eller (2000). For a counter response to Eller, see Dashu (2000) and Marler (2005).
5. Papers from First World Congress on Matriarchal Studies: http://www.second-congress-matriarchal-studies.com/1st_congress_submenu.html; Web site of the Second World Congress on Matriarchal Studies: http://www.second-congress-matriarchal-studies.com; Web site of A (M)otherworld Is Possible conference: http://www.motherworldconference.org/; Web site of the International Conference on the Gift Economy: http://www.gifteconomyconference.com/.
6. See, e.g., papers in Goettner-Abendroth (2009) and those available on the Web sites mentioned in n5.
7. This theory received yet another confirmation in the summer of 2007 by the Mount Lykaion Excavation and Survey Project, which uncovered evidence of the worship of a pre-Olympian deity in the archaeological layers under an altar to Zeus on the summit of Mount Lykaion in Arcadia in Greece (Wilford 2008).
8. Although controversy surrounds Gimbutas's methods and conclusions, (e.g., Goodison and Morris 1998; Hayden 1993; Meskell 1995; Tringham and Conkey 1998), the viewpoint I adopt is in accord with those of archaeologists and other scholars who are verifying and expanding on various aspects of Gimbutas's theories (e.g., Nikolov 2009; C.-M. Lazarovici 2008; G. Lazarovici 2008; Dergachev 2007; Yakar 2007, 1997; Brukner 2006; Christ 1996; Keller 1996; Spretnak 1996). Like

these scholars, I find that Gimbutas's theories have tremendous heuristic utility for the interpretation of not only archaeological artifacts, but also iconography, mythological motifs, and historical texts. I believe that, because prominent classics scholars such as those cited earlier independently held to similar theoretical views, the assumption of an early matriarchal substratum in Greece, upon which my analysis is based, is built on firm, if not conclusive, footing.

9. Also of interest is Hwang's (2005) comprehensive analysis of the parthenogenetic aspect of an early East Asian goddess, Mago, in which she observes the similarities between this deity and the Virgin Mother goddesses of Greece and elsewhere.

10. The notion sometimes proffered that indigenous spiritualities, whose paradigms may be in accord with those of the pre-patriarchal Europeans, embrace strictly abstract rather than personified images of great cosmic forces (e.g., the "Great Spirit") may be misinformed. Mann, a scholar who is also Native American, for example, notes (2000, 302–3), "At least as regards the Iroquois, the now familiar 'Great Spirit' is *bogus dialect*, the minstrel version of Native religions.... Instead, Iroquoian Creation was awash in multiple Creators, female as well as male, animal as well as spirit." The idea of a "Great Spirit" was, she says, conjured by "self-designated Friends of the Indians bent on describing 'their Indians'' so-called progress in civilization."

Chapter 1   In the Beginning: Chaos, Nyx, and Ge/Gaia

1. Since the names *Ge* and *Gaia* are both used in ancient Greek texts to denote the Earth Goddess, I will use the conjoint Ge/Gaia to refer to this deity.

2. Readers accustomed to using Graves (1960) as a source of Greek myths may wonder why I do not include discussion of Eurynome as an early parthenogenetic goddess, as he does in his so-called "Pelasgian Creation Myth" (27–30). This is because in fact there is no evidence in any of the ancient texts that Eurynome was parthenogenetic. Graves's intuition that early Greek goddesses were parthenogenetic seems correct, but his details in this case are incorrect.

3. The problem of Orphism's authenticity and antiquity has been a hotly disputed area in the field of Greek religion (see, e.g., Guthrie [1952] 1993, 69–147). Presumed fragments of Orphic myth have been collected in a compilation known as the *Rhapsodies*, which, when taken together, present a semi-coherent theogony. No indisputable evidence indicates a pre-Hellenistic origin for Orphism, but numerous indirect indicators in the works of Pindar, Empedocles, and Herodotus, and, later, Plato suggest that its myths were known much earlier (Burkert 1985, 297–98). I thus refer to Orphic material throughout this book with the assumption that, like the Hesiodic and Homeric material, it reflects a mixture of authentic archaic beliefs and androcentric theological invention.

4. The theory of wind impregnation of animals was accepted by Aristotle (*History of Animals* 6. 2.559b–60a), and was referenced by Homer (*Iliad* 16.149–51, 20.223–25), Virgil (*Georgics* 3.271–76), Aelian (*On Animals* 4.7), Pliny (*Natural History* 8.67, 4.35), Plutarch (*Table-Talk* 8.1.3), and others.

5. Aristophanes' reference is also in contrast with Orphic frag. 70 (in Guthrie [1952] 1993, 138), which credits Cronus with fashioning the divine egg from which Phanes was born. However, as mentioned previously, frag. 129 (in Guthrie, 139) still places Nyx/Night preceding Cronus in the cosmogonic lineage. It states, "above all others it was Cronus whom Night reared and cherished." Thus, even if Cronus were responsible for the egg out of which Phanes emerged, Nyx/Night still enjoyed precedence and primacy of position.

6. Phanes resembled in every way the legendary first bisexual human beings as described by Aristophanes in Plato's *Symposium* (189d–90c). Such beings were said to have been born of the moon (190b), which was always understood by the Greeks to have been a goddess, either Selene or Artemis. Thus in Plato's story, as well, the progenitor of the bisexual being was rendered female.

7. Translation by E. D. A. Morshead, in Oates and O'Neill (1938, 1:234).

8. Such ancient beliefs contrast with what I propose are later, patriarchal stories such as that recounted by Hesiod (*Works and Days* 60–95, 176; *Theogony* 570–616), in which Zeus made the present race of men from iron, and in which humanity originally consisted of one sex, the male. In Hesiod's blatantly misogynistic account, the first woman, Pandora, was supposedly made out of clay and given to man as a punishment by the gods. In this conception, woman is thus materially different from naturally born men. In the *Timaeus*, Plato similarly states that the first humans were males. He relates, "all those creatures generated as men who proved themselves cowardly and spent their lives in wrong-doing were transformed at their second incarnation into women" (90e–91a, 1925, trans. Lamb). However, in the *Symposium* (189d–90c) he refers to another probable ancient belief that humans originally included a hermaphroditic strain, which Zeus cut in two as a result of humanity's rebelliousness toward the gods.

9. The Danaids' status as priestesses of Demeter and Persephone may be surmised from Herodotus (2.171), who says they brought from Egypt to Argos the Thesmophoria, a mystery festival dedicated to these two goddesses. Their status as priestesses of Athena may be surmised by the fact that one of the Danaids founded a temple to Athena on Rhodes (Herodotus 2.182). I return to this aspect of their story in chapter 5.

Chapter 2   Athena/Neith/Metis: Primordial Creatrix of Self-Replication

1. For a full discussion of the predominance of Neith during the early and very late dynastic periods, see Sayed (1982).

2. Ancient Saïs is now modern Sa el-Hagar, earlier named Ha-Nit, a name that indicates its connection with Neith/Nit (Hagan 2000, 48).

3. See, e.g., Lhote (1959, figs. 35, 48; 1963, 23, fig. 27). In these rock paintings, human figures wear horns (or crescent moons?), and oxen are often
   depicted with attributes above their horns such as large crescents studded
   with oxhide disks. Lhote confirms that these are religious symbols.

4. Hathor assumed the following characteristics of Neith: she was imaged as
   a cow; came to represent the entire sky; and, as the autogenetic "mother
   of the light," birthed herself as the first act of creation and subsequently
   produced Shu and Tefnut. She is also described as "the great cow that
   gave birth to Re." See Budge ([1904] 1969, 1:428–38) for a comprehensive
   discussion of Hathor. Hollis (1994–95, 49–50) also affirms that Hathor
   adopted many of Neith's characteristics. However, Neith's primary characterization was as autogenetic creatrix (which I argue that she retained
   down to the Graeco-Roman period). In contrast, Hathor, who also
   retained the identity of "mother of the god," came to be defined in terms
   of her relationship to the god as mother, wife, or daughter, rather than as
   sovereign in her own right. I argue this represents an ontological demotion
   of the Great Goddess.

5. The claim of Neith's primacy of position in creation is not documented
   until the Nineteenth Dynasty (c. 1224 B.C.E.), when it appears on the
   stone sarcophagus of King Merneptah, and the only text for the story of
   Neith as the creator of all appears quite late, in the Ptolemaic and Roman
   Periods (c. 304 B.C.E.–395 C.E.), in the temple associated with her in
   Esna. Moreover, the same primacy of position was claimed for Atum, for
   Ptah of Memphis, and for Thoth of Hermopolis (Lesko 1999, 57–58, 59).
   Nevertheless, as Lesko (59) writes, "it was perhaps with more justification
   that this was done for Neith, for she, at least, was female [and thereby pos-
   sessed the logical attributes required to be a bearer of creation] and can be
   documented much earlier than any of the aforementioned gods."

6. By the time of Plutarch's writing (first century C.E.), Neith at Saïs was also
   known as Isis (*On Isis and Osiris* 9).

7. The phrasing implies, in particular, that she was never *violated* sexually by
   another. This connotation would have had meaning in Hellenistic Greece,
   where, as I demonstrate throughout this book and *CDB*, the rape of goddesses, nymphs, and mortals by gods was a regular part of religious story,
   pointing to the disempowerment of the feminine in the patriarchal era.

8. This epithet appears on the stone sarcophagus of King Merneptah of the
   Nineteenth Dynasty (Lesko 1999, 57).

9. We saw a reference to this earlier in the Saïtic inscription dedicated to her,
   in which Neith is said to have given birth to the "sun," a manifestation of
   Re. She is also imaged in this way in the previously mentioned inscription on the statue of Utchat-Heru, in which she is declared to have given
   birth to herself as well as all of creation. The stone sarcophagus of King
   Merneptah of the Nineteenth Dynasty similarly refers to her as one who
   was present at "the beginning" and as the mother of the major gods Re and
   Osiris (Lesko 1999, 57). In her depiction as a cow with eighteen stars, also
   mentioned, she is again described as "Net, the Cow, which gives birth to

Re" (Budge [1904] 1969, 1:451). In *The Book of That Which Is in the Beyond*, which describes the journey of Re as the sun through the underworld during the twelve hours of the night, Neith appears as a pregnant goddess in the eleventh hour. This points to her role as the one who continually gives him rebirth (Lesko 1999, 58). In a hymn on the walls of the temple of Hebet, in the Great Oasis, Net (Neith) as cow is depicted as "rejoicing in the Bull of his mother"—that is, Re (Budge 1:464). Mysliwiec (1998, 18) and Roth (2000, 193) note that the expression "bull of his mother" means "*impregnator* of his mother," which expresses the idea that Re coupled with his own mother to create himself. Still, I argue that such a concept necessitates the preexistence of the mother. Thus, Re's creation is more a parthenogenetic act on the part of the goddess than on the part of the god. Sometimes, as son of Neith, Re was identified with Sobek, the ancient deity whose zootype was the Nile crocodile (see, e.g., Lesko 1999, 50–51).

10. See, e.g., Budge ([1904] 1969, 1:308–21) for a fuller account of Re/Khepera's role in creation. This story is also attributed to the creator god Atum. See, e.g., Troy (1986, 15–16) for textual excerpts depicting Atum's act of creation.

11. See Plutarch (*On Isis and Osiris* 10); Aelian (*On Animals* 10.15); Porphyry (*On Abstinence* 4.9.8); and Horapollo (*Hieroglyphics* 1.10).

12. I also disagree with Troy's (1986, 18) assertion that Neith's attribute of crossed arrows reflects her "masculine aspect," as ancient Libyan rock art regularly depicts women wielding bows and arrows in hunting and combat situations. To my mind, this indicates that this equipment was, in the time of Neith's earliest emergence, as much practically and symbolically associated with the female as the male (see Lhote 1959, 148; Lajoux 1963, 163–67). Moreover, as I discuss later in this chapter, in what Meyerowitz (1958, 13–56; 1960, 23–30) argues may be the oldest substratum of Akan theogony in Ghana, and a probable survival of ancient Libyan religion, the universal creatrix was considered an autogenetic Mother Goddess. Visible as the moon, she was also known as Atoapoma, the "Ever-Ready Shooter." As creatrix and "shooter," she is likely identical with Neith of Libya. Atoapoma was thought to vivify humans, animals, and plants by shooting into them a particle of her life-force energy, conceived as a moon ray. Meyerowitz is clear that in its earliest form, this divinity, also known as Nyame, was seen as unequivocally female and that it was not until a later period that she came to be regarded as bisexual. Nyame's male aspect, when thought of separately, was personified as a moon god, her son; in time Nyame also came to be personified as her son's sister and wife. The male life-force energy of the god was eventually seen as being incarnate in the sun, whose life-giving power came to be regarded as greater than that of the moon. We have here the precise theological trajectory of divinity moving from wholly female, to bisexual, to "partner of" the masculine that I am suggesting for Neith. (Note, however, the critiques of Meyerowitz's work, mentioned below.)

13. As I argue throughout *CDB* was the case in Greece, it is possible that Neith's most holy priestesses originally were considered practitioners of pure parthenogenesis. There is little evidence by which to construct an argument to this effect, but it is interesting to note that Neith's early priesthood was mainly, if not exclusively, female, and that a number of these women had extremely high political status (Lesko 1999, 58). Numerous stele from the First Dynasty name priestesses of Neith, and several queens bore names that demonstrated they may also have been her priestesses: Neith-Hotep, Merit-Neith, Her-Neith, and Nakht-Neith. These were politically powerful women, as evidenced by the fact that some had tombs as large as or larger than those of the male rulers (49). Moreover, since at this time the king's *serekh*, an identifying glyph surmounted by the Horus falcon, symbolized the linking of humankind with the world of the gods, the depiction of two queens' names (Meretneith and Hetepneith) in a *serekh* surmounted by Neith's standard of the shield and crossed arrows suggests the queen of this era held power comparable to that of the king (Hollis 1994–95, 48). Neith's bee totem also likely connected her with "female powers of divination, sooth-saying and oracles" (Hagan 2000, 70), given various associations of the bee with ancient female oracular activity. For example, as mentioned earlier, the oracular priestess at Delphi in Greece was known as *Melissa*, or "bee." This suggests that her priestesses had a divinatory role, also. That divination and parthenogenesis may have gone hand in hand in Egypt would be consistent with the phenomenon of parthenogenetic stories throughout Greece frequently being associated with oracular priesthoods, as I argue in *CDB*, where I discuss possible parthenogenetic cults associated with Dodona and Delphi (Rigoglioso 2009, 139–204). I discuss the bee as a symbol of oracular priesthood more fully in *CDB* (Rigoglioso 2009, 192–202).

14. Faraone and Teeter (2004) present the case that Metis should be identified with the Egyptian Maat. While their argument is interesting, I contend that the iconographic, mythological, and cultic associations between Metis/Athena and Neith are much stronger than any associations between Metis/Athena and Maat, as I attempt to show here.

15. Frazer (Apollodorus 1967, 1:24–25) incorrectly, I believe, interpolates "Ge" into the text where it was not originally present, basing his construction on Hesiod (*Theogony* 891).

16. The Hesiodic detail of Ge telling Zeus to swallow Metis furthermore suspiciously suggests a later patriarchal revision to the myth, given that, as I have argued, Ge belonged to the older, matriarchal, parthenogenetic layer of cult.

17. This fragment is retained in Lattimore's translation of *Theogony* 925 (Hesiod 1959, 179–80), which I use here.

18. Other feminist scholars have also intuited that Metis's conception of Athena was parthenogenetic, among them Daly ([1978] 1990, 13), Shaktini (1982, 36) (who has similarly interpreted the Chrysippus

fragment, in particular, to reference Metis's ability to conceive independently of Zeus), and Dexter (1990, 172).

19. E.g., Chrysippus (frag. 908/Hesiod 1959, 929a); Tzetzes *On Lycophron* 355; Philostrates (*Imagines* 2.27); and the scholiast on Apollonius Rhodius 4.1310.

20. Other locales in Greece, some of which had rivers or wells named *Triton* or *Tritonis*, subsequently asserted that Athena was born there, such as Alalcomenae in Boeotia, and Argos (Pausanias 9.33.5; Strabo 9.2.36). The bulk of the mythological stories and ethnographies, however, place Athena as originating in Libyan Africa. Nilsson ([1950] 1971, 484–500) argues for a Cretan origin for Athena, a view that seems to have been widely accepted (see, e.g., Guthrie 1967, 106). I am in strong agreement, however, with Bernal (1987–2006, 3:540–82), who uses historical, cultic, and linguistic evidence to support the argument for a Libyo-Egyptian origin for Athena, and for the transfer of her cult to Greek soil. My argument here overlaps with his to some degree, but goes further in looking at mythological and ethnographic evidence. Although they do not discuss Athena's Libyan roots, excellent feminist analyses of this goddess include Spretnak (1978, 97–101); Dexter (1990, 118–20); Baring and Cashford (1991, 332–45); and Downing (1992, 99–130).

21. It should be noted that other figures by the name of Pallas are associated with Athena in various myth fragments. There is, for example, a giant named Pallas whom she killed, and out of whose flayed skin she made a shield (Apollodorus 1.6.2). Cicero (*De Natura Deorum* 3.23) relates that this Pallas was her father, and that Athena slew and flayed him on account of his attempting to rape her. However, given my argument for Athena's African origins, I contend that the dominant figure to whom her epithet "Pallas" should be attributed is that of the maiden of Libya.

22. Diodorus states he derives his own account from that of Dionysius of Mitylene. It is conjectured that the latter, surnamed Scytobrachion, lived either shortly before the time of Cicero (c. 106–43 B.C.E.) and was instructed at Alexandria, or as far back as the fifth century B.C.E. Attributed to him were works recounting the military expedition of Dionysus and Athena and a prose work on the Argonauts in six books. He may also have been the author of the historic cycle poems, lost epics recounting ancient history up to the twelfth century B.C.E. (Smith 1870, s.v. *Dionysius, literary* 34). One translator of Diodorus's history, C. H. Oldfather (Diodorus Siculus 1935, 246n2), dismisses Dionysius's purported account of the Libyan Amazons as a mere "mythical romance." However, that the work of Xanthus the Lydian, a source cited by Dionysius Scytobrachion, was once regarded as fictitious but is now thought to be both genuine and reputable (Brown 1946, 268 n46) opens the door to the possibility that the latter's other sources could have reflected authentic historical material, as well. This may have included any source from which he obtained his information about the Libyan Amazons.

23. A few lines later, Herodotus conjectures that both shields and helmets were in fact introduced to Greece from Egypt.

24. For a discussion of these and related customs as being indicative of matriarchy, see, e.g., Göttner-Abendroth (1987, 2; 2001). Refer also to the definition of matriarchy I provide in the introduction, which is drawn from Göttner-Abendroth.

25. See, e.g., Dodds (1951, 28–63) for discussion of the archaic tendency to assume that human misfortunes represented acts of justice on the part of supernatural powers.

26. Göttner-Abendroth (1987, 2) notes that in the social condition of matriarchy more broadly, "the relationship between the mother and daughter is the core relationship of the family."

27. The description of the Akan in the following paragraphs is taken from Meyerowitz (1958, 13–45, 145–50).

28. Meyerowitz's work on this topic, which appears with variations in her four other volumes (1951, 1952, 1960, 1974), has been criticized on several counts. Danquah (1952, 364), although otherwise appreciative of Meyerowitz's first volume, suggests there is no evidence that the primary Akan deity Nyame was acknowledged as exclusively female in its earliest conception. Nor, he maintains, is there any evidence that the queen mother ever ruled alone. Goody (1959) argues that Meyerowitz naively took material from her informants without adequately corroborating or qualifying it, generalized from what may have been merely localized or idiosyncratic accounts, and misunderstood and/or distorted certain terms and concepts owing to her lack of knowledge of local languages and her reliance on interpreters. Robertson (1976) complains that her 1974 volume "seems to have contradicted, with dignity but with passion, almost every scholar who has written anything of substance on the history of Ghana."

However, that Meyerowitz's work, carried out in the field in the 1940s and 1950s, was supported by the Royal Anthropological Institute, the Colonial Development and Welfare Fund, and the University College of the Gold Coast suggests that it was undertaken seriously, contains a good deal of merit on at least some counts, and should not be simply dismissed. John Patton, a scholar of African history at the University of London, remarks (personal communication via email, May 30, 2007), "I think Eva Meyerowitz is an interesting and perhaps unjustly neglected scholar. Her work on the Akan tends to use oral traditions too liberally and is overly concerned with 'origins' and migrations, many of which are highly contested and dubious. But the books do contain a wealth of material on the states of the northwestern frontier of the Akan world, much of which was derived from valuable oral sources dating back to the 1940s. Like [Robert] Rattray, she was a pioneer fieldworker, and like Rattray her work should be regarded as primary material rather than secondary." I would add that, although Meyerowitz indeed may have lacked training in anthropology and linguistics (she was herself an art supervisor at Achimota College), her perspective as a non-specialist—and as a woman—may, in fact, have helped her to discern details and intuit patterns that her male colleagues missed or ignored, as is frequently the case when female investigators turn their attention to territory that has primarily been the province of male scholars. Bearing in mind the critique, I include her work here for the intriguing kernels it provides in relation to my thesis, particularly given that it corroborates hypotheses about ancient North African matriarchy and its relationship to Neith/Athena (or related goddesses) as a virgin mother that I developed independently.

29. Athena herself was, from Homer on, frequently given the epithet *glaukō-pis*, which has been translated as "owl-eyed" because of its similarity with *glaux/glaukos*, "owl" (see, e.g., Homer *Odyssey* 13.420; Hesiod *Theogony* 895, 924). Athena's attribute became the owl, as well (e.g., Harrison [1903] 1957, 304).

30. E.g., *Hymn 5 to Aphrodite* (7–9); Diodorus Siculus (5.3.4); Ovid (*Metamorphoses* 5.375), etc.

31. Used rarely, the term *monogenês* is employed to describe two other goddesses whom I suggest also represent daughter-bearing parthenogenesis: Demeter and Persephone (Orphic *Hymn to Ceres* and Orphic *Hymn to Proserpine*), as I note in chapter 5. As Long (1992, 49) observes, the term is applied to Jesus in the prologue to the Fourth Gospel (John 1:14) and, as such, serves as "an early indicator of the process of [Female] Wisdom becoming absorbed" into the male godhead. That Jesus was one in a line of *parthenioi*, children of holy *parthenoi*, as described in *CDB*, emphasizes the associations between the term *monogenês* and the concept of parthenogenesis.

32. In *CDB* (Rigoglioso 2009, 60–61), I suggest that in the context of the Panathenaia, the *peplos* similarly was a symbol of Athena's original (and, by later times, long forgotten) capacity as virginal creatrix.

33. Dexter (1990, 172) terms the male-assumed capacity for parthenogenesis *androgenesis*.

34. The entire fragment, some of which Guthrie does not include but I add here at the end, referring to Metis, can also be found in Eusabius (*Preparation for the Gospel* 3).

35. Daly ([1978] 1990, 13) eloquently denounces this ontological state of affairs for its broader ramifications for women.

36. Harrison ([1903] 1957, 281, 283–85) argues that, in earlier mythology, Pandora was likely "the Earth, giver of all gifts" and that her name "is a form or title of the Earth-goddess in the [maiden] form," to whom men made sacrificial rituals. In the patriarchal mythology of Hesiod, Harrison writes, "her great figure is strangely changed and [di]minished. She is no longer Earth-born, but the creature, the handiwork of Olympian Zeus." Hesiod "has shaped [her story] to his own *bourgeois*, pessimistic ends," and in his telling "gleams the ugly malice of theological animus."

37. Connelly (1996) has made the interesting argument that another scene on the Parthenon frieze, whose meaning has baffled scholars, represents a prelude to the sacrifice of three daughters of Erechtheus, legendary

grandson of Erichthonius and an early king of Athens. According to Greek legend, that sacrifice was carried out so as to ensure the Athenians' victory in the war against Eumolpus (Apollodorus 3.15.4). Certainly the scenario of virgin sacrifice for the purpose of patriarchal warfare would correspond further with the misogynistic theme I am arguing was illustrated elsewhere on the Parthenon. The west pediment of the Parthenon shows the original contest between Athena and Poseidon for patronage of the city, which seems to be the only scene to hint at Athena's original connection with North Africa and Neith.

38. Constructed between 447 and 432 B.C.E., the Parthenon was designed as a replacement for the temples the Persians had destroyed when they sacked Athens in 480 and 479 B.C.E. (Blundell 1998, 49).

39. In Sparta, the sanctuary of Athena Poliouchus (City Protecting) was similarly befitted with scenes depicting the disempowerment of the matriarchy. These include some of Heracles' twelve labors, many of which, as I demonstrate in chapter 4, symbolized the vanquishing of Amazony and the female parthenogenetic cult. Also rendered is the story of Hephaestus releasing his mother Hera, who bore him parthenogenetically, from the fetters in which he had angrily entrapped her. Other scenes include the rape of the two daughters of Leucippus, who were priestesses of Athena and Artemis, and Perseus's military engagement against Medusa in Libya, who I argue in *CDB* was most likely an historical Amazon queen and parthenogenetic priestess in her own right (Rigoglioso 2009, 71–74). For these details, see Pausanias (3.17.2–4).

40. See, e.g., Diodorus Siculus (3.70.1–6); Homeric *Hymn to Aphrodite* (10–12); Homeric *Hymn to Demeter* (424); Callimachus *Hymn 5, Bath of Pallas* (43–45).

41. See, e.g., Apollodorus (3.12.3, E5.10–13); Dionysius of Halicarnassus (*Roman Antiquities* 1.68–69); Pausanias (1.28.9).

Chapter 3   Artemis: Virgin Mother of the Wild, Patron of Amazons

1. See Apollodorus (E.3.21, E6.26), Pausanias (1.43.1, 9.19.6), and Euripides (*Iphigeneia in Aulis* and *Iphigeneia Among the Taurians*) as possibly connecting worship of Artemis at Tauris and Boeotia with human sacrifice. Pausanias (9.17.1) similarly refers to an occasion of the sacrifice of maidens to Artemis at Thebes. Philostratus (*Life of Apollonius of Tyana* 6.20) indicates that the Spartans adopted the custom of whipping human victims to draw blood offerings for Artemis in lieu of human sacrifice. The festival to Artemis at Patrae also included a gruesome rite, though one not involving humans: live animals of all kinds were thrown on a massive pyre on an altar and immolated (Pausanias 7.18.11–13).

2. Among them, e.g., Guthrie (1967, 99–101); Harrison ([1903] 1957, 299–300; [1912] 1963, 502); Nilsson ([1950] 1971, 503; 1961, 16); Farnell ([1896–1909] 1977, 2:425–26); and Rose (1959, 112–14). For feminist

analyses positing a pre-Greek origin for Artemis and presenting many of the characteristics I argue for here, see, e.g., Spretnak (1978, 75–76); Dexter (1990, 115–19); Baring and Cashford (1991, 320–32); and Downing (1992, 157–85).

3. Pindar (*Heracles or Kerberos for the Thebans*, Dithyramb 2.20), for example, depicts Artemis as yoking savage lions together during Dionysian revels, a likely reference to her identification with Cybele.

4. Artemis's identification with Britomartis can be seen, for example, in Pausanias (3.14.2), who notes that in Sparta, Artemis was "not really Artemis but Britomartis of Crete." Britomartis was a goddess of eastern Crete (Nilsson [1950] 1971, 510–11; Guthrie 1967, 105). Artemis is identified with Dictynna in Euripides (*Iphigeneia in Tauris* 126), Aristophanes (*Frogs* 1356), and Orphic *Hymn 35 to Diana*. Dictynna was a goddess of western Crete (Nilsson [1950] 1970, 510–11). For Artemis's identification with Eileithyia, see Orphic *Hymn 2 to Prothyraea*. According to Pausanias (1.18.5), the Cretans believed Eileithyia was born at Amnisus in the Cnossian territory, and that she also was the daughter of Hera.

5. For Artemis being accompanied by such creatures, see, e.g., Pausanias (5.19.5, 8.37.4–5); Apollonius Rhodius (*Argonautica* 3.879); Suda (s.v. *Arktos*); Aelian (*On Animals* 12.4). For iconographic images that have been identified as possible depictions of Artemis as Mistress of the Animals, see, e.g., Harrison ([1903] 1957, 264–66) and Farnell ([1896–1909] 1977, 2:522 pl. 29).

6. The conflict between the older religion of which Artemis was a part and the newer religion of the Olympian gods into which she was absorbed may be intimated, for example, in the Homeric episode (*Iliad* 21.470–514) in which the Olympian goddess Hera beat Artemis about the head with her own bow and sent her off the battlefield in tears (Guthrie 1967, 101n2).

7. Leto's presumed genealogy is also outlined in Apollodorus (1.9.2) and Diodorus Siculus (5.67.2).

8. For Leto's persecution, see, e.g., Callimachus (*Hymn to Delos* 55–65); scholiast on Euripides *Phoenissae* 232; Hyginus (*Fabulae* 140).

9. This island is not to be confused with Ortygia in Sicily, where a cult to Artemis was also located.

10. Strabo (14.1.20) similarly places Artemis's birth in Ortygia, but says Leto gave birth to Apollo there, as well.

11. Whether Leto and Artemis in fact belong together or whether their "pairing" was also a manipulation of the patriarchal age is a valid question, but I will not explore it here.

12. Pindar (*Pythian Ode* 4.90); Callimachus (*Hymn 3 to Artemis* 110); Apollodorus (1.4.1).

13. See, e.g., Homeric *Hymns to Artemis* (9.1–2 and 27 *passim*); Homeric *Hymn 5 to Aphrodite* (15–20); Callimachus *Hymn 3 to Artemis* (6–10); Orphic *Hymn 35 to Artemis*.

14. See, e.g., Homer (*Odyssey* 6.100); Homeric *Hymns to Artemis* (9, 27 *passim*); Homeric *Hymn 5 to Aphrodite* (15–20); Callimachus (*Hymn 3 to Artemis* 10–15 and *passim*); Orphic *Hymn 35 to Artemis*.

15. This theme was the centerpiece of Euripides' plays *Iphigeneia in Aulis* and *Iphigeneia in Tauris*. Similarly, the legendary maiden daughters of Antipoenus, Androclei and Alcis, were willingly sacrificed to Artemis to ensure victory to Heracles and the Thebans in their battle against the Orchomenians (Pausanias 9.17.1).

16. Although the lunar aspect was not emphasized for Athena, it was expressed in the Panathenaia, which was held in conjunction with the new, or dark, phase of the moon (Kerenyi 1978, 40–41, 58). See also Rigoglioso (2009, 61).

17. For references to the Greek war against the Themadon Amazons, see, e.g., Herodotus (4.105–19); Diodorus Siculus (4.16); Justin (2.4); Plutarch (*Theseus* 27–28); Isocrates (*Panathenaicus* 193, 194); Demosthenes (*Funeral Oration* 8); Lysias (*Funeral Orations* 4, 6); Aristides (*Panathenaic Oration* 83–84), etc.

18. The placement of Artemis under an oak tree calls to mind the oracle of Dodona, which was centered around a large oak tree, and which was originally dedicated to a female deity, possibly an early version of Ge/Gaia. I argue in *CDB* that Dodona was once the location of a divine birth priesthood. See Rigoglioso (2009, 139–40).

19. Among the legendary Thermadon Amazons, for example, was Lysippe, who led the Amazons around the Black Sea to the Thermadon River; there they formed three tribes, each of which founded a city. To Lysippe is attributed the founding of the city of Themyscyra and the defeat of every tribe as far as the river Tanais. Her descendants extended the Amazonian empire westward across the river Tanais to Thrace and Phrygia. Two other famous legendary Amazonian queens, Marpesia and Lampado, are said to have seized a great part of Anatolia and Syria. Other cities they are said to have founded include Sinope, Paphos on the island of Cyprus, and Thiba. Later Thermadon Amazon queens Antiope and Melanippe also were said to have founded and ruled cities in Anatolia. For these and other details about the Thermadon Amazons as depicted by the ancient authorities, see, e.g., Bennett (1967), duBois (1982), Kleinbaum (1983), Sobol (1972), Tyrrell (1984), Wilde (1999), and Noble (2003).

20. According to Bennett (1967), this was particularly true of Artemis of the Tauric Chersonese, of Brauron, and of Laodicea, as well as of Artemis variously surnamed *Tauropolos*, *Laphria*, *Agrotera*, and *Hegemone*.

21. It has its analog in the Semitic *Hallelu*, which has survived in the Christian *Hallelujah* (Herodotus 1920, 4.189.2n2, trans. Godley).

22. W. R. Smith (1907, 431) conjectures that the Libyan *ololugê* was generally a cry of ritual lamentation for sacrificial victims.

23. The verb Pindar uses is the aorist *alalaxa*, formed from the cry *ololugê* (Liddell and Scott 1889, s.v. *alalazô*).

Chapter 4   Hera: Virgin Queen of Heaven, Earth, and the Underworld

1. Cf. Apollodorus (1.1.5), who calls Hestia the eldest daughter of Cronus and Rhea.

2. Aristophanes (*Women at the Thesmophoria* 970); Plutarch (in Eusebius *Preparation for the Gospel* 3 Preface = *Moralia* 15.157).

3. Euboia: Stephanus Byzantius (s.v. *Karustos*); Samos: Varro (in Lactantius *On False Religion* 1.17); Cnossus: Diodorus Siculus (5.72.4); Mt. Thornax: scholiast on Theocritus 15.64, Pausanias (2.36.2).

4. See, e.g., Müller (1857, 249–55); Harrison ([1903] 1957, 315–21); Kerenyi (1975, 123, 132–36 and *passim*); O'Brien (1993, *passim*); Burkert (1985, 130–31). For feminist analyses of Hera, see, e.g., Spretnak (1978, 87–84); Baring and Cashford (1991, 310–19); Downing (1992, 68–98).

5. "Queen of gods": Homeric *Hymn to Hera* (2); seasons: O'Brien (1993, 116–17); earthquakes: Homer (*Iliad* 8.199, 14.285); atmosphere: Cicero (*De Natura Deorum* 2.26); rain: Pausanias (2.25.10); wind: Homer (*Iliad* 14.249), Apollodorus (2.7.1), Orphic *Hymn to Hera*; stars: Hyginus (*Poetic Astronomy* 2.3, 2.43). Hera's association with the moon was more oblique, expressed in her connection with the cow. As Kerenyi (1975, 127) notes, the horns of cattle were a symbol of the crescent moon in nearby West Asia. Moreover, Hera's triple titles at Stymphalos of *Pais* (Child), *Teleia* (Fulfilled or Full-Grown), and *Chera* (Widow) (Pausanias 8.22.2) may reflect the waxing, full, and waning periods of the moon (Kerenyi 1975, 121–22, 128–31). Cook (1914–40, 1:455–57) notes other scholarly arguments that Hera was identified with the moon, although he questions whether this identification took place before 625 B.C.E.

6. Willow: Pausanias (7.4.4, 8.23.5); asterion: Pausanias (2.17.2); lily: Clement of Alexandria (*Christ the Educator* 72); pomegranate: Pausanias (2.17.4), Philostratus (*Life of Apollonius of Tyana* 4.28); wheat: *Etymologicum Magnum* (s.v. *zeuxidia*, in Farnell [1896–1909] 1977, 1:242n13a), which calls wheat "flowers of Hera."

7. Peacock: Pausanias (2.17.6); see O'Brien (1993, 38–39) for discussion of coins depicting Hera and peacocks at her central cult location of Samos; hawk: Aelian (*On Animals* 12.4); doves: O'Brien (229–30).

8. As the story continues, upon the arrival of the threesome, the Argives praised the young men for their strength and courtesy. Flushed with pride, their mother prayed that Hera would grant them the best thing possible for men. When the youths were found dead in the temple the next morning, it was clear to all that the goddess's message was that death was the greatest blessing that could befall a human being. The story underscores Hera's early association with death and the underworld, as Argos was the location of one of her oldest cults.

9. See Antoninus Liberalis (*Metamorphoses* 16); Aelian (*On Animals* 15.29); and Ovid (*Metamorphoses* 6.90).

10. See, e.g., Aristotle (frag. 570, in Cook 1914–40, 3.2:1027n1); Pliny (*Natural History* 5.37); scholiast on Apollonius Rhodius 1.185–87; Callimachus (*Hymn 4 to Delos* 49); Strabo (10.2.17). Kerenyi (1975, 156) argues that the claim that *Parthenia* was the "original" name of Samos was false. Regardless, the important point is that the name came to be associated with Hera there at some early date.

11. See Strabo (10.2.17); Eustathius on Dionysius Periegeta 533, scholiast on Apollonius Rhodius 1.187, and scholiast on Homer's *Iliad* 14.295–96, all in Cook (1914–40, 3.2:1027n1).

12. See, e.g., Neumann (1963, 240–67) for an analysis of the tree as a symbol of primal female generativity, and the implication of its specifically parthenogenetic nature.

13. It should be acknowledged that the expanded term *parthenios anêr* could refer simply to a man who married a virgin (Plutarch *Pompey* 74.3). This usage is obscure, however, and evidence for this particular meaning is lacking in the early Heraian context.

14. See, e.g., Aelian (*On Animals* 9.26); Pliny (*Natural History* 24.33); Dioscorides (*Greek Herbal* 1.135, s.v. *Agnos* [1934] 1968, 73, ed. Gunther). Also see Cook's (1914–40, 3.2:1030n5) citations of Galen (*De Simplicium Medicamentorum Temperamentis* 6.2), scholiast on Nicander's *Theriaca* 71, and Eustathius on *Odyssey* 1639, 2ff.

15. For a discussion of bride abduction, or *klepsigamia*, in ancient Greece, see Brumfield (1981, 129n37). I also refer to this term in chapter 5.

16. Hera's wedding on Samos is also spoken of by Varro (in Lactantius *On False Religion* 1.17) and St. Augustine (*City of God* 6.7).

17. Farnell's interpretation of Hera ([1896–1909] 1977, 1:179–204, especially 190–91) is hampered by the same restrictive notion, which prevents him from resolving the paradox of Hera's having being seen simultaneously as a *parthenos* and a mother figure in antiquity. It also causes him to disallow Hera's original identification as a generative earth goddess (181–84).

18. Pliny (*Natural History* 24.38); Dioscorides (*Greek Herbal* 1.135, s.v. *Agnos*, ed. Gunther [1934] 1968, 73).

19. Argos is depicted as Hera's "home" in Pindar (*Nemean Odes* 10.1) and is intimated as being such by Homer (*Iliad* 5.908, 4.51–52).

20. See Rigoglioso (2009, 184–85), where I discuss women's practice of vaginal fumigation and the possible chemical role of "vapors" in the trance/impregnation of the Delphic priestess.

21. For Hera's parthenogenetic birth of Hephaestus, see Hesiod (*Theogony* 927–28), Chrysippus (frag 908, in Hesiod *Theogony* 925, 1959, 179), and Apollodorus (1.3.5). Apollodorus notes, however, that Homer claims Zeus was the father. In another myth, Prometheus was also Hera's son, by the Giant Eurymedon (scholiast on *Iliad* 14.296), which further points to her connection with the pre-patriarchal, pre-Zeusian order.

22. The story is also mentioned by Stesichorus (frag. 239 *Etymologicum Genuinum* in Campbell 1991, 167).

23. Typhon's name in myth also appears as *Tuphaôn* (Typhaon), *Tuphôeus* (Typhoeus), and *Tuphôs* (Typhos). In Hesiod's *Theogony* (270–306, 825, 870–80), he was born of Ge/Gaia, not Hera. Given that, as mentioned earlier, Hera was identified with Ge/Gaia, this mythologem only serves to underscore the possible identification of the two goddesses.

24. Hesiod (*Theogony* 869, 824–26); Homer (*Iliad* 2.782–83); Pindar (*Pythian Ode* 1.15–28); Aeschylus (*Prometheus Bound* 353ff); Apollodorus (1.6.3).

25. Even the Hesiodic variant that Ge/Gaia was Typhon's mother supports the "resistance" theme, as Ge/Gaia is said to have borne Typhon in anger over Zeus's defeat of the Titans. Thus, the stories of Typhon's birth from Hera and Ge/Gaia both depict an attempt to restore matriarchal order via the son.

26. Homer also further detaches Hera from her parthenogenetic powers by depicting Hephaestus not as parthenogenetically born, but as her offspring by Zeus (*Iliad* 1.578, 14.338; *Odyssey* 8.312).

27. This seems to be a variant on the story, mentioned earlier, that Zeus shackled Hera over her efforts to cause trouble for Heracles. Given that Heracles was a son of Zeus by a holy *parthenos*, Semele, he could be seen as a "double" of the god; hence, the two stories are not incompatible.

28. Guthrie (1967, 22) echoes the idea that goddesses such as Hera and Athena originally may have been imagined in the form of the animals with which they were associated (which include the cow for the former and the owl for the latter). The idea of Old European goddesses originating in serpentine and aviary form has been further developed by Gimbutas (see, e.g., 1989, 3–17, 25–41, 63–65, 121–37).

29. See, e.g., Callimachus (*Hymn to Delos* 55–65); scholiast on Euripides *Phoenissae* 232; Hyginus (*Fabulae* 140).

30. For discussion of Hathor's role in this regard, see Rigoglioso (2007, 79–80).

31. See Rigoglioso (2009, 68–70, 100 103), where I argue that various rites may have represented propitiation to Athena and Artemis for the violation of their parthenogenetic priesthoods.

32. See, e.g., Apollodorus (3.6.7); Phlegon (*Mirabilia* 4); Tzetzes *On Lycophron* 683; Eustathius on Homer's *Odyssey* 10.492; scholiast on Homer's *Odyssey* 10.494; Antoninus Liberalis (*Metamorphoses* 17); Ovid (*Metamorphoses* 3.320–35); Hyginus (*Fabulae* 75).

33. For further discussion of "shape-shifting," or "metamorphosis," as a standard power of holy persons in the Graeco-Roman world, see Rigoglioso (2009, 93–94).

34. For a powerful and convincing argument that the archetypal symbol of "two snakes intertwined," so often witnessed by those who engage in trance journeys, is a homolog for DNA and the very mystery of incarnation itself, see Narby (1998).

35. Some traditions name only three (Apollonius Rhodius 4.1427; Servius on Virgil's *Aeneid* 4.484), whereas others name seven (Diodorus Siculus 4.27.2; Hyginus *Fabulae* Preface).

36. In other traditions, they are called daughters of Erebus (Hyginus *Fabulae* Preface), or of Phorcys and Cato (scholiast on Apollonius Rhodius 4.1399), or of Atlas and Hesperis (Diodorus Siculus 4.27.1–2). Sometimes also they are named daughters of Hesperus, or of Zeus and Themis (Servius on Virgil's *Aeneid* 4.484; scholiast on Euripides's *Hippolytus* 742).

37. E.g., Apollonius Rhodius (*Argonautica* 4.1390); Diodorus Siculus (4.26.2); Hyginus (*Astronomica* 2.3). Apollodorus (3.5.11) notes the tradition that

the Hesperides were located in Libya, but places them instead "with Atlas among the Hyperboreoi."

38. Faraone (1990), for example, presents a wide-ranging analysis of how apples, quinces, pomegranates, and other fruit designated by the Greek word *mêlon* were used to these erotic ends.

39. It may be due to its parthenogenetic associations that the pomegranate was sometimes linked with the Virgin Mary, the most famous holy *parthenos* of all, as in Botticelli's painting "The Madonna of the Pomegranate" (see, e.g., Starbird 1993, plate 18). Interpreting the apple as a parthenogenetic symbol also allows for an entirely new reading of the schema of Eve, the apple, and the snake found in *Genesis* 3. Could this triad refer to human women's knowledge of virgin birth? That the ancient Hebrews indeed believed in divine birth through *hieros gamos* between women an incorporeal entities is indicated in *Genesis* 6, where it is written, "The Nephilim were on earth in those days...when the sons of God resorted to the women, and had children by them. These were the heroes of days gone by, men of renown" (*New Jerusalem Bible* 1990, 9). That the apple was a reference to parthenogenetic knowledge is supported by the idea that the eating of it rendered humans as gods. Here, we will recall my assertion that the holy *parthenos* who gave birth in virgin fashion was rendered divine, as was, in many cases, her progeny. Thus the negative treatment of Eve for having eaten of the apple suggests that such knowledge was, under patriarchy, made transgressive, particularly in that it was the province of women. In Sethian Gnostic theogony, the taboo against female parthenogenetic capacity was maintained in the legend of Sophia, whose parthenogenetic production of Achamoth and Ialdabaoth was depicted as a grave violation in a male-headed universe and was accordingly punished by virtue of the offspring being "imperfect" (like Hephaestus) and, in the case of Ialdabaoth, a powermonger (like Typhon). See *The Secret Book of John* (in Barnstone and Meyer 2003, 146–49). See also chapter 6 in this volume, on Sophia, as well as Rigoglioso (2009 38n17), regarding the ancient parallels between mythological and biological deformity in certain cases of parthenogenesis.

40. For Peleus's pursuit of Thetis, see Apollodorus (3.13.5) and Pindar (*Nemean Ode* 3.32–36). Cf. Philostratus (*On Heroes* 45.2–4), who relates a legend that another marine divinity appeared to Peleus on Mount Pelion, testified her love to him, and promised to present him with a son who should be more illustrious than any mortal. The bulk of the legends suggest that Thetis's marriage occurred against her will. Poseidon and Zeus are said by some to have sued for Thetis's hand (Pindar *Isthmian Ode* 8.27–29), but when Themis declared that the son of Thetis would be more illustrious than his father, both suitors desisted.

41. For the relationship of Thetis to Achilles, see, e.g., Homer (*Iliad* 1.351–63, 495–543, 18.70–148, 381–467).

42. See, e.g., Proclus (*Chrestomathy* 1, in West 2003a, 68); Apollodorus (E3.2–3); Pausanias (5.19.5); Hyginus (*Fabulae* 92); Colluthus (*Rape of Helen* 59–221).

43. I suggest this episode may point to a period of time in which the cult of divine birth was losing status, possibly in favor of the Aphroditian cult of sacred prostitution. Strabo (17.1.46) mentions an Egyptian custom whereby a prepubescent girl of high birth who was dedicated to Zeus seems to have freely engaged in sexual relations with men until the time of her menarche and marriage. Budin (2003, 151–52) questions the interpretation that such a girl "concubined" herself, suggesting, instead, that she served as a handmaiden. Nevertheless, if the Theban maidens' role indeed was sexual, it may signal a devolving over the centuries of the original role of the virgin "God's Wife" into that of cult prostitute. For Herodotus (1.81–2), it is clear that the priestess of his day who was dedicated to Theban Zeus did not engage in sex with other men. On the other hand, it may be that a priesthood of sacred prostitutes had (always?) existed alongside that of the virgins. I offer the conjecture that in such a case, each priesthood would have had a separate function: the latter, to engender the divine child; the former to unite with him sexually to create his earthly lineage. A serious consideration of the cult of the sacred prostitute, of which Aphrodite was the tutelary goddess in the Greek context, is beyond the scope of this work. For suggestions of the practice of sacred prostitution in ancient Greece and West Asia, see, e.g., Herodotus (1.199); Strabo (6.2.6, 8.6.20, 12.3.36). Cf. Budin (2008), who argues that sacred prostitution did not in fact exist in the ancient world.

44. For discussions of the hero cult of Greece and categories of heroes, see, e.g., Farnell (1921), Rhode ([1925] 1966, 115–55), and Burkert (1985, 203–15).

45. As Rhode ([1925] 1966, 141n23) points out, divine parentage was not necessarily a *requirement* for being made a hero. Nevertheless, many heroes indeed were believed to have had a divine parent, as is evident in works such as Hesiod's *Theogony* and the Hesiodic *Catalogue of Women*, as well as in many of the myths discussed throughout *CDB*. Burkert (1985, 207–8) affirms that sons of gods were regarded as heroes.

46. Alcmene's ancestral connection to Io can be traced through Perseus back to Io's son, Epaphus, founder of a family from whom sprang Danaus, Perseus's grandfather, and the father of the Danaids, whom I discuss as priestesses of divine birth associated with Demeter and Persephone in chapter 5. See Smith (1870, s.v. *Io*) and Apollodorus (2.1–4) to piece together this lineage.

47. For other mentions and versions of this story, see Hyginus (*Fabulae* 29); Pindar (*Isthmian Ode* 7.6–7; *Nemean Ode* 10.11–14); scholiast on Homer's *Odyssey* 11.266.

48. Homer (*Iliad* 19.98–133); Apollodorus (2.4.5); Diodorus (4.9); Pausanias (9.11.3).

49. Pausanias (9.25.2); Pseudo-Eratosthenes (*Constellations* 44); Hyginus (*Poetic Astronomy* 2.43).

50. Other scholars have also argued that Heracles' divine conception and suckling were influenced by Egyptian royal iconography and inscriptions, e.g., Burkert (1965, 166–77), and West (1997, 458–59). Such correspondences suggest that the Egyptian motifs of the New Kingdom could have made their way into pre-Homeric Greece as early as c. 1473 B.C.E. (Faraone and Teeter 2004, 200).

51. Other traditions place this madness at a later time and give it different circumstances. See Euripides (*Heracles* 914ff.); Pausanias (9.11.1); Hyginus (*Fabulae* 32); scholiast on Pindar's *Isthmian Ode* 3.104.

52. It should be noted that Diodorus (1.24; 3.74.4–5) says that *Heracles* is the name given to three heroes in ancient times whose legends were combined in the story of the "twelve labors" of the prince of the Greek city of Tyrins. The most ancient Heracles, Diodorus says, was born in Egypt, subdued a large part of the inhabited world, and set up pillars on each side of the Straits of Gibraltar to mark his conquests on each continent. Herodotus (2.42–44) confirms that Egyptians believed Heracles was of Egyptian origin; according to Diodorus (1.24) the Egyptians dated this Heracles to what we may determine was c. 10,000 B.C.E. The second Heracles, according to Diodorus, was a priest on Crete and the founder of the Olympic games. The third and last hero of this name was born of Alcmene and Zeus "a generation before the Trojan War." After his death, the twelve labors, which included some of the exploits of the previous two Heracles figures, were attributed to him. Even if the Heracles of the twelve labors myth was an amalgam character, however, this does not invalidate my basic point that what essentially is being described in the myth is the assailing of the divine birth priestesshood by the forces of patriarchy.

53. Hesiod (*Theogony* 313–25); Apollodorus (2.5.2); Diodorus (4.11.5–6); Ovid (*Metamorphoses* 9.70ff); Virgil (*Aeneid* 8.300); Pausanias (2.37.4); Hyginus (*Fabulae* 30).

54. See Cooper (2003) for an extensive analysis of the self-generating qualities of the hydra.

55. Anaxagoras in the scholiast on Apollonius Rhodius (in Cook 1914–40 1:456–57) tells the same story.

56. See also scholiast on Pindar's *Olympian Ode* 3.53; Apollodorus (2.5.3); Diodorus (4.13.1;) Aelian (*On Animals* 7.39); Virgil (*Aeneid* 6.803).

57. As I discuss in *CDB*, according to another tradition, Taygete was unable to avoid Zeus, and by him became pregnant with Lacedaemon (Rigoglioso 2009, 165–66). The latter became the legendary king of the country to which he gave his own name, and of which Sparta was the capital (Apollodorus 3.10.3; Pausanias 3.1.2). According to the scholiast on Pindar's *Olympian Ode* 3.53, Artemis turned Taygete into a cow, which further suggests a link with Hera, given Hera's own bovine associations and the metamorphosis of her priestess Io into a cow.

58. E.g., Herodotus (4.10.1), where it belongs to Heracles, and Apollodorus (2.5.9), where it is said to be a gift to Hippolyte from Ares in exchange for her prowess in warfare.

59. Apollodorus (2.5.11); Diodorus (4.26.2–4); Pliny (*Natural History* 5.8); Apollonius Rhodius (4.1396); Hyginus (*Fabulae* 30, *Poetic Astronomy* 2.6); Pseudo-Eratosthenes (*Constellations* 4).

Chapter 5   Demeter and Persephone: Double Goddesses of Parthenogenesis

1. For the sake of convenience sake, I will refer to this poem simply as *Hymn* throughout this chapter.

2. For a comprehensive listing of these and other versions of the myth and ancient literature whose treatment of Demeter and Persephone seems to have been influenced by the *Hymn*, see Richardson (1974, 68–86).

3. Diodorus Siculus (3.62.7–8); cf. Callimachus (*Hymn* 6.136); Farnell ([1896–1909] 1977, 3.29–34; 48–51).

4. See, e.g., Farnell ([1896–1909] 1977, vol. 3); Zuntz (1971, 75–83); Richardson (1974, 16ff.); Suter (2002 121ff.). See Suter (2002, 229–36) for a survey of major classicists' conjectures about the prehistory of the Demeter and Persephone myth and their cults, including those of Farnell, Nilsson, Burkert, Bert, and Zuntz.

5. Lincoln (1981, 79) suggests that Kore's name was changed to Persephone as a result of her sojourn in the underworld, and was indicative of female pubertal initiation.

6. Cleanthes (fr. 547, in Plutarch *Moralia* 377D); Cicero (*De Natura Deorum* 2.66); scholiast on Hesiod *Theogony* 912, Tzetzes on Hesiod *Works and Days* 32, and Cornutus 28 (all in Foley 1994, 59n99).

7. Diodorus Siculus (3.64.1); Hyginus (*Fabulae* 167); Nonnus (6.155–65); Clement of Alexandria (*Exhortation to the Greeks* 2.14).

8. See also Suter (2002, 169–207) for a critical assessment of detailed archaeological evidence possibly attesting to the existence of figures representing Demeter and Persephone throughout the Aegean basin, its surrounding coastlines, Greek colonies in Magna Graecia, and North Africa.

9. Mellaart (1967, 236, 238); Gimbutas (1982, 121 [fig. 86], 122 [fig. 90], 127 [figs. 100–101]; 1989, 171 [fig. 271]).

10. Jerry L. Hall, ViaGene Fertility director, personal communication, August 19, 2004. One important exception is the honeybee, which I discuss at length in *CDB* (Rigoglioso 2009, 192–94).

11. Jerry L. Hall, personal communication, August 19, 2004. What would have been stressed in the ancient condition of daughter-bearing parthenogenesis was the symbolism of the mother essentially "creating (herself) out of herself," not technical scientific details (which may or may not have been understood).

12. See Rigoglioso (2007, 205–7) for discussion of scientific experimentation with parthenogenesis and human eggs.

13. Plutarch (*Face of the Moon* 28/943B); Orphic *Hymn to Ceres* 40.21; Orphic *Hymn to Proserpine* 29.3.
14. Pausanias (8.31.2); Diodorus Siculus (5.2.4); Hyginus (*Fabulae* 146).
15. Note that some sarcophagi and other myth fragments portray the goddess's companions as deceiving her (Richardson 1974, 290). I contend that these few portrayals reflect later insertions to the story, as they seem strikingly at odds with the theme of female solidarity that dominates the myth.
16. This detail may derive from a fifth century B.C.E. Pythagorean source (Richardson 1974, 78). Diodorus Siculus (5.3.4) says she is weaving it for Zeus, but the weaving of a robe for a male god seems to be an anomaly; most *peplos* weaving was done for goddesses, at least in cult practice.
17. Scholiast on Aristophanes' *Woman at the Thesmophoria* 298; Hesychius (s.v. *Kalligeneia*) (all in Smith 1870, s.v. *Calligeneia*).
18. Scholiast on Theocritus 15.94 (in Richardson 1974, 288); scholiast on Pindar's *Pythian Ode* 4.106 (in Cook 1914–40, 1:443); Porphyry (*On the Cave of the Nymphs* 18); Callimachus (*Hymn 2 to Apollo* 110).
19. Heliodor, in Harpocration, s.v. *Nikê Athêna* (in Kerenyi 1978, 87n109).
20. Cf. Pauanias (7.17.11), who relates the tradition that the tree in question was the almond.
21. It is highly interesting that another figure whom I discern in *CDB* was also a priestess of divine birth, Nicaea, was also said to have been fathered by the Sangarius. Nicaea's mother was said to have been Cybele/Artemis herself, which I similarly interpret to mean she was a priestess of divine birth dedicated to this goddess. This genealogy indicates that Nana was related to Nicaea, and affirms that both were from a lineage of divine birth priestesses. See Rigoglioso (2009, 99).
22. In this regard, it is fascinating to note that, in antiquity, the pomegranate was used as an abortifacient (Riddle 1992, 25–26). Given its strong mythological connections to parthenogenetic fertility, however, I agree with Nixon (1995, 87–88), who suggests that it and other plants associated with the Demeter and Persephone myth and rituals, including the narcissus, crocus, and *agnus castus*, may have more broadly symbolized women's agency in regulating their reproductive lives. I would go so far as to suggest that such regulation may have been extremely necessary in the divine cult priestesshoods that I argue in *CDB* were associated with goddesses, where, in terms of conception, timing indeed may have been (nearly) everything. In this, as in everything else related to divine birth discussed in relationship to Persephone, I contend that this goddess again served as the divine "template."
23. The term *entheogens* was coined by Ruck et al. (1979). It derives from the Greek *entheos,* "full of the god," "inspired," or "possessed," and connotes a state in which both the imbiber was "in the god" and the god was "in the imbiber" (Cook 1914–40, 1:673).
24. Euripides (*Helen* 1307) and fr. 64 in Nauck *TGF*; Carcinus, in Nauck *TGF* fr. 5, line 1 (all in Kerenyi 1967, 26).

25. Cf. the "daughters of humans" who mate with the "sons of god" in Genesis 6:1–4, and related stories in *1 Enoch* and *The Testament of Reuben*, discussed in Collins (2008, 259–74).

26. Cf. Zeus's purported impregnation of the historical Olympias, mother of Alexander, in such a form (Rigoglioso 2007, 522–24).

27. Orphic *Rhapsodies* frag. 303 Kern, Orphic frags. 58, 153, 195, and 303 Kern (all in Foley 1994, 110); Orphic *Hymn to Proserpine* 29.11; Orphic *Hymn to Dionysus* 30.6–7; Diodorus Siculus (3.64.1); Hyginus (*Fabulae* 167); Clement of Alexandria (*Exhortation to the Greeks* 2.14); Nonnus (*Dionysiaca* 6.1–168).

28. See, also, Cook (1914–40, 3.913–14n4), who discusses the cult of Aeon as "the product of a comprehensive religious movement, which in some ways recalls the all-embracing ontology of Neo-Platonism."

29. It may also be important that we not try to tie Persephone's rape to a specific "moment" in historical time. While I am proposing that her rape was the cosmic marker for the commencement of patriarchy and the usurpation of the virgin birth priestesshoods on earth, I contend that it would be counter to the mystical tradition to state that Persephone's rape "occurred" at any specific "human" date, such as 5,000 B.C.E., to which the origins of patriarchy have been assigned in some quarters (see, e.g., Gimbutas 1989), I suggest that it will be more productive to embrace the correlation between the goddess's rape and the breaking of the earthly matriarchy more loosely and obliquely, seeing the rape as an *analogue* for what happened on earth, rather than to demand literal dates and timeframes.

30. I wish to thank Shannon Werner for this insight.

31. It is instructive here to note the striking parallel with the Virgin Mary, who, according to the *Infancy Gospel of James* (10–12), was also weaving when the angel announced her miraculous conception of Jesus. I will discuss further similarities between Mary's motifs and elements found the Greek cult of divine birth in my third volume, *Miraculous Birth across the Ancient Mediterranean World*.

32. The loom is mentioned here as a sacred symbol, as well, which has resonances with my interpretation of Homer's portrayal of the "cave of the nymphs," in which the loom also appears in relation to various partheno-genetic motifs, such as nymphs, bees, and so forth. See Rigoglioso (2009, 197–99).

33. For more on the comparison, see Richardson (1974, 27); Foley (1994, 52n79).

34. See also Frazer's commentary on customs around the world involving passing a child above or close to fire or smoke to purify it of evil spirits (in Apollodorus 1967, 2:311–17). I suggest that such customs *derive* from original fire rites intended to seal a miraculously born child's divinity.

35. See Richardson (1974, 232). Here, details from the life of Jesus being baptized by John the Baptist and being anointed by a figure some identify with Mary Magdalene come to mind.

36. The crucifixion of Jesus also comes to mind here.

37. Foley (1994, 52n79), however, notes that the latter is not attested.

38. See also Foley (1994, 41) for affirmation of these associations.

39. Other traditions list him variously as the son of Eleusis, of a hierophant named Trochilus and an unnamed woman of Eleusis, of Dysaules, or of Rarus and the daughter of Amphictyon. In the verses of Musaeus, he was apparently named the son of Ocean and Earth. See Apollodorus (1.5.2); Pausanias (1.14.2–3).

40. Sophocles (fr. 83, in Richardson 1974, 76); Apollodorus (1.5.2); Pausanias (1.14.2). Richardson (1974, 195–96) details the development of Triptolemus as the teacher of agriculture and Attic hero.

41. It is relevant here that Pausanias (1.38.7) notes a tradition in which the hero Eleusis, after whom the city came to be named, was considered a son of Hermes and of Daeira, daughter of Ocean. This once again points to a divine birth story behind a major eponym associated with the Demeter/Persephone complex.

42. As I discuss further later, however, such legends may simply reflect a cultural memory that agriculture was instituted on a large scale under his reign, rather than a claim that he was its inventor.

43. IG i^2.76.38, ii.140.20 ff. (in Richardson 1974, 196); Pausanias (1.14.1, 1.38.6).

44. When applied to Hades, the epithet "Good Counselor" is likely euphemistic, however.

45. In Euripides' *Erechtheus*, Eumolpus is killed in battle, and it may be his descendent whom Athena predicts will found the Mysteries at Eleusis. Richardson (1974, 198, 78) notes that "two Eumolpoi" were probably devised to account for the legend that made this figure the son of the so-called Thracian poet Musaeus.

46. Again, see Richarson (1974, 201) and Foley (1994, 138) for several mentioned earlier.

47. See also Ruck (in Wasson et al. 2008, 98–102) for an extensive catalogue of ancient references attesting to the narcotic and psychotropic nature of wine in Greek antiquity.

48. Independently, Ruck (in Wasson et al. 2008, 108) has discerned that Demeter refuses the wine because she did not want to "partake herself of the body of the abductor," that is, Dionysus.

49. See Rigoglioso (2009, 62–71) for an analysis of Erichthonius in the context of the divine birth cult to Athena.

50. Indeed, certain myths relate that Demophoon actually died as a result of the interruption of the rite. See Apollodorus (1967, 2:311–12, ed. Frazer).

51. It is a story that continues as of this writing, with a rising genetic-engineering establishment and the attempted appropriation of all seed production by certain corporate entities.

52. I will not discuss other festivals dedicated to Demeter and Persephone that included private women's rites: the Proerosia, Haloa, Skira, Kalamaia. For details on such rites, see, e.g., Brumfield (1981).

53. For more detailed discussions of the Thesmophoria, see, e.g., Brumfield (1981), Zeitlin (1982), Burkert (1985), and Goff (2004).

54. Aelian (frag. 44, in Foley 1994, 74n33); Suda (s.v. *Thesmophoros* and *Sphaktriai*); Pausanias (4.17.1); Aristophanes (*Women at the Thesmophoria* ff.).

55. The Thesmophoria is attested in at least thirty other cities in Greece, Asia Minor, and Sicily. See Brumfield (1981, 70).

56. Hesychius (s.v. *Anados*); scholiast on Aristophanes *Women at the Thesmophoria* 80, 585; Alciphron (2.37.2); Photius (s.v. *Thesmophoriôn*) (all in Brumfield 1981, 82n48).

57. Plutarch (*On Isis and Osiris* 69/378E); Pliny (*Natural History* 24.59); Aelian (*History of Animals* 9.26). See also Smith et al. (1890, s.v. *Thesmophoria*).

58. Scholiast on Aristophanes *Women at the Thesmophoria* 80, Alciphron (2.37.2); Photius (s.v. *Thesmophoriôn*) (all in Brumfield 1981, 83n56).

59. Clement of Alexandria (*Exhortation to the Greeks* 2.14–15); Diodorus Siculus (5.4.7); Plutarch *On Isis and Osiris* (69/378F).

60. Scholiast on Sophocles *Oedipus at Colonus* 681 (in Brumfield 1981, 84n63); Ovid (*Metamorphoses* 10.438).

61. Diodorus Siculus (5.4.7); Apollodorus (1.5.1); Aristophanes (*Women at the Thesmophoria* 533ff.); Hesychius (s.v. *Stênia, stêniôsai,* in Brumfield 1981, 80n35).

62. See, e.g., Aelian (*On Animals* 9.26); Pliny (*Natural History* 24.33); Dioscorides (*Greek Herbal* 1.135, s.v. *Agnos* [1934] 1968, 73, ed. Gunther). Also see Galen (*De Simplicium Medicamentorum Temperamentis* 6.2), scholiast on Nicander's *Theriaca* 71, and Eustathius on *Odyssey* 1639, 2ff. (all in Cook 1914–40, 3.2:1030n5).

63. Archaeological evidence for use of ritual libations at Thesmophoria rites may be found farther afield, in the sanctuary of Demeter at Bitalemi in Sicily near Gela. There, where the celebration of a Thesmophoria is indicated, rows of overturned cups were found in the sanctuary, lying on the earth with a female figurine propped up among them (probably a representation of the goddess). These may indicate that a *kykeon* was drunk as part of the rite (Stehle 2007, 169).

64. Scholiast on Lucian's *Dialogues of the Courtesans* (in Brumfield 1981, 74); see also Brumfield (72).

65. See Farnell ([1896–1909] 1977, 3.75–77) for a discussion of references in this regard, although he misses the point I make in what follows about what type of "law" might be associated with Demeter.

66. Observing that poppy capsules, from which opium was extracted, are commonly represented on ruins from Eleusis, Kerenyi (1967, 180) conjectures that an opiate may have been one ingredient in the *kykeon*. Cf. Wasson et al. (2008), who think the drink contained a hallucinogen extracted from ergot, a fungus that grows on grain, and Taylor-Perry (2001), who proposes that the psychoactive substance was either the fly agaric or psilocybin-containing species of mushroom, or Syrian rue.

67. It may be significant that in the later Platonic tradition the soul's ascent *to* the One was simultaneously experienced as a descent *from* the One, as

divine manifestation. As Iamblichus expressed it, "there is no opposition between the descents of souls and their ascents" (*On the Mysteries*, 8.8; 272.7–9). Since the later philosophic tradition understood itself as an extension of the Eleusinian Mysteries—and its teachers as mystagogues—it is not surprising that the fusion and paradox of the ascent and descent associated with Demeter's rites was reflected in their philosophic discourse. I wish to thank Iamblichus scholar Gregory Shaw for these insights into Neoplatonism.

68. Photius (s.v. *magaron*); Hesychius (s.v. *anaktoron*, *megara*); Suda (s.v. *megara*) (all in Brumfield 1981, 100n53); Eustathius 1387 (in Harrison [1903] 1957, 125).

69. Although it is confusing exactly which rite the scholiast on Lucian's *Dialogues of the Courtesans* is describing (see, e.g., Brumfield 1982, 73–78 and accompanying notes discussing various academic opinions), I follow the generally accepted tradition that all of his comments are relevant to the Thesmophoria, as well as any other rite he may be discussing.

70. Brumfield (1982, 74–75) notes that the scholiast may be Arethas of Caesarea, a tenth century bishop and student of Photius. He may have derived his information from Didymus, a grammarian of the first century B.C.E.

71. It is interesting to note that at the Eleusinian Mysteries, the day known as the "Banishing" (*Elasis*) involved the ritual procession of initiates to the sea with pigs. Harrison ([1903] 1957, 152) posits this procession was intended to dispel negative spirits prior to the Mysteries.

72. Cf. Foley (1994, 171), who cites more recent archaeological evidence questioning the presence of an Eleusinian cult of Demeter in the Mycenaean period.

73. Scholiast on Aristophanes *Ploutos* 1013 (in Foley 1994, 66n6); Athenaeus (*Deipnosophistae* 6.253D); Hippolytus (*Refutation of All Heresies* 5.3); Harrison ([1903] 1957, 559).

74. Scholiast on Aristophanes *Ploutos* 1013 (in Harrison [1903] 1957, 559). Kerenyi (1967, 52–59) also presents the possibility that the Lesser Mysteries may have been instituted to purify Heracles of his murders before being initiated in the greater rites.

75. Kerenyi (1967, 62–64, 155); Aristophanes (*Frogs* 324); Plutarch (*Camillus* 19.6, *Phocion* 28.1).

76. See Clinton (1974) for an exhaustive discussion of the sacred personnel at Eleusis.

77. *Dromena:* Homeric *Hymn to Demeter* (474), Plutarch (*Alcibiades* 22.3, *Moralia* 81E), Xenophon (*Hellenica* 6.3.6); *deiknumena:* Hesychius (s.v. *hierophants,* in Brumfield 1981, 200n36); *legomena:* Sopatros *Rhetores Graeci* 8.10 Walz, Andocides 1.132 [Lysias] 6.51 (both in Brumfield 1981, 200n36).

78. Clement (*Exhortation to the Greeks* 2.13, 2.18); Lactantius (*Divine Institutions* 18 [23].7); Gregory of Nazianzus (*Orations* 39.4); Plutarch (*Moralia* fr. 178, Loeb).

79. See my remarks toward the end of the chapter on the meanings associated with the name *Brimo*.

80. Cf. the persistent ritual use as a phallic symbol of a vegetable similar in shape, the leek, by Greek women into contemporary times (Brumfield 1982, 125).

81. Cf. the scholiast on Plato's *Gorgias* (in Harrison [1903] 1957, 158) who affirms that such "disgraceful" things were done but attaches them to the Lesser Mysteries.

82. This point has been much debated. See, e.g., Richardson (1974, 26ff., 27n2, 316ff.); Kerenyi (1967, 117–18).

83. Kerenyi (1967, 117–18) insists that the Church fathers commenting on the phenomenon were mistaking what took place during the mysteries at Alexandria for what took place at Eleusis. His reasoning is that the secrecy around the Eleusinian rites was so tight that information about such sexual rites never would have been revealed. I see no convincing argument in this regard, however, particularly given that the Church fathers were hostile to the Mysteries, no doubt had their ways of ferreting out information, and had no compunction about publicizing any of their rites. Mylonas (1961, 314) objects to Asterius's statement on the grounds that no underground chamber was found at Eleusis below the Telesterion where the nights of the Mysteries took place. However, as with the *megara* of the Thesmophoria, I suggest that the "subterranean passage" was one that took place on the subtle planes in an altered state of consciousness. See also Richardson (1974, 27n2), who notes other scholars who have argued for or against the idea that a *hieros gamos* took place at Eleusis, including Nilsson and Deubner.

84. Scholiast on Aristides 3.648 (in Wasson et al. 2008, 119n3); Lucretius (4.1160), Suda (s.v. *Iakchos*) (in Richardson 1974, 320).

85. Hippolytus (*Refutation of All Heresies* 5.7.34); Proclus (*In Platonis Timaeum Commentaria III* 176.28), IG ii–iii² 4876 (in Foley 1994, 69).

86. Clinton (1974, 98) disputes the existence of such priestesses at Eleusis. Cf. Foucart (1914, 214–15), who is of the opposite opinion. Hesychius identifies them as priestesses of Athens (Turner 1983, 185). Whether they were associated with Athens or Eleusis proper, their *Melissa* title still suggests that they were part of the larger Demetrian cult.

87. Scholiast on Pindar's *Pythian Ode* 4.106 (in Cook 1914–40, 1:443); Callimachus (*Hymn 2 to Apollo* 110); Lactantius (*Divine Institutes* 1.2); Hesychius (s.v. *Melissai*).

88. See *Moralia* (fr. 178, Loeb), for one location of this excerpt, with an alternate translation.

89. See, e.g., Wasson et. al. (2008); Eyer (1993); Taylor-Perry (2001). See also Hillman (2008) and Scarborough (1991) on the widespread use of plants to induce altered states of consciousness in the ancient world.

90. See also Richardson (1974, 167) for a list of purposes behind fasting in the ancient world and many contemporary societies.

91. This discussion of Dieterich, Kern, and Picard is taken from Mylonas (1961, 296). Other scholars have conjectured that ritual joking that occurred at the Mystery rites may have had a scatological component that was also related to the handling of the sacred objects (see Richardson 1974, 215–16).
92. Again, see Rigoglioso (2009, 46–50, 97–98) for discussion of Dionysus as an initiator of women into the cosmic erotic mysteries.
93. Proclus on Hesiod's *Erga kai Hemerai* 389, excerpting Plutarch, in Kerenyi (1967, 127).
94. Again, see Hillman (2008); Ruck (in Wasson et al. 2008, 90–108); Scarborough (1991) for discussion of the widespread use of entheogenic plants in antiquity.
95. Clement (*Exhortation to the Greeks* 2.12); Lactantius (*Epitome of the Divine Institutes* 18 [23].7); Gregory of Nazianzus (*Orations* 39.4).
96. Apollonius Rhodius (3.861–62); Smith (1870, s.v. Brimo); Kerenyi (1967, 92–93). Harrison ([1903] 1957, 551–53) says that Brimo was an underworld goddess from Thessaly and that her name may be connected with *obrimos*, "raging," the epithet of Ares.
97. It is important to emphasize that the interpretation being offered here is not one asserting that "rape," trauma, or the imposition of masculine power are necessary on any level (cosmic or human) for the "evolution" of the human race or of "consciousness" more broadly. The argument being made is far more subtle and paradoxical.

Chapter 6   The Gnostic Sophia: Divine Generative Virgin

1. Joan O'Brien and Wilfred Major (1982, 195) note that both the *Enuma Elish* and *Genesis* 1:1 use "a clause beginning with 'when'" to describe the time in which "the formless world...existed prior to creation."
2. I have relied on the translation by the Christian Classics Ethereal Library, Ante-Nicene Fathers, vol. 1, as well as the description and summary provided by Gnostic scholar Robert Grant (1961, 162–77) of the Valentinian system from Harvey's 1857 translation. I have chosen to use this particular text because it is the most widely available representation of the basic Valentinian origin story, and it contains many of the elements found in other Gnostic creation myths. Irenaeus was one of the prominent leaders of the early Christian church who branded the Gnostics as heretics. He attributes his version of the myth to the teachings of Ptolemy (*Against Heresies* preface, 2), a disciple of Valentinus and perhaps the most well-known systematic theologian of the Valentinian school.
3. The text that follows in this section is my summary of the works of Irenaeus and Grant, as noted in n2.
4. The Pleroma, which is essentially the totality of divine characteristics, is sometimes known as the Perfection. According to Williams (1996, 10),

"At this point in the myth, the scene portrayed in this divine realm is one of complete order, peace, and reverence, with the entire population of entities/attributes glorifying the Invisible God from whom they all ultimately emerged as if from a mysterious spring. When God images himself/herself, the imagination is this household full of Perfection."

5. Hippolytus, in his third-century *Refutation of Heresies* (6.26), notes that among the various beliefs held by different Valentinian groups, some maintained that the Father, Depth, the primal source, was a monad, not united with Silence as Mother in a dyad. Therefore, it is only with the appearance of Christ and Holy Spirit that the *aeons* reach the number thirty, still the number of completeness within the Pleroma.

6. Note that her conception of Ialdabaoth is also depicted as being parthenogenetic in the Gnostic text *The Secret Book of John* (in Barnstone and Meyer 2003, 146).

7. The only extant copy, one of the tractates of the Nag Hammadi collection, is written in Coptic and dates to approximately 350 C.E. There is evidence that it is based on a Greek language version of earlier origins, most likely pre-Christian, according to Arthur (1984, 157). For this study, unless otherwise noted, I use the English version of the hymn from *The Nag Hammadi Library*, 3rd ed., translated from the Coptic by George MacRae (1988).

8. Observing the ancient Greek tendency to envision abstract forces (wind, anger, sleep, fear, and so forth) as anthropomorphized deities, Rigoglioso suggests that these attributes were also understood in anthropomorphic terms throughout the ancient Mesopotamian and Mediterranean world. Personal communication, February 2010. See also the introduction to this volume.

9. For a more extensive examination of the text in relation to Sophia, see Campra (2001, 80–91).

10. See also hymns to Inanna in Sumerian texts that contain statements similar in tone, dating c. 2500 B.C.E. See, e.g., Wolkstein and Kramer (1983).

11. For further discussion of other ancient female deities during cultural transitions, see Campra (2001, 126–50).

REFERENCES

Adams, Barbara. 1988. *Predynastic Egypt*. Aylesbury, UK: Shire Egyptology.

Adams, Douglas O. 1987. Hrôs and hra: Of men and heroes in Greek and Indo-European. *Glotta* 65:171–78.

Aelian. 1959. *On the characteristics of animals*. 3 vols. Trans. A. F. Scholfield. Cambridge, MA: Harvard University Press.

Aeschylus. 1926. *Aeschylus*. 2 vols. Trans. Herbert Weir Smyth. Cambridge, MA: Harvard University Press.

Allen, James P. 2000. *Middle Egyptian: An introduction to the language and culture of hieroglyphs*. New York: Cambridge University Press.

Apollodorus. 1967. *The Library*. 2 vols. Trans. Sir James George Frazer. Cambridge, MA: Harvard University Press.

Artemidorus. 1975. The interpretation of dreams (*oneirocritica*). Trans. Robert J. White. Park Ridge, NJ: Noyes.

Arthur, Rose Horman. 1984. *The wisdom goddess: Feminine motifs in eight Nag Hammadi documents*. Lanham, MD: University Press of America.

Bachofen, Johann Jakob. [1861] 1897. *Das mutterrecht*. Basel: B. Schwebe.

———. [1861] 2005. *An English translation of Bachofen's mutterricht (mother right)*. Trans. David Partenheimer. Lewiston, NY: Edwin Mellen.

———. 1973. *Myth, religion, and mother right*. Princeton, NJ: Princeton University Press.

Baring, Anne, and Jules Cashford. 1991. *The myth of the goddess: Evolution of an image*. London: Arkana.

Barnstone, Willis, and Marvin Meyer. 2003. *The Gnostic bible*. Boston: Shambhala.

Bates, Oric. 1970. *The eastern Libyans: An essay*. London: Frank Cass.

Bennett, Florence Mary. 1967. *Religious cults associated with the Amazons*. New York: AMS.

Bernal, Martin. 1987–2006. *Black Athena: The Afroasiatic roots of classical civilization*. 3 vols. New Brunswick, NJ: Rutgers University Press.

Bethge, Hans-Gebhard. 1988. Introduction: On the origin of the world. In *The Nag Hammadi library*, 3rd rev. ed., ed. James Robinson, 170–71. San Francisco: Harper Collins.

Bethge, Hans-Gebhard, Bentley Layton, and Societas Coptica Hierosolymitana, trans. 1988. On the origin of the world. In *The Nag Hammadi library*, 3rd rev. ed., ed. James Robinson. 171–89. San Francisco: Harper Collins.

Bleeker, C. J. 1975. *The rainbow: A collection of studies in the science of religion.* Leiden: Brill.

———. 1983. Isis and Hathor: Two ancient Egyptian goddesses. In *The book of the goddess past and present: An introduction to her religion,* ed. Carl Olsen, 29–48. New York: Crossroad.

Blundell, Sue. 1995. *Women in ancient Greece.* Cambridge, MA: Harvard University Press.

———. 1998. Marriage and the maiden. In *The sacred and the feminine in ancient Greece,* ed. Sue Blundell and Margaret Williamson, 47–70. London: Routledge.

Brouscaris, Maria S. 1978. *The monuments of the Acropolis.* Athens: General Direction of Antiquities and Restoration.

Brown, Truesdell S. 1946. Euhemerus and the historians. *Harvard Theological Review* 39 (4): 259–74.

Brukner, Bogdan. 2006. Possible influences of the Black Sea flood on the formation of Vinča culture. *Journal of Archaeomythology* 2 (1): 17–26. http://www.archaeomythology.org/journal/read_article.php?a=0306_3_brukner.pdf (accessed July 14, 2008).

Brumfield, Adair Chandler. 1981. *The Attic festivals of Demeter and their relation to the agricultural year.* Monographs in Classical Studies. Salem, NH: Ayer.

Budge, E. A. Wallis.[1904] 1969. *The gods of the Egyptians.* 2 vols. New York: Dover.

Budin, Stephanie Lynn. 2003. *Pallakai,* prostitutes, and prophetesses. *Classical Philology* 98, no. 2 (April): 148–59.

———. 2008. *The myth of sacred prostitution in antiquity.* Cambridge: Cambridge University Press.

Bullard, Roger A. 1988. Introduction: The hypostasis of the archons. In *The Nag Hammadi library,* 3rd rev. ed., ed. James Robinson, 161–62. San Francisco: Harper Collins.

Burkert, Walter. 1965. Demaratos, Astrabakos und Herakles: Königsmythos und politik zur zeit der perserkriege (Herodot 6.67–68). *Museum Helveticum* 22:166–77. Cited in Faraone and Teeter 2004, 198n55.

———. 1983. *Homo necans: The anthropology of ancient Greek sacrificial ritual and myth.* Trans. Peter Bing. Berkeley: University of California Press.

———. 1985. *Greek religion.* Trans. John Raffan. Cambridge, MA: Harvard University Press.

Cady, Susan, Marian Ronan, and Hal Taussig. 1989. *Wisdom's feast: Sophia in study and celebration.* San Francisco: Harper and Row.

Callimachus. 1975. *Aetia, iambi, lyric poems, hecale, minor epic and elegiac poems, and other fragments.* Trans. C. A. Trypanis. Cambridge, MA: Harvard University Press.

Campbell, David A., ed. and trans. 1991. *Greek lyric III: Stesichorus, Ibycus, Simonides, and others.* Cambridge, MA: Harvard University Press.

Campra, Angeleen. 2001. *Sophia, divine generative force: A Gnostic representation of divine image. Dissertation Abstracts International,* publ. nr. AAT3034813, DAI-A 62/11.

Canan, Janine, ed. 2004. *Messages from Amma: In the language of the heart.* Berkeley, CA: Celestial Arts.

Christ, Carol P. 1996. "A different world": The challenge of the work of Marija Gimbutas to the dominant world-view of Western culture. *Journal of Feminist Studies in Religion* 12 (2): 53–66.

Cicero. 1933. *De natura deorum; academica.* Trans. H. Rackham. New York: G. P. Putnam.

Clarke, John Henrik. 1988. African warrior queens. In *Black women in antiquity,* ed. Ivan Van Sertima, 123–34. New Brunswick, NJ: Transaction.

Clement of Alexandria. 1919. Trans. G.W. Butterworth. Cambridge, MA: Harvard University Press.

Clinton, Kevin. 1974. *Sacred officials of the Eleusinian Mysteries.* Philadelphia: American Philosophical Society.

Collins, John J. 2008. The sons of God and the daughters of men. In *Sacred marriages: The divine-human sexual metaphor from Sumer to early Christianity,* ed. Martti Nissinen and Risto Uro, 259–74. Winona Lake, IN: Eisenbrauns.

Connelly, Joan B. 1996. Parthenon and parthenoi: A mythological interpretation of the Parthenon frieze. *American Journal of Archaeology* 100, no. 1 (January): 53–80.

———. 2007. *Portrait of a priestess: Women and ritual in ancient Greece.* Princeton, NJ: Princeton University Press.

Cook, Arthur Bernard. 1914–40. *Zeus: A study in ancient Religion.* 3 vols. Cambridge: Cambridge University Press.

Cooper, Melinda. 2003. Rediscovering the immortal *hydra*: Stem cells and the question of epigenesis. *Configurations* 11 (1): 1–26.

Corradini, Anna Maria. 1997. *Meteres: Il mito del matriarchato in Sicilia.* Enna, Sicily: Papiro Editrice.

Daly, Mary. [1978] 1990. *Gyn/Ecology: The metaethics of radical feminism.* Boston: Beacon.

Danquah, J. B. 1952. The culture of the Akan. *Africa: Journal of the International African Institute* 22 (4): 360–66.

Dashu, Max. 2000. Knocking down straw dolls: A critique of Cynthia Eller's *The myth of matriarchal prehistory: Why an invented past won't give women a future.* Suppressed Histories Archive. http://www.suppressedhistories.net /articles/ eller.html (accessed July 25, 2007).

Davis, Elizabeth Gould. 1971. *The first sex.* New York: Penguin.

Davis-Kimball, Janine. 2002. *Warrior women: An archaeologist's search for history's hidden heroines.* New York: Warner.

Dergachev, V. A. 2007. *About Scepters, horses, war: Sketches in defence of migrational conception by M. Gimbutas.* St. Petersburg: Nestor-Istorija.

Detienne, Marcel, and Jean Pierre Vernant. 1978. *Cunning intelligence in Greek culture and society.* Trans. Janet Lloyd. Atlantic Highlands, NJ: Humanities.

Dexter, Miriam Robbins. 1980. The assimilation of pre-Indo-European goddesses into Indo-European society. *Journal of Indo-European Studies* 8 (1–2): 19–29.

———. 1990. *Whence the goddess: A source book.* New York: Teachers College.

Dillon, Matthew. 2001. *Girls and women in classical Greek religion.* London: Routledge.

Diodorus Siculus. 1935. *Library of history: Books 2.35–4.58.* Trans. C. H. Oldfather. Cambridge, MA: Harvard University Press.

Dioscorides. [1934] 1968. *The Greek herbal of Dioscorides.* Ed. Robert T. Gunther. London: Hafner.

Dodds, E. R. 1951. *The Greeks and the irrational.* Berkeley: University of California Press.

Downing, Christine. 1992. *The goddess: Mythological images of the feminine.* New York: Crossroad.

duBois, Page. 1982. *Centaurs and Amazons: Women and the pre-history of the great chain of being.* Ann Arbor: University of Michigan Press.

Ehrenberg, Margaret. 1989. *Women in prehistory.* Norman: University of Oklahoma Press.

Emery, Walter B. 1961. *Archaic Egypt: Culture and civilization in Egypt five thousand years ago.* London: Penguin.

Engelsman, Joan Chamberlain. [1979] 1987. *The feminine dimension of the divine.* Philadelphia: Westminster Press.

Eyer, Shawn. 1993. Psychedelic effects and the Eleusinian Mysteries. *Alexandria* 2:65–93.

Faraone, C. A. 1990. Aphrodite's *kestos* and apples for Atalanta: Aphrodisiacs in early Greek myth and ritual. *Phoenix* 44 (3): 219–43.

Faraone, C. A., and Emily Teeter. 2004. Egyptian Maat and Hesiodic Metis. *Mnemosyne* 52, fasc. 2:177–208.

Farnell, Lewis Richard. [1896–1909] 1977. *The cults of the Greek states.* 5 vols. New Rochelle, NY: Caratzas Brothers.

———. 1921. *Greek hero cults and ideas of immortality.* Oxford: Clarendon.

Foley, Helen P., ed. 1994. *The Homeric hymn to Demeter.* Princeton, NJ: Princeton University Press.

Fontenrose, Joseph. 1959. *Python: A study of Delphic myth and its origins.* Berkeley: University of California Press.

Foucart, Paul. 1914. *Les Mystères d'Éleusis.* Paris: Picard.

Georgopoulos, Neoklis A., George A. Vagenakis, and Apostolos L. Pierris. 2003. Baubo: A case of ambiguous genitalia in the Eleusinian Mysteries. *Hormones International Journal of Endocrinology and Metabolism* 2 (1): 72–75. http://www.hormones.gr/preview.php?c_id=87 (accessed February 1, 2010).

Gimbutas, Marija. 1982. *The goddesses and gods of Old Europe 6500–3500 B.C.: Myths and cult images.* Berkeley: University of California Press.

———. 1989. *The language of the goddess.* San Francisco: HarperSanFrancisco.

———. 1991. *The civilization of the goddess.* San Francisco: HarperSanFrancisco.

———. 1999. *The living goddesses.* Ed. Miriam Robbins Dexter. Berkeley: University of California Press.

Goettner-Abendroth, Heide, ed. 2009. *Societies of peace: Matriarchies past, present, and future.* Toronto: Inanna Press.

Goff, Barbara. 2004. *Citizen bacchae: Women's ritual practice in ancient Greece.* Berkeley: University of California Press.

Goodison, Lucy, and Christine Morris, eds. 1998. *Ancient goddesses.* London: British Museum.

Goody, Jack. 1959. Ethnohistory and the Akan of Ghana. *Africa: Journal of the International African Institute* 29, no. 1 (January): 67–81.

Göttner-Abendroth, Heide. 1987. *Matriarchal mythology in former times and today.* Freedom, CA: Crossing.

———. 1995. *Das matriarchat, bd.1, Geschichte seiner erforschung.* Stuttgart: Kohlhammer.

———. 1999. *Das matriarchat, bd.2/1, Stammesgesellschaften in Ostasien, Indonesien, Ozeanien.* Stuttgart: Kohlhammer.

———. 2000. *Das matriarchat, bd.2/2, Stammesgesellschaften in Amerika, Indien, Afrika.* Stuttgart: Kohlhammer.

———. 2001. Modern matriarchal studies: Definitions, scope and topicality. Paper presented at Societies in Balance, the First World Congress on Matriarchal Studies, September 5–7, 2003, Luxembourg. http://www.second-congress-matriarchal-studies.com/goettnerabendroth.html (accessed May 24, 2007).

Grant, Robert. 1961. *Gnosticism.* New York: Harper and Row.

Graves, Robert. 1960. *The Greek myths.* New York: Penguin.

Griffis-Greenberg, Katherine. 1999. Neith: Ancient goddess of the beginning, the beyond, and the end. http://www.geocities.com/skhmt_netjert/neith.html (accessed December 19, 2006).

Guthrie, W. K. C. [1952] 1993. *Orpheus and Greek religion.* Princeton, NJ: Princeton University Press.

———. 1967. *The Greeks and their gods.* Boston: Beacon.

Hagan, Helene E. 2000. *The shining ones: An etymological essay on the Amazigh roots of Egyptian civilization.* n.p.. Xlibris.

Harrison, Jane Ellen. [1903] 1957. *Prolegomena to the study of Greek religion.* New York: Meridian.

———. [1912] 1963. *Themis: A study of the social origins of Greek religion.* London: Merlin.

Hartland, Edwin Sydney. 1909–10. *Primitive paternity: Or the myth of supernatural birth in relation to the history of the family.* 2 vols. London: David Nutt.

Hayden, Brian. 1993. An archeological evaluation of the Gimbutas paradigm. *The Pomegranate* 6:35–46.

Herodotus. 1920. *The histories of Herodotus.* Trans. A. D. Godley. Cambridge, MA: Harvard University Press. Perseus Digital Library. http://perseus.mpiwg-berlin.mpg.de/cgi-bin/ptext?lookup=Hdt.+1.1.0 (accessed May 30, 2007).

———. 1972. *The histories.* Trans. Aubrey de Sélincourt. New York: Penguin.

Hesiod. 1959. *Hesiod.* Trans. Richard Lattimore. Ann Arbor: University of Michigan Press.

———. 1987. *Hesiod's theogony.* Trans. Richard S. Caldwell. Cambridge, MA: Focus Information Group.

Hillman, D. C. A. 2008. *The chemical muse: Drug use and the roots of Western civilization.* New York: Thomas Dunne.

Hippolytus. 1885. *The Refutation of All Heresies*. In *Ante-Nicene Fathers*, vol. 5, *Christian Classics Ethereal Library of Calvin College*. http://www.ccel.org/ fathers2/ANF-05/anf05–10.htm#P1593_473699 (accessed February 4, 2010).

Hollis, Susan Tower. 1994–95. Five Egyptian goddesses in the third millennium B.C. *KMT: A Modern Journal of Ancient Egypt* 5, no. 4 (Winter): 46–51.

Hwang, Helen Hye-Sook. 2005. *Seeking Mago, the great goddess: A mytho-historic-thealogical reconstruction of Magoism, an archaically originated gynocentric tradition of East Asia*. Ph.D. diss., Claremont Graduate University. *Dissertation Abstracts International*, publ. nr. AAT3159640, DAI-A 66/01 (July 2005); 218.

Irenaeus. 1885. *Against heresies*. In *Ante-Nicene Fathers*, vols. 1–2, *Christian Classics Ethereal Library of Calvin College*. http://www.ccel.org/fathers2/ANF-01/ anf01–58.htm#TopOfPage (accessed February 4, 2010).

Jacobsen, Thorkild. 1976. *The treasures of darkness: A history of Mesopotamian religion*. New Haven, CT: Yale University Press.

Jacoby, Felix. 1957–. *Die Fragmente der Griechischen Historiker*. Leiden: Brill.

Janko, Richard. 2001. The Derveni papyrus ("Diagoras of Melos, Apopyrgizontes Logoi?"): A new translation. *Classical Philology* 96 (1): 1–32.

Jung, C. G. [1963] 1973. *Essays on a science of mythology*. Princeton: Princeton University Press.

Kees, Hermann. 1961. *Ancient Egypt: A cultural topography*. Chicago: University of Chicago Press.

Keller, Mara Lynn. 1996. Gimbutas's theory of early European origins and the contemporary transformation of Western civilization. *Journal of Feminist Studies in Religion* 12 (2): 73–90.

Kerenyi, Karl. 1967. *Eleusis: Archetypal image of mother and daughter*. Princeton: Princeton University Press.

———. 1975. *Zeus and Hera: Archetypal image of father, husband, and wife*. Princeton, NJ: Princeton University Press.

———. 1978. *Athene: Virgin and mother in Greek religion*. Dallas, TX: Spring.

King, C. W. 1887. *The Gnostics and their remains, ancient and mediaeval*. 2nd ed. London: D. Nutt.

Kipp, Godehard. 1974. Zum Hera-kult auf Samos. In *Kristische und vergleichende studien*, vol. 18, ed. F. Hample and I. Weiler, 157–209. Innsbruck: Institut für Sprachwissenschaft, Universität Innsbruck. Cited in O'Brien 1993, 57n25.

Kleinbaum, Abby Wettan. 1983. *The war against the Amazons*. New York: New Press.

Lajoux, Jean-Dominique. 1963. *The rock paintings of Tassili*. Cleveland, OH: World.

Larson, Jennifer. 2001. *Greek nymphs: Myth, cult, lore*. Oxford: Oxford University Press.

Layton, Bentley, trans. 1988. The hypostasis of the archons. In *The Nag Hammadi library*, 3rd rev. ed., ed. James Robinson, 162–69. San Francisco: Harper Collins.

Lazarovici, Cornelia-Magda. 2008. Symbols and signs of the Cucuteni-Tripolye culture. *Journal of Archaeomythology* 4 (1): 65–93. http://www.archaeomythology.org/journal/read_article.php?a=0108_4_clazarovici.pdf (accessed July 14, 2008).

Lazarovici, Gheorghe. 2008. Database for signs and symbols of spiritual life. *Journal of Archaeomythology* 4 (1): 94–125. http://www.archaeomythology. org/journal/read_article.php?a=0108_5_glazarovici.pdf (accessed July 14, 2008).

Leland, Charles G. 1892. *Etruscan Roman remains*. Blaine, WA: Phoenix.

Lesko, Barbara. 1999. *The great goddesses of Egypt*. Norman, OK: University of Oklahoma Press.

Lhote, Henri. 1959. *The search for the Tassili frescoes*. London: Hutchinson.

Lichtheim, Miriam. 1973–80. *Ancient Egyptian literature*. 3 vols. Berkeley: University of California Press.

Liddell, Henry George, and Robert Scott. 1889. *An intermediate Greek-English lexicon*, 7th ed. Oxford: Oxford University Press.

Lincoln, Bruce. 1981. *Emerging from the chrysalis: Studies in rituals of women's initiation*. Cambridge, MA: Harvard University Press.

Lindsay, Jack. 1970. *The origins of alchemy in Graeco-Roman Egypt*. New York: Barnes and Noble.

Long, Asphodel P. 1993. *In a chariot drawn by lions: The search for the female in deity*. London: Women's Press.

MacRae, George, trans. 1988. The thunder: Perfect mind. In *The Nag Hammadi library*, 3rd rev. ed., ed. James Robinson, 295–303. San Francisco: Harper Collins.

Malalas, John. 1986. *The chronicle of John Malalas*. Trans. Elizabeth Jeffreys, Michael Jeffreys, and Roger Scott (with others). Melbourne: Australian Association for Byzantine Studies, University of Sydney.

Marler, Joan. 2005. The myth of universal patriarchy: A critical response to Cynthia Eller's *Myth of matriarchal prehistory*. In *Prehistoric Archaeology and Anthropological Theory and Education*, ed. L. Nikolovna, J. Fritz, and J. Higgins, 75–85. Salt Lake City: International Institute of Anthropology.

Mann, Barbara Alice. 2000. *Iroquoian women: The Gantowisas*. New York: Peter Lang.

McGuire, Anne. 1994. Thunder, Perfect mind. In *Searching the scriptures: A feminist commentary*, ed. Elisabeth Schussler Fiorenza, 39–54. New York: Crossroad.

Mellaart. James. 1967. *Çatal Hüyük: a neolithic town in Anatolia*. New York: McGraw Hill.

Meskell, Lynn. 1995. Goddesses, Gimbutas, and "New Age" archaeology. *Antiquity* 69:74–86.

Meyer, Marvin. 2007. *The Nag Hammadi scriptures*. San Francisco: HarperOne.

Meyerowitz, Eva L. R. 1951. *The sacred state of the Akan*. London: Faber and Faber.

———. 1952. *Akan traditions of origin*. London: Faber and Faber.

———. 1958. *The Akan of Ghana: Their ancient beliefs*. London: Faber and Faber.

———. 1960. *The divine kingship in Ghana and ancient Egypt*. London: Faber and Faber.

———. 1974. *The early history of the Akan states of Ghana*. London: Red Candle.

Müller, Heinrich Dietrich. 1857. *Mythologie der griechisschen stämme*. Vol. 1. Göttingen: Vandenhoeck and Ruprecht. Cited in Harrison [1903] 1957, 315n1.

Mylonas, George E. 1961. *Eleusis and the Eleusinian Mysteries*. Princeton: Princeton University Press.

Mysliwiec, Karol. 1998. *Eros on the Nile*. Ithaca, NY: Cornell University Press.

Narby, Jeremy. 1998. *The cosmic serpent: DNA and the origins of knowledge*. New York: Tarcher.

Neumann, Erich. 1963. *The great mother: An analysis of the archetype*. Princeton, NJ: Princeton University Press.

The new Jerusalem Bible. 1990. New York: Doubleday.

Nikolov, Vassil. 2009. On the semantics of Neolithic altars. In *Signs of Civilization*, ed. Joan Marler, 141–44. Sebastopol, CA: Institute of Archaeomythology.

Nilsson, Martin P. [1950] 1971. *The Minoan-Mycenaean religion and its survival in Greek religion*. New York: Biblo and Tannen.

Nixon, Lucia. 1995. The cults of Demeter and Kore. In *Women in Antiquity: New assessments,* ed. Richard Hawley and Barbara Levick, 75–96. London: Routledge.

Noble, Vicki. 2003. *The double goddess: Women sharing power*. Rochester, VT: Bear.

Oates, Whitney J., and Eugene O'Neill, Jr., eds. 1938. *The complete Greek drama*. 2 vols. New York: Random House.

O'Brien, Joan V. 1993. *The transformation of Hera: A study of ritual, hero, and the goddess in the* Iliad. Lanham, MD: Rowman and Littlefield.

O'Brien, Joan, and Wilfred Major. 1982. *In the beginning: Creation myths from ancient Mesopotamia, Israel, and Greece*. American Academy of Religion Aids for the Study of Religion Series, no. 11. Chico, CA: Scholars Press.

Pagels, Elaine. 1979. *The Gnostic gospels*. New York: Vintage Books.

Parrott, Douglas M., ed. 1988. The thunder: Perfect mind. In *The Nag Hammadi library*, 3rd rev. ed., ed. James Robinson, 295–303. San Francisco: Harper Collins.

Petrie, W. M. F. 1901. *Diospolis parva: The cemeteries of Abadiyeh and Hu*. London: Egypt Exploration Fund.

Pindar. 1997. *Nemean odes, Isthmian odes, fragments*. Ed. and trans. William H. Race. Cambridge, MA: Harvard University Press.

Plato. 1892. *The dialogues of Plato*, 3rd ed. 5 vols. Trans. B. Jowett. London: Oxford University Press. Also available online at http://oll.libertyfund.org//files/766/0131–02_Bk.pdf.

———. 1925. *Plato in twelve volumes*. Trans. W. R. M. Lamb. Cambridge, MA: Harvard University Press. Perseus Digital Library. http://perseus.mpiwg-berlin.mpg.de/cgi-bin/ptext?lookup=Plat.+Hipp.+Maj.+281a (accessed June 1, 2007).

Plutarch. 1970. *Plutarch's de Iside et Osiride*. Ed. and trans. J. Gwyn Griffiths. Cardiff: University of Wales Press.

Proclus. 1820. *The commentaries of Proclus on the Timaeus of Plato*. 2 vols. Trans. Thomas Taylor. London: The author.

Ransome, Hilda M. [1937] 2004. *The sacred bee in ancient times and folklore*. Mineola, NY: Dover.

Reis, Patricia. 1991. *Through the goddess: A woman's way of healing*. New York: Continuum.

Rhode, Erwin. [1925] 1966. *Psyche: The cult of souls and belief in immortality among the Greeks*. 2 vols. Trans. W. B. Hillis. New York: Harper Torchbooks.

Richardson, N. J. 1974. *The Homeric Hymn to Demeter*. Oxford: Clarendon Press.

Riddle, John M. 1992. *Contraception and abortion from the ancient world to the Renaissance*. Cambridge, MA: Harvard University Press.

Rigoglioso, Marguerite. 2007. *Bearing the holy ones: A study of the cult of divine birth in ancient Greece*. Dissertation Abstracts International, publ. nr. AAT3286688, DAI-A 68/10.

———. 2009. *The cult of divine birth in ancient Greece*. New York: Palgrave Macmillan.

Robertson, A. F. 1976. Review of *The early history of the Akan states of Ghana* by Eva L. R. Meyerowitz. *The International Journal of African Historical Studies* 9 (1): 169–70.

Rose, H. J. 1959. *A handbook of Greek mythology*. New York: Dutton.

Roth, Ann Macy. 2000. Ancient Egyptian beliefs about conception and fertility. In *Reading the body: Representations and remains in the archaeological record*, ed. Alison E. Rautman, 187–201. Philadelphia: University of Philadelphia Press.

Ruck, Carl A. P., Jeremy Bigwood, Danny Staples, Jonathan Ott, and Gordon Wasson. 1979. Entheogens. *Journal of Psychedelic Drugs* 11 (1–2): 145–46.

Ruether, Rosemary Radford. 1992. *Gaia and God: An ecofeminist theology of earth healing*. San Francisco: HarperSanFrancisco.

Sanday, Peggy Reeves. 1998. Matriarchy as a sociocultural form. Paper presented at the 16th Congress of the Indo-Pacific Prehistory Association, July 1–7, Melaka, Malaysia.

Sayed, Ramadan el-. 1982. *La déese Neith de Saïs: Importance et rayonnement de son cult*. Cairo: IFAO.

Scarborough, John. 1991. The pharmacology of sacred plants, herbs, and roots. In *Magika hiera: Ancient Greek magic and religion,* ed. Christopher A. Faraone and Dirk Obbink, 138–74. New York: Oxford University Press.

Schliemann, Heinrich. [1881] 1968. *Ilios and the city and country of the Trojans*. New York: Benjamin Blom.

Schroer, Silvia. 2000. *Wisdom has built her house: Studies on the figure of Sophia in the Bible*. Trans. Linda M. Maloney and William McDonough. Collegeville, MN: Liturgical Press.

Sethe, Kurt. 1906. Der name des göttin Neith. *Zeitschrift für Ägyptische Sprache und Altertumskunde* 43:144–47. Cited in Lesko 1999, 47.

Shaktini, Namascar. 1982. Displacing the phallic subject: Wittig's lesbian writing. *Signs* 8 (1): 29–44.

Sjöö, Monica, and Barbara Mor. 1991. *The great cosmic mother*. San Francisco: HarperSanFrancisco.

Smith, W. Robertson. 1907. *Religion of the Semites*, 3rd ed. London: Adam and Charles Black.

Smith, William, ed. 1870. *Dictionary of Greek and Roman biography and mythology.* Boston: Little, Brown. The Ancient Library. http://www.ancientlibrary.com/smith-bio/ (accessed April 18, 2007).

Smith, William, William Wayte, and G. E. Marindin. 1890. *Dictionary of Greek and Roman antiquities,* 3rd ed. London: J. Murray. The Ancient Library. http://www.perseus.tufts.edu/cgi-bin/ptext?doc=Perseus%3Atext%3A1999.04.0063 (accessed September 18, 2007).

Sobol, Donald J. 1972. *The Amazons of Greek mythology.* New York: A. S. Barnes.

Spencer, A. J. 1993. *Early Egypt: The rise of civilization in the Nile Valley.* Norman: University of Oklahoma Press.

Spretnak, Charlene. [1978] 1981. *Lost goddesses of early Greece: A collection of pre-Hellenic myths.* Boston: Beacon.

———. 1996. Beyond the backlash: An appreciation of the work of Marija Gimbutas. *Journal of Feminist Studies in Religion* 12 (2): 91–98.

Starbird, Margaret. 1993. *The woman with the alabaster jar: Mary Magdalen and the Holy Grail.* Santa Fe, NM: Bear.

Stehle, Eva. 2007. Thesmophoria and Eleusinian Mysteries: The fascination of women's secret ritual. In *Finding Persephone: Women's rituals in the ancient Mediterranean,* ed. Maryline Parca and Angeliki Tzanetou, 165–85. Bloomington: Indiana University Press.

Suter, Ann. 2002. *The narcissus and the pomegranate: An archaeology of the Homeric Hymn to Demeter.* Ann Arbor: University of Michigan Press.

Taylor-Perry, Rosemary. 2001. Renewing *Ta hiera,* the holy mystery rites of Eleusis. *Shaman's Drum* 60 (47–60).

Theoi Project. 2000–2007. http://www.theoi.com (accessed April 16, 2007).

Tringham, Ruth, and Margaret Conkey. 1998. Rethinking figurines: A critical view from archeology of Gimbutas, the "goddess" and popular culture. In *Ancient goddesses,* ed. Lucy Goodison and Christine Morris, 22–45. London: British Museum.

Troy, Lana. 1986. *Patterns of queenship in Ancient Egyptian myth and history.* Boreas. Uppsala Studies in Ancient Mediterranean and Near Eastern Civilization 14. Stockholm: Acta Universitatis Upsaliensis.

Turner, Judy Ann. 1983. *Hiereiai: Acquisition of feminine priesthoods in ancient Greece.* Ph.D. diss., University of California, Santa Barbara. *Dissertation Abstracts International,* publ. nr. AAT8401758, DAI-A 44/10 (April 1984); 3135.

Tyrrell, William Blake. 1984. *Amazons: A study in Athenian mythmaking.* Baltimore: Johns Hopkins University Press.

Vermaseren, Maarten J. 1977. *Cybele and Attis: The myth and the* cult. Trans. A. M. H. Lemmers. London: Thames and Hudson.

Versnel, H. S. 1992. The festival for Bona Dea and the Thesmophoria. *Greece & Rome* 39, no. 1 (April): 31–55.

Wasson, Gordon R., Albert Hoffman, and Carl A. P. Ruck. 2008. *The road to Eleusis: Unveiling the secret of the mysteries.* Berkeley, CA: North Atlantic Books.

West, M. L. 1997. *The east face of the Helicon.* Oxford: Clarendon.

————, trans. 2003a. *Greek epic fragments from the seventh to the fifth centuries BC.* Cambridge, MA: Harvard University Press.

————. 2003b. *Homeric hymns; Homeric apocrypha; lives of Homer.* Cambridge, MA: Harvard University Press.

Wilde, Lyn Webster. 1999. *On the trail of the women warriors: The Amazons in myth and history.* New York: Thomas Dunne.

Wilford, John Noble. 2008. An altar beyond Olympus for a deity predating Zeus. *The New York Times*, February 5. http://www.nytimes.com/2008/02/05/science/05zeus.html?pagewanted=1&8dpc&_r=2 (accessed July 8, 2008).

Williams, Michael Allen. 1996. *Rethinking "gnosticism": An argument for dismantling a dubious category.* Princeton, NJ: Princeton University Press.

Wolkstein, Diane, and Samuel Noah Kramer. 1983. *Inanna, queen of heaven and earth: Her stories and hymns from Sumer.* New York: Harper and Row.

Yakar, Jak. 1997. Did Anatolia contribute to the neolithization of Southeast Europe? In *From the Realm of the Ancestors: An Anthology in Honor of Marija Gimbutas*, ed. Joan Marler, 59–69. Manchester, CT: Knowledge, Ideas and Trends.

————. 2007. Interview with Jak Yakar. *Journal of Archaeomythology* 3 (1): 25–31. http://www.archaeomythology.org/journal/read_article.php?a=0607_4_marler_yakar.pdf (accessed July 14, 2008).

Zeitlin, Froma I. 1982. Cultic models of the female: Rites of Dionysis and Demeter. *Arethusa* 15 (1, 2): 129–57.

————. 1984. The dynamics of misogyny: Myth and mythmaking in the *Oresteia.* In *Women in the ancient world: The Arethusa papers*, ed. John Peradotto and J. P. Sullivan, 159–91. Albany: State University of New York Press.

————. 1996. *Playing the other: Gender and society in classical Greek literature.* Chicago: University of Chicago Press.

Zuntz, Gunther. 1971. *Persephone: Three essays on religion and thought in Magna Graecia.* Oxford: Clarendon Press.

INDEX

Printed in the United States of America